# DISTURBER OF
# THE PEACE

Books by Harrison E. Salisbury

*A Journey For Our Times*   1983
*Without Fear or Favor—The New York Times*   1980
*The Unknown War*   1978
*Russia in Revolution 1900–1930*   1978
*Black Night, White Snow: Russia's Revolutions 1905–1917*   1977
*Travels Around America*   1976
*The Gates of Hell*   1975
*To Peking—And Beyond*   1973
*The Eloquence of Protest—Voices of the 70's* (Editor)   1972
*The Many Americas Shall Be One*   1971
*War Between Russia and China*   1969
*The 900 Days—The Siege of Leningrad*   1969
*The Soviet Union—The Fifty Years* (Editor)   1967
*Behind The Lines—Hanoi*   1967
*Orbit of China*   1967
*Russia*   1965
*The Northern Palmyra Affair*   1962
*The New Russia?*   1962
*Moscow Journal: The End of Stalin*   1961
*To Moscow—And Beyond*   1960
*The Shook-Up Generation*   1958
*American in Russia*   1955
*Russia On The Way*   1946

# DISTURBER OF THE PEACE

## Memoirs of a Foreign Correspondent

Harrison E. Salisbury

UNWIN

HYMAN

LONDON    SYDNEY    WELLINGTON

First published in Great Britain by the Trade Division of Unwin Hyman Limited 1989.

This book is a condensed version of two volumes, *A Journey for Our Times* (copyright © 1983 by Harrison E. Salisbury) and *A Time of Change* (copyright © 1988 by Harrison E. Salisbury) originally published in the United States of America by Harper & Row.

This one volume edition copyright © 1989 by Harrison E. Salisbury

**UNWIN HYMAN LIMITED**
15–17 Broadwick Street
London W1V 1FP

Allen & Unwin Australia Pty Ltd
8 Napier Street
North Sydney
NSW 2060
Australia

Allen & Unwin New Zealand Pty Ltd with the Port Nicholson Press
Compusales Building
75 Ghuznee Street
Wellington
New Zealand

**British Library Cataloguing in Publication Data**
Salisbury, Harrison E. (Harrison Evans), *1908–*
    Disturber of the peace: memoirs of a foreign correspondent.
    1. United States. Journalism – Biographies
    I. Title   II. Salisbury, Harrison E. (Harrison Evans), *1908–*. Journey from our times
    III. Salisbury, Harrison E. (Harrison Evans), *1908–*. Time of change
    070'.92'4

    ISBN 0-04-440389-5

Printed in Great Britain by The University Press, Cambridge

# Contents

# Acknowledgements

In writing of a life that spans eighty years it is hard to get all the credits tucked in neatly. Let me say that my greatest debt is to my parents, Percy P. and Georgiana Salisbury, to my sister, Janet, to my aunt, Susan Salisbury, to my sons, Michael and Stephan and to my great comrade, companion and love on so many of these pages, Charlotte.

I owe a debt to my many colleagues at *The New York Times*, especially to Clifton Daniel, Turner Catledge, Charlotte Curtis, David Halberstam, Iphigene and Arthur Hays Sulzberger, James Reston and David Schneiderman.

I must thank, too, President Yang Shangkun and too many other Chinese friends and helpers to list, but I especially appreciate the aid of two recently demised old friends of China and myself, Rewi Alley and George Hatem. And special appreciation to John S. Service, the premier Old China hand of the U.S. State department, who accompanied Charlotte, myself, General Qin Xinghan and Zhang Yuanyuan on the retracing of the Long March.

A word for London war-time friends like Paul Winterton, Frank Owen, Michael Foot, Harold Hutchinson, Claud Cockburn, Jennie Lee and Hilde Marchant. A bouquet to those great Russians, the poets Yevgeny Yevtushenko, Andrei Voznesensky and Bella Akhmadulina and, to be sure, a special word for Aleksandr Solzhenitsyn.

# Introduction

I have spent a lifetime on the fault lines of the world, those stressed areas of war, conflict, bloodshed and revolution. Bombs have sometimes seemed the metaphor of the age in which I have lived.

In World War II I walked over the blasted ruins of London's East End, the rubble of Stalingrad, the frozen corpses of Leningrad after the 900-day siege, the broken bricks of Warsaw's ghetto and of Berlin's Wilhelmstrasse.

I missed the Korean War but I cowered in a Hanoi shelter as the American B-52s thundered over.

The echo of bombs first became familiar to my ears in my own America—the rumble of blasts in Al Capone's gang wars of Chicago, the terror bombs of the sit-ins of Depression and the New Deal, the dynamite of Alabama and Mississippi in the Civil Rights strife.

Nor was it only bombs. There were the assassin's bullets which took the lives of John F. Kennedy, Martin Luther King and Robert F. Kennedy, a litany of violence which I still find hard to credit.

My life began in peaceful, cherubic Victorian surroundings in the American Middle West. Victoria was a few years gone but her aura lingered on at 107 Royalston Avenue, Minneapolis, where I grew up. In childhood I am afraid war was to me much as it was to Winston Churchill, a bright adventure, chivalry, sacrifice for noble principles. It was many years before I saw the bloated bodies of German soldiers slowly bobbing up and down in the placid waters off Sevastopol, the metallic frozen bodies of Leningrad, and smelled the pungent odor of death in the jungle.

But I have not written a cavalcade of horror in these pages excerpted from my two published volumes of Memoirs, *A Journey for Our Times* and *A Time of Change*. I have throughout my life sought to be where the action was, political, economic, social. I have gone into the slum streets of New York to try to understand the violent adolescent street gangs of the Shook-Up Generation. I have learned more than I really want to know about the asphalt de-humanized metropoli of the future, the Los Angeles' and Houstons. I have gotten as close as I could to political figures like Zhou Enlai, Stalin, Nikita Khrushchev, Jack Kennedy, Adlai Stevenson, Lyndon Baines Johnson and Richard

Nixon. Of them all I found Nixon the most talented, the most flawed. And then there was that most unexpected President, a true artifact, Ronald Reagan.

Somehow I have managed to retain a sense of optimism even while being forced to concede that Murphy's Law seems to apply to the world we live in—if anything possibly can go wrong it will go wrong.

Early in life I nourished the hope of going to the Orient. I was fifty-four years old before I made it to China but I've not been idle since then. I have retraced with my wife, Charlotte, the 6,000-mile course of Mao Zedong's Long March of 1934–35, I've explored Tibet, Mongolia and almost every obscure spot in China. I have talked for hours with the leaders of that turbulent emerging society. I never expected to go to Russia but was plunged into the maelstrom, willy-nilly, in World War II and went on to live through the final terrible years of Stalin. And I have seen both great Communist societies struggling to get back into the mainstream from their Marxian backwater.

So, despite skepticism, I think the world will survive. I wish my own profession of journalism had more guts. I'd like to see it hold high the torch of truth or something like that. But the thought is, I fear, naïve. At least it manages to do better than it did in the days of the "yellow press" and the egocentric Press Barons.

I have one hope for this book: that it will stir some hackles. As I say in its pages I feel uncomfortable with too many bouquets. I must, I feel, be missing part of the story—the best part.

## Chapter 1

# Child of War

To a working man, head tucked into collar against the wind, hurrying home in the dark Minnesota November, the figure of a small boy slowly stomping across the snowy lawn beyond the yellow arc of gaslight was almost invisible, a blur against the crepuscular shadows of the gabled house. A flint-edged wind discouraged curiosity, but if, despite wind, and cold, and winter twilight, the man had taken note, he would perhaps have been puzzled at the boy's movements, trudging a dozen paces toward the naked thorn apple hedge, feet squeaking on the dry snow, abruptly reversing and repeating his maneuver again and again, almost as though he was standing guard.

The small boy was myself, and in fact I *was* standing guard. It was late November 1917. The Revolution had triumphed in Petrograd and that evening I was a member of the Children's Regiment. I wore my high-peaked Budenny helmet of gray felt with its red star, and a long-skirted uniform coat over Cossack boots. I thrust my hands deep into black gauntlets and on my shoulder I bore a Berdan rifle. Back and forth I paced before the Winter Palace; back and forth beside the parapet beyond which lay the expanse of Palace Square and the shaft of the monument to Alexander I. Occasionally, I glanced at the glowing windows of the palace and saw my silhouette on the crust of snow: the peak of my helmet, the long point of my bayonet, black against the white. The scene was more real than life. I was a boy soldier on sentry duty.

Then, as I knew it would, came the voice of my mother at the kitchen door. "Bunny! Bunny!" she called. "Time to come in. You'll catch your death of cold."

I hesitated a moment to show that I was not hungry, not cold, not beginning to get a bit frightened by my fantasy, then I turned, left the parapet of snow I had built, and with a last look to the dark curve of Royalston Avenue, where the enemy lay hidden off toward the coalyards, I hurried to the house which my grandfather had built and where I had lived since I was born, on November 14, 1908. Stacking

1

beside the door the rifle I had fashioned from a two-by-four, I brushed the snow from my feet and passed into the radiant sphere of the kitchen, with its coal range and the copper sink so veined with solder it looked like a relief map of Europe. The room was filled with smells: beans and molasses bubbling in an earthen crock, the scent of brown bread, coffee heating in a granite pot and the spice of fresh gingerbread pinching my nostrils.

I hung up my helmet, a white-and-red stocking cap, and my uniform greatcoat, a sheep-lined mackinaw, and put away my gauntlets of rabbit fur with the skin outside. I stood there a nine-year-old fourth grader, wearing itchy wool union suit, flannel shirt, dark brown corduroy britches, long black stockings, heavy wool socks neatly folded over the tops of my soft elkskin boots, suddenly hungry and cold, cheeks chapped, nose running, Petrograd, the Winter Palace, the Children's Regiment vanishing as I sat down at table with my father, my mother and my seven-year-old sister, Janet, to a steaming plate of pork and beans.

"What were you doing out in the yard?" my father asked.

"Just playing," I said, keeping my eyes down and reaching for the ruby red flask of ketchup.

I've looked back a hundred times at that nine-year-old youngster, particularly during my long years in Russia, wondering whether, in fact, I was "just playing."

I think I first heard the names of Lenin and Trotsky a month or two later, in early February 1918, about the time Trotsky submitted to the astonished German plenipotentiaries at Brest Litovsk his proposal of no war, no peace. I could not have guessed that they would run through my life like a red thread.

Afternoons now were growing longer in Minneapolis, and one day when I came home from school I saw a new boy outside a house across the street, a verandaed house of fading red which was being rented to rooms, the original owners, the Dericksons, who like my grandfather had bought a lot in the fashionable Oak Lake Addition in the 1880s, having, as had most of the others, sold their place and moved away.

On this afternoon I was busy behind my snow fort, laying by a supply of icy snowballs with which to repel attack by youngsters passing down Royalston Avenue or issuing from the alley which was my left flank. I glanced occasionally at the boy across the street, a slight youngster, dark, olive-skinned, a bit taller and older than myself, wearing tan muffler, black cap and a torn red sweater over a dark blue woolen work shirt. On his feet were rubber boots, the thin knee-high glossy kind that kids wore when the ice melted in spring. He was fashioning the snow figure of a slender young girl, and even to my rude eye it had a grace that set it apart from the slushy yard, the dingy house, the stains of yellow horse piss and brown droppings from the heavy teams of sledges that passed by.

A sense of envy seized me. I picked up a snowball and threw it across the street. It scudded into the snow and the boy went on working. I threw another. No response. I threw a third. It hit the slender figure, smashing away her shoulder. The boy turned and cried: "Why did you do that?" I saw tears in his brown eyes. Filled with shame, I stood a moment, then crossed the street. "Maybe we can fix it," I said. "No," the boy said. "No. It can't be fixed." He gave a kick and the snow maiden crumpled. "What's your name?" I asked. "Reuben," he said. "What's yours?" "My name is Bunny," I said. I hated that name. I hated it when my mother and sister called me Bunny. I fought any boy who called me Bunny, but now I gave it to the boy as a kind of penance. "Bunny," I said, "that's my name." The glance he gave me burned into my mind, and years later, describing him in a sketch which I called "Christ Was Born in Asia," I wrote that he looked like the figure of Jesus in a Pre-Raphaelite painting.

"Would you like a glass of tea?" he asked. "My father is upstairs."

I had never heard of drinking tea from a glass. "Yes," I said. "I'd like that a lot."

Reuben's father was Nathan Rosen. He told me about Lenin and Trotsky and Russia and the Revolution and the Czar and the Jews and the pogroms and so many things that my head almost burst. He had fled Russia to escape the pogroms and the Czar's twenty-five-year term of military duty and more importantly because he had become a revolutionary. He had been born in a village in Belorussia between the rivers Dnieper and Sozh, names that meant nothing to me until I went to Russia during World War II. Fierce battles were fought there in 1941 near Gomel, at the hinge of Belorussia, the Ukraine and Russia proper.

Nathan Rosen, slim, dark, lively, had a talent for painting. A local aristocrat offered to send him to St. Petersburg to study, but his family could not spare him. It was the time of the pogroms. Young

Nathan looked more Italian than Jewish. He hung about the tea-houses where police agents and Black Hundred toughs gathered and he tipped off Jewish self-defense groups about their plans. When he was conscripted for the war against Japan, his regiment mutinied. He made his way to London, where his fiancée joined him. They were married at a registry office on Piccadilly Circus and came to Winnipeg. When war broke out in August 1914, they moved to Minneapolis, Nathan fearful that he might again be conscripted.

Now he was starting to work as a painter—houses, signs, decorations, paperhanging. They lived in three rooms on the second floor, Nathan and his wife, Edith, baby Harold, Reuben and his sister, Bessie, whose sculpture in snow Reuben had been making.

That afternoon we sat in a kitchen crowded with a tall armoire and a magnificent chair that had carved griffins, claw feet and a black leather seat. Reuben loved to run his hands over the silken sheen of the mahogany. I imagined it must have come from Russia. A kettle simmered on the stove, the air was filled with steam and the windows had glazed with frost. A huge brass engine hissed away, a samovar, the first I'd seen. Everything was mysterious and foreign and unknown. I felt very brave to be sitting in so strange a place. Mr. Rosen poured me a glass of black tea and gave me a lump of sugar. "Here," he said, "drink it the Russian way. Put the sugar in your mouth." He took a lump and sucked the tea through it. I had never tasted tea. Children weren't supposed to drink tea. It stunted their growth. So did coffee. Children drank milk and cocoa. Mr. Rosen didn't seem to know this. Nor did he care whether I drank my tea or not; he was too excited, talking about Russia in words and accent that I didn't always understand.

"Enormous things are happening," he said. "The world is changing. The Czar is finished. So is Kerensky. Trotsky and Lenin are changing the world. When the war ends, revolution will sweep Europe—Germany first, then France and England. Even here in America. You'll read about it in the newspapers." I could see that Reuben was a little embarrassed at the torrent of his father's words. "Maybe not here, Papa," he said quietly. "You wait," Mr. Rosen said. "You read the papers. Even here. The Revolution has started. Nothing will be the same again. Remember what Karl Marx said, and Engels too."

I wanted to tell Mr. Rosen how I had stood guard at the Winter Palace, but he was talking about the *real* Revolution. He came from the *real* Russia. He was a *real* revolutionary. I had just been playing, making up a story from the dispatches of Floyd Gibbons, the *Chicago Tribune* man who wore a black patch over one eye. Gibbons was my hero, along with General Blackjack Pershing, Lord Kitchener (my favorite—I could not believe he had been lost on the *Hampshire*), Edith Cavell, the King of Belgium and Colonel George E. Leach of Minnesota's own 151st Field Artillery, who had gone to Central High with my mother, very handsome but very dumb, she said. At exam time she had had to whisper the answers to him. Later George Leach would become mayor of Minneapolis, campaigning in his uniform, very handsome, but he still didn't know the answers.

World War I was my life. I learned to read sitting in Unk's lap, picking out headlines about the battle on the Marne in the *Minneapolis Journal*. Unk was James Pritchard, my father's uncle, and he had fought at Shiloh and endured the hell of Andersonville prison. It left him a little fuzzy and sometimes he put sugar in his soup, thinking it was oatmeal. He was a gentle-hearted man who lived with us and looked after the furnaces—two because the house was so big—until one day when he kept starting fires in the toilets, complaining that somehow they didn't draw very well. After that he went to live in a nursing home.

When I launched my literary career in 1918, my first work was a historical treatise called "The Great War." It filled seven pages (including penciled illustrations and maps) of my old green copy-book. I began with these words: "1914—Germany declared war on France August 1, 1914. All France was astire."

I didn't stay long that day at the Rosen flat. I refused the garlic sausage, the spiced cakes, the dill pickles encrusted with salt, the black bread and herring. My mother had laid down a strict rule. I was never, never to visit a boy's house without first getting permission. Quickly I retreated outside, across the street past the lamp, its gas mantle glowing soft and yellow and into my house. I had had my first experience of Russia. I guess I was a Bolshevik before I was ten, but by the time I was eleven I was wearing a Pershing for President button.

When I finally found myself in Russia in 1944 and began a long career as correspondent, a specialist in Soviet affairs and a historian, I came to realize that nowhere in that gray wasteland would I ever taste the wine of the Revolution as pungent and pure as that of my childhood in the Oak Lake Addition.

I was born a Victorian child. Edward had ascended the throne by the time of my birth, but Victoria still reigned at 107 Royalston Avenue. My grandmother, Mary Pritchard Salisbury, dressed my father in a black velvet suit with gold embroidery like Little Lord Fauntleroy's and had Mr. Schuesler, the photographer on Hudson Street in Mazomanie, Wisconsin, take his picture on a little rattan chair, looking woeful. My father dressed me in the same suit and took my picture. I hated that Fauntleroy outfit, but when the time came, I dressed my son Michael in it, posed him on the curlicued walnut sofa that had stood in the parlor at 107 and took his picture. Continuity.

In his heart, my father never left the house on Royalston Avenue. There are times when I wonder whether I have. Father sold the house just before I went to college and we moved to Kenwood Hill, but when Father walked home from the factory at night, his legs occasionally took him over the Seventh Street bridge, across the railroad tracks, past the coalyards and up to 107 before he realized that he didn't live there anymore. It was home for him and home for me and hardly a day of my life was to pass without my thinking about it. In strange cities I put myself to sleep walking through the rooms at 107, remembering the long yellow Dagestan runner on the hall floor, the red of the Khiva in the parlor, my mother's favorite picture, "The Age of Innocence," over the sofa, the seven-branched candelabra on the mahogany table that had belonged to my great-great-aunt in Cincinnati (or was it Philadelphia?), the gentle head of a deer (how could my father have shot it?) over the fireplace in the dining room; remembering my grandfather's cherrywood library, the folios of Shakespeare lying flat under Milton's *Paradise Lost* with the Doré engravings. Later I was to discover plain-brown-wrapper copies of *What Every Boy Should Know* and *What Every Girl Should Know* hidden back of Milton; the juxtaposition of Doré's naked men and women amid the flames, and the giddy perils of adolescence, convinced me, for a time, that hell was real.

On the library shelves stood volumes of *Scribner's, Harper's* and *Century* magazines, bound in black leather by my grandfather. He was a doctor and he read these volumes, sitting in the carved cherrywood rocking chair where he spent the last year of his life, knowing from his own diagnosis that his heart had worn out, reading and drowsing and waiting for it to stop beating, as soon it did. Here were Gibbon's Rome and the Green's history of England, Grant's memoirs, Charles Dickens and William Makepeace Thackeray, John Greenleaf Whittier and Henry Wadsworth Longfellow, Louisa May Alcott and Ralph Waldo Emerson, Henry Thoreau, James Fenimore Cooper and William Cullen Bryant, a nineteenth-century litany. I read them all, serially, in continuous wonder, shelf by shelf, between the ages of nine and thirteen. I grew up knowing what culture was—it was the books on the walls of my grandfather's study.

On New Year's Day in 1966, I found myself in the North Vietnam countryside, eighty-five miles south of Hanoi. It had been a long day, spent driving down narrow bomb-pitted roads, with the threat of more American bombers at any moment. Now I was spending the night on a slat-bottomed bed with a straw mattress in a barracks with open sides and clay floor. I was too tired to sleep. I thought I could hear the rustle of people moving past the compound and wondered what was happening. I was an enemy deep behind the lines. I did not even know the name of the place where I was staying. It was cold under the thin blanket and I lay half awake and a little frightened. Finally, I turned my mind away from Hanoi, away from the war and the bombs, and back to the security of Royalston Avenue. I sat again in our light carriage, the black-painted trap, my father driving Dolly, our old bay, I sitting beside him, my mother and Janet in the rear, clop-clop, neatly around the curve under the elms, Dolly's hooves falling rhythmically on the soft brown earth of the street freshly watered by a yellow sprinkling wagon. My father, dark and handsome, pulled up at 107, the reins taut in his hands, and my mother, broad-brimmed straw hat with mauve veil sheltering her blond hair and pale complexion from the sun, alighted to the granite stepping-stone, Janet and I following her, scrambling up the five wooden steps of the veranda, overhung with grapevines, bursting through the double oak doors with their brass fittings and into the entry, past the half-glass doors, etched with flowers, into the front hall with its elk's head, shot by my uncle Scott Evans on his way to the Klondike in 1900, grim, menacing and sprinkled so heavily with red pepper against moths that I could not come close without sneezing. A crystal-faceted chandelier sparkled over the oak staircase with its polished newel and banister, whose smooth surface first gave me a warm masturbatory pleasure and made me think of my girl cousin Eleanor Evans, who liked to slide down the rail, thin legs clenching its rotundity, short skirt pulled back and panties riding up narrow thighs.

7

That night in the Vietnam countryside, I walked through the house on Royalston Avenue as I had so often, and finally I sat on the floor beside the window box in my grandfather's library, pulling out of its depths the architectural journals my father kept there, looking at the plans for the house on the Mississippi riverbank which he dreamed of but never built, taking out the Frederic Remington engravings and the lithographs of the Philadelphia Exposition, and finally a worn purple-and-gold book, *Dick Whittington*, my father's childhood favorite. I listened again to the words: "turn, turn again, Dick Whittington, Lord Mayor of London Town," and at that moment the Bow Bells sounded as they had for Dick Whittington. I awoke. It was not yet dawn, but the iron bells in the shattered tower of the bombed-out Cathedral of St. François Xavier across the rice paddies were calling black-pajamaed peasants to mass before daylight, before the first flight of American bombers appeared in the sky. Pulling aside the mosquito net, shivering in the early coldness, I saw the peasants moving along the willow-lined roadway almost without sound on inner-tube sandals, shuffling past the barracks on their way to pray. In an instant I was transported from my Victorian dream to the reality of grass-cutter bombs, of napalm and Agent Orange, to the deadly imposition by my loved America of pain and horror on an ancient Asian people.

## Chapter 2

# The Making of a Patriot

War was the glory of my childhood. I must confess there was not a hint of moral outrage in my being, nor have I ever been a pacifist. I could say with FDR: "I hate war"; I can say that I have feared war and have opposed war, notably the Vietnam war; but until nuclear war was born, I never believed in a world without war. Now no other kind of world is imaginable.

As a youngster I surrounded myself with lead soldiers, guns, toy cannon, cap pistols. I compelled my complaisant sister, Janet, to play war with me, once keeping her so long in the shallow trenches we had dug in the hot sun that she almost suffered sunstroke.

(I was amused later to learn that Vladimir Lenin and his brothers and sisters played war endlessly in the parlor of their house high on the Volga River bluff at Simbirsk.)

After supper each evening, our family gathered with my uncle Andrew and aunt Mary, who lived on the second floor of our house. We wound up the mahogany Victrola and played "Madelon," "Tipperary," "Over There" and the rest. My father and uncle gravely discussed military strategy.

A Red Cross unit headed by my mother and my aunt met at our house to roll bandages, the ladies in white uniforms and turbans. They rolled hundreds of muslin bandages, knitted 1,194 pairs of socks, 1,003 sweaters and twelve dozen face masks. We children learned to knit too. I shudder to think of the soldiers who had to wear our socks.

I dreamed of Allied victory. My aunt Sue Salisbury was in France with the YMCA. Letter after letter flowed back from Paris, full of the *Boche* and his bestiality. I began to feel ashamed that my father was not Over There; that he was in the Home Guard—in uniform, true, but no tin hat, drilling on Monday evenings and on Wednesdays serving ice cream cones and sodas to Our Boys at the Army and Navy Club. He would come home tired on Wednesday evenings but lugging a gallon of left-over ice-cream, a consolation for not being at the Front.

9

I was totally chauvinistic. When I saw in the atlas the enormous globs of British Empire red spread over the continents, it made me angry that the American green covered only Hawaii, the Canal Zone, Puerto Rico, Alaska and the Philippines. I yearned for an American Empire on which the sun never set. My father was a Teddy Roosevelt Republican, a Bull Mooser, and so was I. In 1916, at the age of seven, I was against "Yellow Dog" Wilson, who was "too proud to fight." I agreed with my father and my uncle Andrew, who said that Wilson was afraid to fight.

I could not believe my ears when I heard my uncle John Dort, sitting on the porch of his house in St. Paul (living in St. Paul was bad enough in those days of Twin City rivalry), tell my father that he was voting for Woodrow Wilson. John Dort—a locomotive engineer, a hero—a Wilson Democrat? I was stunned. Only town drunks and Irishmen were Democrats.

When we entered the war, no one was more vigilant that I against the "pros," that is, the pro-Germans, secret enemies of Our Cause. Minnesota had a large population of Scandinavians, many Germans and a small Irish minority. The war was not a "Crusade for Democracy" to them. Many of the Germans and Scandinavians were socialists. They believed the war reflected the rivalry of capitalists eager to grab each other's wealth.

None of this was perceived by me. I listened with rabbit's ears to my elders talking about the "pros"; about old German friends who were suspect, especially a prosperous family that ran a big liquor store. The test was Liberty Bonds. If you didn't buy bonds, you were a "pro." Even if you did buy bonds, you might be trying to mask your secret sympathy for Kaiser Bill. I visioned the Kaiser as a death's head, bony fingers dripping blood, a necklace of skulls, wolf's teeth, spiky helmet, devil's tail. My image may have derived from one of John McCutcheon's cartoons in the *Chicago Tribune*. I believed every atrocity story invented by the British—the nuns used as bell clappers, the little girls with hands chopped off (because they threw stones at German soldiers), the martydom of Edith Cavell. God knows what I didn't believe. Every letter of Aunt Sue's from Paris told of horrors—destruction of the Rheims cathedral, desecration of Louvain, *Schreckenskrieg*, poisoned chocolates dropped by zeppelins (I was instructed never to accept chocolate from a stranger on the street), Big Berthas shelling orphanages.

Friday was War Savings Stamp day at Sumner School and I took a quarter to buy a big purple stamp and paste it into my stamp book. When I got one hundred purple stamps, I could turn the book in for a twenty-five-dollar Liberty Bond. Each Friday morning, I glanced around the classroom to see if anyone didn't buy stamps. The children who attended Sumner School were mostly poor. Nickels and dimes were scarce, quarters they never had. But on Friday, each had a coin or two, often pennies carefully tied up by their mother in the corner of a handkerchief. One boy (myself) had a small black leather coin purse with a metal clasp. There was a Swedish girl named Marie in my class who always seemed a bit older than the rest of us (in fifth grade she had real breasts). One Friday she had no money: "My mother said she didn't have any money for savings stamps," and she tossed her blond braids defensively. When I brought this news home, my mother and my aunt Mary exchanged looks. My father started to say something, but was shushed by my mother. I knew this meant a scandal not fit for children's ears and kept mine fine-tuned. Later that evening, I overheard a whispered exchange about Marie's mother. She kept a rooming house on Sixth Avenue around the corner from us. One of the roomers was a black man. "What do you expect from her kind?" my aunt remarked. "Something ought to be done." My mother solemnly agreed: "For the children's sake." The next evening, my father, dressed in his Home Guard uniform, and my uncle Andrew, solemn in a black suit, left the house. They returned a bit later looking pleased and closeted themselves with my mother and aunt. The following Friday, Marie appeared in class with a dollar bill and pushed to the head of the line saying, 'Put four purple stamps in my book. A whole dollar's worth!"

My mother and father and aunt often went to houses door to door, to be sure people were buying Victory Bonds. There were signs in front windows, saying: "We subscribed." And Red Cross stickers too. My father and my uncle Andrew thought well of the board of directors of the Minneapolis Symphony Orchestra when they drove from his position the respected conductor Emil Oberhoffer, who refused to drop German composers from the repertoire.

Of course, I ate spareribs with liberty cabbage instead of sauerkraut, and when I got sick it was with liberty measles. No voice was raised in dissent in our house when the teaching of German was banned by the Minneapolis public schools. My father and my uncle were fluent in German, enjoyed reading German novels and switched to German if they were speaking of "naughty" matters (like the

Swedish lady and her black roomer). But they abandoned the language except for an occasional *Donner und Blitzen, Dummkopf* or *Gott im Himmel.*

All this seemed right as rain to the small chauvinistic patriot who was me. I was not a thoughtful child and I enthusiastically joined the chorus of hate. I had never, I am certain, heard of the Bill of Rights or the First Amendment. I loved parades, especially military parades with lots of guns and bands, such as the Stars and Stripes Parade of August 16, 1917, not just an ordinary flag-waving demonstration. The Stars and Stripes Parade touched off—and was designed to touch off—a violent wave of xenophobic, prowar vigilantism in Minneapolis and in the state of Minnesota.

Its leader was a man named Fred B. Snyder. There were bands galore—the Donaldson's department store drum corps, Captain Sinclair and his bagpipe corps, the white-uniformed young women's marching corps of Dayton's department store, led by George D. Dayton himself, the Zurah Temple band, the Maccabees, Modern Woodmen, Shriners, uniformed firemen, the Pillsbury Flour Company band and the band of Glencoe, Minnesota, somewhat crippled because the bass drummer had beat his drum so vigorously both drumheads broke.

The martial music was matched by the martial oratory. On the parade grounds, Snyder whipped up the crowd against the officials of New Ulm, Minnesota, a German community in the southern part of the state, where a temperate attitude toward the war prevailed. "What shall we do with the copperheads?" Snyder demanded. "Shoot 'em! Hang 'em!" the crowd roared. Snyder wound up by pleading that "nothing should be left undone to win this war even though it requires harsh treatment of friends and neighbors."

The hit of the day was William H. Morris, described as "colored" by the *Minneapolis Journal.* He spoke for the "Black Sammies." He declared that the "Black Sammies" already in France and those about to follow would prove that "no braver, better, more patriotic loyal soldiers" had ever lived than the Sammies and that their guns and swords would "always be true to the country that has given them a voice in government for the first time."

Minnesota's governor, a lumbering Republican, J. A. A. Burnquist, had set up a Commission of Public Safety, which could supersede local officials and mayors. It was empowered to do anything it

12

pleased with persons it accused of disloyalty. The powers of the commission make those of the late Senator Joseph McCarthy look like a kindergarten teacher's. Three days after the Stars and Stripes Parade, the commission ousted the town officers of New Ulm "so that liberty, equality and humanity might endure."

There was no pretense of constitutionality about the commission. One of its sponsors privately wrote Minnesota's Senator Knute Nelson: "The bill has teeth in it eighteen inches long. There are provisions in it that are unconstitutional and palpably so."

The commission closed saloons and dance halls in working-class areas. Soon it had created the Home Guard, in which my father enlisted, to "protect private property in this period of unrest and disorder."

My father's finest hour came when the Home Guard was ordered to break a streetcar strike in 1917. Issued a long oak ax handle and a nickel-plated pistol, he rode with strikebreaking motormen and, as he swore, cracked the skulls of strikers who tried to interfere. Put him in uniform, give him a weapon, issue an order, and even a gentle man like my father obeyed.

The commission published a weekly called *Minnesota in the War*, which was circulated to the public schools. The issues were loaded with atrocity stories and incitements against "pros," "traitors," "treason." No wonder my mind reverberated with the sadism of the Huns.

After the war, case after case came to light in which the Home Guard had led mobs against supposed traitors, particularly A. C. Townley's Nonpartisan League and the IWW. I grew up believing that the Nonpartisan League was a branch of the Kaiser's war apparatus and that the initials IWW stood for "I won't work."

So it was that the liberal state of Minnesota was transformed into a pre-fascist fief. The powers vested in the Minnesota Public Safety Commission were totalitarian powers; the commission established a dictatorship in Minnesota; the ideology of hatred, racism, xenophobia, was as naked as in Nazi Germany.

As a child, I understood nothing of this. Nor, so far as I can see, did my father and mother and their friends. They believed the propaganda. My aunt Sue wrote my father that German agents every night were shooting American soldiers in the training camps, that spies were dug in so deep it would take years to root them out. These good people believed in the threat of "subversion from within." It never entered their minds that a groundwork for authoritarian rule was being laid under the cloak of "protection of democracy and liberty," as Fred B. Snyder so often declaimed.

The lesson of the Minnesota dictatorship is a frightening one, and it was not until I was preparing to write this book that I took a clear look at what was going on behind those red-white-and-blue banners of which I was so proud. It would have served me well if at least I had paid some heed to Fred B. Snyder, for he was to appear dramatically in my life during my years at the University of Minnesota. He was then, had been since 1914, and would until 1950 continue to be chairman of the University Board of Regents. When as a feisty student editor I challenged the conduct of the Administration and Board of Regents, Fred B. Snyder took the lead in ousting me from the university.

This lay to the future. With war's end, the hysteria slowly died, leaving me only a faint perception that something had been wrong, but I did not yet understand that it was America's own principles that had been savaged. I was beginning to be influenced by Henry Mencken, George Jean Nathan and *The American Mercury*, and I found in the banning of Heine, Schiller and Goethe, the silencing of Mozart, Beethoven and Bach, a comedy of the absurd which demonstrated the banality of the American booboisie. I never thought to question my own bigotry.

A decade after the war, I had become a cub reporter on the *Minneapolis Journal* and my first out-of-town assignment was to report a convention held at Austin, a small town in southern Minnesota. Not long before this, I had stood one afternoon in May 1927 beside a Morse telegraph operator in the city room of the *Journal* and listened as the sounder clicked away, a Prince Albert tobacco tin wedged against it to enhance the sound, and the operator typed out the news that Minnesota's Slim Lindbergh had made it to Le Bourget field in Paris. It was an extraordinary moment, the biggest moment for me since the armistice of November 7, 1918, the "false" armistice which I and everyone in Minneapolis thought had ended World War I. Now came this remarkable adventure of the skinny young serious-eyed boy from Little Falls, Minnesota, flying alone across the Atlantic, landing precisely where he said he would, thirty-three hours and twenty-nine minutes after takeoff at Roosevelt Field, Long Island, carrying letters of introduction so that people in Paris would know who he was.

Lindbergh was light-years older than myself—that is, he was twenty-seven and I was eighteen—but I experienced a surge of empathy. But for... well, let's face it: I could never have flown across Lake Minnetonka, let alone the Atlantic, but my emotion was there, never quite to vanish.

On this hot evening in August 1928, I was sitting in a breezeless room of the Fox Hotel at Austin with half a dozen men in their upper thirties or forties, elderly in my eyes, members of the American Legion. These were Prohibition days and some had plain pint bottles of Minnesota Thirteen, the best moonshine whiskey in the state, distilled from a corn called Minnesota 13, developed by the State Agricultural Experiment Station. The rest of us were drinking spiked beer, that is, near beer, spiked with grain alcohol—hospital alcohol, we always called it. We poured off an inch of beer, poured in an inch of alcohol, put a thumb to the top, shook the bottle and drank.

The legionnaires were telling stories, mostly stories about the broads they had bedded—the Frenchwomen they claimed to have laid in Paris, whores in Chicago and Minneapolis, gang fucking in the nearby countryside and other brutalities. Lynchings—well, they hadn't actually killed a nigger. There weren't any niggers or hardly any niggers in Minnesota, but once, during the war, they had "run ol' man Lindbergh outa town."

I listened as they talked, tilting back the clean glass pints of Minnesota Thirteen, capping the near beer with a thumb, draining the brown bottles into gullets, sitting on the sagging beds, shirts unbuttoned, shirttails out, belching and farting, sitting and sweating and talking. Yup, old man Lindbergh had come to town, the election was on, shee-it, we wuzzin gonna let him get away with that shee-it, that goddamn commie pro bastud passafist. Agin the war. The boys got tugetha, got some tar and feathers, good olfashioned taranfeathers, chicken feathers, came up to the hotel, dragged that olbastud down to the street, pulled his pants right off, poured the tar on him, put the feathers on him and run him outa town, right outa town. Took him on a truck down the road bout three miles and dumped him and that was the end of Lindbergh. Yup. That wuz plumb the end. He juskinda wentoff his rocker afta that, never made anutha speech, never heard anutha yip outa that olpassafist bastud.

What about Charley, what about Slim? I heard myself asking. One of the legionnaires took a long swig. Charley was justa kid. Can't blame his olman's craziness on Charley Lindbergh. Charley

Lindbergh, he's one of the greatest. The greatest, fact of matter. The greatest. Was he here in town with the old man that night? I asked. Another pause. Damif I know, the legionnaire said. Seems to me he wuz. Course he wuz justa kid then. Yup. I kinda think he wuz here. Seems to me I remember him, cussin', cryin' and throwin' his fists around, and one of the boys had to take him aside an quieten him down. Yup. Kinda think that's what happened that night.

I woke up the next morning early. I had a black taste in my mouth. The sun was shining into my room and it was Sunday morning, the hotel very quiet. I still had the smell in my nostrils of vomit and sweat and alcohol and beer, and the noise of the legionnaires shouting, glasses smashing on the sidewalk outside, women giggling and screaming and the thumping of beds in the rooms next door, hours and hours of it after I left the old veterans with their bragging of great days, the fucking in Paris, the tarring and feathering in Minnesota.

I have searched out the records and they show that mobs trailed Charles Lindbergh, Sr., during his 1918 campaign for the Republican nomination for the Minnesota governorship. He was arrested on charges of conspiracy along with the Nonpartisan Leaguers; a rally at Madison, Minnesota, was broken up with fire hoses; he was hanged in effigy in Red Wing, dragged from the speaking platform, threatened with lynching, and he escaped from one town amid a volley of shots. I could find no record of an incident exactly matching the tale of the legionnaires; probably they exaggerated. What the record does show is the vicious, vituperative, life-threatening mob action against a man who had fought against the war but once he got into it had said: "A few would destroy democracy to win the war and the rest of us would win the war to establish democracy."

The image of the beer-bellied bullies of Austin floods back in my mind each time I hear patriotic flannelmouths ranting against those whose protection is the sacred function of our democracy.

Ten years passed. The kidnapping, the Hauptmann trial, the self-exile to Europe, the trip to Moscow, dinners with Göring, the long days with Alexis Carrel, the Astors, Cliveden, and the speeches against America getting into World War II—people couldn't understand Lindbergh now. He didn't seem like the man who flew to Le Bourget, didn't seem like the kid who grew up in Little Falls, Minnesota, and quit the University of Wisconsin to be an aviator. The Lindbergh who joined General Robert E. Wood of Sears,

Roebuck in the America First Committee, who belittled England's chances against Germany, who thought the Luftwaffe would smash Russia in six weeks, who made remarks about Jewish bankers and Jewish influence—this didn't sound like our American hero who rode up Broadway in the greatest ticker tape parade of all and then married Anne Morrow, the ambassador's daughter.

I did not get to know Lindbergh until the last years of his life. Lindbergh hated newspapers and reporters. He never forgave their scrofulous treatment of his family and himself at the time of the kidnapping, the Hauptmann trial and the afteryears, but for a long while he made an exception for *The New York Times*. Adolph Ochs had taken him up; the *Times* had exclusive rights to his articles about the flight and gave him all the profits; Deak Lyman, the *Times*'s aviation writer, became his personal friend and worked with him in the terrible kidnap days; but Lindbergh had not been in the Times Building since Mr. Ochs's death in 1935, until he lunched with me and Alden Whitman there a few times in the late sixties. He came only because he wanted to talk privately about conservation. There had been something mystical, almost pagan, in his relationship to the earth, his feeling for the sea, for continental space, for the crystalline upper air. No one had a more precise, exact, scientific and practical mind. It was this that made him a magnificent flier and gave him his remarkable grasp of aeronautic technology. He was both a theorist and a craftsman. He checked out a Hertz rental car at La Guardia Airport with the meticulous care he gave to the controls of a Boeing 707.

But science and technology were not enough. His mind was forever pushing the unknown regions that lay beyond demonstrable fact. Now, at least partly through the stimulation of his son, Jon, he had come to see the threat man had brought upon his environment and particularly the danger implicit in aeronautics. His sense of concern had been raised to a pitch by the supersonic aircraft, with its potential for irreversible desiccation of the atmosphere.

Lindbergh was never a man to turn from cruel facts. He had made his decision. What was left of his life (very little, as it turned out), and all his determination (enormous) and world prestige (great), would be thrust into a struggle to save the earth he worshiped.

It was, I thought, a heroic decision, consistent with the heroic image he possessed of his role in society. He was prepared, if necessary, to go against the whole of that aviation which had been his

17

life. It was the radical decision of a radical man, a man almost too complex to analyze but one whom I believed I understood. I was nourished in the same soil as he. I had lived close to those giants in the earth of which Rölvaag wrote, the giants that hurled and clawed at the generations which came first to Minnesota and the Dakotas from Sweden, Norway, Denmark and Iceland. I knew now a good deal about Lindbergh's father, about the socialist agrarians of Sweden and Germany, the Nonpartisan League, the Farmer-Labor party, the passions, prejudices and hatreds that swept Minnesota in 1917 and after. I understood, I thought, why Slim Lindbergh, America's fair hero of 1927, had taken the same implacable stand against the majority, against war in 1939, that his father had taken against war in 1917. Others could assess the influences of Carrel, of the Astors, of Munich and Göring, of Truman Smith, of Hoover, Borah and Byrd, of the American politicians who sought to use Lindbergh. To me, he did not seem so different from the teenager who had watched his father, humiliated, defiled, run out of town by bully boys, driven to nervous breakdown because he had dared to stand up for his socialist principles and say what few other men in that day would say: that war was wrong, that America had no business entering Europe's quarrels, that it was, after all, a feud among greedy empires, a contest of lordly jackals over the corpses of ordinary men and women.

# Chapter 3

# Dr. Salisbury's Son

It was a crisp February Saturday, sun shining on a white world of snow new fallen, sky blue, no wind—the best of Minnesota days. I watched at the bay window for my father. Saturday was a half day at the factory, the Northern Bag Company, where he would work his whole life, starting out dark, thin, aristocratic, looking very young, working until, gray, worn, thin, tired, sad, bent, he died June 6, 1944, D-Day in Normandy, lingering only a few days after the stroke felled him as he walked out of the factory. I was at an American shuttle bombing base at Poltava, deep in the Ukraine, the cherry trees in blossom, hopelessly distant, when I got the news that he was ill; a few days later I was in Moscow, trying to figure out how to get back to Minneapolis. It was midafternoon and I was whiling away the time playing poker in the Metropol Hotel with my friends Bill Lawrence of *The New York Times*, Ed Angly of the *Chicago Sun*, Dave Nichol of the *Chicago Daily News* and Dick Lauterbach of *Life* magazine. Mike Handler, my UP colleague, walked into the room, motioned me over and said: "Your father is dead. The cable just came." "Thanks," I said, turned, picked up my hand and threw a chip into the pot.

Back on that diamond of a February day I saw my father coming around the curve of Royalston Avenue, walking fast, a steady countryman's gait, his head high, wearing a dark winter fedora and a velvet-collared black overcoat. All his life he wore fedoras, a woolly fedora in winter, a sleek gray fedora in spring and autumn; in June he donned a panama with black band and wore it until Labor Day. He was a Victorian in dress, and wore striped cambric shirts with detachable collars and starched cuffs, brass collar buttons, plain gold cuff links, and a small gold lion's head stickpin with a tiny ruby eye in dark blue, dark purple or dark, dark carmine figured silk ties. He preferred pin-stripe suits, and I never saw him with his coat and vest off in the office, even in steamy August. In summer he changed to tan linen suits, never baggy, never wrinkled. I thought he was very handsome with his Indian high cheekbones, aquiline nose, black hair, blue eyes, set chin. When he grew older he looked like Lincoln, not so tall, but with Lincoln's deep-set eyes and melancholy, the melancholy of a man who believed he had failed—failed his wife, his family, his heritage. He could not have been more wrong.

On this particular bright Saturday as he rounded the curve, his step was that of a comfortable paterfamilias who soon would experience his greatest pleasure, reunion with his wife and children in his own home. I saw that he was carrying a small packet and I knew what it contained. I jumped from the window, away from the bubble that stared back at me, and I ran to my mother: "Daddy's coming!"

Then he was at the front door being kissed by his wife, herself happy and gay, her waist-long hair a golden mass, blue eyes sparkling behind golden pince-nez attached to gold button on frothy white shirtwaist. He put the packet in Mother's hands, reached into an inner pocket, extracted a small manila envelope sealed with waxed red string, handed this to her, then looked at Janet and myself in mock surprise as we jumped up and down, shouting: "What's for us?"

This was the Saturday ceremonial. It occurred every two weeks. We went into the dining room, the sun sweeping through the stiff Brussels curtains and pocking highlights on the black carved furniture. Mother's quick fingers untwisted the red twine and out sparkled a handful of golden coins, six of them, six twenty-dollar gold pieces, heavy, almost greasy to the touch, rolling out on the sunlit table, my father's salary at the factory. No one was paid by check, it was always by cash—factory people once a week in big green bills and silver coins, office heads twice a month in gold. Class-conscious money. Mother turned to the packet. "And what is this?" she asked as she always asked. "Open it! Open it!" Janet and I demanded. Slowly she pulled away the white paper, exposing a box covered in crinkly gold imprinted with the name "Ivy." It was, as we all knew it would be, the pound of chocolate which Dad brought home from Ivy's shop on Nicollet Avenue every two weeks. We were permitted one chocolate each, one for Janet, one for me. This was grownups' candy. When we were put down for naps, Dad came into the room. We appealed for candy. He had none. Then, mysteriously, he pulled back the pillow and a gumdrop was discovered; doodle candy I called it, God knows why. How did he do it? I never figured it out.

The plant closed at 1 P.M. on Saturday. Every day the factory shift went to work at seven. You could hear the seven o'clock factory whistles all over town. The office started at seven-thirty. Dad's day ended at five. He spent his life on that schedule. I do not believe there was a single day in fifty years of work that gave him pleasure.

The Northern Bag Company was an extension of the flour-milling industry. Minneapolis was two things: lumber and flour. It was the biggest milling center in the world. I grew up to the smell of sawdust burning, mountains of sawdust endlessly burning at the Camden Place mills above St. Anthony's Falls, the pungent pitch itching my nostrils. One cold spring day in 1919, I watched the last log drive down the Mississippi, the logs filling the river bank to bank, great booms to corset them, the jacks leaping log to log, timber to timber, jam to jam, spikes on heels, peaveys and cant hooks in hand. The air was thick in spring with the smoke of sawdust fires and thicker in autumn with the smoke of forest fires, the Hinckley fire (which my mother narrowly escaped—it killed more than four hundred people —riding out on the Northern Pacific train; the train carried three hundred fifty people, and engineer Jack Root's hands were burned to the throttle when they got to Duluth), the Moose Lake–Cloquet fire, which darkened Minneapolis and drove deer, bear and birds a hundred miles south, a horned owl sitting one morning in the oak tree, staring in my window. My father's Home Guard regiment went north and he helped stack burned bodies on the railroad platform. The smell of the charred corpses haunted him for years.

Before I was born, northern Minnesota had been cut over, burned over, ravaged by the timber barons. Minnesota was the happy land of barons: timber barons, Shevlin, Heffelfinger, Walker, Weyerhaeuser; milling barons, Washburn, Crosby, Bell, Pillsbury; railroad barons, Jim Hill, who fought Jay Gould and E. H. Harriman to a standstill; iron barons, Gary, Frick, Carnegie. The timber barons beat all. They slashed away the lordly Norway pine which mantled northern Minnesota, Wisconsin and Michigan, slamming the logs down rivers to the mills, leaving behind the raddled earth, a ruin that had no equal until our petrochemicals turned the forests of Vietnam into hell. So technology advances. Forty years after the devastation, I began to canoe in the North Woods along the Canadian border. My friends and I had to pick our trails with care to bypass tamarack swamps, log-choked streams, square miles of stumps that looked like Belleau Wood, a monument to the Almighty Dollar.

The milling business was different. No one thought badly of milling wheat. No one thought badly of turning the prairie, of bringing the plow to the soil. This was man's duty. Man lived by the

21

sweat of his brow and bread was the stuff of life. No one regretted the high grass that extended like a sea from the Mississippi to the Missouri and beyond, the grass that nourished the buffalo, the Sioux, the Chippewa, in a symbiotic life. No one thought of that. To bring plow to prairie, to break the sod (and break the men)—this, as I grew up to understand, was civilization, progress, turning land to use; *use* was the word. I could not have imagined dust bowls, erosion, red gullies that bloodied the hills, irrevocable annihilation of earth and plant and animal. To be American, I understood, was to be hell-bent for change. Away with the prairie that stretched to the horizon and on to the next horizon. Bring in the plow. Rip the earth. Endure in a sod hut with your bone-skinny wife and the bone-skinny children. Build a log cabin. Bury your wife and get another, a strong young one. Work. Work. Work.

This was the philosophy on which I was raised, the pioneer spirit, boosterism, as Sinclair Lewis called it, the American way, as Henry Luce would say. Not until I read the novels of Willa Cather, O. E. Rölvaag and Frank Norris did I begin to see what was wrong. The grain poured into the mills at St. Anthony's Falls. I remember my pride, my wonder and my fear when my father showed me the falls, turbulent brown water, and the gray mills that lined the river like battlements. (St. Anthony's Falls does not turn a wheel today; not a flour mill, not one, remains; water power is out; Washburn Crosby is General Mills, big on fast foods, toys, electronics and frosted cornflakes.) St. Anthony's Falls ground the wheat of Minnesota, the Dakotas, Montana, all bound together by Jim Hill's iron rails, the Northern Pacific, the Great Northern, the Burlington. Into Minneapolis poured the wheat and from the mills flour flowed to the world.

The North Dakota farmers took a different view of all this. They saw the millers as part of a crooked combine with the railroads, the elevator men, the bankers, the speculators of the Chicago wheat pit, an unholy alliance that rigged prices and drove the farmers to the wall. The monopoly was the blight of humanity, capitalists ruled the world by money, by money-love. The oratory of the Populists, the Nonpartisan League, was florid but it made the point.

Untimely thoughts. So these would have seemed in the living room at 107 Royalston, where my father and my uncle smoked their cigars and pondered the state of the world. Untimely? Revolutionary! But the blood sagas of the barons were ready meat for my greedy ears. These were told and relished: the seven Merritt brothers, who

22

discovered the Mesabi iron range, and the steel barons who stole it and sent them to ruin; Jim Hill, sitting in his St. Paul castle and hurling back the challenge of Jay Gould, devils condemning each to perdition and Archbishop Ireland saving Jim Hill's soul on his deathbed, a pretty penny for the Church; the bold young logger who married the old timber baron's daughter and then tossed the old man into the river with a twist of his peavey, deaf to his cries, and inheriting the fortune. What was truth? Did it matter? These were tales of giants that illuminated the lust, the greed, the plunder.

I do not suppose a man less apt at business existed than my father; an artist; not a great artist, but a wonderfully satisfying one, with a sure hand, an eye for likeness. He enjoyed sketching still lifes, dogs, cats, horses and children, and made a hobby of rather elaborate wood carving, for he loved the textures of woods. He enjoyed the work of William Morris and the handicrafts of the Oneida community. He liked color and succumbed to the 1880s rage for Rosa Bonheur, Edwin Landseer, Delacroix, Henri Rousseau; he collected exotica: Persian rugs, Armenian brasses, Turkish water pipes. He pored over architectural journals and books and planned every detail of the house he hoped to build on the Mississippi riverbank. His bent was well developed before he entered the University of Minnesota in 1889, son of a moderately well-to-do and popular doctor, an attractive young man with attractive friends, men and women. He was a sensitive amateur photographer, and left a collection of plates that exquisitely illuminate the life of Oak Lake Addition and the early years of his marriage, not unlike Leonard Dakin's record of Cherry Valley, New York. He developed and printed his own work. His pictures were tart, simple, evocative, often humorous. He had a good voice, loved to sing, strummed a good banjo and a sentimental mandolin. Later he taught himself to play a squeaky violin to accompany my mother's rather boisterous piano. She played the "Warsaw" Concerto with such gusto that I grew up thinking it portrayed the Battle of Warsaw. Dad took romantic leads in amateur theatricals. He was very fond of pretty girls. He was a fine hunter, spending afternoons in the nearby countryside shooting partridge and ducks. He owned a beautiful English shotgun, which he sold when he was desperate for money. He taught me to shoot and shoot well. He believed in guns and would stand for no nonsense where they were concerned, a lesson I learned from him. He never raised his voice.

23

He told me once that he had expected to study medicine and go into partnership with his father, but when Dr. Salisbury fell ill he told Percy that the life of the doctor was too hard. You could not do your duty to your patients without neglecting your family. He forebade his son to take up medicine. So Percy Pritchard Salisbury, a little solemn, shy, reticent, twenty-one years old, standing in the red cherry library where Dr. Salisbury spent his last year of life, swore to his father that he would not become a doctor. I think he would have been a grand doctor. His gray-blue eyes could see into your soul. But I think his father was right. A family doctor ninety years ago needed an iron constitution and an iron will. My father was not made of steel. The profession would have killed him as it did his father.

Now my father was free to follow his bent, to become an architect. But Grandfather Salisbury's death coincided with the panic of '93. His money was tied up in two Minneapolis banks which failed. The money his patients owed him was in the same closed banks. My father took up the unpleasant task of bill collecting. He did not do well. Mary Pritchard Salisbury was a demanding woman in the Victorian tradition. With the death of her husband, she took to her bed and never emerged, placing her son Percy in thrall for seven years until she died, in 1900. He turned away from the mandolin, blackface theatricals, sketching still lifes, picnics in the country with saucy Maude Derickson or pretty Josie Mann. He spent a year or two trying to collect bills and then found a job with a firm run by an upstate New Yorker and a handful of men from Dundee. They had set up a bag business in Minneapolis. Dundee was the milling center of Scotland; Minneapolis, of the U.S.A. There was bound to be a profit, and indeed, there was a smart ha'penny and a deal more for the Christians, the Falconers and the Skinners. They knew their business to the last strand of jute, the toughest hemp and the stoutest cotton. Into the ranks of this cold-eyed company Percy Salisbury entered and there he was to remain for the rest of his life. There could not have been a greater misfit.

I didn't know that. I was fascinated by my father; by the six doubloons twice a month; by the miniature flour samples he gave us, doll sacks bearing the Gold Medal label just like the big sacks; by the curious stamps ripped off letters from Scotland and India. Mother loved the lengths of Osnaburg Dad brought home, seconds, and the misprints, the flour sacks with wrong labels or bled colors. Bleach them and they made dish towels or even curtains. I loved the mill: the pounding of the presses, the huge stamping machines, the automatic sewing machines, the looms, the smell of jute and Osnaburg and ink.

Very early I knew that my father was different from other men. My uncle Andrew, handsome, brown-haired, pipe-smoking, loved to talk about his receiverships; sometimes he brought home a suitcase of dress materials, thread, ribbon, buttons, buckles, linings, from a bankrupt shop for my aunt Mary, who was a dressmaker. He talked of crooks and crookedness, of sly tricks and coups. John Dort would talk all afternoon about the Milwaukee railroad, and Charley Gaskill, who sold coats and jackets on the road, couldn't wait, relaxing in the front porch swing, lighting up his seegar, to begin talking of "conditions." "Conditions" were never, never good, but they were always expected to get better. Dad loved a good Havana cigar. He smoked with the rest. But I never heard him say one word about "conditions" or the bag business. He listened. More likely he didn't listen, his mind far away in that secret place I never penetrated.

I think the men from New York State and Scotland with whom he worked liked my father in their dry, dusty way. Of course, they would have been the last to say it. I think they liked him because he was totally loyal, totally conscientious. He did everything he was asked and did it promptly and accurately. I don't think he ever initiated anything.

I believe the men from Dundee knew that Dad didn't belong with them, that he marched to another tune, but they respected him because he never complained, and could be depended upon. I don't know how many times he told me: "If a thing is worth doing, it is worth doing well." Usually he said this after I had made a mess of something—splitting the wood I was driving a nail into or failing to shake out the clinkers before putting coal on the fire. He was not given to aphorisms and this is the only one I remember his repeating. I think he lived by it and the Scots respected him for it.

To this day I do not know what Dad did at the factory. Oh, I know one thing: he locked up the safe at night. The safe was Dad's responsibility. He closed it in the evening and opened it in the morning, last man out, first man in. A responsible job—well, a servitor's job, as became clear after they put him out on the factory floor, on his feet all day at nearly seventy and made to understand it was just a matter of charity, keeping him on. I never knew what he did in the factory. I didn't want to ask, because I knew he didn't want me to know. But he continued to lock the safe at night and open it in the morning. At 2 A.M. he would awaken, possessed with certainty that he had not locked the safe. He could see it standing open. He would slip from bed, quickly dress and walk to the plant, a three-mile walk in the dead of night, often in the dead of winter, temperature twenty below zero. He would walk to the plant, let himself in with his passkey, check with the night watchman and visit the big safe. It was always locked. So he would sit in the office from 3 A.M. or 4 A.M., shivering in his overcoat until the first shift began arriving and he could get a cup of coffee. Dear, dear man.

The gold pieces. The war years were golden for the millers. For the farmers, as well. Wheat two dollars a bushel. Before the war it had been fifty cents, and there were times when you couldn't give wheat away. Two-dollar wheat! Minneapolis couldn't ship enough flour to match the U-boat sinkings. Grain poured like a golden river into the elevators, siphoned from the boxcars, the chaff filling the air. Wheat, wheat, wheat, the combines working through the night, migrant labor in Gateway Square, shipping by the thousands to North Dakota and the Red River of the North, every empty freight car filled with the 'boes, going north to work the harvest, to Fargo, to Bismarck, to Great Falls, golden grain pouring into Pillsbury A, pouring into Washburn Crosby Main, twenty-four hours a day, bags, bags, bags, never enough, bags for flour, bags for grain, bags for the army, three shifts a day, the money rolled in. Yes. By now there must have been another gold piece or two in the manila envelope.

One day I heard my father telling my mother the news. Old George H. Christian had died, the founder of the mill. He had left the business to the "boys," all the stock, and Dad along with the others. "We will never have to worry again." I could hear the sound of his voice. Bubbling. Happy. "How much? How much?" Mother asked. Dad's reply meant nothing. It was—what?—fifteen thousand, twenty thousand, a little more, a little less. It was just grand. I don't know what Mother and Dad did that night. Probably they went to Rogers' Café, *the* night spot in Minneapolis, the only one, the one with the artificial waterfall and the mirror as you went downstairs from the street, and they drank champagne.

That night Dad laughed. Well, you know, he said, George H. was a skinflint to the last. He didn't *give* us the stock, as he could have just as well. What he did was to let us *buy* the stock. Not that it makes any difference. It pays for itself from the dividends. Isn't that like him?

26

Mother couldn't understand. I couldn't. But it didn't make any difference. Don't bother. It's just a technicality. The dividend is so high it will buy the stock in three years. It's just one last Scots touch—from beyond the grave. Dad laughed. He loved the Scots that night.

Dad was easy, relieved. We'll pay off the mortgage on 107, the one Dr. Salisbury took out, he said, and he began looking over the plans for the Mississippi River house. The house would be a clean white colonial. I was disappointed. I had fallen in love with England and I longed for a house of exposed beams, plaster and fake thatch, Anne Hathaway's cottage.

Happy days. There must have been more gold pieces in the envelope. I heard all the talk and then it stopped. Just like that. The grain boom burst. In Minnesota, 1929 happened in 1920. The mills ground to a halt. You couldn't give bags away. Government contracts were canceled. Business—there was no business. But what difference did it make? The stock put Dad on easy street and it paid for itself, didn't it? Just an old man's whim against giving something away, wasn't it?

Like hell it was. There were no dividends. Not in 1920. Not in '21. Not in '22. If you wanted your stock, you put up your money. If you didn't have the money—too bad. You couldn't expect the company to go broke paying for stock that was supposed to be bought, could you? That busted it. No more dream. Oh, it was 1929, all right, but nobody yet knew there would be a 1929. For Minnesota it would be 1929 until 1929, and then 1929 would go on forever.

What was a man to do? The look that came to my father's face would stay there for the rest of his life. It just settled down. Not a mask, just a tiredness, a terrible tiredness.

27

# Chapter 4

# Going to War

I was a few months shy of thirty-one when World War II started; my son Michael was not quite six months old. I was a certified star writer and reporter for the UP Press Agency and had, I thought, a working grasp of Washington and national politics. I had been attending the national political conventions since 1932 and I knew the Senate well, particularly men of the old populist tradition like Nye and La Follette. George Norris was my hero. I had become fond of Eleanor Roosevelt, an affection that would continue to the end of her life.

I spent a good deal of time at the State Department. I respected the crusty Cordell Hull, though I knew the secretary of state had little influence with FDR. Under the tutelage of Arnold Gingrich, for whose magazines I had written, I had lost some of my insularity.

Washington was a more comfortable, more commonsensical place than it is today. The security mania had not taken over. The only credential you needed to cover the White House was a plain white pasteboard issued by the Correspondents Association and signed by Stephen T. Early, FDR's press secretary. No plastic idents on a chain, no four-color laminated photos, no background checks, no metal detectors, no fingerprints, and you never even showed your card. There were no guards at the White House gates, just a friendly White House policeman at the pressroom door who knew everyone. In the New Deal years, I never saw him stop a single person. At the State Department, there were no credentials at all, no guards; anyone could enter and wander from floor to floor of that wonderful General Grant pile. The floors were marble parquet and there were beautiful mahogany slatted doors at each office so the breeze stirred up by the ceiling fans could circulate in summer. Sleepy black servitors sat outside the offices of the secretaries of state, war and navy (all three in the building then) and nodded to visitors.

A few years ago, I read a study of the Alger Hiss case which described how difficult it would have been for anyone on the outside to have got access to secret State Department documents. The author, a man named Epstein, mentioned guards, credentials, clearances. There were no such things. Corridor after corridor was lined with old wooden filing cabinets, no locks, stuffed with State Department documents. Anyone could stroll down the halls, stop, pull out a drawer and select what he wanted. Secretaries, clerks and minor officials did it all the time. War brought a little change to this; not much.

Nothing was more inevitable than the outbreak of World War II. By September 1, 1939, it had become totally unavoidable. But nothing was so amazing to me, to the country and to the world as the signing by Molotov and Ribbentrop of the Nazi-Soviet pact on August 24, 1939. True, rumors had circulated in Moscow, since shortly after the May 1 dismissal of Maksim M. Litvinov as Soviet foreign minister, that a deal with Germany might be possible. But they had been dismissed by all reputable commentators including *The New York Times*'s Walter Duranty. After the event, a dozen clues to what had been developing were quickly identified, but until August 24, nobody paid heed to them.

Forty years would pass before I would discover that the inside story of this event, the negotiations between Hitler and Stalin, had not been secret at all. The whole thing had been made known in meticulous detail to the governments of the United States, Great Britain, France and Italy, all this through the daring of a young German diplomat, Hans Von Herwarth, or Johnny, as he was known to my old friend Charles ("Chip") Bohlen, who told me much of the story and presented what he knew in his memoirs in 1973.

What Chip knew was that Johnny, an attaché of the German embassy in Moscow as Bohlen was an attaché of the American embassy, had briefed him, step by step, as the secret Nazi-Soviet diplomacy progressed. Bohlen did not learn until after the war that Johnny in 1939 was a member of an anti-Hitler underground desperately hoping to keep Hitler from starting a war. Nor did Bohlen know that Johnny had talked with anyone else. It was not until 1981 that Johnny revealed he had first tried to alert the Italians, hoping that Mussolini might halt Hitler. He tried agonizingly to convince the British and the French that unless they unfroze the glacial talks they were conducting with the Russians in Moscow, Hitler would leave them at the starting post.

None of these efforts succeeded. Mussolini was only mildly

interested. London and Paris gave no sign they even read the dispatches instigated by Von Herwarth. Only in Washington were Bohlen's reports taken seriously. Late in the game, very late, Secretary Hull called in the British and the French to warn what was impending. There is nothing in the record to show that Hull influenced the Foreign Office or the Quai d'Orsay in the slightest. As Von Herwarth told me in 1981: "They lacked the imagination to perceive that a Nazi-Soviet pact was possible, and even had they foreseen this, they had nothing to offer the Russians"—that is, they were not prepared to conclude a genuine alliance. The fatally feckless course of Chamberlain and Daladier continued. Neither Cordell Hull nor Franklin Roosevelt, both of whom understood the implications of the German-Soviet talks, gave thought of leaking the information to the press in order to compel the British and the French to derail the Hitler-Stalin talks. Such publicity would have delayed the outbreak of war or at least put the world on warning as to what lay ahead. Neither Hull nor Roosevelt acted, and Von Herwarth's courageous attempt to alert the West constituted, in the end, the first great intelligence disaster of World War II.

I asked Von Herwarth later why, in his view, no one followed up on the rumors of Soviet-German contacts which had circulated in Moscow during that pleasant summer of 1939. He had no answer. He could not understand it. He had risked his life by leaking the details, in the belief that any experienced diplomat would draw the obvious conclusions. They had not. The episode reinforced my belief in the eternal rightness of those words of Abraham Lincoln that Gingrich had put on the masthead of *Ken*, "Let the people know the truth and the country is safe."

It was not and would not be leaks that would do us in, but suppression of the facts of what was happening in the world.

The war changed my life. Six months after the outbreak, I was transferred to New York to handle the cable and wireless reports from London, Paris, Berlin and Moscow. I got to New York just in time for the transformation of the "phony war" to the real war, to write of Hitler's invasion of Denmark and Norway, the Low Countries, the fall of France. I didn't have a moment's free breath. In the summer of 1940 came the political conventions, the nomination of Willkie at Philadelphia and Roosevelt for a third term at Chicago. I covered both, torn between my liking for Willkie and a sense that times were too dangerous to change leaders. My then wife, Mary, and I took a vacation in Minneapolis after FDR was nominated. It was a quiet interlude. Dad and Mike played together in the backyard, we took drives in the Minnesota countryside, the harvest at full swing, the great red combines cutting golden wakes across the endless fields.

While we were in Minneapolis, we got a letter from a woman named Lucy, who with her husband had been looking after our house in the New York suburb of Mamaroneck: "House has been searched by an unknown person." Nothing seemed to have been taken. She had called the police but apparently only my papers had been disturbed. The police wanted to know if I had left behind anything important, "especially Mr. Salisbury's papers concerning the war."

Of course, I had no important papers about the war, and when we found that our war bonds—$475 worth—and my insurance papers were intact, we stopped worrying. I talked to the police when I got home and they minimized the affair: probably just some high school kids who wanted to use the house for a party.

I dismissed the matter myself. The question about war papers lingered in my mind, but I thought that was a product of the growing hysteria. France had fallen. The battle of Britain was beginning. Soon we would be listening to Edward R. Murrow saying: "This—is London."

The Luftwaffe seemed all-powerful. Hitler had invented the blitz-krieg. Would he invade England? The world had suddenly grown dark and dangerous. I was working harder and harder. We bought a lovely old Federal house, at 303 North Barry Avenue in Mamaroneck, from Henry Steele Commager. He refused to make any profit, sold it for what he had paid, $7,500. "I don't believe in taking advantage of a hard-working young newspaper-man." We put in a garden and played badminton with our next-door neighbors. I learned about suburbia and commuting. We had no car. Once again I felt restless and frustrated. Sometimes I missed my train and had a martini or two with a young magazine editor. I told her I wanted to be a war correspondent. I was sick of sitting at my desk and pounding out roundups and new leads all day, going home on the commuter train. She sympathized a lot.

Saturday, June 21, 1941, was a lovely early-summer day. We had invited Bernie Geis, the editor of *Coronet*, and his wife, Darlene, to spend the weekend. I worked late at UP and after dinner we sat on the back porch, drinking rum swizzles and talking about the war. I said that the Germans were going to attack Russia that weekend. Bernie was skeptical. I told him every report that had come in indicated the Germans were massed on the Soviet frontier, ready to invade. This was the word from London, from Washington, from Switzerland, from Sweden, fromTokyo, from Turkey and even from Berlin—if you read the dispatches carefully. The only place where the news seemed to be totally bland was Moscow.

"I just can't believe it," Bernie said. "Why would Hitler do that?"

"Well," I said, "he's always wanted to and now he's made up his mind on the *Drang nach Osten*—the drive to the east." I told Bernie that I had written flatly in my war lead—flatly without qualification—that the German assault would come this weekend.

"As a matter of fact," I said, looking at my wristwatch, "it's ten-thirty now. That's four-thirty A.M. Sunday in Moscow. I wouldn't be surprised if they were going across the border right now."

The telephone rang. "O.K., Bernie," I said, "there it is."

It was. The office was calling me to say the Nazis had attacked Russia all along the frontier. I dashed for the train. By the time I got home again, it was noon Sunday. The Germans were deep into Russia and had already destroyed most of the Soviet airforce.

For the second time, a massive intelligence failure had occurred. Now, because Stalin stubbornly, insanely, had refused to credit the reports submitted to him, the world faced a catastrophe. Stalin had not believed the evidence of his own remarkable spy network in Berlin and Tokyo, he had disregarded warnings from Churchill, Roosevelt and even Mao Zedong (although, of course, we did not know this then). Thus the Soviet almost collapsed under the Nazi blitz and was saved only by the sacrifice of twenty to thirty million lives of her citizens.

The Nazi-Soviet pact had caught me by surprise. Not so the Nazi attack of June 22, 1941. I had seen the evidence mount up. For nearly three weeks I had been predicting the attack and on that Saturday afternoon of June 21 I had taken all the facts and put them before Earl Johnson, the UP news director. "I want to do something we have not done before," I said. "I want to write tonight without qualification— without any qualification—that the German war against Russia will begin this weekend." Johnson read the reports carefully. "O.K." he said finally. "But remember it's your ass if you're wrong." I grinned. I didn't have to remind him that it was his ass too.

The Western news agencies and newspapers were caught badly off base when war came to Moscow. Because of intense American partisanship for the Finns, they had pulled their correspondents out during the Russian winter war with Finland and hadn't sent them back. Even the news agencies had only bare-bones staffs. UP had Henry Shapiro and AP had Henry Cassidy. That was all.

I was appalled as Hitler's Wehrmacht swept into Russia. There seemed to be no stopping them. The military experts in Washington and London predicted it would be over in six weeks. Not until later was it revealed that Colonel Faymonville, long-time American military attaché in Moscow, alone among military specialists insisted from the start that regardless of losses, the Red Army would prevail. He was to pay a heavy penalty for being right, for betting on the Russians and not the Germans. In 1943, he was yanked out of Moscow, and finally he was drummed out of the army, because his colleagues considered him "pro-Soviet"—one more example of the fate of men who report an uncomfortable truth.

I could not believe Stalin had been caught by surprise. Of course, neither I nor anyone outside the Kremlin realized that he had fallen into a trauma, had run away to his dacha and locked himself within, convinced that "all that Lenin created for us had been lost forever," as Nikita Khrushchev was to reveal.

Of all this there was no hint in 1941. True, the Red Army was falling back; true, the Germans were advancing; but Stalin was receiving the emissaries of Churchill and Roosevelt—Harry L. Hopkins, W. Averell Harriman, Anthony Eden, Sir Stafford Cripps. He admitted his problems, but radiated confidence.

It was clear that Roosevelt and Churchill saw the war as a common cause. I knew that we were going in sooner rather than later. I knew that we were not going to permit Hitler to destroy England or possess Russia. Somehow I was convinced that the invasion of Russia had sealed Hitler's downfall. How did I convince myself of that? Well, Napoleon's example was the main thing. Another was my conviction that the United States would shift the balance.

Yet as I came in each morning to write the war leads and watched Hitler's armored forces race across the Ukraine (they claimed they inflicted two million casualties in taking Kiev), storm up to the gates of Leningrad (would the Russians be able to hold the northern capital?) and in early October drive to the suburbs of Moscow, I could not but wonder. Then toward the end of October 1941, it began to seem to me that the Nazis had been slowed; they had not taken Moscow as Goebbels had proclaimed they would; they had not broken into Leningrad. Maybe, just maybe, the tide was beginning to turn, and I reflected this feeling in my dispatches.

Saturday, December 6, was a beautiful springlike day, the grass still green on the Mamaroneck lawns, and when I went to work that morning I saw buds opening up on the lilacs. In the newsroom, December 6 was another day of crisis. We had become inured to weekend crises because Hitler had made them a cliché. If something was going to happen, it happened on a weekend. Every dispatch that reached my desk from the Pacific spoke of imminent war: Japanese convoys, Japanese warships, ominous preparations. This was the word from Frank Hewlett in Manila, from Robert Bellaire in Tokyo, from Pepper Martin in Shanghai, from Dick Wilson in Hong Kong.

I had been watching closely the talks in Washington between Mr. Hull and the Japanese. It seemed clear that they had broken down. That the crisis was coming to a head I had no doubt.

As always, I wrote a general lead on Saturday night, wrapping up the war news. I said: "War in the Pacific seemed powder-close Saturday night." But I qualified this, raising the question of whether the Japanese would attack this weekend or a bit later.

There were two reasons for my qualification. The first was that the Japanese had permitted a freighter, the *Tatuta Maru*, to sail from Yokohama for the United States four days earlier. The second was that the dispatches from Moscow made clear that the Red Army had gone over to the offensive and was beginning to drive the Germans back—the first time the Germans had retreated since Hitler unleashed the Wehrmacht, September 1, 1939. I thought the Japanese might delay action until after January 1, 1942, in order to observe developments on the eastern front. I had convinced myself that war was to Japan's disadvantage and that Japan's civilian cabinet opposed war. Of course, I was right on both points, but I did not understand the strength of the militarists who actually ran Japan.

Sunday, December 7, the weather changed. Mary and I went to the Polo Grounds with our friends Nordau Schoenberg and his wife, to watch the big pro football game, the Brooklyn Dodgers versus the New York Giants. There was a huge crowd and a stiff cold wind. We left before the end of the game and went to Nordau's apartment for a drink. We turned on the radio as an announcer cut in with "additional details on the Japanese bombing of Pearl Harbor."

Nordau was deeply moved. I had a curious reaction. "Those poor little Japanese bastards," I said. "The suicide boys have got them in the soup. They are finished. They are through. They haven't got a chance."

By attacking Pearl Harbor, I said, the militarists had cast the die for war, and war with the United States meant defeat for Japan. That was true. But defeat was years away and would cost many lives.

I went into the office and heard how heavy the fleet losses were—though the figures were only a fraction of the real total.

I had no notion that the United States had broken the Japanese purple code and was able to follow the government's secret movements and decisions, but immediately after Pearl Harbor I began to hear from friends in Washington sensational reports about our real losses and the failure of the army and navy in Hawaii to maintain an alert. They had, I was told, lowered vigilance over the weekend of December 6–7; though the attacking Japanese planes had been detected by radar or sonic devices, the signals had been ignored. The smell of a major intelligence breakdown was strong. Before December 1941 was out, I understood that while we had anticipated an attack by Japan that weekend, we had not imagined that it would strike Pearl Harbor. Southeast Asia, Hong Kong, Singapore, Manila, Indonesia—yes, all this was anticipated, but not Pearl Harbor. Even though MacArthur had been strongly reinforced with planes in anticipation of war, the Japanese had managed to destroy his air arm.

As would be revealed in due course, Pearl Harbor was the third intelligence disaster of the war. War, it would seem, almost by definition consists of intelligence failures; World War II would provide extraordinary evidence of this.

In the first week of January 1942, I went to Washington to handle the big war stories there, principally the battle of the Philippines, which MacArthur was fighting gallantly but obviously was doomed to lose. I handled reports of the battle in Malaysia, the rapidly deteriorating situation in Indonesia and the threat to Burma. I got the full story of the Pearl Harbor losses from Wallace Carroll, UP's London correspondent, who arrived in Washington after a journey around the world via Russia, Iran, India and the Pacific. He had much information about the incredibly careless conduct of the U.S. command in Hawaii. Naturally, none of this could be published.

I was dismayed by the lack of public understanding of war; the wild expectations of immediate victory; the ignorance of basic logistics. People could not see why we didn't just rush troops to Southeast Asia and shatter the Japanese. I found to my surprise that I had acquired some notion of war's reality from studying the Civil War during my Washington days. I had read and reread Douglas Southall Freeman's classic four-volume biography of Robert E. Lee, and G. F. Henderson's study of Stonewall Jackson. I had visited the battlefields at Gettysburg and Chancellorsville, walking over the terrain. This gave me some understanding of the importance of preparation and surprise. The side that was ready to strike possessed an extraordinary advantage, which could not quickly be overtaken by the other side. It might hold good for a year or two years; it might even cause defeat. I applied this principle to the Russians and concluded that not before late 1942 or 1943 would they be able to make up the damage inflicted by the initial Nazi attack. I put the same measure against the United States in the Pacific and inferred that it would take us equally long to begin to turn the tables against the Japanese.

I don't pretend that all my conclusions were farseeing. Many were not. Some were childish. Since I wrote them down, I can cite them against myself. I predicted in early January 1942 that Singapore would be lost by February 1, the Dutch islands by March 1. These were good guesses. I suggested that the next big battles would be in Burma (correct) and in Alaska and Australia (totally wrong). I thought the Germans would attack Cyprus and Malta, but that their main target would be Ireland (totally wrong). I thought that the Pacific east of Hawaii was gone. I thought the Nazis would drive deep into the Caucasus in the spring of 1942, aided by Turkey. The Germans went for Stalingrad and the Caucasus, lost both. I thought Rommel would cut the Suez. He tried and failed.

I was disturbed to find that my friends in army intelligence and in the State Department didn't seem to think much of the Soviet achievement in halting the Germans before Moscow and successfully counterattacking in December and January. The Red Army had driven back the Nazis fifty or sixty miles, the first land defeat Hitler had suffered since moving into the Rhineland in 1936. In Washington, this was attributed to General Winter, not the Red Army. I thought the Moscow victory plus the aid that we and the British would give Stalin marked a turn in the war. I was more right than the military intelligence people, but it would not be until the Russian counterblow at Stalingrad late in 1942 that the outcome of the war would be finally fixed.

I was depressed by Washington. The capital seemed overwhelmed in bureaucratic struggle. FDR was dominant over Congress and setting the pace, but the congressional isolationists still held powerful positions and were only biding their time. Already the shape of America First policy had begun to emerge—fight the Pacific war and leave the British and Russians to cope with Germany. I thought the isolationists' real objective was to arrange a peace between the West and Germany, permitting the Nazis to polish off Russia while we wiped up Japan.

The strongest impression I had—and this came in large measure from some of the air corps men whom I knew, men like General Carl ("Tooey") Spaatz, Colonel Henry Berlinger and others—was what I called the "mass ignorance, stupidity and ineptness of the top American [military] staff." I thought this condition would prevail until the wear and tear of battle cleared out the deadwood. I didn't know much about General George C. Marshall, but what I did know spoke well for him. I formed a high regard for General MacArthur despite his loss of air force to the Japanese—it was a regard I retained throughout the war, intensified when late in 1944 I got to his command headquarters in New Guinea, met him and observed the extraordinary military machine he had welded together—in his own image.

For the generals in Washington, I am afraid, I had little but contempt. As I noted at the time: "[They] seem to have learned little or nothing from the war so far; [have] no comprehension of the significance of Pearl Harbor; are more inclined than ever to keep their heads down, do nothing (especially nothing new) to avoid presenting a moving target." It was, alas, a picture I would see many times during the war and after.

"It is almost impossible," I wrote, "to locate an offensive-minded, realistic, hard-boiled thinker in the army high command. To a suggestion that propaganda might be utilized as a military weapon, they throw up their arms in horror, exclaiming: 'Of course, we wouldn't think of using a Nazi method!'"

It was almost certainly Tooey Spaatz who gave me that vignette. The air corps in January 1942 was in revolt. They talked gloomily of the loss of the whole Pacific and the complete collapse of the British,

even of heavy German air attacks on the U.S. coast if the drift of the
early days was not quickly halted. The navy, of course, was in a state
of shock.

I was back in New York at the end of February, determined that I
would go abroad as a war correspondent. The UP had on January 21,
1942, applied for my credentials to go overseas. This didn't mean that
I was going. The UP asked accreditation for a group of us, just to be
prepared. But I was moving toward a resolution of my personal and
professional life. I did not see how I could stay out of the war, feeling
as I did about Hitler, believing as I did that the future of the world
depended on the defeat of Nazi Germany and the Japanese. I was
capable of great hypocrisy, that I knew, but I did not see how I could
live with myself without taking a hand in the struggle of our time.
There was a lot of old-fashioned American patriotism in my makeup.
TR and Blackjack Pershing had not been my youthful heroes for
nothing. And, it should be added, patriotism was not a dirty word in
1941. Perhaps I should simply volunteer for the army. But this did
not seem right to me. I might or might not be a good soldier. I knew I
was a good reporter and could serve the war effort by reporting from
the front. This was the story of my lifetime and I wanted a part of it.

There was building up for a second time a crisis in my personal life.
Mary and I were not getting on. I had, or thought I had, fallen in love
with another girl. I didn't know how this would work out, but I
believed that if I threw myself into the war I could clarify my feelings;
distance and involvement in the fighting would give me perspective.

Mary was not warm to the idea of my going abroad as a foreign
correspondent, but she was not hostile either. Many of my friends
were preparing to go. The young woman who had captured my
affections thought I should go. "Let's face it," she said. "You are a
writer. The only place for a writer in these times is at the front."

It took six months for the details to be worked out, but by autumn
1942, UP had decided to send me to London. The situation in the
London bureau was chaotic. A remarkable correspondent, Webb
Miller, had headed London before and after the outbreak of war, but
in the spring of 1940 he was killed when he fell from a British train
during a blackout. Miller, a gifted, poetic writer who felt that the war
would destroy the England (and Europe) he loved, had been deeply
pessimistic about the future, and embodied much of his pessimism in
a brilliant book, *There Is No Peace*. Miller drank a good deal but was

not a man to lose control. The autopsy said he fell from the train as he stood between cars to relieve himself. I always thought it was suicide.

The bureau then had been placed in charge of a hard-hitting war correspondent, Edward W. Beattie, Jr., but Beattie had gone off to the front. The store was not being minded and Joe Alex Morris, UP foreign editor, was sent over to straighten things out. He and Earl Johnson finally decided I should go to London and take over the bureau.

So I found myself in December 1942 dashing about New York getting inoculations, loading up on vitamin pills and sulfa drugs, buying a money belt, into which the UP business office stuffed God knows how many beautiful white English ten-pound notes, each almost the size of a double damask dinner napkin, to help finance our London bureau. (No one told me that bringing in these black market notes was a violation of English wartime currency regulations, for which I might go to prison. When I got to London I turned them over to our startled English bookkeeper. He locked them away in a safe, almost afraid to touch them.) I picked up my war correspondent's credentials on December 14, got my plane ticket, had a multiple-martini luncheon at the old Ritz grill with the sympathetic young woman who had encouraged me to go abroad. My father, mother and sister Janet came east from Minneapolis for Christmas (my departure was scheduled for December 29). It was the last time I would see my father. I had a deep premonition of this. He looked thin and worn. I knew he shouldn't still be working at the factory, but there was no persuading him.

And then—nothing. I did not take off for England. I went out to the Marine Air Terminal at La Guardia to board the American Export clipper. All the formalities had been completed; my passport was to be handed to me at the plane. But it was not. The passport control office said it had been withdrawn. There was no explanation. I went back to New York. The UP raised hell. Lyle Wilson, my friend and UP's Washington manager, took up the matter with the formidable Ruth Shipley, for many years director of Passport and Emigration for the State Department. A couple of weeks later, the passport was issued. A bureaucratic mix-up, Wilson told me. "You've no idea how fouled up things can get," he said. "They had an order out to pick up Cy Sulzberger's passport if he tried to leave the country. He's gotten into a row with the British command in the Eastern Mediterranean. When you came along, somebody got the names confused." Well, the story didn't make much sense, but I caught the next available plane, a Pan-American clipper, and at 9:30 P.M. February 4 I arrived in London.

I don't know whether Lyle Wilson ever got the true story of why my passport was blocked. I didn't get it until some forty years later, when, applying for my FBI records under the Freedom of Information Act, I uncovered a twisted chain of events which led back to that late July of 1940 when our house at 714 Bradley Street in Mamaroneck was broken into and "searched," as the letter from Lucy had reported with such excitement. I still don't know if I have the whole story, so much has been suppressed in the documents the FBI turned over. But here is what I believe happened.

Someone, a neighbor lady, I believe (her name has been carefully blacked out in all the FBI documents), was possessed of a vivid imagination. She had, according to the Mamaroneck police, occasionally reported "things" to the police, who paid little attention to them. On this occasion, she seems to have told the police that I was a "code expert" for United Press and an "employee of the German government," and that I had attempted to recruit other individuals (possibly including herself) for "undercover work." She reported that I had installed hidden microphones in my living room and recording devices in the attic. My electric bills, she said, were astronomical.

We were absent from Mamaroneck for about a month, and it was during our absence that the gossip passed on her suspicions to the Mamaroneck police. I cannot entirely reconstruct what followed, but I think I have it worked out pretty well. On July 25, 1940, between 1 P.M. and 4:15 P.M., someone forced open the front door and searched the Bradley Street house. Lucy and her husband, keeping an eye on the house, were absent and had taken our two dogs with them, so she wrote at the time. When they returned, they found the door forced but nothing apparently taken. Only my desk had been disturbed and my papers scatterred around.

They called the police, who investigated. The lock of a trunk in the basement had been forced, but there was no evidence of burglary.

Who made the search? Forty-two years after the event, I managed to track down Lucy. The occasion was still present in her memory. "Well, they were government men, weren't they?" she said. "And I think the police came too, didn't they?"

"Why do you suppose, Lucy, they wanted to search the house?" I asked.

"Well," she said, "I think somebody thought you were a spy."

There it was. Somebody did, all right. Regardless of who that somebody was and who conducted the first search or the second search, it is clear from the surviving documents that the Mamaroneck police did not take the matter seriously. When I got back in early August, they told me not to be concerned about the incident, and later they were to tell army intelligence that the lady who was the source of the rumor was unreliable, of "a very imaginative mind," her reputation in the community not of the best. They said she came from a family that they described as "known to be nefarious prevaricators." They thought the story was a figment of her imagination. They told the army they had taken the precaution of inspecting the Bradley Street house (presumably this was the search to which Lucy referred on July 25) from attic to cellar and found no recording devices, microphones or bugs. They checked our electrical bills and found they averaged about $5.50 a month, not high enough to pay for the elaborate equipment the lady said had been installed.

Looking back on the dusty reports, I think the Mamaroneck police did their work competently, efficiently and with intelligence. They never told me about the lady's allegations, but that seems fair enough—why create trouble?

Fair enough except for one circumstance. On September 10, 1940, a routine report of the incident was received by the FBI in New York City from the Mamaroneck police. An FBI agent went to Mamaroneck, visited police headquarters, got a rundown on the affair and on September 16 submitted a report to E. E. Conroy, special agent then in charge of the FBI's New York bureau. The New York office of the FBI gave no further attention to the allegations and a year later, on September 10, 1941, notified Washington that the matter had been placed on "deferred status."

I have not been able to retrieve from the FBI the full text of the agent's report, but the action of the New York office is commentary enough—obviously the FBI took the allegations no more seriously than did the Mamaroneck police.

Or did they? Once the agent's report of September 16, 1940, had been turned in, certain events inexorably followed.

The first occurred January 30, 1941, when B. E. Sackett, the special agent in change of the FBI's New York office, forwarded to

J. Edgar Hoover in Washington, my name for inclusion in a list of "Persons for Custodial Detention: Internal Security." The grounds: "Pro German... Is a code expert for the United Press Association and stated he is in employ of German government." This memorandum was sent to Mr. Hoover in response to his telegram of June 15, 1940, requesting field bureaus to forward to him names of "Communist, Fascist, Nazi and other nationalistic background" to be placed on a master list of persons who would be "apprehended and interned immediately upon the outbreak of hostilities between the U.S. Government and the Government they serve, support or owe allegiance to."

Mr. Hoover's action was taken on his own initiative. He established his list in September 1939, without reference to any other branch of the government. When the existence of the lists was discovered by Attorney General Francis Biddle, on July 13, 1943, Mr. Hoover was ordered to dismantle them. This Mr. Hoover did not do. He simply changed the heading in his files. Instead of being listed for "Custodial Detention," the names were placed on a "Security Index."

The Security Index under various permutations was maintained by Mr. Hoover during all the years in which he headed the FBI—that is, until his death, on April 2, 1972.

Congress ordered the list (or lists, there now being several such) destroyed in 1971. But under new titles—"Administrative Index," or "ADEX," and "Reserve File"—they merrily persist to this writing.

When United Press in January 1942 submitted by name to army public relations for accreditation as a war correspondent, the provost marshal in his routine check submitted my name to the FBI. On April 20, 1942, the FBI furnished the provost marshal the information that I was a code expert and an employee of the German government.

Because, perhaps, of the complexity of the federal bureaucracy, this report did not halt the wheels of army public relations. In due course, they accredited me to serve as a war correspondent.

There the matter rested until the eve of my departure for England, when, on December 19, 1942, Captain Wallace, the Visa and Passport officer of Military Intelligence, pulled out of the file the Mamaroneck report and sent it to the Passport Division of the State Department. The wheels of bureaucracy move slowly—so slowly that I almost took off for England before the security alarm was sounded. On December 21, still unaware of Captain Wallace's report, the redoubtable Ruth Shipley sent my passport file to Michael McDermott, the State Department's press chief—a good friend of mine and an even better friend of the UP's Washington bureau head, Lyle C. Wilson— for approval. McDermott signed it and sent it back to Mrs. Shipley, who received his O.K., according to the stamp on the letter on December 24.

Only after the Christmas holiday, as I was about to board the clipper at La Guardia, did the warning come through to hold me up.

I knew nothing of this, nothing of the blazing bureaucratic row which broke out between army intelligence, the provost marshal's office, army public relations, the State Department and the FBI over what manner of person I might be. I did not know that intelligence agents had been sent scurrying to interrogate the unflappable Mamaroneck police, who patiently led them through the case of the gossipy woman from the family of "nefarious prevaricators"; I did not know that the late police captain Louis Giancola had painstakingly drafted a two-page statement giving me the highest kind of references; I did not know that Captain Earle of military intelligence had submitted a comprehensive report clearing my record; nor that the FBI, when all this was over, would launch its own investigation and decide that it had done all the right things, a report carried out at the very top of the agency by none other than Mr. Hoover's right-hand man Louis B. Nichols, which he submitted to Mr. Hoover's other right-hand man, Clyde B. Tolson, a report which like all the others cleared my name but failed to mention that I had been put on the "Custodial Detention" list and that it was the raw, unverified bureau version of the Mamaroneck police report which had caused the whole imbroglio.

A tempest in a teapot for certain, an incident that happened long ago and had such trivial consequences that it does not seem worth mentioning. Except for two chilling facts: the placing of my name on a list for "Custodial Detention" and the possibility that to this day, so far as I have been able to ascertain, it may still be carried on one of the secret FBI lists.

One more thing not of trivial consequence. At intervals over forty years, one government agency or another has requested of the FBI a rundown on what their records show about me. Once, President Johnson gave a dinner party for Burma's leader Ne Win and his wife, Katie, who had lavishly entertained my wife, Charlotte, and myself in Burma at a time when Americans were not welcome in that country.

Our names went to the FBI for a routine check. Invariably the FBI résumés begin with the passport incident, invariably noting that I was "cleared," but of course the aura of the "charges" hung over my name and continued to do so for years and years and years without my being aware of it.

I don't think anyone in the last four or five years has bothered to ask the FBI for a security check on me. But the last time one was run, in 1974, the "nefarious prevaricator" report still topped the résumé.

Not a pretty story. I have spent a good deal of my life behind the iron curtain, where the presence of police surveillance, wire-tapping, censorship and all the rest is the conventional business of the day. I hesitate to think of the thousands of miles I have been tailed in the years of travel I have undertaken in the Soviet Union. But it never occurred to me that all during this period I had, in the Russian expression, an American *khvost*, an invisible tail, planted on me secretly and irresponsibly by our own public servants the FBI.

## Chapter 5

# There Will Always Be an England

A cockney porter had me out from under the gloomy fretwork of Paddington Station before I knew it and into a taxi. It was nine-thirty of the night of February 4, 1943, and I had never seen anything like London in blackout, stars sparkling in the dark sky, around me the thousand fireflies of pedestrians' torches and in the street the Christmas wink of red and green traffic lights. And the quiet—a quiet so deep I heard every footstep, the soft civilian steps and the rasp of hobnail boots, whispers floating over the pavement and a cough that sounded like a revolver shot. I could not take my eyes from the cab window, straining to see the skeletal silhouette of the blitz as the taxi chuffed through unknown streets into the Strand, Fleet Street and up to No. 30 Bouverie, under the clock that marked the home of *News of the World*. Here United Press had quarters.

London in blackout made my heart ache. One evening in early spring, walking back from Haymarket and looking up to the gambrels of St. James's Street, the lead-and-copper gutterwork gleaming like molten emeralds, the chimney pots old as King Arthur and gray as carp, a low moon making a rather stagy appearance, I turned to my companion, a young woman, and said: "You know, after the war London must go on blackout every summer so people will not forget how this looks." It was a silly remark, because no one could forget the beauty of the London blackout any more than they forgot the beauty of the blitz, London burning against a velvet sky, remarkable coups d'oeil, the sensations heightened by the adrenaline of war.

Here I was in the heart of it. Forty-eight hours ago, I had taken off from New York in a flying boat, a kind of aerial yacht with white-jacketed mess boys, berths for the night, a lounge for gin rummy and cocktails, had made languorous pauses at green-and-sapphire Bermuda, tropical Horta, the Hotel Aziz in Lisbon, a haunt of spies and intrigue, the river Shannon, sunshine and showers and the smell of burning peat, blasted Bristol—and now London. I could not believe I had arrived in this extraordinary city at this extraordinary moment. The hunchbacked taxi with its tiny beam of light, its worn leather seats, its cricket of a driver, maneuvered through the crowds of Piccadilly, overtook an elephant that was, in fact, a two-decker bus and deposited me at the Park Lane, where a handsome man in silk hat, green uniform and gold braid took my bag and ushered me over Turkey red carpets to the reception desk, glowing with mahogany, steeped in quiet broken only be a distant hubbub which was, as I later learned, the sound of Canadian officers at their nightly drinking in the Park Lane's formal lounge.

London. It was, I thought, the Paris of World War II. Excitement throbbed through my body. *Everything* was new. I arrived at the office before eight in the morning. A boy was going to the Black-and-White across the street and a deskman asked what I'd like. A cup of coffee, I said. The youngster was back in no time with a steaming mug. I tasted it tentatively. Then I tasted again. It wasn't coffee nor did it seem to be tea; possibly it was some ersatz substitute. The boy obviously could no more understand my Midwest American than I his Bow bells tongue. I said to the English deskman: "I asked for coffee. I guess he misunderstood." The deskman had a word with the boy. "Well," he said with a quizzical smile, "he says that *is* coffee."

I had quite a few misunderstandings. I caught a double-deck bus in front of the Park Lane to Fleet Street, buying a tuppenny ticket. On the third day, a conductor gently explained that I should buy a thruppenny ticket. He wouldn't let me give him the extra penny. I was puzzled the first time a girl said, "Knock me up in the morning." I was surprised to learn you never ordered a single whisky in a pub, always a double, and a double was only half an American drink. And I didn't have to say Scotch. There wasn't any other kind, not even at the Savoy's American bar, so pastel gray and chic I kept looking to my shoes, fearing I was tracking mud over the pale carpet.

El Vino's was *the* Fleet Street pub, a place of dark woods, sherry casks, cobwebbed bottles (not many left on the racks in those days), gleaming brasswork and a cozy room to the back, with a round table and Queen Anne chairs, one of which bore a brass plate with the legend: "The incomparable Bob Davis, Friend of Man, sat here." In

1943, the name of Bob Davis was at the fringe of memory: a long-dead correspondent of the long-dead *New York Sun*. There was no brass plate in Bleeck's in New York to recall his existence. I was awed by the sentimentality of the English.

Aneurin Bevan was sitting in Bob Davis's chair the day I met him. I did not like him and never was to. I thought there was a vainglory to him that reminded me of Ernest Lundeen, the Farmer-Labor senator from Minnesota, who shared some of the same views of the world. But Lundeen was a sloppy man. He did not have a hard core. Probably I was wrong about Bevan; certainly no one at the table that day would have agreed with me—not Bevan's wife, the magnificent Jennie Lee, straight as a King's Lancer; not Michael Foot, the diffident, intelligent editor of the *Evening Standard*, who, improbably, would ultimately lead the Labor party; not Hilde Marchant, the gingery imp from Hull who had worked for Beaverbrook and was now the star of the *Daily Mirror*. One member of the band of brothers of the left, as I came to think of them, was not there that day. He was Frank Owen, whom Foot had succeeded as editor of the *Standard*. Owen was now in the tank corps. I think—but I am not sure—that Frank might have come closer to agreeing with me about Bevan.

This company, I quickly concluded, made up the next generation of England's leaders, the men and women on whom the future of the scepter'd isle would depend. It was they, more than anyone, who would determine whether, indeed, there would always be an England. While I later developed serious doubts about England's left, I at that moment believed in it. Even in my brief days in and en route to London, I had been struck by impressions that badly dented the idealized picture I had drawn of Churchill's England, bright and noble, organized for total warfare, ready to fight on the beaches and in the hills, prepared to sacrifice all for the cause of freedom. Already my eyes told me that the case was not so simple. True, I had arrived in London after the crisis had passed. Since June 1941, the war on the eastern front, the titanic battle of the Wehrmacht and the Red Army, had taken the Luftwaffe off the backs of the British. England's skies had become almost peaceful; no more fire raids devouring London, blasting Coventry, turning Hilde's port of Hull to ashes.

Even before I reached England I was vibrating to images of Europe's poverty: the earth-floored huts, barefoot peasants and scrawny cattle of the Azores; the rosy-cheeked ten-year-old bellboys at the luxurious Aziz; Irish peasants tilling stony fields. True, these were Europe's outposts, but they had given me a dimension by which to judge the social balance.

Now in London I was beginning to see the pinched faces of the English underclass, their thin bodies. I heard the hack of catarrh-raddled lungs, saw the chilblains, the acne, the snot of dwarfish children. And I saw something that shocked me more—the un-mobilized manpower (as I believed it to be). There were the silk-hatted doormen at the Park Lane, the Dorchester, the Savoy. A healthy lad (not a maid) wearing white tie and tails brought me tea and *The Times* at 7 A.M. (I paid a one-pound bribe to get on the list for *The Times*; Lord knows whom the hall porter scratched off.) The Strand, Fleet Street, the City, were filled with morning-coated messengers; bank clerks rode in dark maroon phaetons, delivering bonds and stocks and titles and deeds from one Dickensian business house to another. The Law Courts and Lincoln's Inn Fields abounded with well-fed servitors. True, there were young women ticket takers and even a few women lorry drivers, but not many. The police were male. In the countryside, men of military age worked the fields. Fair enough, but they also held on as gatekeepers, butlers and gamekeepers. They drew the ale at country inns and spun the roulette wheels in the gambling hells of London. They were doormen at the ancient men's clubs along St. James's.

Of course, I did not know Mayfair; I did not know English society. But in the swirl into which I was quickly drawn, it seemed to me that countless wealthy men and women were leading lives totally divorced from the ordinary people. They filled the luncheon tables at the Ivy and they danced at the Savoy dining room, they gathered at the Connaught for tea and the Embassy after the theater. I tried to assure myself that perhaps the men had physical disabilities, but what of the pointless duties they were performing? I repeated to myself what I knew was the truth: that the British had sacrificed without stint while America dawdled in peace, while Detroit spun off automobiles for the most profitable year in its history—1941. I knew the British were brave, indomitable people. Yet there was something amiss, this nagging evidence that I saw all around me of something wrong, of an unfairness in the social order, privilege for the privil-eged, the continuing toil of a serving order.

I connected this with class. In spite of reading Veblen, I had not been personally aware of class in the United States.

But it was different in England. I found myself, because I was head of a large and important American news agency, propelled into the upper class. I dealt with cabinet ministers, ambassadors, the Astors, Lord Camrose, Lord Kemsley, Lord Beaverbrook, the great newspaper proprietors. I dealt with Sirs, with Mark Twain's belted knights. I came to know duchesses (but no dukes). London was, in a sense, just like Washington. These men had the power; they ran England. But there was something different about it. The cockney kids in the UP office whose talk I couldn't make out; the quiet English clerks and tape punchers; the English on the desks and in the back office—they were working class, they were, I suddenly realized, the proletariat of whom the Marxists spoke. They were locked into their class and there was nothing that would get them out. This was true of those clerks with the top hats and morning trousers. They were locked into their station in life and nothing, nothing would get them out of it.

I was fresh from the exhilaration of John L. Lewis, Walter Reuther, Philip Murray, Sidney Hillman, the CIO organizing drives, the sit-down strikes in Flint, the bloody battles in South Chicago, the struggles of Youngstown—the revolution that had swept American labor out of the stodgy cigar smoke of Samuel Gompers and William Green into the cresting wave of industrial unionism, organizing the unorganized, the National Labor Relations Act, the New Deal transformation, that had made the American labor movement the most dynamic social force in the world.

English labor as epitomized by Clement ("good old Clem") Attlee, Ernest ("good old Ernie") Bevin and Sir Stafford Cripps seemed to me archaic, trussed by the bonds of class, tradition and rote. No spark, no spunk. It had not used the war—as it could have—to press its demands, to trade high production and round-the-clock effort for political and social goals. It was, I thought, moribund. Churchill ran rings around Attlee. I thought Churchill a holy wonder; I thought his social views medieval.

But the bright band at the table in the rear of El Vino's was something else. I admitted to myself that my doubts about the moon-faced, tousle-haired Nye Bevan might, in part, reflect deep prejudice against my fellow Welsh. He was the member for Ebbw Vale, authentically Welsh, authentically a coal miner, brilliant, ambitious, with a rare gift for language and speech. I have puzzled for years over why I never felt attracted to him, never trusted him, always thought of him as Ernie Lundeen (as I wrote at the time) and not Minnesota Governor Floyd B. Olson, who remained for years my benchmark for pragmatic radicalism. I was to see a fair amount of Bevan at El Vino's, which was a favourite base for him, as Jennie Lee was to write in her memoir, and later at their home at 23 Cadogan Place. But the initial reaction never vanished. He made the hair bristle on the back of my neck.

Jennie Lee was pure delight. I loved her the moment I saw her and loved her to the end of her life. Her heart was right and her mind had no trouble following it. She laughed easily, but she was very serious, very much a fighter. There couldn't have been a better moment to meet her, for after a decade out of Parliament she was engaged in a gallant campaign to win a by-election in Bristol. Jennie was running as an Independent, not on the Labor ticket. Labor had ousted her for membership in the left-wing Independent Labor party. Nye could not openly support her candidacy in Bristol, but of course he was in her corner. Michael Foot and Hilde Marchant were campaigning for her. None of them expected Jennie to win, but her challenge was notice to Churchill and the Conservatives that they would not win postwar England without an all-out fight from the left. It carried a similar notice to the dozing dons of Labor—the Attlees, the Bevins and the rest. The left was throwing down the gauntlet for an England that would not repeat the experience of the years after World War I. They would not permit England to go back to sleep and allow a new fascism to rise. Nor would they repeat the tragedy of the 1920s— social sloth, industry stagnation and, ultimately, the dole, in which half the country idled on a pittance of a few shillings a week. Jennie was sounding the clarion of the new England, a clarion that thrilled me. These were people who believed Churchill was deliberately delaying a second front in order to drain Russia's strength. They knew that there were those in England who still hoped that Hitler and Stalin would fight until each destroyed the other. They were not going to let the reactionaries get away with this.

I was wiped out by Hilde Merchant. She must have been twenty-five or twenty-six years old, with rusty blond hair, firestruck eyes of green, and so much verve in her small body she seemed not to walk but to bounce from step to step on springs, a whirlwind of energy, fierce opinions, anger and pity. She had been the chief feature reporter for the *Daily Express*, working for its great editor, Arthur Christianson, becoming his mistress, then leaving him in a fiery quarrel and joining the *Mirror*, the hottest paper in London, a tabloid guided by the erratic genius of Guy Bartholomew.

Hilde was the *Mirror*'s star, headlined, front-paged day after day. Jennie had come from a labor background in North Lanark in Scotland. Her grandfather had been with Keir Hardie, Bob Smillie and the others. Hilde came from Hull. She had the grit of that gray port ground into her being. Her temper flared like a torch. Once I rode from Fleet Street to Hyde Park Corner with her on the upper deck of a bus. She started talking about England's tormented coal mines, talking so fast I could hardly pick out the words as they poured from her mouth. But I got the point. It was a dying industry and if it died England might die with it. Every year it needed thirty thousand replacements for the rheumatic men who had given their lives to the pits. No more than eight thousand young men were following in the traces of their fathers. The industry would peter out if new machinery, safe, sanitary conditions, were not brought in—but was there an economic base to support rationalization of the pits? Hilde had just been in Wales and had done a sensational series on the miners, the old men of seventy-six and seventy-nine still in the pits, earning less per week than young girls in the munitions plants. She painted sad pictures of the working people of Hull; she told of the terror of the dole; of her efforts to pull herself, the daughter of a working-class family, up by her fingertips. I looked at her small hands and their tiny, ink-stained, nail-bitten fingers.

Hilde had been living with Bill Dickinson, my friend and right-hand man in the UP's London bureau, for a year when I first met her. She was riding the crest. She had her own five-minute spot on the BBC every evening after the nine o'clock news. She had a daily column in the *Mirror*. She wrote front-page features. She went to northern Ireland to explore the life of the Irish at war and to Scotland to explore bombed-out Glasgow. She wrote shilling pamphlets every few months on subjects like "Women at War." Her name was plastered on the sides of every *Mirror* truck. She was as widely known as any woman in wartime England. She made twice as much money as Bill and, improbably, they planned to be married, at the end of the war if not sooner. She loved Bill's flat Kansas City voice, his big, easy way of moving, even his homemade pot-baked beans, of which he was very proud. Hilde delighted in Americans. She thought they were enchantingly naive children. The first time she met Tom Wolf she danced up with a pert face and said, "Hello, old cock." He had just landed in London and had not heard the Briticism before. She saw his jaw drop, and looking him in the eye, said, "That's O.K. You can call me old cunt if you like."

When I met her in El Vino's, she was going down to Bristol almost every evening to campaign for Jennie Lee. She was a blazing orator. Many expected her to follow in Jennie's footsteps and herself stand for Parliament on the Labor ticket once the war was over. Bill, of course, dreamed of bringing her back to the U.S.A. He wrote pages to his family about this wondrous mite of a woman.

But it did not happen. Sometime, somehow, in the late autumn of 1943, the implausible romance of the girl from Hull and the romantic American came to an end abruptly. Bill left London and went to the Southwest Pacific, where he took over UP's coverage of General MacArthur. Hilde flung herself into her reportage, her pamphlets, her work. But did not run for the House of Commons after the war and soon she began to drift. She was drinking now, and when I went to London and asked about her, people looked a bit uneasy, a bit guilty. They didn't know just what she was doing. By the 1960s, she had begun to haunt the pubs of Gray's Inn Road near the printing offices of *The Times*. A friend of mine was in El Vino's one night when a shabby old lady crept through the door and sidled up to the bar. "We thought she was a beggar," he told me, "and gave her a few shillings." It was only as she slipped away that he realized it was Hilde. One morning in 1970, the police found her on a bench on the Embankment, back of the Savoy Hotel. She was dead. I cannot bear to think of that bright imp snuffed out in the deadly wastelands of life.

Frank Owen was not at El Vino's on the day I met Jennie Lee, Aneurin Bevan, Michael Foot and Hilde Marchant. I met Frank late one April day in his Westminster Gardens flat. His wife was there, a long-stemmed American beauty, a real one, a statuesque blond showgirl, Grace Stewart McGillivray of Boston, who had come to London, and married Frank on the eve of the war. One night, a German bomb crashed through the glass skylight of the Savoy dining room and Gracie's face was badly cut. The scars were barely visible, but the wounds to her psyche did not heal and the blast of Frank's personality had already begun to unsettle her nerves.

Frank was asleep when I arrived at the flat. He had come up from his tank unit, training somewhere in the countryside, and was tired and dusty. He grinned, apologized and said he'd take a tub and wake up. Gracie drew the tub, Frank flung off his clothes and invited me to talk while he relaxed in the boiling water, a black Welshman, with black gleaming hair, his face, neck and shoulders red from the sun, and muscles that rippled across his chest—a physical man, all gristle and hairy body, his mind racing a mile a minute, deep blue eyes sparkling with profane comment about the bloody government, the bloody army, the bloody war, the bloody tanks. He was having the time of his life.

Owen was a Liberal, but he thought very much as did the Laborites Bevan, Lee, Foot and Marchant. Beaverbrook had picked him up as he picked up Foot, as he was forever picking up the brightest left-wing minds, and made him editor of the *Evening Standard*. The Beaver got a bit more than he counted on. Owen's *Standard* fought Munich and the Cliveden set. It fought Chamberlain. It fought Hitler and questioned the phony war. After Dunkirk, Owen, Foot and a man named Howard wrote an overnight pamphlet called "Guilty Men," which they signed "Cato." It excoriated Chamberlain and the appeasers. It swept England like a prairie fire and swept Churchill into office. It was the most powerful political jeremiad of the war.

The *Standard* supported Churchill before he came into power. It supported Russia after June 22, 1941. It backed the second front. To all this Beaverbrook agreed. But the bite of Owen's words was more than the government could take. When Owen was suddenly called up to the army and entered the tank corps, there was talk on Fleet Street. The government was getting a tiger off its back. Was the Beaver ducking too? It was a question that never got answered.

When I met Owen he was full of swagger, a muscular man with a daredevil's courage. You knew he would pick up any challenge thrown down. I was never satisfied with the words I chose to describe him, not then, not now. Words were poor instruments to capture his animal movement, the computer speed of his mind, the robustious-ness of his style, the grin on his face. There was nothing he couldn't do. I thought if he had been given charge of the war, he would have run Hitler off the planet within a year. I wrote once that he was an Irishman who happened to be Welsh, a careless son of a bitch.

I had only to meet Frank Owen to pick him as the best man in England's future. Owen drove himself day after day after day, taking only an hour or two of sleep until he collapsed. There was no one on the left or the right (I thought) to compare with him, not Bevan, not

Foot, not Morrison, certainly not Cripps or Bevin, not Attlee. I hadn't heard of Harold Wilson and would not meet him until he began to come into Moscow in the late forties and early fifties on timber-buying missions for some Scottish syndicate. He did not win my favor with his slippery statements and I quickly put him at the bottom of my list of English pols. In the end, I was by no means certain that Owen or anyone could pull off the postwar transformation England needed, but I was certain he would come closest. He inspired instant loyalty. His army chums swore by him from the day he donned his uniform. The *Evening Standard* staff loved him. I could believe that there were those on high who thought it better to dress him in the khaki of the tank corps than let him lead the editorial cry of the *Standard*, preparing for a left-wing takeover.

One night I sat in Jack's Club, a black market eating place favored by American journalists, a clothes closet of a place, tucked into No. 14 Orange Street, just behind the Haymarket. There were half a dozen of us—Ray Clapper, the Washington columnist and my old friend, Jack Knight, editor of the Akron paper and later head of Knight-Ridder newspapers, Walter Cronkite, who covered the Eighth Air Force and worked with me in UP, and a couple of others. We got to talking about Frank Owen. What would happen to him when the war was over? One of three things, we agreed: He would become prime minister, commissar of a revolutionary England—or a bum. Each fate was within his grasp.

Owen went to India. He served on Mountbatten's staff, fought in Burma, then came back to London. At the end of the war, he became editor of the right-wing *Daily Mail*. Somehow he had lost his edge. He was drinking heavily. The copybook romance with the long-stemmed American Gracie had foundered in alcohol and boredom. A succession of young Americans occupied Gracie's life; Frank slept around, a different bed almost every night. No longer was he the wonder of Fleet Street and the fear of Whitehall.

Owen, it began to become apparent, was a broken man. Had he broken himself or had Beaverbrook, that Machiavelli, spotted Owen's weakness, prized open the crack a bit and let nature take its course? What happened to Frank Owen? This is not just a personal question; it is a national question. How had his talents been destroyed; how could his country have been deprived of his remarkable energies? His friends did not understand it. It was easy to say, as many did, "It was the drink that did it." To be sure, the drink did.

54

But Owen possessed the ability England needed above anything, that careless talent for inspiration, the courage that could have set the country on a new course. I do not think this is just my romantic image, the fancy of a young American hardly landed in London, inexperienced in the world. I go back to that conversation in Jack's Club and the fearful accuracy of our prediction—prime minister, commissar or bum.

Frank was never again to do anything memorable. He held on at the *Mail* for a while and when that blew up he wrote some potboilers. Beaverbrook came to the rescue and commissioned his biography; Owen turned out a piece of boiler plate, with some difficulty. Then amazingly it was all over; this lion of a man became a drooling hulk, his mind a gray swamp, his body wasting. Gracie died in 1968. I have always thought she should have died in the Savoy bombing. Her life had not been worth living since her face was cut. Frank lived until the summer of 1980, finally dying of cancer. Better he had been killed forty years before in Burma with Wingate and left his legend for young England to burn a candle to.

It was not easy to know and understand Michael Foot, and even now I am not certain that I do. At El Vino's I saw him thin, dark, shy and taciturn, as waves of talk swirled about him. It would have seemed outrageous to suggest that this young editor of the *Evening Standard* might head the British Labor party, one of the most formidable political forces of the Western world.

Surely I did not expect that to occur, but before I left England I recognized that he had greater qualities of leadership than I first imagined. But I still considered Owen the only man on the left capable of capturing the British masses.

One afternoon, Beaverbrook invited me to the Mayfair apartment to which he had removed after a fire at his house at Cherkley. Max Aitken was a gnomish man with a small boy's grin which gave many people the impression that at heart he was more mischief-maker than menace. He invited me into his study, where he was using a Dictaphone. Two secretaries walked in and out with papers. Most of his messages were to his general manager, a man named Robertson. "Robertson," he dictated, "I see that you have not yet cut down on the advertising in the *Express*. Cut it down. Immediately." He chatted a bit about John Cowles, the publisher of the Minneapolis papers, and his brother Mike, publisher of *Look* magazine. Then another memo: "Mr. Robertson, the advertising rates in the *Evening Standard* are too low. The *Evening Standard* must be the most expensive advertising medium in England. Come and see me about this. Tomorrow." I had begun to ask him about his campaign to revive the authority of the House of Lords (in which he sat) and his bitter battle for a second front, when Michael Foot walked in, in horn-rimmed spectacles, gray cardigan sweater, looking like so many people in England, a little shabby. In an instant Beaverbrook was setting me at Foot, encouraging me to ask sharp questions about the Labor party and the left and what Foot thought would happen after the war. I fell to it with a will. Afterward I felt that I had been unfair, but I excused myself by saying that I wanted to strike sparks. Foot was a Socialist and I pressed him on his ideas of what the political temper of the country would be after the war. Would it be 1918 all over again? Would there be another khaki election? Beaverbrook intervened to say that he believed Britain was fundamentally conservative and the United States was also conservative. It was his view that Conservative power would be retained after the war and go on and on. He called Hugh Baillie, the head of United Press and my boss, a "bloody Tory." Wallace Carroll, the former UP London chief, now with the Office of War Information in London, was a "leftist." What, he said to me, was I? I responded that I was a newspaperman who wanted to know what made people tick. That was not a complete answer, but I did not want to get into an ideological match with this sharp-tongued man. Tiring of this pastime (never having let Foot give me a fair answer about postwar England), Beaverbrook took some scrapbooks from his shelves and began to read quotations from English statesmen of recent years, especially embarrassing attacks by Churchill on Russia and Stalin. Beaverbrook said he had volumes on everyone, filled with deadly parliamentary ammunition.

As Michael Foot watched, he took a copy of the day's *Evening Standard*, spread it on the floor, pointing to the headlines with his foot, criticizing the makeup and the placement of stories. It was, I realized, a show for my benefit and designed to chastise Foot, but the Beaver's criticisms were apt. This was a brilliant editor at work, and in each instance I thought he was right and Michael woefully agreed. It was not, he admitted, a particularly good paper. Another idea struck the Beaver. He turned to his Dictaphone: "Mr. Robertson, the *Daily Express* must have the best newspaper library in the world. I want you to see that this is done." Michael interjected that the *Standard* library did not possess several important series of government documents. Back to the Dictaphone: "Mr. Robertson, Mr. Foot informs me that the *Evening Standard* does not have such and such. Get them." (A day later, I saw a want ad in the *Standard* inquiring for the needed government volumes; Mr. Robertson was carrying out his instructions.)

Michael Foot and I lunched soon after this at the Cheshire Cheese. He had just read Wendell Willkie's *One World.* We found we had a mutual admiration for Willkie and similar views on many things. We talked about his hopes for England after the war and I began to realize better the mettle of which he was made. He was a newspaper editor largely by chance, by the chance of Frank Owen's being called up to the army, but he was a writer and a publicist born. He was a scholar from a scholarly family, one of five sons of Isaac Foot, a remarkable, largely self-educated solicitor in Plymouth, a sometime Liberal member of Parliament, an iconoclastic observer of life and an orator of such appeal that crowds turned out whether he spoke from stump or pulpit and whether they agreed with what he was saying or not. Four sons entered politics—Hugh (later elevated to the peerage as Lord Caradon), Dingle and Michael—who were sometimes called "left" Foot (Michael), "right" Foot (Hugh) and "center" Foot (Dingle)—and John, who never acquired a designation, not that these designations were necessarily accurate. Each Foot shared the iconoclasm of the father. Party whips were forever having trouble with them.

Within the year, Michael would leave Beaverbrook, leave the *Standard,* for the left-wing *Tribune,* established by Bevan, and at war's end he would enter the House of Commons, first winning at Devonport, and with Bevan's death in 1950 taking his place at Ebbw Vale.

Michael was no ordinary politician. He never lost his literary taste, his love for books, inculcated by his father. I thought that he was more comfortable with pen and typewriter than with the speaker's lectern, but he came to be as effective on the platform. I never thought Michael possessed the killer's instinct that seems characteristic of powerful politicians. He was a humane man, he respected his fellows, he did not employ the big lie or the little lie, as did so many rivals. Nor did he turn his back. There was some estrangement between himself and Beaverbrook after he left the *Standard.* But Foot never forgot what Beaverbrook had taught him about editing and, even more, about life. Beaverbrook had after all, as he said, been a second father to him. Toward the end of the Beaver's life there was a reconciliation and a second honeymoon of these two men whose personalities clashed so vigorously, whose views differed profoundly but who shared a warmth of human understanding.

After I had seen Foot and Owen together, I understood each much better. They complemented each other, they respected each other's strengths. I had been wrong to suppose that Foot's diffidence meant weakness. Each man had guts.

"Both of them," I wrote April 26, 1943, in my journal, "are the sort who would tell Beaverbrook or Churchill or anyone else where to get off in a real showdown. But Owen would do it with a string of bloody, cuss words and Foot would say it very quietly, very firmly."

There was courage enough to go around within the "band of brothers," but this did not suffice to give any of them or the group (minus Owen) immediate postwar leadership in the Labor party. They tried, and certainly Bevan tried hardest, to reshape the party and its views, but they did not succeed, Bevan no more than Foot. As years passed, Foot slowly rose within the party, and with the death of Bevan he emerged as the spokesman for the left. But basically the old guard prevailed, just as I had feared, and none of the group at El Vino's could change its course, nor could they change the course of England. There was not the postwar renaissance that had to be if there was always to be an England capable of holding the substance of power and glory. In one form or another, Churchill's formula of England as a junior partner to the United States prevailed.

Steadily year by year, the figure of Foot loomed larger. His integrity, his courage, his intellect, lifted him toward the top of his quarrelsome, divided party. In the main, the Conservatives provided England with such leadership as it had. I did not believe the decline of England could be blamed upon the Conservatives. They did the best they knew how, but Labor languished in the flabby hands of the Bevins and the Wilsons, who did not possess the imagination to understand the breadth and depth of England's decay. They were wedded to preservation at any cost of the small trade union gains of the past; they quailed at the notion of extricating themselves from the bear hug of American economic and foreign policy.

Long before I left England in 1943, I had concluded that the chance for a real comeback was almost nil. I went back to London briefly in late 1945, and the sight of that great city, absent the exhilaration of war, grubby, tired and grim, tore my heart. I could see no signs of hope, nor could I hear them. The faces in the Strand and in the City were pallid; I saw dull eyes, heads down, coat collars turned up against the chill. Mayfair was frightened of the loss of capital; the East End feared the loss of jobs. No one could face the fact that the United States had become *the* world power and was taking England's markets and production away. Churchill's boast that he had not become the Queen's first minister in order to preside over the dissolution of empire had become a pitiful joke. England was losing, as I had understood it would (and not myself alone), India, the colonies, South Africa. Canada and Australia were cuddling up to Washington. China and the rich trade of the Yangtze and the treaty ports was going down the drain. Soon the fierce competition of Germany and of Japan would resume. (Mistakenly in 1943 I had thought that Russia also would assault England's markets with low-cost goods, but the Kremlin was as rigid and stupid as Attlee and Bevin.)

I saw by 1945 that my belief that Foot and Owen and Bevan and Lee and Marchant would put it all together was a lost vision. Even my deepest wishful thinking could not make that seem very likely. For the first time, as I flew home from the joyless London of 1945, I was beginning to understand that it was not holy writ—nowhere was it written large that there had always to be an England.

# Chapter 6

# A London Diary

Early on the morning of February 27, 1943, three weeks after I arrived in London, I met Hal Leyshon and Jack Redding, public relations officers, and Colonel Gates, the chief army censor, and the four of us in a command car drove out into the English countryside, my first sight of the soft green fields, the hedges, the narrow roads, the sleepy sheep and fat red cows. Sprouts and cabbages thrust through the muddy earth, daffodils were beginning to show yellow faces; the sun tucked in and out of the clouds but was not quite as warm as it looked. We lost our way and stopped a dozen times to ask directions. Everyone was helpful. They told us just what to do: "Down the lane to the King and Keys, then first right, second left, you ca-a-an't miss." And so we would go until we asked the next person. The English had taken down all road signs when they thought the Germans were going to invade, and they had not put them back. We were headed for an Eighth Air Force base called Molesworth, from which shortly after dawn the UP's correspondent Walter Cronkite had taken off on a bombing mission over Germany, the first time correspondents had been permitted to go on a raid. It had been set up before I arrived in London. I was not happy about it, but a dozen elephants could not have kept Walter out of the B-17 Flying Fortress.

It took us so long that when we got to Molesworth the planes were back and the fliers just coming out of the interrogation room. Soon Walter appeared, looking serious. No wisecracks. I had never been so relieved. I was too new to England to understand the full danger, but I knew enough to be frightened to death for him. I had spent the evening before talking with two youngsters, a Royal Air Force lad from the Bronx and an Australian. Both had the DSC and the Bronx boy had the bar as well. I knew long before the end of the evening that they did not expect to survive. They had to kick each other into the planes and their only prayer was for bad weather. I don't know what the odds were on returning from a daylight bomb run over

Germany, but they were not very good. Five of the seventy-six Flying Fortresses did not return that day; two of the seventeen Liberator B-24s were lost, one of them carrying Robert Post of *The New York Times*.

I clucked over Walter like a hen. He was the star of our staff and my close friend. Now he was wound up like a top. It was so cold in the windowless room where he was writing that he kept his coat on as he typed. I hovered about, trying not to interfere, trying to be of help. People kept coming in with reports about Post. It was definite that he was missing. I fed Walter some headline phrases, out of which he constructed a memorable lead: "I flew through hell today." Then I retreated to the lounge, where a handful of crew members lolled about, trying to read *Life* magazine, their attention span very short. A radio played quietly in the background. Blond English WAAFs strolled past in their blue uniforms. I remember two of them skipping down a corridor, arms around each other's waists, their faces innocent as choir girls', singing: "When the lights come on again all over the world." I spoke to a WAAF about the young fliers on the base. Her face became solemn. Oh, our lads, she said, there is nothing we can do for them but hold them very tight and tell them we love them and we know they will come back, but most of them won't. She began to cry and I felt like a fool. I wondered how many boys she had held in her arms and how empty those arms must feel when the flights limped back and the boys did not return. "Don't make friends with the kids," Walter had told me. "Don't get to know them too well. It's just too much when they are lost, and most of them, you know, will be."

It was very late when we left for London. Homer Bigart had even more trouble than Walter writing his story. (It was on one such occasion that Bigart said: "I hate to write, but I love punctuation.") It was a long ride back to London, ten of us in the command car built for four, everyone on edge. Gladwin Hill, the AP man and later my *New York Times* colleague, had a talking jag. Walter kept poking sarcasms at Gladwin, who never noticed, he like everyone in deep gloom over the loss of Post. Two parachutes had been seen, but no one believed either was Post's. We didn't get to Bouverie Street until 11:30 P.M. and started pouring the copy in to the censor. There was the inevitable snafu. AP's copy cleared briskly, Walter's was held up. We lost a lot of play, but his "Hell" headline swept the British press. Peter Daniell of the *Times* was on the phone, sore at me because I had told New York that Post was missing before he could nerve himself to do it. Peter was clogged with guilt; felt he should have flown the assignment; feared people would say he pushed Post into it because he and Post didn't get along; to make things worst, Post's wife had just arrived in London, intending to stay with her husband for the duration. It was a mess.

More than a mess—it was a scandal, but it took me considerable time to understand the extent of it. The origins ran as deep as General William ("Billy") Mitchell's fight for an independent air force in the early 1920s. It involved some tricky politics between the RAF and the USAF as well.

I had heard a lot about the air corps in long evenings in Washington at Lyle Wilson's, listening to Tooey Spaatz and other air officers. They were true believers in air power and their convictions had been reinforced by Japanese bombings in China, Mussolini's in Ethiopia, Spain, and the Luftwaffe's success in the early phases of the war. Spaatz's first objective had been to win independence for the air corps. His second was to demonstrate that air power was supreme, stronger than all other military arms. He had the independent air force now and in England he and his men were building a strategic air force which they believed would win the war.

Germany's bombing of England had been primarily by night. The daylight air battles were designed to wipe out the British fighter command. The Germans lost that one—by a hair's breadth. German night bombing was quite successful. It was a not, of course, accurate, but no bombing was. Though it did not knock out British industry, it laid waste workers' housing. It was a terror weapon, except that the English did not panic.

I didn't understand how air power worked until one Sunday when I took a bus with Ellen to Petticoat Lane to see the East Enders at the street fair, with its sparse remnants of the blitz: secondhand shoes with inch-thick soles, mangy furs, five-and-dime jewelry, clocks and watches (stolen), plaster dogs, musettes, a few flowers; there were men doing card tricks and lots of tarts, not out for business, just shopping for pleasure in tattered finery; and all around, the desert left by the bombers, a desert that encircled St. Paul's, the Liverpool Street station, the City and down Commercial Road to the East India docks. The docks were working, cranes overhead, lift machinery battered but operating, yet all around lay the rubble of the dockers' grimy barracks. I understood then why it was said that the East Enders had great respect for bombs. The East End no longer existed. God knows where the people lived; lots of them, of course, lived in the underground stations. We went into a pub which stood alone in a row of smashed tenements. It was filled with men, men with thin faces, chicken necks, pinched shoulders, nasal voices. They looked at us with sullen eyes. I didn't blame them. There was not enough beer to go around, let alone whisky or gin, without strangers barging in. We slipped away without a drink.

It was my first glimpse of successful bomb warfare. I understood now what Tooey Spaatz was talking about. This was what they wanted to do to Germany.

Had there been no RAF Bomber Command, no Air Marshal Harris, I believe the American Eighth Air Force would have established itself in England and embarked upon a merciless night campaign to savage the Germans, to wipe their cities off the earth. The air force insisted that the Norden bombsight made hitting a German target like shooting fish in a barrel. I remember how we parodied that phrase until the PR men stopped using it. (The same claim, of course, was made during the Vietnam war and trapped Lyndon Johnson into the contention that American bombs were destroying only "steel and concrete," a claim my Christmas trip to Hanoi in 1966 would demolish.)

But the RAF had preempted night bombing. It was doing very well at it, thank you, and would be glad to have the U.S. Air Force join in too. By no means had the Eighth Air Force been established to become an appendage of the RAF. That was not for the likes of General Ira C. Eaker, or a young cigar-chomping, tough-talking colonel named Curtis LeMay, or the others. The Eighth Air Force was a high-octane outfit. It was run by ambitious men and backed by an ambitious command in Washington. It had set up a large public relations staff—men from newspapers, publicity firms, advertising agencies—and made use of Hollywood celebrities. They were not attracted to the air force because they thought it was going to take directions from the English.

Although no one would admit it, that, I thought, was why some one had invented the daylight bombing doctrine. Later on, when the air force grew so large that it could saturate the German defenses and fly almost at will through German skies, starting fire storms at places like Hamburg and Dresden, daylight bombing became something different. Under such conditions, daylight bombing was an effective military weapon, particularly for destroying cities and civilians. It was necessarily imperfect, but it followed the well-trodden tradition of Attila the Hun and prefigured Hiroshima.

On February 27, 1943, the Eighth Air Force was flying its third daylight mission over Germany. The target was Bremen, but because of poor weather, the planes were diverted to Wilhelmshaven, which undoubtedly was why losses were so low. The total force of ninety-three planes mustered that day was just about maximum capability, a long way from the numbers needed for saturation. The day's toll of seven planes lost was trivial; missions frequently lost a third of their planes, sometimes half of them or more, and in the case of the terrible Regensburg disaster, all but one. These were not what a military man would call "acceptable" losses. Again and again the bombing had to be halted or slowed in order to build up the backlog of planes. To fly in the Eighth Air Force in those days was to hold a ticket to a funeral. Your own.

The command tried to justify daylight bombing in every possible way—by exaggerating results, by lying about losses, by long-winded theories of how the day-and-night pressures produced by round-the-clock British and American bombing were driving the Germans to the brink. I thought there was a lot of mush in the theory and I could tell by talking to generals like Eaker and air marshals like Harris what the real competitive issues were between the British and the Americans. They were the issues that had compelled my hero, Blackjack Pershing, to insist on an independent American command in World War I despite the pressures and blandishments of Marshal Foch and Lord Haig.

Not until I got to Russia and saw war on the eastern front did I learn what was really wrong with the U.S. strategic bombing "theory." There was no such thing as strategic bombing in the East. The Germans had given it up almost immediately after the start of war, June 22, 1941, and the Russians never tried it, except for a few splashy morale raids on Berlin. Neither side could afford it. The results were two skimpy. They were too busy fighting the real war on land, a struggle of men and guns and tanks. Air power was used as it should be used, as long-range artillery and close-support artillery. The Germans at Stalingrad didn't bomb the internal railroad systems of

Russia or plaster the steel mills of Magnitogorsk. They pulverized the broken factory buildings in which the Russian troops had taken shelter and tried to smash pontoon bridges, a few yards away across the Volga, by which the Russians got their ammo and grits. When the Red Army turned the tables and broke the Nazi armored strength at Kursk-Orel in the summer of 1943, they didn't strike at the supply routes far behind the fighting zone; they plastered the German tanks with every bomb they could drop.

Of course, in 1943 we had no second front. Our land battles were in Africa, Sicily and Italy. But the air force had little interest in joint operations and had never learned to collaborate intimately with ground forces. Many remarkable air-infantry operations, particularly use of helicopters as mobile fire platforms and for quick movement of troops, were developed in Vietnam, but the air force's heart still was locked into strategic bombers, B-52s whose powers were irrelevant in the jungle.

The glimmering of this that I got on the eastern front was confirmed by the U.S. strategic bombing survey at the end of World War II, which spotlighted the military uselessness of much of the spectacular strategic operations of the Eighth, the Fifteenth and other air forces. But the lesson was never accepted by the heirs of Billy Mitchell.

The important thing, as the Eighth Air Force saw it in 1943, was to establish a presence, to prove a doctrine, to stake out a position in public consciousness. If this cost the lives of many fine young men and inflicted no really serious damage on Germany's fighting capability, that was too bad. War was war and people were bound to be killed.

And they were killed. Bob Post was killed. There was nothing special about his death except that he happened to be a newspaperman and the first one to be killed on an air mission, flying, of course, in total violation of the Geneva conventions. All the correspondents spent three or four days in indoctrination. They were instructed in how to handle a machine gun. They were combatants and automatically lost their civilian status. All this was part of the campaign begun so long ago by Billy Mitchell, one more building block in the relentless drive to establish public belief in the invincibility of air power.

Years later, Homer Bigart was musing over the operation. He thought it was total luck that it had not come off more badly. He wondered how many of his colleagues had shot their machine guns. None had had more than three hours' practice, just enough to learn how to point the gun and pull the trigger. "I used mine," Homer said. "I just hope I didn't shoot down one of our planes. I saw one of the B-24 Liberators go down. Wouldn't it be awful if it was one of us who shot down the B-24 with Bob Post in it?"

Freddie Chapman was killed sometime on May 4, 1943, when the plane in which he was flying with General Andrews, the U.S. commander in England, was lost on a flight over the North Atlantic en route to Iceland. Freddie was a lieutenant colonel, just promoted from major, General Andrews's personal aide, a boy from Alabama full of "Thank you, ma'am"s and "Yes, sir"s, whom I had known in Washington. He arrived with General Andrews from Cairo to take up the London post and we met the next day, each thinking it a lucky omen. In no time, I was on first-name terms with the general. By accident, I had an inside track on U.S. military operations from England. Freddie watched over his general like an adoring son, and the general, a gruff, tough, exquisitely professional old-army man, treated Fred like his boy. They lived at the Dorchester, but Fred had found the general a big English house in Hampstead. The general could hardly wait to get into it. First, he thought he would make an inspection trip to Iceland, where his old friend General Bonesteel was commander. I wanted to go along, but at the last moment I couldn't break away from the office. I had been writing in my journal and had dropped off to sleep when the telephone rang. It was 12:30 A.M., May 5, and the office was calling to tell me General Andrews had been lost on a flight to Iceland. I phoned the Dorchester to see if by chance Fred had missed the plane, but no luck. I got dressed, went to Bouverie Street and wrote the story. It was the first time in the war I had lost someone close. I could hear Fred's slow, slow drawl wondering whether his mama and his papa had heard that he had made lieutenant colonel. He didn't think anyone in his little home-town had ever risen so high in the army.

I began to wobble; London was too much. I ran about town all day. I was up half the night. I was drinking too much. I began to sleep with girls, sometimes because I was fond of them, sometimes because we found ourselves together at the end of an evening. Entries began to appear in my journal: "Terribly sloshed last night"; "Must cut out these evenings and get to work." Once I noted a remark by Jeff Parsons: "How much whiskey in the world can a man drink?" To which I had replied: "We're finding out."

I had to change this pattern. I went down to the country to spend a weekend with Constance Spry. She lived in a rambling brick house with stone floors, possibly two hundred years old, in Kent; it was twenty miles southeast of London, about five miles from Orpington station. She had just enough gasoline on the ration to get to the station once a week.

I'd never met a woman like Mrs. Spry. She must have been sixty years old and had been part of that sophisticated, almost precious set which dominated English social life in the late twenties and thirties, something like Fleur and her friends in the last of Galsworthy's Forsyte novels, a member of the crowd that eddied around the Duke and Duchess of Windsor. With a difference. Constance Spry was as energetic, as talented a woman as I had ever met. She reminded me of my aunt Mary (as unsophisticated a woman as lived) because she was so chipper in the face of adversity, so warm, so human. She had won international recognition for growing flowers, for arranging them, the Cecil Beaton of her profession—had set up a shop in South Audley Street and another on Park Avenue, had commuted between Southampton and New York on the *Berengaria*. When England went to war in 1939, Constance Spry threw her energy into traveling the country from Lands End to John o'Groat's, she and her friend Rosemary Hume, teaching recalcitrant British housewives how to cook, how to cook without boiling the last vitamins out of their Brussels sprouts, their cabbages, their potatoes. She hymned the virtues of greens, of cucumbers, of coleslaw and raw cabbage. She taught that lettuce was edible, that tomatoes could be grown in backyards, that life was possible without roast beef and Yorkshire pudding.

I went down to her quiet household, she in a pink calico apron, living in the kitchen with its copper and tiles, serving on the kitchen table, a Brussels lace tablecloth over the old boards, ancient silver and five-and-dime utility china. Her greenhouses were filled now with tomatoes and corn, but she had acres of flowers. We picked sixty bunches of roses and I can't guess how many other flowers, to be brought up to London early Monday morning by horse and cart. She had no coupons to send them by truck, and the railroads wouldn't accept "nonessential" freight.

I lay in the sun, pulled weeds in the rose garden, played with the four-year-old son of a gardener, taking "trips" to London in the cart, inspected the cross goose that chased him, admired a flock of yellow chicks and petted a rabbit which he looked forward to eating at next Christmas dinner.

In the evening I sat by a gray-stone fireplace and talked with Shed, Constance's husband, recuperating from a ghastly heart attack, a onetime India civil servant, about the Civil War, his hobby and mine, about Douglas Southall Freeman's Lee and what a guide it was to the real nature of war, Henderson's Jackson and Carl Sandburg's Lincoln, which he was then reading.

The weekend at Constance Spry's transported me a long way from the complexities that were pulling my life apart, but on Monday morning I was back in the midst of them.

One evening I dined in London with Storm Jameson and her husband, Guy Chapman, and lost my heart to the two of them. Margaret (Storm's true name) was rather small, quiet, very intelligent and possessed a fiery spark that lighted up her whole being. I described Guy then as a cherubic man with a puckish sense of humor who talked very openly and freely, with lots of laughter, lacking the reserve I had seen in so many English. But I don't remember him that way, probably because later images were superimposed on that first one. I remember him as wry, ironic and, ultimately, tragic. That evening Guy and Margaret talked a lot about Wales, where he was teaching in an army school. He had plunged into World War II supposing he would find again the golden days of World War I, a comradeship of men and duty and danger in the hell of Flanders, about which he wrote his classic account, *A Passionate Prodigality*; but 1940 was not 1914 and the past is quicksilver that can never be held in the hand. In our postwar meetings, this was starkly apparent. For many complicated reasons, Guy and Margaret were turning inward on themselves, a relationship so close, so total, I have never seen another like it.

Margaret was looking that first night, as was Guy, toward the future, toward the England that would emerge with the peace, and neither of them liked the face of what they saw coming; nor that of Europe. They dreamed of an island where they could loll in the sun and read and talk and write, but certainly they did not find it. Nor did Guy achieve his ambition of living again in his beloved France. He was a scholar of France, a great one, but so dedicated, so precise, he could hardly bear to turn in a manuscript to the printer.

They hated the Wales in which they were condemned by the war to live, a narrow, secular people, clannish, tight, raw, uncomfortable, and living was harsh, a primitive inn with scant food and abominable cooking.

Margaret was already one of England's finest novelists, with a spare, strong prose and a relentless honesty which was her strength. The tragedy of her life was Guy's death. He left her alone in a world that only the two had shared. She never got used to it. For reasons of their own, they had never had a home, always living in rented quarters, moving from pitch to pillar, she winding up at Cambridge in the late years and abhorring it, she said, although I think she got a warming comfort from her fierce refusal to accept the banality of life.

I had breakfast with Ellen one Sunday at the South Audley Street mess (once it had housed London's Bachelor Club). We walked in Rotten Row, not many horsemen out, and the barrage balloons cuddled close to the ground. I thought it was because of the wind, but Ellen said an ATS girl had told her it cost too much to let them go up unless there was a good chance of a raid. The Serpentine was alive with flowers, ducks and geese swimming by, so peaceful and appealing we decided to go to the country. We caught a train to High Wycombe, a Westchester kind of town, then clambered onto the second deck of a great red London bus and were off down country lanes. We alighted at a crossroads and rambled into a rather unattractive Gypsy camp inhabited by what looked like extremely business-like Gypsies, Romany without romance. Over fields and muddy paths, we found ourselves at the Crown. I thought it must date back to Richard the Lionhearted, a stout, half-timbered building with low ceilings, paneled walls, hunting prints, pewter mugs and a fireplace with deep corner seats, harness brasses and a slow oaken log burning. I could have stayed forever. At midnight we were back in London, chilly, tired and rested. How pleasant it would be, I thought, to wander over England with Ellen, how easy I felt with her and she, I knew, with me. But I closed my mind to these thoughts because Ellen was the friend of a friend and this kind of thinking was not loyal.

There was no peace in London. Hugh Baillie, the President of UP and the man on whom my career depended, was headed for England. He had not been to London since the start of the war. The news filled me with apprehension. Baillie must have the best. He must stay in the best suite at the Savoy. He must meet Churchill and Eden, the air marshals, the U.S. brass. He must go to Parliament (where I had been only once). He must see the countryside (which I hardly knew). I must take him to dinner every night at the best restaurants and he must be seated at the best tables. There wasn't much on at the theater, but he must have the best seats at the best shows. The UP bureau must impress him with its get-up-and-go. We must have exclusive stories every day. I must be suave, sophisticated, tough. I must show him I had entrée to the highest circles, that there was nothing I couldn't do, no one I couldn't see. I must come up with a world-beating story. Maybe more than one.

When these thoughts raced through my mind I felt I was bouncing off the ceiling. My God! It was all I could do to keep my head above water—and now Baillie. I could handle the American military all right and the Eighth Air Force, I was confident of that, but what about the English, the Foreign Office, Churchill, his mean-spirited aide, Brendan Bracken, and those restaurants so chic my knees wobbled as I encountered the maître d'hôtel, and how would I wangle the suite at the Savoy?

I was beginning to worry about money. Mary was crisscrossing the United States, moving every two or three weeks. She had rented out the Mamaroneck house, moved to Washington, gone to Minneapolis, left for Florida, and now was back in Minnesota. It cost a fortune. I counted up how much I owed one night—it was more than a hundred dollars, and I didn't dare draw more from the office. I stayed home three nights that week, ate cold Spam and soda crackers, and held my living expenses to eighteen shillings a day. If I could do that for two weeks, I might square my accounts.

I met Baillie at Paddington Station and hired a car to drive him to the Savoy. He behaved exactly as I had on my first night, his head out the window all the way to the hotel. He loved his suite. He should have—it was delicate blue and white, with graceful curved windows looking out on the Embankment and the Thames. He didn't want a drink, he didn't want anything to eat, he just wanted to get rid of me and get out on the street and see London, *his* London. He didn't want anyone sharing that first impression. I hadn't understood that Baillie loved the city as only a colonial Scotsman could love it. Before his visit was over, he had walked my legs off. He took me to the City and showed me where the Great Fire had halted. He showed me how the German bombs hit almost exactly the same area. We walked it street by street and he told of the buildings that had been turned to dust. He took me to Westminster Abbey and led me past the graves of the mighty and the poets. He knew every one. We went to St. Paul's and he marveled at the great bomb that had fallen through the sacristy and been defused. He inspected the ruins of the Wren churches, ate at the Cheshire Cheese, and we went up to Hyde Park to look at the antiaircraft installations and the searchlights by night. He attended Commons and heard Churchill. He spent two days with Walter Cronkite at Eighth Air Force bases and would have flown a mission if General Eaker had let him. He thought the spirit of the fliers was like that of a University of Southern California football team before the big game. He talked to General Devers, who had replaced General Andrews, he met Eden and Air Marshals Harris and Peck. He dined with Beaverbrook and Lord Astor and all the rest. He came with me to Sandy's, had late drinks at the Savoy, he loved the UP bureau, never had met such correspondents, never been so thrilled, he even loved me, gave me a raise and promised to promote me to the post of European News Manager. I was walking on air. My worries vanished.

But Baillie had a protégé named Virgil Pinkley, a Southern Californian like himself, a salesman who was doubling in brass on the news side in North Africa. Virgil had won a place in Baillie's heart by the simple trick of putting in the hands of the desk each Saturday during football season two telegrams. One said: "Congrats, we won again!" The other read: "Tough luck, we'll lick 'em next time." The desk waited until the USC score came in, then dispatched the appropriate sentiment. Whatever Baillie's mood, win or lose, Pinkley had it covered. Virgil flew up, took Baillie back to Algiers, and was named General European Manager. When Baillie told me he was going to promote me, I had written a sad note in my journal: "I hope he does but he might forget. Really." Well, he did forget and I found myself working for Virgil. I didn't handle that very well, but there was no way I could. We were strange dogs, sniffing and growling at each other.

One Sunday in September, I called Ellen and invited her to spend the day with me. I had hardly seen her all summer. My life had become too complicated and I thought I should put some distance between us. We took the train to Maidenhead, rented a canoe and started up the Thames. It was a winy autumn day, and we relaxed beside each other and let the canoe move very gently. There were many swans sailing, majestic and white. I had never seen a swan except in a park. Now they floated up to the canoe, looking at us with great curiosity, arching their necks. I took some peppermints from my pocket and tossed them to the swans. They turned out to be peppermint freaks. I switched to chewing gum. They liked gum too. It was an enchantment—the river, the swans, the countryside and the girl beside me. My worries floated off into the white clouds that lazily passed overhead. We fell in love that day. We spent the next weekend together in her flat in Weymouth Mews. There was a rather sharp air raid, the guns awakening us, heavy gunfire, the drone of the planes overhead, searchlights. We watched it, holding each other, and went back to sleep before the all clear. I should have been in seventh heaven. I was. But I wasn't. I was more filled with guilt than ever. Ellen was my friend's girl (well, I knew that had faded). I was betraying Mary (well, I had done that before). I was betraying Ellen, because there was no chance of a future together (well, we had talked about that; we each knew it). What else? There was my gnawing ambition. This was no time to fall in love. I should be clearing up my life, not bringing in something new and overwhelming. (Since when had logic and reason held back the heart?) I didn't know what to do, so I began spending every possible moment with her.

Something happened a week later that I could not have imagined. I was invited to lunch with the directors of *The Times* of London—the paper that long ago my mother had hoped I might be editor of. I've no notion why Lord Astor sent the invitation, but to me it had a solemn, almost sacred import. To be sure, I was ill at ease in the faded red-brick building across from the *Times* offices in Old Victoria Street, just down from Blackfriars Bridge, but no matter. I was there in the house that had been for so many years the home of the Walters family, publishers of *The Times*. Here was John Walters himself, old and spare, and Lord Astor, tall, handsome, with a shy smile and a severe limp, who apologized that only five of the directors could be present. Nothing happened at this luncheon. Nothing of significance was said. No matter. I was served by two old butlers whom I had often seen around London at formal affairs. The food was excellent, a tomato puree of real tomatoes, not from a tin, a very good chicken which had been allowed to run and peck a bit, peach Melba, Stilton cheese, port and cigars. I have always been sorry I didn't take a cigar.

Most of the directors wore proper morning clothes with waistcoats, pin-striped trousers and gates-ajar collars. I was very aware of my Bond's suit (walk a flight–save ten dollars) and my scruffy shoes. A proper coal fire burned in the grate and after the port and some small talk with Colonel Astor about the postwar problem of newsprint, we broke up. Later, writing a schoolboy's account of the occasion to my uncle Andrew, who had read *The Times* of London all his years, I bathed again in the aura of the occasion. I might be in sixty-nine kinds of trouble, but I had been taken into the bosom of the Old Thunderer. It was something to cherish through a lifetime.

Luncheon at *The Times* did nothing to dispel my problems. They stood impacted, impossible of resolution, when on October 12 a cable arrived from Earl Johnson in New York. He ordered me to leave London immediately, proceed to North Africa, reorganize the UP's coverage there (left in a mess by Pinkley), go east to Cairo, to Moscow, to New Delhi, and await instructions. Perhaps I would return to London, perhaps I would go on to Chungking. I did not have to read the cable twice to understand that Johnson had come to my rescue. He had saved me by sending me into orbit. I only realized how desperate I had become when the surge of excitement hit my brain. Johnson had given me an open-ended invitation to cover the war all over the world; no one had had such an opportunity. My imagination took off, my blood tingled. I was not doomed to purgatory in my beloved London. I had been cut loose just as the express train thundered down the tracks. No one could stop me now. I was on my way.

So I thought in one grand rush. Then bittersweet flooded my heart. My new love! What of her! Had I found her just to lose her? But wasn't it always thus? When the hero pledged his love he must go forth and slay the dragon. This nonsensical Arthurian imagery actually flashed through my head. I had been right and so had Ellen to understand that there could be no future for us. This was war. Now I began to feel like Hemingway. Farewell, Catherine! I had army orders to fly from Prestwick in Scotland to Marrakesh in Morocco. I booked a compartment on the *Flying Scotsman* and at 8:40 P.M. on the evening of October 23, 1943, my love and I left London, holding each other all through the night. At 6:40 A.M. (we were always so precise during the war with our travel notes), the train arrived at Prestwick, the air chilly, fog creeping about, heather hidden, the sun not yet up. We stood on the platform and kissed an endless farewell. Then I caught the army bus for the air base, leaving Ellen standing at the station, looking back as long as I could at this woman with chestnut hair, red cheeks, pert nose, brown eyes and my heart in her hands, standing alone in her dark blue uniform.

# Chapter 7

# Russia!

I spent my first night in Russia in the old, old city of Astrakhan, at the head of the Caspian Sea. It was January 13, 1944, and I had been waiting since before Christmas in Teheran for the weather to clear so that a Soviet DC-3 could fly over the sixteen-thousand-foot Elburz Mountains and into Russia. My North African experience had been fleeting. True, I had met General Eisenhower, a frosty, rather unpleasant meeting. He called me in a couple of days after I arrived in Algiers, to warn me to mind my conduct. Anyone who cut corners or violated rules was consigned to a slow boat back to the U.S.A. I think the lecture was instigated by my AP competitor Ed Kennedy, a tough agency man who later won ignominy when he violated a pledge to Eisenhower and secretly transmitted to AP word of the war's end, on May 7, 1945. I was not taken by Eisenhower nor by his headquarters, ridden by cliques and rich with intrigue. The war had moved up to Italy and Ike was marking time for the shift to England and preparations for the landing in France on June 6, 1944. I never got to know Eisenhower, but I did get to know his brother Milton, whom I liked and respected. I believe we will always be in Eisenhower's debt for his farewell address, with its warning against the military-industrial complex. The language was written by Milton, but it was Dwight Eisenhower who understood the danger, spoke the words and left it as his legacy to the American people.

I took off from Teheran for the Soviet Union, my mind imprinted with images of poverty and disease. Algiers, Tunisia, Cairo and Persia, the contrast of incredible riches and horror: dirty little girls of eight or nine being offered for twenty-five cents by their eleven-year-old brothers; the stores of Cairo filled with symbols of American good living—Campbell's soup, Quaker oats, Del Monte peaches, seventy-five cents for Heinz tomato juice, an astronomical dollar a pound for Maxwell House coffee, everywhere English woolens, Paris jewelry, perfume, furs, silks, a selection that I thought could not be had in New York, and the streets stinking of human excrement. But

Teheran—Teheran had to be the worst: beautiful German-built apartment houses, but no sewers, no water system; a ditch beside the asphalt streets carrying mountain-pure water, contaminated every few feet by defecating humans and horses; women washing clothes; women drawing water to drink; a naked seven-year-old with one testicle the size of a walnut, the other big as a coconut; a pubescent girl with green pus dripping from a blind eye. I saw the shah, a nervous youngster, wondering whether the British, the Russians and the Americans would let him keep the Peacock Throne or dump him as they had his terrifying old father.

One day I sat beside the fieldstone fireplace in the U.S. officers' club at Camp Amirabad, aromatic pine logs filling the room with their scent, eating pistachio nuts and sipping vodka and tonic and wondering whether there was a way in which these wretched people could be rescued. No one had an idea. "It's too much," one thoughtful major observed. "We can't get a hold on it. The only ones who can help are the Russians. They are closer to the gooks [yes, we called them gooks]. I think we ought to turn Persia over to the Russians. Maybe they can do it." There was no one around the fireplace—all of us in uniform—who disagreed. We thought that with the end of war, everyone would turn to resolving the world's ills. It would be like the early New Deal days—only on a world scale, the Russians, ourselves and possibly the British. We didn't think the French would take a hand.

Now I was flying over the blue Caspian Sea in our Russian DC-3, first stop Baku. We had some American oil engineers with us and they thought Baku was just like Galveston, Texas, a sprawling town, derricks, refineries and oil tanks scattered over a sandy spit. After a bite to eat and a customs inspection (an apologetic clerk took some lemons away from two English correspondents who had been vacationing in Palestine, then relented and gave them back), we took off and were flying between two thousand and three thousand feet— Russian pilots in those days never took much altitude—when we hit a downdraft. It was like dropping through a hole in the sky. The water rushed up at us and I thought we were going in. But with a tremendous groan the plane stabilized just above the waves and the pilot fought it onward and gradually gained a fair altitude. At midafternoon we bounded down on the dark, cold, windy Astrakhan field.

No stop had been planned at Astrakhan, no arrangements had been made. We were taken to a dismal little hotel with heat only on the third floor, where, thankfully, we were harbored. I dumped my musette on the blue-painted iron bed and rushed for the street. I was in *Russia!* The most exciting place in the world. I couldn't wait to get out, bundled up in an Alpine army parka I had bought at the U.S. Army store in Cairo, and a beaver cap that I had had made in Teheran at a cost of fifteen dollars. Russia—it was too much to believe. When I got my instructions from New York to go to Moscow and run the bureau while Henry Shapiro took a brief vacation, I hadn't quite taken it in. I had to get a visa, and put in my application in Algiers. To my amazement, the visa was waiting for me in Teheran two days before Christmas. Of course, I couldn't read what it said. I didn't know a letter of Cyrillic. The only Russian I knew was half a dozen words I had been given by a girl in Cairo named Zette, whose parents had fled to Sofia at the time of the Revolution. My vocabulary consisted of: *da* (yes), *nyet* (no), *mozhno* (may I), *spasibo* (thank you), *puzhalista* (please) and *ya vas lublu* (I love you). She acknowledged that I didn't really need the last expression. "Russian girls are very realistic," she said. "But it will amuse them if you say 'I love you.'"

The first thing I did on the cold, windy streets of Astrakhan was to look at people's feet. They all wore shoes or felt boots, except for one woman, rather elderly, who wore a pair of rubbers over three pair of stockings. I had remembered the first dispatch of my friend Cy Sulzberger when he got into Russia in late summer 1941. It started out: "The Russians have shoes." A curious fact to report, with the Germans pounding toward Moscow, but a significant one. What Cy meant was that despite Hitler's attack and the terrible losses, Russia was still able to feed and clothe itself. If the Russians wore shoes they were capable of fighting. This was big news. Astrakhan was down-at-the-heels, but the kids looked healthy, well-fed, red-cheeked, warmly dressed. They had just got out of school for the day and tagged after us, fascinated by the sight of foreigners. There were few trucks, no passenger cars, no troikas. But I saw one smart-looking Russian officer driving a spanking mare in a droshky and thought of *Anna Karenina.* Crossing a bridge to get back to the hotel, I encountered a blind musician, a pale young man with upturned collar, playing a violin with wool-gloved fingers. Passersby were dropping kopecks and ruble notes into the fur hat at his feet. My first day in Russia, my first beggar. I saw two more, women begging at a factory gate, as I walked around Astrakhan like a prospecting miner. Every little speck was gold.

At the hotel there was chaos. We had no money to pay for our rooms or meals. Our Intourist tickets were good only in Baku or Stalingrad. The hotel manager talked to one official after another. After an hour she got permission to feed us. It was my first lesson in Russian bureaucracy. The manager said she'd had the same problem with the Archbishop of York. He'd sent her the rubles from Moscow. She had entertained Anthony Eden too, but he paid cash. She liked him a lot. She fed us black bread and tea and a slab of tough beef, some vodka and watery beer. I was running a fever and slipped off to aspirin and bed under a pile of blankets, but not before I had heard her tell about the Germans. They were very strong, the strongest people in Europe, and the Russians were not nearly so cultured, not nearly so advanced. But, she said, "We are very cunning people. The Germans will not be so strong again." I thought about that as I sweated my fever away. She had screwed up her face and her eyes squinted a Mongol squint. I was too ignorant to know that Astrakhan was an old Tatar city, one of their last strongholds (as well as the birthplace of Lenin's father, Ilya Ulyanov, from whom Lenin derived a measure of Tatar blood), and I did not recognize in her remarks an echo of the peasant tradition—to appear ignorant, blockheaded, stupid, but in the end to use cunning to overcome educated, cultivated, cultured people.

I pondered that night about those beggars. How did they fit into the workers' paradise? And our landlady's preoccupation with money—what about that? Certainly there was a lot to learn in the Soviet Union. No sign thus far of the new Soviet Man or the humanistic society of which, I had been told, Lenin dreamed.

Between the fever and the excitement of arriving in Russia, I did not sleep for hours. I had never felt so far from London and New York. In the two months since Prestwick, I had been cut off, no word from Mary, none from Ellen. I had been working like spit. I knew I had made a hit at Cairo, handling the Teheran Conference story; this was the kind of professional job at which I was a master. Now I stood on the doorstep of a new world. Tomorrow I would be in Moscow— the Kremlin, Stalin, the Red Army. Headlines danced in my mind. Every kind of person had come to Russia: correspondents with red stars in their eyes, romantics hunting the Revolution, seekers of utopia, believers, scoundrels, men on the make. I thought I had a big advantage. I was not going to Moscow with a bagful of illusions. I was a hard-headed newsman. That was what I thought, and it was pretty true, pretty true. But not entirely true. I had infinite regard for the Red Army and the Russian people. I had seen those banners in London's East End: "They gave us Quiet Nights." Or just little signs in windows saying: "Quiet Nights." A lot of emotion rode in that. I distrusted Stalin, feared him, but I respected him. So far as I knew, he had done a brilliant job of fighting Hitler. He was a tough, hard dictator, of that I was certain, but he had had the guts to stand up to the Nazi armies (how little I really knew!). Already the Russian bureaucracy was rubbing me the wrong way. But what I could not then comprehend was the real depth of my ignorance, not only about Stalin and Communist Russia, but about the eternal Russia that had existed long before the Romanovs and would persist long after the Soviets. What I knew that night, huddled under my mountain of blankets, sweat turning me into a soggy mass, was that I had started on a new path. I did not know where it would lead or what it would bring, but I had finally cut loose. I was on my own. I felt very much as I had that frosty January morning thirteen years before when I had stalked up Michigan Boulevard on my first day in the Chicago bureau of the UP. Russia was the big one and I was going to make it my own.

It was my fifth day in Moscow and I was at Spaso House, the merchant's palace that George F. Kennan had acquired in 1933 as a residence for the American ambassador, when a telephone call came from the Foreign Office: A trip had been set up for the correspondents to visit Katyn Forest. The name Katyn rings soundless in minds that today react instantly to the name Auschwitz, but it is one that is not forgotten in Poland. Katyn is a pleasant wooded region not far from Smolensk, where in a place called Goat's Hill some thousands of Polish officers, possibly 4,500, possibly more, were killed in 1940 or 1941, each with a pistol bullet in the head. The officers had surrendered after the brief hostilities that followed the Nazi-Soviet partition of Poland in September 1939. They had been placed in internment camps in Russia and then brought to Katyn. The Germans announced the discovery of mass graves and bodies April 13, 1943, and put the blame on the Russians with a propaganda flourish overseen by Goebbels. Forensic specialists, academicians of various countries, an international commission of inquiry, foreign journalists, were hurried to the scene, graves were opened, bodies exhumed, autopsies performed, letters and newspaper clippings presented, to suggest that the men had been killed in April and May of 1940—that is, when still in custody of the Russians. The sensation was tremendous. In occupied Poland, the German version was generally accepted. Families of the officers, it was said, had not heard from them since spring 1940. Relations with the Poles and the Russians, always stormy, became impossible. Moscow broke diplomatic contact with the Polish government-in-exile in London. The Soviets maintained that the Germans had committed the atrocity.

Kathy Harriman was in Moscow with her father, now ambassador to Moscow. She had a job with the Office of War Information and acted as her father's hostess, bringing life and gaiety to a banal scene. She turned the embassy ballroom into a badminton court and found a cache of old Hollywood films in the Spaso attic. They were so britttle they broke a dozen times during a showing, but we ran them just the same.

Kathy was present when the Katyn announcement was made and said she'd like to go along. The Russians promptly invited her and John Melby, a young embassy attaché. They laid on a special train—international wagon-lits, a mahogany-paneled dining car, quantities of caviar, champagne, butter, white bread, smoked salmon, cake, beef Stroganov, cutlets Kiev—and we were off to look into one of the war's great tragedies.

The Russians had recaptured Smolensk in September 1943 and now they were about to explode their own propaganda bomb. The Western correspondents were invited as part of the stage setting. I don't think the participation of Kathy Harriman and John Melby was calculated U.S. policy. I think it was spur-of-the-moment impulse, but it is true that Averell Harriman was fed up with the "London" Poles and when we came back from Katyn he told me he had been convinced for a long time that the Poles had fallen for a German atrocity story and what we had seen strengthened his conviction.

I am deeply grateful to the Soviet press department for arranging this expedition. It was (and remains) a vivid lesson in Soviet methodology. There was the embarrassing extravagance of the train, outfitted with snowy linen, perfumed soap, down quilts, white-jacketed waiters, luxury fit for the Czar. In fact, it may have been one of the Czar's special trains. To sit in the dining car, tables laden with bottles, crystal and silver, plates heaped with *zakuski*, and look through lace curtains at wooden freight trains where wounded Red Army men, heads in bloody bandages, arms in splints, legs amputated, gazed from the next track, shivering around potbellied stoves, was almost

80

too much. As Dick Lauterbach, the *Time* correspondent, said, turning away from the stare of the young soldiers, many of them not more than fifteen or sixteen: "Comes the revolution..." What he meant was that once the war was over, there would *be* a revolution, times would change, the young veterans would come back determined to end the inequality, the suffering, the terror, the ugliness of Russian life. That seemed plausible to me. How could they fail, no matter what repressions the regime imposed? As we now know from the examples of Solzhenitsyn and others, that was what Stalin feared; that was why SMERSH, the front-line secret police, ferreted the young Solzhenitsyns out of the army and sent them to prison camps long before war ended; that was why Red Army men released from starvation and torture in Nazi POW camps were sent straight to Stalin's camps in Siberia; no intermediate halts; that was why the end of the war signaled new and sharper repressions. Stalin had never seen the eyes of the young Russian soldiers. He had never visited the front, from first day to last. But he knew what to fear. "When these boys come back from the front there are going to be lots of things different here," I wrote in my journal. I was right but, alas, the more things changed, the more they became the same.

I think we all wanted to believe that the Germans had done Katyn. Whatever their idiosyncrasies, the Russians were our allies. We hated the Nazis. Atrocities were what the Nazis were all about. What more natural than to kill the Polish officers, blame it on the Russians and sow trouble? But the Russian expedition got off on the wrong foot and never changed. I didn't like the fact that the inquiry was being conducted by a "Commission to Investigate the German Atrocities at Katyn Forest." That established the verdict in advance. Perhaps the Nazis did it, but I wanted to hear the evidence and make up my mind. The Russians couldn't understand what we were talking about. Of course the Germans did it. Why would we be having this hearing? That was a topsy-turvy world to me. The man was convicted before the evidence was presented. Some of my colleagues told me that Russian law was based on the Code Napoleon. First a thorough inquiry was conducted, and unless the man was guilty, he was not put on trial. I didn't buy that.

When we got to Smolensk we drove out to the forest, out a well-laid road through pine woods and new-fallen snow. At Katyn there were log fires everywhere, tents, doctors in white smocks and surgical caps, nurses, Red Army men with shovels and entrenching instruments. It took some time to see the bodies, neatly stacked like cordwood, hundred after hundred of them in precise, rectangular excavations in the sandy soil. It was hard to believe that these were bodies, that they had been men, that this was not some kind of outdoor festival in the north woods of Minnesota.

But it was real enough and we went from tent to tent, watching the surgeons perform autopsies, trepanning skulls with fine-tooth medical saws, cutting open stomachs and depositing the contents in flasks of yellow and blue fluid, an anatomical laboratory suddenly transported into a snowdrift. The sweet cheesy stench and the sight of the carcasses were too much for some of my colleagues, Henry Cassidy of the AP for one, but Kathy seemed unaffected. So was I. There was something about the mass of bodies that deprived them of humanity.

I was struck by the neatness of it all. Every man executed exactly in the same way, a pistol bullet fired close up at the base of the skull. Almost all the men wore their army greatcoats and had been buried with their boots on. This did not impress me. I was too new to Russia. But it struck my colleagues. "I can't believe the Russians would bury those boots and that warm clothing," Alex Werth said. After I had seen Russians scavenging on the battlefields, I was inclined to agree.

The evidence of the commission was poor and its presentation worse. The witnesses were a dreary lot. After much argument, the correspondents were given the right to ask questions through the commission. I did not please my hosts by my insistence on finding out the prior and present status of the witnesses. (It seemed apparent to me that they had been arrested, were prisoners and probably headed back to prison—potent incentives for them to tell the story as their captors wanted them to tell it.) When I asked the quisling deputy burgomaster of Smolensk if he had been arrested and whether he was now in prison, the commission refused to put my question. Finally, the novelist Alexei Tolstoy, a relative of Leo Tolstoy and a member of the commission, said that the man had indeed been arrested but that he was presently at liberty and was going to Moscow. Not much of an answer. The commission was ill at ease with our sharp inquiries. Finally, they called the thing off at midnight and we were hustled back to our train luxe for our fifth banquet of the day. We stayed up until 4 A.M., arguing and drinking. I told Apollon Petrov, a Chinese-archaeological specialist, who for some reason was deputy chief of the Press Department, that Russia would get better American public support if it let U.S. war correspondents go to the front. "Mr. Salisbury," he told me soberly, "if the Red Army's victories have not won American support, I don't think your stories will help." One of our colleagues was a newspaperman who represented something called the "Free Polish Press." He had looked pale and ill all day and when we got back to the train went straight to his berth. Small wonder. He had once been a Polish officer.

We had embarked on the trip expecting that the Russians would have an airtight case. The evidence had been poor and the presentation sloppy. "Our verdict," I wrote in my journal, "was: A lot of Poles have been killed by revolver shots in the back of the head. They have been dead for some time. We wished we knew who killed them." In other words, the old Scots judgment: "Guilt not proven." That was the tenor of the dispatches we filed. The censors killed all skeptical remarks and deleted references to the caviar.

The tragic evidence of Katyn has been pawed over time and again, almost entirely by "London" Poles and others antagonistic to the postwar Polish regimes and to the Soviets. The Soviet government made a halfhearted effort to submit the case to the Nuremberg War Crimes Tribunal but never pushed it, and no indictment was returned. Forty years after it happened, Katyn remains in limbo, but few, indeed, are the Poles who do not believe it was Stalin's secret police who committed the crime. Once, Stalin let drop a remark in talk with the Poles which convinced some that the execution had been carried out by accident, by chance, by misinterpretation by Beria of a casual remark Stalin had made. That seems nonsense. Nor is there support for another report, that Nikita Khrushchev at the time of the Twentieth Party Congress contemplated making public the evidence about Katyn but was dissuaded because the consequences on Polish-Russian relations would be so catastrophic.

The truth is that at any moment the Polish government wants to establish and make public the facts about Katyn, it has the means to do so. The same is true of the Soviet government. Had the Germans committed the massacre, the sober bookkeeping evidence, the orders, the statistics, the whole dreary business, would long since have turned up, no matter how cleverly it had been hidden. Yet some things nag—the burial of the overcoats and boots and one bit of evidence never publicized: The bullets the Poles were shot with were

German bullets fired from German pistols. But, it is said, the Russians bought a shipment of these handguns from the German firm of Gustav Genschow & Co. in 1929. Who knows? Until someday an impartial commission gives the final verdict, Katyn will remain dark, bloody and tragic as it was in the January days of 1944 when I first saw it.

By the time I returned from Smolensk, I knew that the task of understanding and interpreting Russia was going to be more difficult than I could have imagined.*

I went to the Foreign Office one afternoon and met Max Litvinov for the first time. He was one of my heroes. Since the days when he stood up in the League of Nations in the 1930s and thundered "Peace is indivisible," I had seen him as a champion against fascism. Henry Shapiro, the UP's permanent Moscow correspondent, took me to the Foreign Office, housed in a warren of old buildings off Lubyanka Square, across a narrow street from the vast headquarters building of the GPU, the secret police, and its enormous Lubyanka Prison. I did not then know it, but the whole area around the Foreign Office was honeycombed with police institutions and, as it later would emerge, the Foreign Office itself for practical purposes had been in the hands of the police since May 1, 1939. To see Litvinov, we did not use the main entrance of the Foreign Office; instead we entered by an obscure side entrance. I never figured out the significance of that; there was an armed guard at this entrance just as at the main one. But each time I called on Litvinov, he had instructed me to use this entrance. It was the same with his other foreign visitors. We liked to think there was something conspiratorial about it. Litvinov had been on the shelf since his recall from Washington to Moscow in August 1943. Now I sat down with him in a little office somewhere behind the back stairs of the ministry and he talked long and frankly, just as "twinkling, beaming, rotund" to quote my journal, as I had always imagined him. "It was nice," I noted, "to meet a Western mind again." When I brought up the diplomatic problems of the day (there was a great flap on over rumors of separate British peace talks), he smiled wearily and said that if we got the main question of collective security resolved, the smaller problems would fall into place. Then he

* As part of its *glasnost* policy the Gorbachev regime for the first time admitted Soviet responsibility for the massacre.

led the conversation away from politics into a tale about the twelve-day trip he had taken from Washington to Moscow via Montana on his flight back to the Soviet Union. A plane-ferrying route via Montana, Alaska and Siberia was then functioning.

I wasn't certain of the validity of his thesis that if the basic relationship could be resolved, the little things would fit into context. I think he was saying that if America and Russia and Britain could construct a solid postwar structure, small problems would not fester so badly.

I saw Litvinov possibly a dozen times before leaving Moscow. Never without profit. Always his talk was civilized, penetrating. Always he managed to distance himself from the pompous rigidity of Soviet diplomacy, giving me an insight into what lay behind it. Sometimes he just shrugged his shoulders and cast his eyes upward as if imploring heaven as his witness that he understood it no better than myself (perhaps he was just drawing my attention to hidden microphones). He never ducked a question; never found a subject too sensitive. He was the only Soviet official I was to meet whom I found unfailingly decent. I knew then that he was a man of courage, but I had no understanding of his real situation. That would not come until long after his death. He visited the American embassy often, attending receptions, dinners, movies. Whatever the company, whether in the presence of Molotov or not, Litvinov consistently spoke with me and the other correspondents, not just diplomatic froufrou, always talk of substance.

When many years later Ivan Maisky told me that Litvinov had slept every night of his life from the mid-1930s onward with a pistol under his pillow (later, Pavel Litvinov told me his grandfather had shown him the gun), that he had confided to Maisky that if they came to arrest him he would shoot himself, I was not surprised. This was in Litvinov's character. Perhaps that is why the knock never came.* When I returned to Moscow in 1949, I wrote letters and made calls to men in official positions whom I had known during the war. Only Litvinov replied. I had sent him a letter suggesting that he write for *The New York Times* a brief memoir of FDR on the fifth anniversary of his death, in April 1950. I promptly got a note back, thanking me for the

---

* Nikita Khrushchev revealed that plans had been made by the secret police to kill Litvinov by running him down with a truck, but they were never carried out (*Khrushchev Remembers*, 1970, p. 262.)

suggestion, assuring me that were it not for "indisposition," he would be happy to do as I suggested.

Not quite two years later, on January 2, 1952, *Pravda* published a five-line notice on its back page that Litvinov had died December 31, 1951. I was shocked. Not by the news—Litvinov had lived beyond his life expectancy in the Stalin epoch—but by the shamelessly obscure notice of the death of one of the great men of the twentieth century, the greatest diplomat of the Soviet era. It was a shabby thing. In my outrage I called the dean of the diplomatic corps, Ambassador Yves Chataingeux of France, to see if the corps had been invited to the funeral. He had not even heard Litvinov was dead. I called the Foreign Office and discovered the funeral was being conducted at that moment. I threw on my coat and raced over to the old building on the Kuznetsky Most, entering the drafty reception room at the moment the cortege was emerging, Andrei Gromyko at its head, and in his train, deputy ministers Zorin and Gusev (who had replaced Maisky in London), Litvinov's wife, Ivy Low, who had dreamed of conducting a postwar salon in Moscow, and Litvinov's son and daughter. His grandson Pavel, who, carrying on the family's tradition of courage, would become a dissident and ultimately settle in the United States, was not there. He was off on a ski trip with his high school class. I was the only foreigner present. What an insult, I thought, to Russia's history this seamy ceremony was. A nation that had no respect for its history could only be a state with no respect for itself.

I did not know in 1944 the reality of Litvinov's position; nor did I in 1951. It was not until his former secretary, Yevgeny Gnedin, published his memoirs in samizdat, that is, in the underground literature which circulates in the Soviet, that some concept of what happened to Litvinov could be established. Litvinov's removal from his post as foreign minister on May 1, 1939, and his replacement by Vyacheslav Molotov, was no mere shift of jobs. It was a takeover of the Foreign Office by the secret police and the opening of an attempt to concoct a case for the arrest and execution of Litvinov. Gnedin was head of the Press Department at the time, probably the man closest to Litvinov on the Foreign Office staff. Like every Litvinov associate, he was summoned to the Foreign Office on the evening of May 2. He didn't even know that Litvinov had lost his job. He had seen him the day before in Red Square, standing with the Soviet leaders at the May Day parade. That evening he was questioned by Molotov, Beria,

Malenkov, and V. G. Dekanozov, a police associate of Beria's who had been named number two to Molotov in the Foreign Office. The questioning went on in the presence of Litvinov.

They were laying the foundation for the case against him. Every man in the Foreign Office, Gnedin among them, who had an association with Litvinov (and many who did not) was arrested. Some committed suicide. Others, including Gnedin, were tortured. Gnedin was interrogated by Semyon Kobulov, Beria's number two in the secret police (who was executed with Beria in 1953). Twice Gnedin was taken to Beria's office, where Kobulov and Beria alternately beat him, knocked him to the floor and kicked him almost into insensibility. Gnedin refused to confess that he was a spy, that Litvinov was a traitor, and finally he was shipped off to the Sukhanov isolator, the most terrible of Stalin's prisons. Later, he was sent into "eternal exile." The effort to concoct a case against Litvinov was still in progress at the time Hitler attacked Russia. It was suspended (but probably not dropped) in order that Stalin might send Litvinov back to the United States to stir up sympathy for Russia. I would guess that the case being fabricated by Stalin at the time of his death in 1953 against Molotov, in which Maisky was arrested, was descended from the Litvinov case; had Litvinov lived, had he not died at the end of 1951, he would have been given a central role in Stalin's grandiose 1953 extravaganza, probably cast as Molotov's "secret agent" in plotting with the United States, just as Maisky had been assigned the role of Molotov's "secret agent" in liaison with the British.

# Chapter 8

# To Leningrad

Three people drank tea with me around a low table in Room 346 of the Metropol Hotel, the UP's office, on the afternoon I arrived in Moscow. A gloomy cave, Room 346 contained two or three tables piled with newspapers; a built-in cabinet full of tea things, canned goods, little hoards of sugar, husks of black bread and snippets of cheese (to be put on the floor for the mice so they wouldn't enter the cupboard); a built-in sofa upholstered in faded brocade; bookshelves spilling over with books and clippings; a two-burner hot plate; a crystal chandelier; and a small sleeping nook and bathroom behind a heavy green *portière*. Windows looked into the courtyard, where women in cotten-padded jackets chopped wood for the Metropol furnaces all day. Room 346 was the crossroads of the hotel, where people came in and out all day and all evening.

One of the three at the table was Henry Shapiro of UP, a chubby little man with broad forehead, Stalinesque mustache and a Rumanian accent. A onetime student in Moscow University's law faculty, he had supported himself for a while as a tourist guide. He had come with his parents to New York at an early age and graduated from Harvard. He was, in his way, a brilliant man, but his Byzantine mind, which often aided him in dealings with the Russians, sometimes affected his relations with his colleagues.

Seated beside Henry was Ludmilla Nikitina, his wife, with her ash-blond hair, pure white skin, almost skeletal face (she was remarkably thin). She was wearing a gray crêpe de Chine dress whose low-cut bodice displayed her white bosom, of which she was rightfully proud. Ludmilla worked for UP as a translator and also acted as a correspondent for Religious News Service. She had graduated from the Gorky Institute of World Literature, and as I later came to understand, she had solid roots in the *kupechestvo*, the Moscow merchant class, so brilliantly satirized in the plays of Ostrovsky.

Beside Ludmilla sat Olga Florentievna Khludova, a striking young woman who, I was to discover, liked to caricature herself as a gaunt borzoi. She was thin enough to make this plausible and there was an air of the aristocrat about her. Before the Revolution, the Khludovs had been one of the great entrepreneurial families that arose in nineteenth-century Moscow. They were closely connected with the Morozovs, an enormously wealthy textile and banking family. Saava Morozov financed Stanislavski's Moscow Art Theater, collected French and Russian avant-garde art and subsidized Lenin and his Bolsheviks with hundreds of thousands of rubles, before finally he drew a circle around his heart with an indelible pencil and put a bullet through it. He left an insurance policy to Maxim Gorky's wife to help the revolutionaries.

Naturally, I knew nothing of this on that January day. I did know that Olga Florentievna possessed a sharp wit, spoke English not very well and worked for UP as a courier—taking telegrams to the Foreign Office, running errands, standing in queues for permits. She and Ludmilla practically lived in 346, although Ludmilla was often absent at her parents' home, caring for her three-year-old daughter, Arisha (Irena). Olga lived with her mother, a medical worker at the big Stalin auto works. She painted with great sensitivity, aquarelles and small oils, and occasionally drew caricatures for Moscow magazines. Professionally she was an animator, a great admirer of Walt Disney. Her studio, the Russian equivalent of Disney's, was shut down because of the war.

I was attracted to Olga the moment I saw her green eyes, *châtain* (the Russians used the French word for "auburn") hair, freckled face and the lilt of her head. She smoked cigarettes in a long amber holder and, as I was to learn, wore most of the time a simple brown jersey dress with a lace collar. Her proudest possession was a brown caracul *shuba*, a warm winter coat with a hood. She made a very stylish appearance, with her long stride and erect carriage.

On *Maslenitsa*, Shrove Tuesday, Ike Patch and Fred Barghorn, young officers at the embassy, had a blini party in their apartment at the chancellery on the Mokhovaya, across Manezhny Square from the Kremlin. The building had been built for artists and the young Americans had a studio with a twenty-four-foot ceiling. There was a good deal of vodka and marvelous blini, caviar and *smetana*, thanks to Pasha, their housekeeper, who spent her life trying to make Ike wear his galoshes so that he wouldn't catch cold. At midevening, Olga decided to leave and I offered to escort her back to the Metropol. We came out onto the Mokhovaya into a swirl of snow,

snow everywhere—in the air, under foot, in our faces—and skipped past the National Hotel, crossed Gorky Street, where scores of *dvorniki*, women with long-handled witches' brooms, were at work, and as we passed the Gosplan Building, we turned to each other and kissed and went down the street, our lips still together, kissing and kissing, past the Hall of Columns, where the purge trials were held, past the big Sverdlov Square metro station, across the asphalt desert in front of the Bolshoi Theater, past the Maly Theater corner, across to the Metropol, only pulling apart as we approached the hotel entrance with its sheep-jacketed militiaman. Into the hotel we went, side by side, across the lobby, past the drowsing "angels," the plainclothes police, up in the wheezing iron-cage elevator to the third floor, got the key to Room 346 from the sleepy woman *dezhurnaya* —floor attendant—entered 346, locked the door, and were in each other's arms without, I think, saying a single word.

Nothing like this had ever happened to me. I woke up next morning not knowing what to think. I was entranced with Olga. More than that I could not say. I made no attempt at trying to fit the evening into logic. It had happened. What would follow I had no idea, but when next I saw Olga, she would hardly speak to me, her eyes smoldering. Somehow I had offended her. It was totally mysterious. I held my peace, hoping that time would give an answer. Days raced by. Every moment I was absorbing sensations, walking through Red Square (much bigger than I had thought), enjoying the chidren skating on the frozen Moskva River (I thought of Mike at home), meeting diplomats (much less formal than London), watching Stalin at the Supreme Soviet (not nearly so tall as I had imagined), visiting the markets (pitiful collections of potatoes, onions and carrots). I found it hard to get an echo of the feeling I had had in the distant days at 107 Royalston Avenue; there was nothing in the Communist Young Pioneers to remind me of the boy soldiers whom I imagined to have defended the Winter Palace. No spark of that enthusiasm which burned in Nathan Rosen's eyes as he told me about the Revolution. It was impossible for me to envision Moscow as the beacon of Revolutionaries from all over the world. I saw the stone in the Kremlin wall with John Reed's name on it, marking the urn where the ashes of the author of *Ten Days That Shook the World* had been placed. I had never read *Ten Days*, although Reed was on my litany. And I saw the stone bearing the name of William ("Big Bill") Haywood, the IWW who had jumped bond in Los Angeles during his trial for dynamiting the *Los Angeles Times* and taken refuge in Russia. The IWW had not and never would lose my romantic interest. I had heard of another IWW, Bill Shatov, who had helped run Siberia and build the Turk-Sib railroad but when I asked, no one seemed to know what had become of him. He had, of course, been shot.

One afternoon I met Ilya Ehrenburg, the author and war correspondent, a man with a mop of gray hair like Einstein's, a fine English jacket, a fawn-colored French pullover, a Gauloise dripping ash over his sweater; he possessed contempt for Americans, total belief that the only good German was a dead German, and a prayerful dedication to Paris, where he had spent more of his life than in Moscow.

In February, I found myself with Olga on a train bound for Zagorsk. The Troitsa monastery, seat of the Orthodox Church, was there, a complex of fortress churches where Russia's fighting monks under St. Sergius had beaten off invading Polish Catholic knights.

We were spending the weekend at Zagorsk, six of us who had formed what whimsically we called the Anglo-American-Russian Walking Club. Olga and Ludmilla were the Russian members, myself and Ike Patch the Americans, and George Bolsover and Pat Kirkpatrick the English. It was just an excuse to get ourselves out in the country on weekends, and Olga was its founding spirit. Russians don't walk for pleasure any more than Americans do. But Olga had been brought up under strong English influence. Her father, an engineer, educated abroad, had taught his daughter to like fresh air, cold baths, dogs, riding horses, walking in country lanes, tweeds, plain shoes, shooting a gun, fly fishing, and what he called "being a gentleman." No matter that his mother was a personal friend of Lenin; that the family had given the Bolsheviks aid and that Lenin suffered the old grandmother to scold him for not taking proper care of tropical plants in the orangery of the family estate, which he confiscated: Olga's father had been arrested.

This was part of the substance of the young woman with whom I was riding that day to Zagorsk, a cold, overcast day with snow spilling into the air. The train was filled with peasant women in *valenki*—felt boots—black coats and black shawls, clutching their *avoski*, their string shopping bags (the nickname means "perhaps"), into which they had jammed whatever they had found in the Moscow markets—mostly onions on this day. Olga and I brought the provisions and would get our quarters in the dirty little Zagorsk hotel ready for the others, who were catching the next train.

Hardly a word was exchanged in the two-hour ride. We sat side by side, she reading a Russian book, its back protected by a paper wrapper, her eyes, I thought, angry, face cold, body rigid. Thinking of the night we had been together, I scraped a patch in the frosted window to stare at the Russian countryside—groves of birches, ghostly against the snow, clumps of pine, small log huts, whole villages of log huts—and in the train the smell of *makhorka*, the peasant's strong tobacco, and of wood smoke and wet wool.

Finally, we arrived at Zagorsk. It was only midafternoon but already getting on for dusk. The hotel manager showed us to the rooms we had reserved, one for the men, one for the women. They were small, three iron beds in each and a big tile Russian stove. In our coats and mittens, we sat on a bed. We could see our breaths. It was about twenty degrees outside and seemed colder within, the stove just beginning to heat up. Olga sat stiff as a kitchen chair. I longed to put my arms around her, but instead tried to make conversation, talking about winters in Minnesota when I was growing up. Olga had nothing to say. Gradually it warmed up a bit and Olga began worrying about our friends. It was full dark now. They should have arrived. Perhaps they had missed the train. I began to hope they had. Olga threw back the hood of her *shuba*. She didn't look angry anymore. Our eyes met and then switched away. Her face was rosy, almost like the blush of a young girl. I was embarrassed too. I knew what we both wanted—that our friends should miss the train. But they didn't. They arrived with shouts and hugs and a draft of cold air. The moment was gone.

Next day we explored the icy old monastery, the churches with their bulbous domes, resounding to the deep chant of the priests, the scent of incense in the frozen air, a tiny glint of candles burning at the altars, peasant women's devout faces haloed by the candles, peasant carts and horses with wooden yokes clattering to the market. This, I knew, must be the deep heart of Russia. We went outside and threw snowballs. Diamonds sparkled in Olga's hair, in Olga's eyes. We rode the train back to Moscow, the train jammed, standing all the way, crushed to each other. Three youngsters had an accordion, they sang *chastushki*, street songs, improvising the verses as they sang, ribald words, the crowd laughing, teasing the boys, Olga and I very close. I put my arm around her. She did not push it away.

Later Olga told me that when she awakened on the morning after *Maslenitsa* she was outraged at what had happened. She had been angry at me from the first afternoon, when, asking a question and not knowing her name, I said, "You, I mean you," and pointed a finger at her. I was, it was clear, another rude, vulgar American, and the morning after *Maslenitsa* this feeling came back very strong. She had got a little tipsy that night and this vulgarian had taken advantage of her, as he would of any whorish Russian girl. He had wanted a quick bounce and that was what she was—another Metropol girl, going to bed for a warm bath, a piece of soap, a little butter. She hated herself and she hated me. She remembered what her father had told her. He had talked to her as frankly as Chesterfield to his son. He told her what men were like; what they thought of women; just an object for their sex; a thing. Women, he had said, played the men's game. They played "the flirt," they led men on, then let men use them. He taught her never to blame a man in her personal relations; she would get what she deserved, no more, no less.

On the evening of February 6, I boarded a train for Leningrad with a dozen correspondents. The nine-hundred-day siege had ended. For the first time we would visit the city where so many had died to keep the Germans from their northern capital. I would, and already I think I knew this, fall in love with the city of Peter and be forever humbled by its people, awed by its beauty and bravery.

We had no fancy train to take us to Leningrad, nothing laid on like the Katyn trip, just a regular train following a very circuitous route. Though Leningrad was free once more, its rail connections were still tenuous. Almost forty years have passed since the cold morning when we debarked at the Nicholas (now, to be sure, the October) station in Leningrad, almost a three-day journey, roundabout through Vologda, moving slower and slower over new-laid tracks as we neared the city. I don't think I have forgotten a detail, standing at a window watching the endless snow, the birches and pines, and saying to the man standing next to me, "That looks like northern Minnesota," and learning that we were both Minnesotans, both graduates of the university. He was Homer Smith, a black who had come to Russia during the Depression as a "postal expert" (having been a clerk in the Minneapolis post office). Now he wished he hadn't. Like all exotic foreigners in Russia, he had been abandoned with the coming of war and was surviving largely through help from the foreign correspondents. His brother and sister were officers in the U.S. Army. His choice of the workers' paradise had proved a bad gamble.

I cannot go back over it all again. I have written so much about Leningrad in *The 900 Days*, which is dedicated to her people. Each of those I met in the winter of 1944 has etched a place in my heart. But a few things must be said. Leningrad was not only a living monument to heroism, to the tradition of "Pyotr," as they called the city in memory of Peter, who founded it. It was not only the little girl at the Kirov works who went out with her friend one afternoon a week to check her parents and her friend's parents to see who was living, who was dead, to put a body on a child's sled and drag it to the mountain that climbed higher and higher near the gates of Nevskaya Lavra. Nor the girls and boys with their dogs and mine detectors in the frosty twilight, slowly crisscrossing the frozen fields beyond the Czar's palace at Peterhof, never knowing when the next mine would blast away their legs or lives; the sudden blast and the column of smoke when they touched off a mine, and the explosions I heard in the distance.

Beneath this façade of courage ran a deadly current of Kremlin politics, more dangerous even than German tanks and bombs. Of this I only occasionally caught a glimpse, as through a door left accidentally ajar, a whiff of the terror that had swept the city after the assassination of Sergei Kirov on December 1, 1934, which set off Stalin's great purges. I knew then (and, of course, much more in later times) that there was something rotten about the Kirov case; just what, I could not say. I caught it in the nuances of remarks, cautious, oblique. *The people did not want to talk about it.* I had been in Russia only a few days, but I already knew that if Russians did not want to talk about Trotsky, for instance, or the Kirov case, something frightening lay behind it.

In Leningrad I saw that Kirov was honored. His name had been given to the great Putilov steel works, owned by a Russian Carnegie named Aleksei Putilov, a friend of the Morozovs and the Khludovs. But no one would talk about the "Kirov case," the purge trials, Zinoviev, Kamenev, Bukharin and the rest of the executed old Bolsheviks or the thousands of Leningraders who had been arrested, shot or exiled. This held no reality for me, I could not grasp what terror meant, until a few months later when in Central Asia, in Tashkent, I met a young Russian composer named Aleksei Kozlovsky and his wife, Galya Geras, an American who had been brought to Russia by her parents, her father having been an important revolutionary before 1917. Galya whispered the story to me during a performance of *Uleg Bek*, an opera she and her husband had written. In 1937, Kozlovsky had been exiled from Leningrad to Central Asia and she had come with him. He had done nothing. By chance he had been in the same high school class with three "Trotskyite" schoolboys. The schoolmates were shot. All that happened to Kozlovsky and his wife was that they were totally cut off from Western culture (she had not spoken a word of English for nearly eight years) and compelled to live in a mud-floored Central Asian house, where they composed "national" operas for the glory of Uzbek culture. What had happened to the Kozlovskys had happened to tens, perhaps hundreds, of thousands of Leningraders.

The terror lay deep under the city. Hitler was not the only enemy. There sat in the Kremlin the most dangerous man of all, Stalin. It would be many, many years before I pieced together the details of this peril. No one outside the tight circle of the Kremlin and the Leningrad leadership knew exactly what had happened in 1934 and the year after. No one outside this circle (and not all within it) knew the inner story of the siege, of Stalin's faithless conduct of the Leningrad defense, the feud between Andrei Zhdanov, Kirov's successor as Leningrad party leader, and his Politburo rivals, Georgi Malenkov and Lavrenti Beria. I was ultimately to learn that Stalin's tactics had almost opened Leningrad to the Germans; that he ordered the city mined and was prepared to blow it up and abandon it to the Germans, halted in this, it would later appear, only by the herculean efforts of Marshal Georgi K. Zhukov, who took command at the critical moment.

Neither I nor any of the correspondents could judge the political standing of Andrei Zhdanov in 1944. We saw his picture everywhere; many, many pictures of Zhdanov, only a few of Stalin. I never saw this kind of iconography anywhere else at any time in Stalin's Russia. Did this mean that in Leningrad Zhdanov was popular and Stalin not? We tried to see Zhdanov but got nowhere. On our last day we met the number three man. Mayor Pyotr Popkov, tired, worn, only forty-one, an engineer who had been at his post all through the siege, cautious and tough, very careful about a question that is still in dispute today, the number of deaths in Leningrad from starvation, cold, disease. Some Leningraders told us that they thought the toll might be as high as 2,000,000 (for years the official Russian total was

632,253, but careful official Leningrad calculations now place it above 1,200,000). Popkov was only willing to discuss the small, almost inconsequential casualties of civilians killed and wounded by bombs and shells—a total of 5,000 killed, 15,000 wounded. He was uncommunicative on how many adults and children had been evacuated. It later became clear that hundreds of thousands of lives were lost in this badly managed, criminally tardy operation; many children were sent to places in the path of the Nazi advance.

Popkov had a right to be wary. When I returned to Russia in 1949, stopping first in Leningrad, I asked to see him. I thought my mention of his name had impressed the hotel manager at the Astoria, but I did not see Popkov. What I did not know and the manager did was that this dedicated, hard-working veteran of the Leningrad siege had been arrested a few days earlier in the so-called Leningrad Affair, which wiped out almost every surviving associate of Zhdanov, dead of a heart attack a year or so earlier. To mention Popkov's name in Astoria was like asking about black spots on a man's face in a city of the plague.

When I got back to Moscow in February 1944, I wrote a story about the future role of Leningrad. Pointing out that Lenin had moved the Soviet capital "temporarily" to Moscow in March 1919 because of the danger of German occupation of what was then Petrograd, I said it seemed not unlikely that Leningrad might be reinstated as capital of Russia. Its palaces and imperial avenues were almost intact despite the siege—they were too grandiose and solid to be wiped out by Nazi bombs. My article was an open plea that Leningrad again be Russia's capital. It was not passed by the censor, nor were similar stories by my colleagues. My article, I confess, was more an expression of my feelings than anything else. True, some Leningraders had spoken of the idea, but no officials, except an architect or two working on plans for postwar Leningrad. I am not certain that one of us did not toast Leningrad as the once and future capital of Russia at a great banquet of the Leningrad intelligentsia given in the Hall of Scientists. There were so many toasts that night that after the seventeenth or eighteenth, the listing kept by one of our number became unreadable. Finally, his pencil simply ran off the page.

There was a good deal of talk among us along these lines and we were, of course, all *foreigners* and all, by definition of the GPU or the OGPU or the KGB or whatever the secret police chanced to call itself at the moment, *shpioni*, spies.

Thus I suppose it was logical that one charge in the Leningrad Affair—invented by Beria and his underlings—should have been a conspiracy of the Leningrad leadership with "foreign agents" to transfer the capital of Russia from Moscow to Leningrad and, of course, to overthrow Stalin and set up a new regime. It was all quite logical to a mind as twisted and conscienceless as that of Stalin.

It would be totally wrong to suggest that in February 1944 I had any suspicion of currents so dark, so deep, so dangerous. At that time I still could refer to Stalin as a great builder in the tradition of Peter the Great. But I did come away from Leningrad with a conviction that there were secrets beneath the tragic city, beyond my ability to probe.

It is also true, as I wrote in my journal, that "I fell in love with Leningrad." It is a love that has endured a lifetime. I vowed that someday that I would write the epic of the city and finally, in 1969, *The 900 Days: The Siege of Leningrad* was published.

After *The 900 Days* came out, after it had become a best-seller in America and in every country in which it was published, the Soviet government wheeled out their greatest general, the man whose ruthless determination saved Leningrad from the Nazis, Marshal Zhukov, and signed his name to a full-page article in *Pravda* attacking me and *The 900 Days* for "vilifying" Leningrad and carrying out anti-Soviet propaganda. I have never met anyone from Leningrad who took this view. Again and again, Leningraders have thanked me for writing the story of their city, for telling the truth about the horror, the sacrifice, the terror, the mistakes, the intrigues that marked their struggle. To this day there has not been published in the Soviet Union an honest or complete account of this siege. Not one. Oh, of course there have been dozens of books, particularly since *The 900 Days*, including a collection of dramatic eyewitness accounts published by my good friend Daniel Granin, the Leningrad author. But what difficulty he had getting out his book; what obstacles were put in its way; what a small edition; how much censorship!

The tragedy and glory of Leningrad sticks like a bone in Moscow's throat, in the throat of the party leaders. Not even Khrushchev could get up his courage to publish the truth about the Kirov case, about Leningrad or the Leningrad Affair. It was too shameful, too black, too odious. But Leningrad will endure. It may never again be Russia's capital, but the full story of the wounds inflicted upon it by Stalin, his henchmen and his survivors will, in the end, see light.

## Chapter 9

# Back to Moscow

It was evening, full dark, a raw evening, the temperature a bit above freezing, when the train from Helsinki reached Leningrad on March 7, 1949, myself burning with anticipation of seeing the city again, fuming at delays, coming in to the old Finland Station where Lenin arrived from abroad on April 17, 1917, and took command of the Russian Revolution. I was going back to Russia for *The New York Times*—a new career, a new life.

I fretted all day. I had routed my return to Russia through Helsinki so that I could go first to that Leningrad I had seen with such awe and, yes, reverence at the end of the blockade in February 1944. Five years had passed. I wanted to enter Russia by way of Leningrad and I wanted to write my first dispatch under that dateline, reciting again the heroism of the city and its people, telling of their return to peace. I thought the spirit of Leningrad was the best in Russia, the best in the world, and I wanted to start my assignment on that note. I wished to find the girl worker at the Kirov plant again, to talk to the architects about their dreams for the northern capital, to meet with Mayor Popkov and see how it was all coming out. I knew that I would not find Andrei Zhdanov there. Leningrad's enigmatic and sometime mysterious wartime leader had died a few months earlier, on August 31, 1948.

The train had made a mule's progress from Helsinki, start and stop, start and stop. We had left about midnight after a big Sunday dinner at the American legation, at which the American minister, Avra M. Warren, presided over a gargantuan roast of beef and a small tub of fresh horseradish, the first of the season, the roots dug from the new-thawed soil and ground for the market stalls by white-aproned Finnish farmwives. The horseradish was so strong it blasted out my sinuses and brought tears to my eyes. The minister ladled it up and got so red I thought he might burst.

He and his wife and an American diplomatic courier joined me on the train.

98

The first delay came when the train approached the Porkkala area south of Helsinki, which the Russians had taken over at the end of the war as a fortified zone. The train halted and heavy wooden "muzzles" were fitted over each window, doors were locked and Red Army soldiers with fixed bayonets stood between the cars. "What are they concealing?" I asked. "Nothing," said the minister. "Absolutely nothing." He explained that occasionally there were cracks in the "muzzles" and diplomats could see out. "We've looked and looked," he said, "and no one has ever seen anything. We think the muzzles are to keep us from finding out that the fortified zone is actually not fortified."

When we had passed through the zone, the train halted again. The wooden shutters came down, then the train was searched and the guards got off. We proceeded very slowly until we reached the Finnish border town of Viipuri. Here Lenin's fellow Bolsheviks had met his train on the night of April 27 and escorted him to Petrograd. The Finnish border control stamped my passport, inspected the train and finally we eased across the border into Russia. It was already past lunchtime and my hopes of an afternoon stroll on the Nevsky Prospekt had gone glimmering.

We halted longer than ever, for customs examination. Everything in the baggage car, including my big trunk loaded with clothing and supplies, electric hot plates, accouterments for the office, had to be hauled into the customs shed. I had twenty or thirty books in my trunk, the *Columbia Encyclopedia*, the *World Almanac*, the *Statesman's Yearbook*, a Rand McNally atlas, Pares's *History of Russia*, Deutcher's *Stalin*, and on top of the heap, Trotsky's *Stalin* and Orwell's *1984*. I knew that Trotsky's name was anathema in Stalin's Russia—but I wanted to see the reaction. I did not know whether Orwell was well enough known to cause his book to be seized. It was, I confess, a minor provocation on my part.

A thin, dour young man came to inspect my trunk. He had only a few words of English and was taken aback by the pile of books. Why did I have so many? I told him in pidgin English that I was a journalist, these were my professional reference works. He stared at the books so fiercely I thought he would have pitched them into a bonfire if one had been nearby. Though he could not read English, he knew that books, particularly foreign books, were dangerous. He stacked the books to one side, painstakingly inspecting the rest of my stuff. Then he sighed deeply, looked at me angrily, said, "*Minut*," and left, to return with a tired, worn woman whose age I could not guess. She spoke English and I knew she must have been through the Leningrad blockade. With a sad smile, she said, "You are a correspondent?" Yes, I replied, I was on my way to Moscow for *The New York Times*. "I was in Leningrad during the war," I told her. "I came there when the blockade was lifted." "Oh," she said, "you know our city." I said that I admired Leningrad more than I could say. "I lived through the blockade," she said, "my daughter and I. We survived. My little girl was eleven years old. She had bright blond hair. I watched it turn gray." I shook my head; what could I say to such a woman? "We have seen war," she went on, "we people of Leningrad want peace. We do not want war with America." I bowed silently and when I wrote my first dispatch from Moscow, I quoted her words. She spoke briefly to the customs man. "I must apologize," she said to me. "My comrade is not a very cultured man. He did not understand. I told him that you must have these books for your work. I am sorry if you have been inconvenienced."

No one, not the little man, not the survivor of Leningrad, had given Trotsky or Orwell a glance. My juvenile stratagem had been a failure.

Finally, we got going again. I was glad that I had telegraphed ahead and asked for reservations at the Astoria. I would need a couple of days to see the city again. We were hustled through the Finland Station so fast I caught only a glimpse of the historic armored car from which Lenin made his first speech on the evening of April 17, 1917. The throngs of people, crowds in the station, crowds in the streets, hurrying along under the dim street lamps, overwhelmed me, the evening bustle of a Russian city, workers, men and women, doing last-minute shopping before going home to dinner.

There had been no crowds in Leningrad in January 1944. There were hardly 500,000 people left of the 3,300,000 who lived there when the war started, June 22, 1941. Now the life of the city seemed normal. Streetcars plowed along, men and women clinging to their sides. There were lots of trucks, a few civilian cars, and many jeeps and command cars still painted army khaki. That was all I could see in the quick passage from the Finland Station, over the Neva to St. Isaac's Square and the Astoria.

It was 6 P.M. when we straggled into the hotel. The Intourist girl told me I was booked to leave on the Red Arrow at 11 P.M. that night. But, I said, didn't you receive my telegram that I would stay over two days? She stared blankly at me and reiterated that I was leaving on the Red Arrow. My latent anger at Soviet bureaucracy boiled up; I had been back in the Astoria less than five minutes. I went to the manager, who was equally unmovable. I had an idea. "You know," I said, "I was here during the war and met Mayor Popkov. He is my friend. I don't think he will like it if he hears that I was not permitted to stay and pay him a call." I saw the manager flinch. Ha! I said to myself, it is the same the world over. If you know the right people . . . I went ahead. "Get me Mayor Popkov on the telephone, please. I will speak to him about this." The manager seemed to tremble at my words. He broke off the conversation and disappeared. I was pleased. Obviously, he had gone to consult higher authority. In fact, he never appeared again. Nor did I talk to Mayor Popkov. We had a hasty meal, then went off to the Mariinsky Theater, where I watched the first two acts of *Swan Lake*. I had not been so embarrassed in my life. Warren, his wife, myself and the courier went to the theater together. By the rules of his job, the courier was not permitted to leave his mail sack of diplomatic correspondence behind. It was, in fact, locked to his wrist. He tried, gently, to dissuade the minister from including him in the party, but the minister was in an expansive mood. "Of course you're coming, man," he declaimed. So off to the Kirov we went with an Intourist guide, a nice young woman who did not exactly understand what lay ahead. When we got to the theater, in we went, courier, bag and all. Naturally, the ushers halted the courier and insisted that he check his bag at the *gvarderobe*—in Russian theaters, everything must be checked. Not a hat or a coat may be worn into the hall, not a *sumka* (shopping bag) or a parcel can be carried to your seat. To do so is *nekulturny*, and whatever else it may be, the Russian theater is *kulturny*. I tried to divorce myself from my companions as the minister bullied his way past the ushers and propelled the unhappy courier and his bag down the aisle, front and center to front row seats. The ushers and the house manager fluttered like sparrows, but finally flung up their hands in disgust. When it was time to leave, I slunk away. What was worst was that the minister and his wife saw nothing wrong with all this. They acted as though they were dealing with the natives of some remote British colony in the days of Queen Victoria. God, I said to myself, let's hope *Krokodil* (the Russian satirical journal) doesn't get hold of this one. They'll murder us.

I checked into the Metropol about noon on March 8. I did not think the omens were good. Leningrad left a bad taste in my mouth and I was worried about the Anna Louise Strong affair. On shipboard en route to taking up my post I had heard the news that this American radical and revolutionary had been arrested in Moscow as a CIA agent and put into the Lubyanka, then expelled over the Polish border. Nor was she the only correspondent who had been expelled. Bob Magidoff, the NBC correspondent, had also been thrown out a few weeks earlier, also branded as an American spy. Bob had come back to the United States, but in the paranoia of the day, he was not hailed as a hero. When he went to Detroit for a speech, the Neanderthals of the auto industry called him a "Commie" because he didn't preach war against the Soviet Union. This kind of blind-siding, as I would learn, was not uncommon in the cold war.

I found the American news colony much diminished, only seven in all, including myself, Eddy Gilmore and Tom Whitney of AP, Henry Shapiro of UP, Joe Newman of the *Herald Tribune*, Ed Stevens of the *Christian Science Monitor*, and Andrew Steiger, who represented U.S. News and the English Exchange Telegraph agency. There was one English correspondent, Don Dallas of Reuters. It was a far cry from the hustle and bustle of wartime.

The Metropol was more grim than ever. Jack Margolis, the London cockney who had managed the hotel since before the war, was gone, his place taken by a Russian woman who called herself Mrs. Grey, an assiduous student of English. At any hour she could be seen at her desk beside the staircase, poring over grammars and exercise books. I don't know where she got her English name. She could not tell me what had happened to Jack, but I later found that he had vanished into the prison camp system.

I had been assigned Room 393. Alec Werth's grand piano was gone, but the room was furnished in the same heavy mahogany, with an enormous bed backed by a carved headboard, a pier glass that reached to the high ceiling, a wardrobe big enough to hide a pony, break-back chairs upholstered in faded brocade that dated to Rasputin's days, a desk of fumed oak filling the space between the window and the French doors which gave onto the courtyard, a settee, a worn and dusty Oriental rug (replaced two years later by a blue-and-taupe Chinese rug about three inches thick, part of a shipment that swamped the Metropol management one day) and a handsome round mahogany table, which had belonged to Alfred Cholerton of the *Daily Mail*, and been left in the care of a succession of correspondents since his departure before the war.

Room 393 boasted an elaborate chandelier fitted with a dim light bulb. When I sat beside Cholerton's table and peered at the shadowy corners of the room, I could see Rasputin's ghost mocking me with obscene gestures. The Metropol had been built just after 1900 (it seemed much older) and was decorated with mosaics by Golovin, which had so deteriorated I was hardly aware of their presence. Before World War I, nothing was more chic than the Metropol. The discreet rooms off the balcony of the dining room were the rendez-vous of the city's millionaires and their most expensive ladies. After the Revolution it became Dom Sovetov (House of Soviets) No. 2 and here were held meetings of the Soviet Executive Committee, including that which approved the execution of the Czar and his family.

It did not take long to confirm my forebodings about Moscow. The U.S. embassy was in a state of siege. The atmosphere had grown poisonous in the last days of Ambassador Walter Bedell Smith. There had been two security scandals: a young woman of Slavic origin named Annabelle Bucar, who had been in the information section, had defected to the Russians (she fell in love with a tenor at the Operetta Theater) and published a small book "exposing" the nefarious deeds of the Americans, their spying, their anti-Soviet plots; and a young man in the code room had recently gone over to the Soviet side. No embassy staff member or member's wife was to walk the streets of Moscow alone. In the hysteria, few poked their noses out of their flats. No ambassador had been named to replace Smith, and Foy Kohler, the able chargé d'affaires, was running a very tight ship. Correspondents, I quickly discovered, were not entirely trusted by the embassy. After all, they lived in the "outer" (Russian) world. Other embassies were not much better. The British were trying to shelter a dozen Russian women who had married Britishers during the war. The husbands had been compelled to return to England and the Russians wouldn't give the wives visas to get out. Originally there had been a hundred cases. One by one, the women vanished. Now many of the remaining dozen were living in the embassy to avoid being picked up by the NKVD (as the Russian police were called at that moment). A British subject was living in the embassy basement, a man accused by the Russians of having trans-mitted venereal disease to a Russian woman. He would go on living in that basement until Stalin's death, the British unwilling to have him go to prison on a false charge. An American sailor was being held in prison in Odessa, serving out a five-year sentence for a minor brawl.

The French had given refuge to several elderly gentlewomen who had come to Russia before the Revolution as governesses, and were now unable to get exit visas. The disappearance of maids, cooks, chauffeurs, clerks or, in the case of correspondents, couriers and translators was a daily event. These hapless people were provided to the foreigners by an agency of the NKVD. After they had worked a year or two, the police considered them "turned," arrested them and sent them to prison camp.

Well, I had known it was going to be bad. I had talked with Magidoff before leaving New York. I had tried to extrapolate from my wartime experience. But not until I set foot in the Metropol did I realize how bad it was—and even then I didn't know the worst things. These took years to put together.

It didn't take long to get the feel of the Anna Louise Strong case. I heard—in whispers—that her old friend Mikhail Borodin had been arrested too, as well as the full staff of the *Moscow Daily News*, on which they had long collaborated. The *Moscow Daily News* itself was closed down.

I quickly learned why I had not met Major Popkov in Leningrad. There had been a lot of changes in Leningrad since the death of Zhdanov. Popkov was now officially described as "no longer in Leningrad." Just where he was and what he was doing I could not find out.

These facts came to light within a week of my arrival in Moscow, when the dismissal from his government and political positions of N. A. Voznesensky, a Politburo member, head of State Planning, a member of the "Leningrad group," was revealed. Along with him went Popkov, A. A. Kuznetsov and others close to Zhdanov. Not even now is the full story of the Leningrad Affair known. In his "secret speech" of 1956, Nikita Khrushchev referred to the "affair" and said that Kuznetsov, Popkov, and Voznesensky had lost their lives. He provided no details. In later speeches in Leningrad in the summer of 1957, Khrushchev and Marshal Georgi K. Zhukov said Malenkov had been afraid to come to Leningrad because he was responsible for the Leningrad atrocity. Malenkov and Zhdanov had been bitter rivals to succeed Stalin. In 1946, by means not yet known, Zhdanov drove Malenkov out of the Politburo and out of Moscow, but within a year he made a comeback and the rivalry intensified. It did not last long. Zhdanov died, so it was announced, of a heart attack on August 31, 1948. He had been suffering from heart disease for some time. Stalin's daughter, Svetlana, knew Zhdanov and his family well. She liked Zhdanov and respected Zhdanov's closest associate, A. A. Kuznetsov. In the last year of Zhdanov's life, knowing Zhdanov's heart was bad, knowing the critical strain on him, Stalin deliberately taunted and reviled him, increasing the pressure. It was at this time, Svetlana once told me, that the Leningrad Affair was building up, fed by reports from Malenkov and Beria, then in alliance. How Stalin could have believed anything bad about these men, Svetlana could not understand.

She felt that her father's conduct hastened Zhdanov's death. Stalin may have gone further. When the "Doctors' Plot" was announced, on January 13, 1953, Zhdanov was listed as a victim of the conspiracy of Kremlin doctors. All his life, Stalin had demonstrated a tendency toward medical murder, first displayed in 1925 when he insisted that M. V. Frunze, the war commissar, submit to an operation that he did not wish and did not need. The operation cost Frunze his life. In the mid-thirties, Stalin blamed "criminal doctors" for the death of Maxim Gorky and others whose deaths he himself hastened if not arranged.

In fact, Stalin's conduct with Zhdanov had a parallel in his attitude toward Lenin during Lenin's illness in 1922 and 1923. Lenin suffered a series of strokes and was increasingly incapacitated. His doctors insisted that he carry only a light work load and that, above all, he be spared stress or strain or emotional upset, which might cause a sudden rise in blood pressure. Stalin was well aware of these medical strictures, yet he deliberately upset Lenin, opposing Lenin's projects in and out of the Politburo and behaving in a rude and vulgar manner with Lenin's wife, Krupskaya. This caused Lenin to flare up in angry outbursts—just the response the doctors wished to spare him. Whether Stalin acted as he did with the intention of imperiling the lives of Lenin and Zhdanov cannot, of course, be determined; the effect was the same.

Without question, Stalin was responsible for the deaths of Kuznetsov, briefly sent to the Far East and then executed in 1949, and Popkov, who may already have been shot when I was trying to telephone him from the Astoria in March 1949 (small wonder the hotel manager hid). Voznesensky was not executed until 1950. No one has ever explained the delay.

Svetlana married Yuri Zhdanov in 1949, only months after his father's death. Stalin had been encouraging this match for a couple of years. Andrei Zhdanov was the man who, it then seemed, Stalin had picked as his successor. The marriage of his daughter to the son of the heir apparent was a way of securing the succession. Stalin's daughter would stand at the side of the new emperor, Stalin's grandson could inherit the throne. Stalin's first son, Yakov, whom he hated, had died in World War II. His second son, Vasily, whom he despised, was drinking himself to death. But through the Zhdanov alliance the dynasty could be secured. Dream stuff? I do not think so. Hardly had Zhdanov died and the ascendency of Malenkov (and Beria) been ensured, than Stalin changed his tune and tried, in vain, to dissuade Svetlana from marrying Yuri. When Svetlana did not get along within the Zhdanov family (Yuri came under severe political pressure after his father's death), Stalin rudely told his daughter he had warned she would not be happy with the Zhdanovs.

Not since Ivan the Terrible had such fear and intrigue gripped the Kremlin. No wonder I found the air in Moscow exuded evil.

In *The 900 Days*, published twenty years after the Leningrad Affair, I managed to collect some details of that shadowy plot, but the fact that neither Khruschev nor anyone since has dared to make public the full record bears witness to its horror. It stands as a monument to the limitless terror political rivalry inspires in the Soviet Union.

Indeed, the political wounds of the affair and the siege were still so fresh and so deep in 1969 that my account of the heroism of Leningrad evoked a violent propaganda attack upon the book and myself. But the people of Leningrad who read smuggled copies of the book were unanimous in their praise and embarrassing in their gratitude that I had erected at least a small monument to their pain and courage.

I knew enough in my first weeks in Moscow to realize that something was badly wrong in Russia. Something was wrong wherever I turned—Leningrad, Anna Louise Strong, Borodin, the Jews. I had stumbled into one of Stalin's worst paroxysms. Anti-Semitism, camouflaged under the title of a drive against "cosmopolitanism," was raging like the plague. The Czar's Black Hundreds and *Okhotnoryadsy*, the masters of the pogrom, would have felt at home reading the names of the victims and looking at the "Semitic" noses in the cartoons. To understand why this was going on was another matter, and I am not sure that I do even now.

On March 13, I sat down at my typewriter in my new office in Room 317 of the Metropol, looking out over the asphalt of Theater Square and across to the Moskva Hotel and the tumbledown pile that housed Moscow's animated-film theater. I began to tap out my first copy for *The New York Times*. I wrote about the mood I had found in Russia. It was, I said, "a preocupied land, preoccupied lest new war break out while the scars of the old are not yet healed." This was my most important impression, that a palpable fear of war colored almost every phase of Russian life, and lay behind the terror. Moscow itelf had not been damaged by World War II, but most of European Russia had been devastated. Leningrad bore deep scars. Its outskirts were a vast ruin. The same was true of the other great cities—Kiev, Kharkov, Stalingrad, Minsk. When you realized the totality of destruction, I wrote, you understood more easily why fear of what would happen if new war came was so vivid in people's minds.

I submitted this dispatch to the censorship. They held it for many hours, then returned it with all conclusions deleted. It was up to me whether to send it forward in this dilapidated form. Finally I affixed a limp kind of lead to it and it ran in the *Times*, referring to "physical and psychological changes" and the preoccupation of the Soviet press with "organizing an international front to protect world peace." I then sketched a picture of what Russia looked like and quoted the Leningrad customs woman on war and peace. But my main conclusions the censor had simply obliterated.

That same day I filed a second dispatch, describing the atmosphere of suspicion and terror that had been created in Moscow by the deterioration of relations between the United States and the Soviet Union.

I called this "a painful and difficult" subject, but insisted that the readers of the *Times* must know the conditions under which the newly reestablished bureau of the newspaper was operating.

All foreigners, and particularly Americans, I said, were subject to harsh restrictions, including a prohibition on direct contact with officials of the Soviet government except as arranged by the Foreign Office. This regulation was backed by a draconian state secrets act. Travel was tightly restricted, some roads leading out of Moscow were closed at the city limits. Many regions of the country were closed entirely to travel. All dispatches were subjected to a rigid censorship.

"There is what might be termed a psychological hazard," I wrote, "arising from repeated suggestions by the Soviet press that the chief function of many foreign correspondents is spying and espionage. In the case of Americans this hazard had been extended to the physical sphere by the expulsion of two correspondents—Anna Louise Strong and Robert Magidoff—within the past year. Both Miss Strong and Magidoff were charged with intelligence operations."

Normal everyday contact between American correspondents and Soviet citizens had become nonexistent.

The result, I observed, was that most American reports were mere rewrites of the Soviet press.

My dispatch was held for two weeks and then killed in its entirety by the censors. I was to learn that no mention of censorship and no negative comments were ever passed.

In my first letter to Edwin L. James, the *Times* managing editor, on March 28, 1949 (sent through the diplomatic pouch), I told him that the censorship was "substantially worse than I have ever seen it." I pointed out that almost everything that did not appear in the Soviet press, as well as much that did, was deleted. Conclusions, analysis, speculation, was cut. So were biographical details, identification of individuals, and comparisons. "Threats to peace" were passed, but "threats of war" were not. "All dispatches emanating from Moscow— *mine* as well as those of the news agencies," I wrote, "are automatically biased. They definitely misrepresent the news and distort it to fit the frequently incomprehensible Soviet propaganda line. These dispatches are printed in the *Times* with no indication to the reader that they have been tampered with."

This, I said, "adds up to a fraud on the American public—a dangerous one under present conditions and a dismal one under the best of circumstances."

I recommended that the *Times* place labels on all my dispatches (and others from Moscow): "Passed by Soviet Censor." Warning that this might bring reprisals, I told Mr. James this was a risk which must be run.

I am sorry that for no reason which was ever made plain to me, Mr. James, Arthur Hays Sulzberger and *The New York Times* in general, individually, collectively and repeatedly refused to follow my recommendation. I know now, having examined the internal files of the *Times*, that Sulzberger on at least two occasions proposed that the *Times* place a "Passed by Censorship" slug on my dispatches as I had requested. His recommendations were not adopted, nor was any explanation ever offered to me, except a suggestion that there were many censorships and if Moscow was slugged, all would have to be. Since the only other permanent censorship (it still exists) of importance was the Israeli military censorship, this did not seem a valid reason, nor does it now. The matter became moot when the Soviet finally abolished censorship in 1961, but it was not a moot question in 1949 and it became less so as the cold war deepened, with serious consequences to readers of the *Times*, to myself and to the paper.

I sent through the diplomatic pouch or by other private means every scrap of my censored copy, along with a commentary on the significance of the cuts. I made weekly recommendations for handling these materials, often proposing that stories be written locally in New York. Sometimes this was done, including an excellent article on "cosmopolitanism" by Harry Schwartz, then a Syracuse University professor free-lancing for the *Times*. The story used my material and carried his name. Taken all in all, however, my efforts had little effect on the executives of the *Times* or the deskmen. They either did not read the record of censorship (or the excellent analyses made of my materials by Will Lissner, a longtime *Times* specialist in Communist affairs) or did not grasp its significance. Nor did the editors seem to understand the distortions they were presenting to the American public. To be certain, my dispatches had great value—if they were read in the appropriate context. But to present them raw, with no reminder that they had been processed by Soviet censors, was a disservice. To this day I cannot understand what was in the minds of men like James and Turner Catledge, assistant managing editor, and the foreign editor, Manny Freedman. Again and again I wrote to them. They sat like bumps on a log and did nothing. When my reports began to be publicly criticized, they flopped around like hens in a chicken coop, forgetting all my warnings, and in some cases even suspecting I was a purveyor of party propaganda. It was a sorry show.

Within a week of my arrival at the Metropol, I began to wonder if I might be in over my head. There was no way in which I could evaluate what was happening behind Kremin walls. But the currents were deep, swift and terrifying. I did not have to understand the Leningrad Affair, cosmopolitanism or Anna Louise Strong to sense that I had landed in a Moscow that was filled with fear. I had in my usual frenetic way dashed off letters or made telephone calls to everyone whom I had met in Moscow during the war. I did not reach anyone, and when I began to bump into people I knew on the street, they looked right through me. Quickly enough I understood that this was only sensible. Contact with an American "spy" was fatal. But understanding did not make my job any easier. The old bureau had been wiped out. There was no secretary, no translator, no chauffeur, no car. I didn't even have letterheads or stationery. Costs were higher than anyone had anticipated, and I was stuck with a living allowance of one hundred dollars a month and an expense account too low for survival. I wanted to bring Ellen to Moscow, but we would have to live, I saw, in the faded splendor of Alec Werth's old room. No doubt, as Eddy Gilmore said, they had popped me into Werth's room to save the expense of bugging another room. Well, I didn't give a damn about bugs. I wasn't going to be saying or doing anything that I wanted to conceal. But I was disturbed by the costs, the fortress mentality and the terror-tinted atmosphere. Could I bring Ellen to this kind of Moscow? What would it do to her or to us? And how would she occupy herself in Moscow? Certainly not playing house in Room 393.

"It is hard to convey the atmosphere of the foreign colony here," I wrote her on March 15, a week after arriving. "I should say, however, that it is the sort of thing that Oechsner and Beattie and Shirer are more familiar with than you and I. Or Howard Smith, for example. You might want to reread that last book of his." All these men had been correspondents in Hitler's Berlin.

I hadn't been in Moscow a month before she wrote to say that she was not coming in June, that she was not ready to make up her mind about coming at all. I was stricken; I cabled, I telephoned, I wrote letters like a madman. After a while, she fell in love with someone else. Then, I think, she fell out of love. Strand by strand, our relationship simply unraveled. It was ending, but it took me a long, long time to believe that.

The *Times* thought I was doing very well, censorship or no censorship. I got glowing letters from Manny Freedman and Arthur Hays Sulzberger and Cy Sulzberger, and I would have been even more pleased if I had been able then to read the analyses by Will Lissner. He started as a skeptic but soon became as powerful a champion as I could have, understanding the problems of my daily struggle with the censorship, the nuances of my writing, the implications of the censor's cuts even better than I did myself. It was a remarkable service and stood me in good stead when, as soon would occur, I badly needed confidence within the good gray portals of the Times Building at 229 West 43rd Street.

110

And, as I have found by consulting the journal I kept of my observations, my grasp of what was going on in Moscow was far better than I thought at the time. I correctly understood that Voznesensky and the other victims of the Leningrad Affair were adherents of Zhdanov; that Zhdanov and Malenkov had been rivals for power; that with the death of Zhdanov, Malenkov was purging the Zhdanov men. (I did not, of course, know that they were being shot.) I knew a great deal more about the cosmopolitanism drive than I could report—the extent of victims, the closing of Jewish theaters, newspapers and cultural institutions, and the dissolution of the Jewish Anti-Fascist Committee. (I did not then know of the murder of the famous Jewish director S. M. Mikhoels in 1948, nor that the members of the Anti-Fascist Committee would, in due course, be arrested and most of them shot.) I had made the correct connection between the arrest of Anna Louise Strong, the closing of the *Moscow Daily News* and the vanishing of Mikhail Borodin. And again, although no one was paying heed, I noted that: "The Kremlin is still very unsure of the situation in China. [China] gets very scanty reference in the press and even statements by the Chinese, laudatory of Russia and the Soviet leadership, are handled most gingerly. My opinion is that the Kremlin has its fingers crossed on its Chinese friends and will keep them that way for some time."

One thing I couldn't figure out. If it had been Stalin who was in such a hurry to see that I got a visa, why wasn't he letting me report what was happening in Moscow? This was a question to which I never would get an answer.

111

# Chapter 10

# Scoop

February 1950 was the month when the long and enigmatic discussions between Stalin and Mao Zedong, begun in early December 1949, finally bore their fruit, a skinflint pact of friendship and mutual aid.

I thought there was something fishy about the treaty. It provided that Moscow would give the Chinese $300 million in loans, not grants, over a five-year period—that is, $60 million a year. Peanuts! And while it professed to restore Chinese sovereignty over all Manchuria, it kept the bases and the railroads in Russian hands. Moreover, the treaty imposed on China joint-stock companies in which Moscow held the controlling 51 percent, not much different from the comprador deals of the nineteenth century. It came as no surprise to me when Nikita Khrushchev revealed in 1956 that Mao would have packed up and turned his face to Washington—if the U.S. had not been even more hostile.

Ambassador Kirk, a canny navy man who had served in China, recommended in November 1949 (along with other U.S. diplomats) that President Truman grant Communist China diplomatic recognition. Truman was not averse, but he felt he had to wait until he got his budget through the Republican Senate.

Kirk had told me his views on China privately. Truman had taken an informal poll of his best diplomats and there was general agreement on going forward with normalization as soon as possible. It seemed clear to me that Russia and China were far from chummy.

I was, thus, more than a little surprised when Cy Sulzberger broke an exclusive story from Paris a few days after the signing of the Sino-Soviet treaty, claiming that it contained secret protocols under which Mao had placed his armed forces at Stalin's command and turned over the Manchurian ports to the Soviet navy. The Kremlin, Cy asserted, now directed a one-billion-man Communist mass extending from the Elbe to the Yellow Sea, a terrifying threat to the U.S. and the world. The *Times*, naturally, gave this chilling intelligence smash play. I was in no position to challenge Cy's story. He had better sources than I, including, as I later understood, access to high U.S. intelligence officials. I had no sources whatever, only my wits. Nonetheless, I didn't think Cy's story was right and I wrote him, tactfully expressing doubts.

I had found it totally impossible to cover the Mao-Stalin talks in any conventional journalistic sense. I never saw Mao, despite many efforts. I even barged into the Chinese embassy, much to their embarrassment. The closest I came was one evening when the Chinese rented the dining room of the Metropol to give Stalin a reception. Even though Mao and Stalin were under my roof, as it were, even though I could hear the murmur of the multitude from the lobby door, I didn't catch a glimpse of the distinguished principals. When I went around to the side entrance of the Metropol, the security men chased me away. For weeks I couldn't even be sure Mao was still in Russia, let along what course the negotiations were taking.

Finally, desperate from lack of information, I took to filing stories about the talks anyway. I just made them up. I reported that Mao was out touring the countryside. That was killed. (I deduced that he was not touring the Soviet Union.) I said the talks concerned trade and security matters. That was passed, but with none of the details I had incorporated (hoping to get some guidance from the censor's cuts). I managed in this way to establish that the talks were continuing; that Mao and Stalin were participating in them; that they were reviewing a whole range of issues; that there was sensitivity about the length of the meeting (all references to "protracted" talks were deleted). In many subtle ways I detected uneasiness. Ordinarily, negotiations in Moscow were totally ceremonial; the chief of state arrived, had his picture taken, attended a Kremlin banquet, paid a few calls, signed the treaty and went back home.

I was impressed by the nuances that could be adduced by careful phrasing and rephrasing of my submissions to the censors. (My fail-safe was that if the censor's treatment was unclear, I did not have to transmit the story.) I decided to try this kind of three-corner billiards on the question of U.S.-Soviet relations. Here I had more materials with which to work. I had a sense that the Soviet Union was ready for a new try at diplomacy with the United States. Moscow had hit a dead end with the Berlin blockade; relations with China were sticky; President Truman's decision to proceed with the H-bomb had plunged the nuclear questions into a new era. Ambassador Kirk was going back home for a month and we talked the situation over. He had been kept on a short leash since his arrival. With nothing to talk to the Russians about, he and Mrs. Kirk had spent their time trying to improve the glacial morale at the embassy. Now he, too, thought the Russians might be ready to talk.

I decided to test this thesis, banking my shots against the censor. I wrote a general story, a sober piece quoting "some diplomatic quarters" (that is, Admiral Kirk and myself), who felt that the Soviet Union was now ready to join with the United States in an effort to solve outstanding problems, including the issue of atomic controls.

I pointed out that there had been "no Soviet statements" to this effect; outlined the differences in positions of the two countries; and cited Soviet declarations that indicated that the differences were not irreconcilable.

I put the dispatch into censorship and waited. It was held up about thirty hours and then passed without a single word being cut. This was significant. If I was flying a kite, it was a kite the Russians wanted flown. For whatever reason, they elected to tell the world they were not averse to talking with the United States.

The *Times* gave the story good play. I then added a twist to my tactics. I sent a letter to Generalissimo Stalin, posing a series of questions on the nuclear arms race, the H-bomb, the possibilities of a joint effort by the U.S. and the Soviet Union to tackle those problems and achieve a general political statement. I waited a few days to allow time for this to reach Stalin's attention (and be answered directly if, as sometimes happened, he wished), I got no reply from the Kremlin. I then read carefully through the current periodicals and spotted in *Soviet State and Law* an article discussing a declaration by Stalin, of a couple of years earlier, that the peaceful settlement of disputes between the United States and the Soviet Union was not only possible but absolutely essential.

I turned up a series of declarations in various contexts which provided possible answers to the questions I had put to Stalin. Incorporating these in four separate dispatches, I filed them one a day, and sent two further questionnaires to the Generalissimo.

My stories went into the censorship on February 13. Just before midnight of the eighteenth, I got a call from the censor's office—most unusual—to tell me they had cleared my materials and they were ready for transmission. I bundled into my sheepskin and hurried through the snow-choked streets to the Central Telegraph Office on

Gorky Street, a fast ten-minute walk. To my astonishment, I found my dispatches bore only a few nominal cuts.

This made it clear that the Soviet Union was, in fact, inviting an American response, as I hastened to advise New York (and the State Department) through private channels.

As in so many examples—past and yet to come—no tangible result emerged from this exercise. A month or so passed and the clouds closed in once more; the censors resumed their arbitrary slashing of my copy and I prepared to go back for a short visit to the United States. But I had learned something that I would employ in the future—the use of the censorship against itself as a device for testing my evaluation of Soviet policy. For a long time to come, there would be diplomats, American and others, who were certain I had a secret, high-level source in the Foreign Office if not the Kremlin. It is possible, I must admit, that there may have been some in the KGB who also arrived at this totally mistaken view. In fact, years later, a defected KGB agent named Yuri Nosenko, told me that the KGB had reached this exact conclusion and had even concocted a plot to do away with me. I never could decide whether this was a figment of Nosenko's lively imagination or the real thing.

I flew to New York in late May, paused briefly to consult the editors of the *Times*, then went to Minneapolis and picked up Michael, now a robust eleven-year-old. We proceeded to Pyramid Lake Ranch in Nevada, where I would spent the obligatory six weeks and then get a divorce. The long matrimonial battle had ended. The ranch was a joy for Mike and me. We rode every morning over the desert and up mountain trails. Neither of us had ridden before, but Mike took to it like a cowboy and galloped circles around me. We swam in the somewhat saline lake in the afternoon and occasionally drove sixty miles into Reno, where I got acquainted with slot machines and roulette. No other guest at the ranch was male, a strange society of women waiting for their decrees, many deeply unhappy, all disoriented. Some years later, Marilyn Monroe's movie *The Misfits*, which Arthur Miller wrote for her, was filmed at this ranch.

I felt disconnected from the world. Russia was in another solar system. New York had vanished. Ellen was going her own way. Somehow none of this mattered. Mike and I rode out on the desert as the sun was coming up and we caught the magical perfume of the flowers and grass awakening in its rays. I had never seen people like

115

the ranchers. One morning a woman drove calmly into the sheriff's office, the body of her husband trussed to the roof of her station wagon like a deer. "Lock me up," she told the sheriff. "I shot the son of a bitch last night. He got drunk once too often." They locked her up for an hour and then she went back to running the ranch. It was a man's world, where a husband could get a divorce by asking for it. A neighboring rancher had had eight legal wives and no one knew how many by common law. Every day a great station wagon, the springs down to the axles, paused at the ranch to fill up with gas. It was a well-known entertainer, on his way up the desert track, where forty miles into the foothills he had a hideaway. Each day he loaded his station wagon with canned goods, preserved hams, corned beef, flour and sugar to help him survive the atom war he thought might erupt at any time.

I was still waiting out my divorce when, totally improbably as it seemed to me, war broke out in Korea. I knew we were in for a long, hard haul and that the freeze in Moscow would get worse and worse.

The place for me was Russia, but some things could not be speeded up. I would not be back in the United States, I felt certain, for a long time. It had taken me six months to persuade the *Times* to let me come home, so fearful were they that if I left I could not get back in. Now I had my return visa in hand and I hurried to get my affairs in order. Mary was selling the house in Mamaroneck; I arranged to have my things put in storage; I made elaborate plans to bring Michael with me to Moscow. To my despair, at the last moment, passports ready, cabin reserved on the *Queen Mary*, Mary refused to let him go. I finally sailed for England in mid-August.

The Korean War had touched off a spiral of war hysteria and anti-Russian emotion. I had been to Washington and found people holding their breaths in fear Russia would intervene. Many felt we were at the edge of nuclear confrontation. The greatest fear was of a Soviet attack on Europe. I had gained confidence in my ability to extrapolate from personal observation. War against the U.S. was no small matter. If the Russians were preparing to take advantage of our preoccupation in the East to strike a sudden blow in the West, there was no way they could hide their preparations along the main railroads.

I made my plans accordingly. I stopped briefly in London, consulted my colleagues in Paris and booked myself first class on the *Orient Express*. I was, I confess, excited—not just because I knew I

116

had the makings of a great scoop, but because I had grown up on E. Phillips Oppenheim: *Le Train Bleu* for romance, the *Orient* for international hugger-mugger. I got on it at midevening, and looked in every direction for the whirl of a black lace skirt, a whiff of exotic perfume, a gentleman in spats and white gloves, the bulge of a pistol in his pocket. The train was almost empty. The iron curtain had descended on classic espionage. In my trench coat, I looked more a spy than did anyone else. There were four or five paunchy Germans who dropped off at points in Bavaria and then I was alone with a young mother and her six-month-old baby all the way to Prague. I had not been in Germany since the war. When the border police knocked at my compartment and asked rudely, I thought, for my passport, I found to my surprise that I deeply resented complying with this simple request by a German. Not until 1966 would I compel myself to visit Japan; the wounds of the war had left deep scars.

From the moment of daylight, my eyes were glued to the window as we rolled across into Czechoslovakia. I saw no troop trains (I hardly expected that), no signs of new construction, no hustle or bustle—just the lazy provincial pace, hardly anything to jot down in my notebook. Well, I conceded, I had passed through most of Czechoslovakia at night. Armies could have been waiting and I would not have seen them. There were no military on the station platforms, none on the train, no Russians, no truck convoys crawling over the hills.

I stopped over in Warsaw a couple of days and found no war fever there. The *Times* man, Ed Morrow, took me around town. I don't know how long Ed had spent in Warsaw, but it had been too long. He had fallen into the disease, so easy to acquire behind the curtain, of playing games with the security detail that had been staked out to keep an eye on him. He had got so deep into ducking and dodging them that he hardly had thought for anything else. Warsaw's air bore the scent of fear. It looked to me as though the Poles were on shorter rations than Moscow, but Ed said there had been no recent changes. A brief flurry of hoarding occurred when the Korean War broke out, but things had quieted down. No sign of troop movements, no new security precautions, no rumors of anything doing in the East, no signs of Russian alert. I thought the testimony of this worried man bore some weight. If anyone was on the lookout for Communist moves, it was Ed. We talked to people in the embassy; no sign of war preparations, and the embassy had reported this to Washington.

I boarded the *Kuriersky Express* in Warsaw with anticipation. The route of the *Kuriersky* across Poland, to the border city of Brest and on to Moscow, was the main invasion route from west to east (as followed by Hitler and Napoleon) or from east to west as followed by the Red Army in its drive to Berlin. Baranovichi, Minsk, Orsha, Smolensk, Vyazma, Mozhaisk—a roll call of the critical battles of 1941. Here, if anywhere, I would find evidence if the Red Army was mobilizing to strike Europe.

We spent a day at Brest, where the train halted, the carriages were changed to the wide Russian gauge, we went through customs. Again the customs man couldn't read English, so my books and luggage were sealed and sent on to Moscow. I was left only *Vie de Bohème* to read. I persuaded the customs officer that it was merely the story of an opera and because it was in French (apparently he did not think French so subversive as English) he let me keep it. I suffered from both lack of reading material and lack of rubles. I had forgotten that I could change no money. I spent the days on a diet of excellent pâté de foie gras which Cy Sulzberger had given me in Paris, some Nescafé and three worm-eaten apples.

During the long halt at Brest, I strolled about the town. It was a major junction. Here if anywhere I should find supplies moving up— guns, munitions, rations, flatcars with weapons concealed under tarpaulins. I had seen the Russian railroads in war. I knew what they looked like, I knew the jams on the sidings, the swarms of troops that collected at every transit point. I found none of that. True, there was a large bustling freightyard. True, there were lots of military, but as far as I could see, as many were coming back from Germany and Poland as going in. The freight traffic was civilian traffic—cars of grain, flatcars of timber, machinery, gondolas of coal. I didn't see a gun except for the rifles and sidearms of the border guards; there were plenty of them. There was the normal range of foodstuffs in the stores and trainside stalls. Something unusual might be going on in Russia—but not here.

It took two and a half days to get to Moscow from Warsaw, and I was all eyes. By the time I arrived in Moscow, however, I had pretty much come to a conclusion. In the entire journey, I had seen not a single piece of artillery, not a tank, not an antiaircraft gun, not an antitank gun, not a troop train, not a food queue. To be sure, people were buying bread from the train's dining car at station stops, but I had never seen a train in Russia where that didn't happen. In those days, there wasn't a place in Russia where white bread was not in short supply except Moscow—and even Moscow sometimes ran out.

I believed I had a first-class, even sensational, political and military story. So far as at least one "reasonably quick observer" (as I was to call myself in my dispatches) was concerned, Russia was not getting ready to jump Europe. She might be preparing something big in the Far East, yet I was dubious of that. From what I knew of the Soviet economy, a prospective major military move in the Far East would have shown up in shortages in the civilian sector as far west as Brest— and probably Warsaw. I determined to explore Moscow thoroughly for further evidence to confirm or upset my hypothesis.

By September 13, I had scoured the city. I could find no sign in the department stores, the food markets, the supply depots, the hardware stores or the drugstores of unusual shortages or hoarding. I heard no rumors, or underground gossip, suggesting the Russians feared they were about to launch an attack. (Soviets were fearful of American attacks.) No unusual call-ups had been uncovered by the U.S. military. The consensus of the diplomatic colony was that the Russians were keeping their heads down, more concerned with being dragged into war against their will than with broadening the conflict by their own design. The city was a scene of unusual construction and reconstruction. New skyscrapers were going up, new efforts were being made to put the city's dilapidated housing into repair. I had seen much the same from the train. I had seen, too, that many concrete bridges demolished during the war had not yet been replaced or repaired.

This did not add up to a picture of Moscow buckling on its sword and girding for battle, and so far as I could ascertain, no one in the American embassy, diplomatic or military, believed they were.

I sat down on September 13 and over the next three days wrote seven or eight detailed, factual articles reporting precisely what I had seen coming into Russia and what was evident within the country itself. As I said: "Naturally one correspondent's railroad car window view is not conclusive but it is recorded here for what value it may have and in a reasoned effort to present a strictly objective account. In view of the present state of world nerves it seems that this is a fact worth recording and possibly even underlining."

I contrasted my present observations with those I had made in Russia-at-war in 1944. I suggested that the program of reconstruction in Moscow was inconsistent with a scenario that would involve the

119

Soviet Union in war with the U.S.A. I laced my copy with warnings that I was aware that the impressions I was offering might conflict sharply with many that the readers held of a trigger-happy Russia that at any moment might lunge into Germany or strike at the American forces in Korea.

Each dispatch was held a day or two in censorship—indicating that it received high-level attention—and then released with fairly trivial cuts, among them, oddly, the description of a dog show at Sokolniki Park (I had seen Olga there). The censor deleted my account of Soviet troop transit traffic in Brest, and cut an important passage dealing with Muscovites' concern that the Korean War might spread and involve Russia in general hostilities.

I thought then and think now, having reread my copy closely, that it was factual reporting of a competent level and that it presented invaluable information for U.S. policymakers and the public. It was conservatively written, loaded with caveats, and it offered a true, realistic and clear picture of a major component in the world situation.

But this was not how it was perceived in New York. First there was an ominous quiet, then a fire storm of inquiries, questions, suggestions for revision, more and more requests, delays, and as I was to become aware, the whole thing began to spill over into the public eye, with the *Daily Worker* and Communist spokesmen charging that the *Times* was suppressing an important series of articles by its Moscow correspondent.

The stories arrived in New York at a moment when Arthur Sulzberger was in Europe and General Adler, the business manager, a staunch patriot, an army man who had never been pleased with my appointment, was in charge. Mr. James was also away. Turner Catledge was sitting in as his deputy. Lester Markel, who had long been a supporter of mine and would be again, now joined General Adler in what I can only describe as a vicious attack on the series and upon me as a Communist dupe. I suspect Lester's motivations lay in his unrealistic ambition to succeed Mr. James and, also, in some problems he was beginning to have over allegations of Communists on the Sunday staff. But that does not show in the record.

Catledge was instructed by Adler to obtain from me a remarkable amount of information, most of which had little or nothing to do with my articles—inserts, elaborations, statistics, new facts galore.

Somewhat to my amazement, I got most of this material and cleared almost all of it through the censorship, except, of course, for prices. The censor never cleared prices.

Adler and Markel apparently thought the articles were Communist propaganda. I can only suppose they did not actually read them. And there was another spoon in the stew, as my later research revealed— that of Irving Brown, who was then the AFL-CIO representative in Europe, very active in anti-Communist doings and later to be described by *The New York Times* as having CIA connections. I've no notion how he got involved, but he did and he stimulated Markel very handily.

Matters had reached a point at which Adler and Markel were demanding that I be recalled from Moscow. When Arthur Sulzberger returned to New York, he was handed a revised and much condensed version of the series, put together by Freedman, which, alas, eliminated a great deal of my factual observations of the state of Soviet military preparedness.

Sulzberger promptly ordered publication of the condensed version, with an editor's note of the type I had been campaigning for from the day I reached Moscow. It pointed out that the dispatches had passed through Soviet censorship and warned the reader that some materials requested by the editors could not be transmitted through censorship.

By this time, considerable hubbub—*shum*, as the Russians would say—had been generated. The stories were promptly seized upon by party spokesmen as a demonstration of a Soviet "desire for peace," which was not the point at all. I had no notion whether the Soviet leaders wanted war or peace. I thought, actually, they had no objection to war if war served their interests. In this case, apparently, they had decided it did not. It was therefore important for U.S. policymakers to know that they could go forward in the Far East without much worry of a Soviet counterblow in the West. If anyone got this point from the mangled articles, I never encountered him.

The row did not die down easily. Years later, I discovered through an FOIA action that poor old Major General R. W. Grow, military attaché in Moscow at the time, had sent the Defense Department a complaint about my report. He thought my stating that there did not appear to be a war scare in Moscow or signs of panic buying was "extremely dangerous" and inclined "to lull the American people to a false sense of security." His superior in the Pentagon, General

Bolling, agreed, and wrote back that he thought the article was a "handout from the Soviet Ministry of Enlightenment."

La, me, here we are again! I didn't know about all this. I didn't know about the row in the top levels of the *Times*, which went on until Arthur Hays Sulzberger put it bluntly to Markel: did he really want Salisbury fired? Markel backed down a bit untidily. I didn't know that General Grow, who within the year would suffer the humiliating disaster of losing his diary in Germany and having it published by the Communists, one juicy, silly passage after another, regarded me as a dangerous "pink." I went on thinking of him as one more gruff, decent military man, produced like sausage from a machine, an American Colonel Blimp, not very well equipped to handle the simple task of observing facts and putting them together in a coherent picture.

I didn't know all this, but I knew enough to recognize that what I thought had been a reporting coup had been turned into a disaster by some rather ignorant cooks. For a long time to come, I could observe in the responses of my editors a touchiness, a reserve, a—well, let's face it—a lack of confidence which held them back from giving my dispatches the play and attention they deserved.

Gradually I began to understand what had happened. Once again I had violated the rules. I had reported an important but unpalatable truth. What I had said about the Soviet Union and its war preparations did not fit the cliché of the day. The fact that what I said gave us a free hand (but for Mao and the People's Liberation Army) in the Far East, that we could go forward with little fear of a European threat, made no difference. The Russia I depicted did not fit the popular image, and without consideration of what I was really saying, a large gob of smear was thrown in my direction. The bearer of unpleasant news was getting his deserts. Once I figured this out, I felt somewhat better. But I remained sore and frustrated. I still am.

# Chapter 11

# George Frost Kennan

A tall, lean, balding man came up to me one afternoon as I was painting the porch at Saltykovka, where Tom Whitney, his Russian wife Juli and I had a dacha. *"Y vas nyet svobodnaya komnata ili mezonik?"* he asked. *"Konechno."* I replied, *"delya vas—vse."* He was the new ambassador, George Kennan, and he was asking if we had a room to rent or maybe an attic, and I was saying, "Of course—for you." It was the same question he had asked when he first came to Russia in 1933 and rambled about the country near Moscow, inquiring at a house for a night's lodging. In those days he had been a third secretary, advance man for the new American embassy, relations having been reestablished after talks between FDR and Maksim Litvinov.

Now Kennan had come to Moscow as ambassador, but a gulf lay between those experiences of a young man, trained for six years in Russian studies, and of this veteran of the diplomatic service, a man of world reputation, author of the extraordinary "Long Telegram" of February 22, 1946, and the "X" article in *Foreign Affairs* in 1947, which fixed the parameters of postwar U.S.-Soviet postures.

I had long awaited this moment. If I had got my original impetus toward Russia from Sir Bernard Pares, I would now sit quite literally at the feet of Kennan, who was henceforward to be my guide, my inspiration, my mentor on Russia.

We talked awhile under the pillar-straight pines, George, Juli and Tom rattling away in Russian, I scrambling to keep up with the conversation. The dachniki strolled past at lazy intervals. It was a sunny day, the air heavy with the scent of spring flowers, an afternoon of peace and quiet. George's family, Annelise and the children, had not yet followed him to Moscow. He was at once nostalgic, a little lonely, romantic and at ease, at least for a moment, deep in that Russia to which he had long ago lost his heart.

As shadows lengthened, we went indoors and lighted our fireplace. The Russian mason had never built one before; in fact, he had never heard of a fireplace. It smoked badly, but it was our joy. The first night we lighted it, Juli burst into tears. "What on earth is wrong, Juli?" Tom asked. She answered, "Here we are, sitting by the fireplace we all dreamed of. We're so happy. I'm crying because we'll never be so happy again."

On this evening, Juli was happy. We sat on the floor around the fireplace and George played his guitar, as he had when he had roamed Podmoskovskoye, the Moscow region, in the early days. He played Russian songs, "Stenka Razin" and "Polyuska Pole" and Juli sang. Then he played his favorite, "A-tisket, a-tasket, a green and yellow basket," and we all sang, smoke in our eyes, hearts overflowing.

We gave George a key to the dacha so he could retreat there whether or not any of us were around, and I arranged my *mezonik* so there was a place for him to stay overnight (which I don't believe he did). He loved to stroll through Saltykovka, listening to the Saltykovka sounds—the talk of the dachniki, an accordion playing in the distance, the sharp smack of ax on wood, the thin whistle of the railroad in the distance. Once on Sunday he went to the market, but this was too much. Everywhere George went, he was accompanied by at least four plainclothesmen. When he drove to Saltykovka, two cars of *shpiks* came with him. A stroll through the village became a parade. It was better to sit under the pines and read Chekhov. For years he entertained the ambition of writing about Chekhov.

George Kennan's return to Russia in 1952 was at once a sentimental journey and a diplomatic mission to which he brought a mystical sense of purpose. Kennan had from an early time (and increasingly with the years) possessed a sense of identification with his relative the first George Kennan. This Kennan—not George's father or uncle, as commonly supposed, but a cousin of his grandfather—was a journalist, a publicist, an agitator, a man of passion who almost by chance committed his life to the cause of a new Russia. He had traveled widely, ranging the country from the ends of Siberia to the salons of St. Petersburg. He had written the single most influential American work about Russia, *Siberia and the Exile System*, published originally in *Century* magazine in 1888–89 and then as a book. The most incisive inquiry into the Russian prison system of the period, it was a work whose worldwide impact can only be compared to that of Aleksandr Solzhenitsyn's *The Gulag Archipelago*. It produced enormous sentiment in the United States and Europe against the

Czar, and within Russia itself gave impetus to the movement for reform and revolution.

Ambassador George Frost Kennan saw himself as his namesake's successor, perceiving parallels between his life and his predecessor's at every turn. But in fact the differences were profound. The second George Kennan came to Russia by way of Germany. He spent six months there at the age of eight, went to school and learned the language. His father spoke beautiful German and George was drenched in pre-1914 German culture. He came from Milwaukee, that city then almost more German than Germany. The summer before he entered the foreign service, he went again to Germany, wandering over the countryside, reading Goethe and Spengler in the original, speaking not a word of English. Then he returned to Washington and tackled the trade of diplomacy. When he embarked on his study of Russia, he went back to Germany of the Third Reich and then to Tallin and Riga, cities strongly under the influence of the Teutonic knights who pushed eastward along the Baltic coast and melded into the Russia of Peter.

It seemed to me in the days when I was getting to know George Kennan that he was more powerfully shaped than he realized by German tradition, more a Lothar absorbing the wonders of Russian life than the Yankee at the court of Alexander III that the first George Kennan was. The earlier George had been a pragmatic, shirtsleeves kind of man (he started life as a Morse telegrapher), but there was in both Kennans a cranky, against-the-grain quality. Kennan seldom accepted anyone's conclusions without testing them. All his life he would be a loner, more comfortable speaking from his own pulpit than joining a chorus. I, having grown up in Minnesota, could see the particularity of this Wisconsin man, born four years earlier, who reflected the independent populist tradition from which I came.

Kennan was a severe judge of Soviet conduct, sometimes an unfair judge, but he was an equally severe judge of American conduct. He insisted that foreign policy could not be carried out on a basis of moral assessments; it must be founded on pragmatic self-interest instead of pontifications about good or evil. But he himself was a stern moralist and nothing disturbed him more in the 1960s than what he saw as the dissolution of moral quality in American youth. He was outraged by the decline in diplomatic ethics and conduct. In a sense, he became a living icon of tradition, wearing fine English-tailored suits with full vests, and, as my father had, a magnificent old gold watch chain. He abhorred the platitudinous rhetoric of John Foster Dulles and could not abide the sloppy solecisms of a Carter or a Reagan. He often stood alone for what he believed, and in this I am drawn to compare him with Charles Lindbergh. They differed profoundly, Lindbergh an isolationist and an America Firster, Kennan an internationalist, but there was in each a standard of values that put his country before any other consideration. If Lindbergh might more properly be described as an international isolationist, perhaps it would not stretch the truth to call Kennan an isolationist internationalist. In each there was a whiff of that climate which produced the La Follettes and the Farmer-Laborites.

Kennan was masterly in the arts of persuasion and skilled in bureaucracy. He might and often did inveigh against the system. He was an open, ardent elitist and once said that in the impossible event of his becoming secretary of state, he would establish a personal foreign service of two hundred specialists, and handle foreign policy through them. He would let the traditional establishment with its thousands of civil servants stay in place, churning out paper. But he would operate through his elite corps. What he was talking about was remarkably like the apparatus that was to grow up around the National Security Council of Henry Kissinger. Though the two men possessed totally different personalities, Kissinger's individualistic style of work was not too different from Kennan's. Neither man possessed much patience with mediocrity; each possessed total self-confidence in judgmental matters. But Kennan was more tolerant of subordinates, and lacked Kissinger's hot paranoia. Both were better working for a President or secretary of state with a coherent grasp of the world than in a position of naked responsibility. The comparison is in a sense unfair to both men. Kissinger's role models were Metternich and Machiavelli; Kennan's philosophy derived in some measure from Heine and Goethe. He was more deeply influenced by Spengler's gloomy doctrine than he realized, and while he loved Chekhov, I always felt there was much more Dostoyevsky in his soul. The Yankee strain which Kennan highly valued, his love of Jefferson and Adams, had been diluted by his long immersion in German culture.

Kennan was antibureaucratic, but he knew how to use the bureaucracy to push his views. In politics he was not strong (nor was Kissinger, for that matter). Knowing what *should* be done, Kennan was not always realistic in what *could* be done. The practical politics that led Acheson and Truman to put the Marshall Plan through Congress by raising the Communist scare was anathema to George. In the Kennedy years, as ambassador to Belgrade, he knew what U.S. policy should be in support of Tito, but the catch-as-catch-can politics of Jack Kennedy drove him up the wall. When he left the State Department in 1953, he toyed with running for Congress from Pennsylvania, as unlikely a babe in the woods in eat-'em alive politics as could be imagined. His very act of listening to such a proposal was a measure of his distance from political reality. There was nothing Congress or the country needed more than Kennan in office; in precinct terms, nothing was less realistic.

Not much of this was evident to me as we sat before the fireplace, George contemplatively strumming his guitar, his mind lost in distant recall. I quickly perceived that he had devoted profound thought to the situation in Russia before he somewhat reluctantly undertook his assignment.

He had believed, as did I, that the chances the Kremlin would give *agrément* were slim. Kennan was identified in the public mind and in that of the Kremlin as the author of the philosophy of the cold war, laid down in his Long Telegram and the "X" article. This declaration (the article was simply a popular restatement of the Long Telegram) analyzed the sources of Soviet conduct, detailed postwar Soviet expansionism and proposed an American policy of "containment" which would erect a dike around the Soviet frontiers, to the end that every Soviet outward push would meet the hard rock of American resistance. It was on the basis of Kennan's theory that Dulles would create a network of anti-Soviet alliances which established a deadline that Soviet aggression would not be permitted to cross.

The "X" article in later years was to involve Kennan in deep controversy. He felt that it had been mistakenly interpreted and militarized, first by Truman and later by Dulles. What he proposed was that by a resolute stand we would discourage the Kremlin and bring it into diplomatic negotiations, not armed conflict. But of course, that was not the way the "X" philosophy was perceived by Washington and Moscow. It was taken as a blueprint for an armed standoff and the diplomatic solution explicitly stipulated by Kennan was overlooked by both sides. (And by revisionist historians who insisted that Kennan had merely offered a euphemism for militarization of foreign policy.)

I was so convinced that Kennan would not be accepted by Moscow that I wrote a long dispatch to this effect on December 26, 1951, drawing liberally on a *Pravda* article which characterized him as directing subversive activities against the Soviet Union. My dispatch was held in the censorship and finally released with almost every aspersion against Kennan removed. Within twelve hours, the Foreign Office informed the State Department that Kennan's appointment had been approved. Once again the censorship had provided a striking clue to Soviet policy, and by killing my adverse speculation it spared me an embarrassing error.

I don't know what conclusions Kennan drew from the Russian acceptance of him as ambassador, but he could hardly interpret it as a negative sign. He had not been in a hurry to assume his post. He wanted time for thought. The number of original thinkers in the world at any moment is small. Kennan is the only one with whom I have ever been close. An original thinker is, to me, someone who turns a problem about in his mind and emerges, not with ideas previously advanced, not with adaptations of or variations on old ideas, but with *totally new thoughts*. Kennan had formed the habit of periodically withdrawing to think and to write. This required a cover device. His was simple. He "came down with the flu," went to bed, put a pad of yellow foolscap on his knees, gazed out of the window, thought, scribbled a bit, and began to dictate to his secretary. Thus he had composed his Long Telegram; thus he had written his dispatches about the Moscow purge trials of the 1930s; thus he had drafted his ideas for George Marshall when he, as secretary of state, put in Kennan as chief of policy and planning. Kennan did not call a committee meeting and emerge with a lot of "consensus" ideas; he locked himself in his bedroom and thought. It was a unique process in our bureaucratic days.

Before coming to Moscow in May, Kennan had formulated his general theses. He had not told anyone in Washington about this; at least, I do not think he had. (There is no hint of it in his memoirs.) I think that he first spoke of his ideas as he sat in a canvas chair under the pines at Saltykovka. He believed that his "containment" theory had succeeded. The outward expansion of Soviet power had been halted all around the periphery, and most notably at Berlin when the U.S. broke the blockade, and in Germany, where the Western powers were moving to consolidate the NATO alliance with Bonn. (Kennan was not very happy about bringing Germany into NATO.) It had been halted in Korea, where the U.S. had finally stabilized the situation on the 38th parallel, where the North-South division would remain for the next thirty years.

Stalin, George said, was no fool. Neither were the men of the Politburo. They might be difficult, dangerous, hostile, but they were, at root, pragmatic, shrewd men. If a policy did not bring results, if it brought defeat after defeat, sooner or later that policy would be changed; sooner or later someone at the Kremlin table would raise the question. Since Kennan assumed that the Kremlin put pragmatism ahead of everything—ahead of precedent, ideology, consistency—he believed that Moscow could change instantly from total antagonism to a willingness to meet and resolve mutual problems, with no embarrassment, no backward glances, no problem in answering questions, just a shift of the gears.

But American policy was now dug in so hard, American opinion had so crystallized, that diplomacy was almost paralyzed. Kennan did not believe that when the Soviets switched signals this would, necessarily, be understood by Washington. It was vital, he felt, that someone like himself be on hand to catch the first hint and be ready to capitalize on the change. In fact, he was prepared, like a good obstetrician coping with a difficult birth, to use the forceps a bit.

He had cleared with the Department one small gambit on which he set great store, a lowering of the decibel level of propaganda. He persuaded the Voice of America to refrain from attacking Stalin; he went to the Luce people in New York and asked them to bear with him for a bit by easing up on stories about Russia. If both sides stopped lambasting each other, a climate for negotiations might be created. He understood this was difficult. He was by no means certain the individualistic American press and radio, not to mention the still-undercover CIA enterprises Radio Liberty and Radio Free Europe, could be kept in line (they couldn't). He didn't get far. He talked to the Foreign Office but got no encouragement, and in fact he became outraged at the level and character of what he came to call the "hate America" campaign. I confess I was so inured (as I am sure the Soviet public was) that I hadn't even noticed it. One day George arrived at the dacha worked up at some posters he had seen. They hadn't even registered with me. They showed Soviet planes shooting down U.S. planes trying to cross the Soviet borders. George issued a public denunciation and refused to attend the Soviet Aviation Day show. In his rage he even accepted the naive statement of our air attaché that the Russians had put a dummy on the reviewing stand in place of Stalin. Some dummy! I was there, and Stalin had looked very snappy in his white summer uniform, talking and joking with his Politburo and his generals.

I did not know, nor was there a hint of it in George's talk, that he had been put on the shortest of reins by President Truman and Dean Acheson. They had, he revealed in his memoirs, given him no policy instructions. He had no functions whatever to carry out in Moscow, except that he must not negotiate or talk about Germany, Korea and nuclear weapons—the three key issues of the day. No wonder he felt frustrated. No wonder we missed an opportunity to resolve the German issue in our favor.

Truman and Acheson were hell-bent to obtain what they called the "contract"—the agreement that was to tie Germany into NATO; to remove Germany, once and for all, from neutrality; to line it up on the U.S. side. It was because of this that Kennan's hands were tied and lips sealed. He disagreed with the Truman-Acheson policy, but had to accept it.

That is why, I should imagine, Kennan failed to respond when I took up with him an intriguing bit of gossip. I had heard it, I believe, from Ralph Parker. It concerned Wilhelm Pieck and Otto Grotewohl, the East German leaders. They had been called to Moscow secretly during the winter and told that Moscow was preparing to sacrifice them and the East German regime in the struggle with the West over Germany. At all costs, Moscow wanted to block the Western effort to tie Bonn into its defense system and was prepared, if necessary, to consent to the reunification of Germany and the end of the Communist regime in the East. Of course, it was more complex than that, but this was the essence. It was news so sensational—if true—that I was totally enjoined against using it in any form, nor would the censors have passed it. I did, however, put it to Kennan as a hypothetical question. I got no response from him and, thinking that it was most likely not true, put it in the back of my mind. But I did not forget it as I observed the frantic offers Moscow began to make in an effort to halt the rapid progress of the "contract."

Suddenly the rumor was published in midsummer 1952 in newspaper reports from Washington. Pietro Nenni, the Italian left-wing Socialist, had been talking with Stalin. He was quoted as saying Stalin had abandoned all hope of a German settlement. The previous winter, the report said, Moscow had been prepared to give up East Germany and accept reunification.

So here it was—indirect confirmation of what I had heard months earlier. The Italian ambassador, Di Stefano, had talked to Nenni and that was the source of the report. Di Stefano told Kennan and Kennan told the State Department and someone leaked it to Joe Alsop. Nenni said Pieck and Grotewohl had told him they had been put on notice during the winter that Moscow might abandon them for the sake of an overall settlement. Now Stalin had given up on this tactic.

Of course, there was no way of being certain these reports were true. But they matched the hysteria of Soviet policy (and confirmed Kennan's estimate that up against the stone wall of containment, the Russians would change stance and negotiate). I wish Kennan and I had known each other better in those times and had been able to talk more frankly. In his memoirs, Kennan paints a woeful picture of a Washington totally frozen against any negotiations. Yet his Saltykovka talks reflected a note of almost mystical optimism. He seemed to believe that change would come in Soviet policy, that it was dialectically certain, and that when the moment came, he would be there to take advantage of it. I must confess I didn't believe a word of this scenario.

Kennan was an optimist and a romantic (he could also be deeply, almost physically gloomy in a Spenglerian sense, and realistic as a surgeon). His optimistic, romantic side was uppermost in his decision to take the Soviet post. He came to Moscow with an empty diplomatic knapsack and a few almost pathetic bits of paraphernalia. One was his guitar. He did not know exactly how he might put that to use, but somehow he saw himself playing his Russian songs as a way to winning someone's confidence—finding a totally irregular and undiplomatic route that would put him in touch with men of the Kremlin. He had his old friendship with Tom and Juli, and I think he imagined that they (and perhaps I) might be in touch with some Russians to whom we could lead him and that this would be the first step. He had one other string to his bow. Before the war, he had been stationed in Prague and had got acquainted with a young intellectual Englishman, correspondent of *The Times* of London—Ralph Parker, not yet in his Communist phase, his wife still alive, a proper and serious and well-informed young man. Ralph had had to get out of Prague quickly when the Germans moved into Poland in 1939, and he left behind with George some of his possessions, or at least one possession—a painting. Kennan had kept it for him. Now Ralph was a medium of Soviet propaganda. In his book about the British and U.S. embassies, he had portrayed Kennan slanderously, saying he came from a rich family, had attended a military academy, and was "the most influential agent of the American warmongers." Never mind. This might even be to the good. Kennan had the picture with him and wanted to give it back to Parker and use him, I think, as a bridge to the Soviets, someone with whom he could talk off the record, totally informally. Parker could pass him on to a designated Russian, an unoffical channel, and words would begin to flow up and down the chain. Perhaps he thought that Tom and Juli might put him in touch with Parker. If so, he was disappointed. Juli would never have become mixed up in anything like that. Her sense of possible peril was too acute. Nor was I eager. Nothing came of Kennan's idea.

Or perhaps something did. It was not known to me then, but on a Saturday in early July, Kennan had a visitor at the embassy, a hysterical young man who dashed past the guards and identified himself as the son of V. S. Abakumov, Lavrenti Beria's right-hand man. He said his father had been purged and that he and several friends would, if given guns and support, be prepared to carry out the assassination of the top Soviet leaders. Kennan, who describes the episode in his memoirs, was appalled. He did not believe a word the young man said, refused his appeal for help in getting away from the embassy and sent him out into the hands of the police. He considered it the crudest of provocations and felt that Stalin himself, having learned Kennan wanted to talk with a Soviet citizen, sent him this queer duck. I believe Kennan acted in the only way he could; he had to get the young man out of the embassy as quickly as possible; he could have nothing to do with him.

But time and my broad acquaintance with Soviet citizenry, particularly young people, over the last thirty years suggests to me that it was totally possible that the man was, as he said, Abakumov's son and that he had come in naiveté to the U.S. embassy, expecting to be greeted with open arms.

George's visits to the dacha became less frequent with summer. His family was now in Moscow and the diplomatic routine began to catch him up. His mood was changing. His nostalgic pleasure in being in Moscow and the secret conviction that a basic Soviet change was at hand may have faded in the harsh cold war reality. This was particularly sad for Juli. She had greeted George with the adoration of a Juliet. Yes, both Juliet and Romeo were as much overage for their roles as were the three actresses at the Art Theater who persisted in playing in *The Three Sisters*, but no one who saw Juli's face light up and her eyes glow in George's presence could mistake the feeling. George was to her, I think, a character out of not Chekhov but Turgenev, sophisticated, wise, urbane, gifted with a philosophy and emotion close to the Russian heart. He was Russian but not Russian, American but a special kind of American. She could talk to him all day and all night, no bounds to the talk—this on Juli's side. It was or would have been much the same, I think, for George except for his feelings for his country and his wife. He understood Russia well enough to understand talk *po dusham*. The time for that was past for him. He was an extraordinarily happily married man, and strongly as he was drawn to this most Russian of relationships, he was not prepared to venture on an excursion down that path. The other consideration, one he felt strongly, he advanced to Juli in simple but, I thought, eloquent terms. He had long since, he said, made a decision of principle; he had placed himself at the service of his country, and this service came ahead of personal desires and inclinations. His life, in a sense, was no longer at his disposal; it was at his country's. This declaration, so similar to that of a priest's in dedicating himself to the service of God, might have sounded presumptuous in another man. But from the lips of the serious and solemn Kennan, one could only respect it. This Juli did. She smiled at him, she gave him her most tender looks, but she made no effort by the arts of her coquetry to woo him from his resolve.

One more act remained to be played out in the drama of Kennan in Russia. He left Moscow on the early morning of September 19, 1952, for a meeting of American diplomats in London. I was at Vnukovo airport to see him off. He was in a silent, withdrawn mood. Kennan's forays into the West had been plagued by unpleasant incidents. Each time, there had been stories and articles (some accurate, some not) attributing to him opinions calculated to embarrass him with the Russians. The tendency of these stories was to suggest that Kennan's private views about the Soviets were much sharper than those he expressed publicly. This would have been of little consequence had he not been engaged in a campaign to lift the norms of Soviet-U.S.

diplomatic behavior. He felt certain that the Russians would assume he was putting out these reports—in a word, that he was a hypocrite and not seriously concerned with improving the diplomatic tone.

Kennan was upset at this; complained bitterly to the State Department; felt someone in Washington was deliberately trying to undercut him. He was uncomfortable in his relations with the Department and this apparent evidence of backbiting disturbed him greatly.

He had talked to me about the problem, but there was little I could advise. On the afternoon before he left, he called in Gilmore, Shapiro, Whitney and myself. He told us of his concern over these leaks, said he would say absolutely nothing while on this trip abroad; if he had something on his mind, he would call us in when he returned.

Meantime, he asked, what could he do with the press? What questions were likely to be asked? What did we think? He would try to develop noncommittal answers which would not offend the Russians.

The discussion went on a long time, more than an hour. Though a bit eerie, it was probably productive. I saw no reason why George couldn't protect himself with reporters; as for department leaks—that was another problem, only too closely related, I felt, to the McCarthyite influence, which even before the advent of John Foster Dulles had appeared within the Department.

In the morning, Kennan took off for London. There was a refueling stop at Tempelhof Airdrome in Berlin, and there Kennan, in answer to a question by reporters, compared conditions of diplomatic life in Moscow to those of Berlin under Hitler. He went on to London, the statement was carried around the world, and when I saw it I knew that Kennan's days in Moscow had come to an end.

How could it have happened? How could so distinguished, so experienced a diplomat, a man so full of foreboding lest any statement by him be misinterpreted—how could he have broken so much crockery? I do not know to this day. I have spoken of it to Kennan. For years he was reluctant to talk about it. I had heard that when he returned to Spaso House after talking to us, he found that one of the Russian employees, a pleasant woman who had worked for several years as a maid, had vanished (as did all Russian employees sooner or later) and that he was deeply upset. Later I heard that his two-year-old boy, romping on the Spaso lawn, had begun to play patacake with a Russian child through the fence at the lawn's edge. As Kennan watched, security guards sent the Russian youngster scurrying up the street. I could understand that either or both of these incidents would have touched Kennan's feelings. It was not until his memoirs were published in 1973 that he revealed that before he left on his trip, U.S. security agents had detected a Soviet bug in the wood-and-plaster great seal of the United States in the ambassador's study. Kennan was disturbed by this, although there was no evidence that anything of value had been picked up by the Russians.

So there is no question that Kennan was in a grim mood that morning of September 19. What happened, then, at Tempelhof? He never contended that he was speaking off the record, although he has suggested that he might have been. In the months after the incident, I took pains to question my colleagues in Berlin. Three reporters had met Kennan at the airport, as well as a representative of HICOG, the U.S. command. The newsmen represented AP, UP and *Stars and Stripes*. Each said the remarks were not placed off the record. The HICOG man confirmed this. Kennan had made similar statements off the record and his statements, of course, were true. Why, though, after the care he had manifested in talking with us the day before, did he throw caution to the winds? The human mind is a complex organ and George Kennan is a complex man. One of the things he began to say immediately after the incident was that there was no role for an ambassador in Moscow under prevailing conditions, no need to replace him. Had that conviction already formed in his mind, did some subliminal impulse impel the conduct that would certainly remove him from Moscow?

There is something even more tantalizing. In that conversation in which Pietro Nenni told Di Stefano about Stalin's views of Germany, Nenni also questioned Di Stefano about Kennan—what manner of man was he, what were his convictions, did he indeed represent the views of Truman and Acheson, could he be trusted? Di Stefano had known Kennan since before World War II, when they both had been young attachés in Moscow. He told Nenni that Kennan was one of the best diplomats he had ever known, totally worthy of trust, that there was no one more professional in conduct, more reliable.

Nenni was most interested in the answer, but made no effort to contact Kennan. Di Stefano told me he would not be surprised if Nenni was simply passing on a question asked by Stalin. If this is true, and it can well be so, it more correctly reflects Stalin's attitude than the enigmatic affair of the young man who called himself the son of Abakumov. It suggests that Stalin was considering taking Kennan

135

up on the private, secret, semiofficial explorations he had proposed. It is further evidence that Kennan's feeling that Russia was nearing the time for a change in policy was not a mystical hunch. Kennan, I believe, left Russia at a moment when his intuition was about to be proved true, a moment when the secret pace of events had already been accelerating for some months and would go on accelerating until March 5, 1953, when Stalin would be pronounced dead.

After that, it would pick up more speed, but by this time Kennan was already being rusticated, John Foster Dulles having told him there was no place in the State Department where his unique talents might be of use.

Kennan retained his abhorrence of the Soviet's police methods and their leaden propaganda. He had no sympathy for Khrushchev, but found Brezhnev's foreign policy advisers surprisingly subtle and sophisticated. The more deeply he plunged into his historical studies of Russia and the Soviet Union, the more strongly he emerged as a backer of diplomacy as the only method of resolving U.S.-Soviet differences and the less patient he became with advocates of force. The raw interference of the military in diplomacy, their emergence as shapers rather than servants of policy, weighed heavily on his mind. He began to speak out for a diplomacy of realism as the only means of assuring the world's survival, by ending the U.S.-Soviet arms race and halting the buildup of nuclear armaments. His personal relationship with the Soviets underwent a gradual evolution; he and they began more clearly to understand each other. Kennan threw his prestige and energy into the establishment of an Institute for Soviet Studies, attached to the Smithsonian Institution. It was named for George Kennan the first, but inevitably would become a living monument to George Kennan the second.

As Kennan reached his seventies, a feeling began to grow in many quarters that his life might well be crowned with the award of the Nobel Prize for Peace, an honor that would have seemed unthinkable in the days when we sat under the pines of Saltykovka and argued about Stalin.

# Chapter 12

# The Plot

I cannot and will not pretend that I had a premonition in those golden weeks of late August 1952 that the Stalin era was rushing toward its end.

My life was lazy—long conversations under the tall pines at Saltykovka, casual bargaining with the babushka who sold icons in the market (she hid them under her long black skirts), hoeing the rows of spindly corn in the garden (the dachniki thought Tom and I had lost our minds), fierce games of *gorodki*, a kind of Russian tenpins, dips in a muddy pond. I described in a letter to my mother the lovely flowers we were growing—dahlias, gladioli, larkspur, asters, marigolds, zinnias, petunias, phlox, nicotiana. I said: "I don't believe anyone in Russia has a nicer dacha. It is a joy and a pleasure to live here."

A joy and a pleasure. I wrote those lines August 11, 1952. The next day, the twelfth, in the basements of the Lubyanka, Stalin did to death twenty-four members of the Jewish Anti-Fascist Committee, which had rallied world Jewry to the Soviet cause in World War II. They had been arrested during the cosmopolitanism campaign of 1948–49 and were secretly placed on trial July 11–18, 1952. Not one hint of that crime would become public until Stalin had been dead nearly three years. Sent to death that quiet August was my old friend Solomon Lozovsky, wartime Soviet press spokesman, whose fiery words and flaming spirit had made Russian surrender seem unthinkable in the terrible days of 1941 and 1942, and with him died a score of poets and writers and artists, Perets Markish, Itzik Fefer, David Bergelson and the rest. Of those put on trial, only Lena Shtern, a physicist, survived. She was given life imprisonment and lived to be released after Stalin's death.

By this 1952 summer, I thought that I had a good grasp on Russia. I had the language down pretty well; living in Saltykovka, wandering over the countryside, talking with Tom and Juli, engaging George Kennan in long discussions; I had learned how Russians behaved,

137

their ordinary lives and attitudes, I had read Tolstoy, had seen Chekhov at the Art Theater (although its Chekhov repertoire was sadly diminished in these last Stalin years), had got acquainted with Ostrovsky and Gogol. I felt the rhythm of Russian life; I knew the terror; I knew about the camps; the thought of the police seldom left my mind. I had become, I felt, competent in my profession as a specialist in Soviet affairs. Of course, I did not put myself in Kennan's class. No one, in my view, could touch him. I did not have Tom Whitney's expertise in economics, but I was willing to match my judgment against that of anyone in Moscow, and I had long since learned the weakness of the offshore specialists, in Washington, London and Bonn.

The quality of the Moscow diplomatic corps was not high. Expertise at the American embassy after Kennan's forced withdrawal was thin. The U.S. chargé was Elim O'Shaughnessy, a marvelously genial man (despite his ulcers), but Moscow was only a way stop for him. The extraordinary skills of the Israelis would soon be lost. They had staffed their mission with Russian-born, Russian-speaking diplomats. They had unrivaled access to friends, relatives, coreligionists—one reason, I thought, why Stalin developed such paranoia about them. When Golda Meir (then Myerson) arrived in 1948 to establish the mission, a two-block-long line of Jews waiting to shake her hand formed outside the Metropol Hotel. That exhibition in central Moscow within sight of the Lubyanka hit Stalin's anti-Semitic nerve and may have touched off the cosmopolitanism drive. In an indirect way, it may have caused Stalin to decree the deaths of the members of the Jewish Anti-Fascist Committee.

The British had a competent embassy under Sir Alvery Gasgoigne, but the brilliant wartime and postwar Russicists like Edward Crankshaw, Arthur Birse and Tom Brebner were long since gone. The French, as so often, were witty but not well informed. There were a few others—the Finns knew a lot but kept their mouths shut, and my friend Sigurd Ekelund of the Norwegian embassy was first-class. Ambassador Rolf Sohlman, of Sweden, who remained in Moscow for many years, never knew as much as he thought he knew.

The United States under the forced draft of the cold war had begun to pour money into Soviet studies and, with the aid of the Russian Research Center at Harvard and the Russian Institute at Columbia, eventually would produce a cadre of specialists second to none. But this was early on. The new Soviet specialists were skewed by the intensity of the cold war and handicapped by nonaccess to the Soviet Union. Their judgments were conditioned by contact with successive waves of Russian emigration: the tremendous outflow (largely Jewish) before 1914; the outpouring after the Bolshevik Revolution—the so-called Whites, that is, the upper and middle classes; and the political enemies of the Bolsheviks, notably the Mensheviks, the Socialist Revolutionaries and the Kadets. And now there had been a new wave, that of Russians displaced by the war, many by way of Germany. This Russian mass was naturally (and rightfully) violently antagonistic to the Soviet regime. In the context of the times, it is small wonder that American expertise tended to be sharply affected.

In this period, unfortunately, popular attitudes which failed to make a distinction between the Russian people and the Soviet apparatus took root, a tendency that would continue into the future and deeply disturb such a man as Aleksandr Solzhenitsyn, as strong an anti-Bolshevik and as strong a Russian patriot as could be found.

I wished in this summer of 1952 that Sir Bernard Pares had been living. I could imagine him sitting under the pines at Saltykovka in a canvas chair, George Kennan in another, myself, Juli and Tom beside them—what conversation! And weak and ungrammatical as was my Russian, I could not have held back from taking part. I thought Pares would not be ashamed of his disciple. I had accumulated a store of information about the Bolsheviks and their terrible master, Stalin. I did not think I could easily be fooled now and in this I was correct, except on one count—Stalin's paranoia, the totality of his crooked vision of the world and his mania that his closest collaborators were engaged in a conspiracy against him. (Later I would ask myself: Was this entirely paranoia? Hadn't at this late date at least some of them begun to *wish* to conspire even if they did not possess the courage?) The vastness of Stalin's suspicions lay beyond my imagination. There was too much hard grit in my mind; I had absorbed too much Midwestern skepticism, down-to-earthism, call it what you will. I could not envision a world leader so psychopathic, even when I used Hitler as a model.

So if someone had come up to me (as the young man did to Kennan) and told me that tomorrow, on August 12, Stalin would wipe from the earth the flower of Russian Jewish intelligentsia and that he had been twisting their limbs, torturing their bodies and flogging their spirits for nearly four years, I would, I am afraid, have thought that my informant was a victim of plotitis, which I understood to be a very common disease in Russia, dating back beyond Ivan the Terrible into the earliest days of Mongol invasions.

Nothing as cosmic as the end of Stalin and his era was on my mind in those splendid August days. Yet I had begun to feel that *something* was in the air—just what, I could not say. In February I had written Manny Freedman, suggesting a revision of the code message I was to send if Stalin died. I had no reason to believe that his death was near, although a spate of stories in the Soviet press about the longevity of Georgians made me think that someone had Stalin's age on his mind (Stalin was then seventy-two). The stories reported that in the Georgian mountains, one not infrequently came upon men in good health at the age of 130 or even 140. I did not think Stalin was likely to live so long; neither did I think his death was at hand; but I wanted to be certain that if I sent a code message, it would not get lost in the paper traffic. The *Times* boasted of handling a million words of copy a day. The danger, I told Manny, was that "the messages are so innocuous that they are apt to be ignored by anyone who is not on the alert."

There is nothing in my dispatches or in my correspondence to suggest that in August there was any rise in my anxiety level. I was writing Cy Sulzberger that "news-wise we are really in the dog days." I told a friend that "everything is peaceful and quiet." I was leading "as uncomplicated an existence as you could find."

In another letter I wrote: "The countryside is lovely in its late summer aspects. The harvest is pouring in. The new buildings are going up. The new dams are functioning and, in general, everything has a rather mid-New Deal aspect."

There were, I must say, a few puzzles in my mind. One was the indication—which I would not confirm until November—that Abakumov no longer was serving as interior minister, that is, as the man in charge of the police. He had, as a matter of fact, been dismissed the previous November, 1951, but until the young "Abakumov" appeared at the U.S. embassy in July, this had been only a vague rumor. Official confirmation that he had been replaced by Semyon D. Ignatiev was still being held up by the censors at the time of Stalin's death.

Any question about the police—the most sensitive apparatus in the Soviet Union—attracted my attention. I didn't know what the rumors meant, but I kept them in mind.

I was very interested in the situation in Georgia, the bailiwick of both Stalin and Beria. In April 1952, a purge of the Georgian political and police leadership had been carried out at a plenary meeting of the Georgian Party Committee. Beria himself was present. This made it an event worthy of study. Moreover, the news did not appear in the Tbilisi newspaper until the end of May; and the censors killed my story out of hand. A couple of days later, *Pravda* ran an editorial commentary about the episode; I filed my story again and this time it went through. New York gave it only a few paragraphs, but I could not blame them. The censor had deleted almost all meaning from the dispatch. To me, however, whatever Beria did was significant. And the curious, finicky conduct of the censors told me that there was special sensitivity to the Georgian events.

But none of this indicated what was really happening, who was behind it, and what roles Beria and Stalin were playing.

Though I knew that some funny business was afoot, I missed the point entirely. I thought Beria had fired Abakumov and was shaking up Georgia. It did not occur to me that *Stalin* had fired Abakumov, *Stalin* was shaking up Georgia and shaking up Beria in the process. I knew that Beria had lasted a good deal longer than either of his police predecessors, Genrykh Yagoda and Nikolai Yezhov, but my conviction that the Stalin regime had reached a kind of plateau of internal political balance blinded me to a realization that by Stalin's timetable, the moment for replacing Beria was at hand; too often had Stalin used Beria to settle his political accounts (as in dealing with the powerful Army marshals, like Georgi K. Zhukov, at the end of World War II). Unless Stalin now dealt with Beria, Beria would deal with Stalin.

Nothing as cataclysmic as the end of Stalin can happen without premonitory signs; the great sphinx does not suddenly topple from its pedestal and shatter in a thousand pieces. There must be preliminary tremors. So there were in this case, but I did not read them correctly nor, I believe, did anyone else except the handful of men who were called Stalin's "closest comrades in arms."

The benign and comfortable Saltykovka days came to an end on August 17, 1952. That evening, we got the announcement of the arrival of a Chinese delegation, headed by Premier Zhou Enlai. They were to negotiate with Stalin and Molotov. The reason for this negotiation I never discovered, and soon it got lost in the cascade of events that spewed forth, one after the other. From that evening until Stalin's death (and for a long time after), there was no peace, no quiet, no rest; just story after story, headline after headline, a mounting crescendo and something else—terror.

At first it was the pounding of the news bulletins, stories breaking like waves on a barrier reef. Hardly had Stalin begun to negotiate with Zhou than we got the announcement that the party would meet in its Nineteenth Congress, the first since 1939, in October. The Politburo, the core of Soviet power since the days of Lenin, was to be abolished and replaced by a Presidium, whatever that might be. The next day, a new five-year plan for industry and agriculture was announced. The next day, Moscow proposed a four-power conference on Germany. Day after day, the *Times* played my dispatches on page one. There was a huge spread on plans for a gigantic power system; there were tough declarations about party discipline and tougher ones on "vigilance." There would be more and more articles about vigilance as autumn wore on. The run of news was so swift I had no time for contemplation. Hardly a moment to mourn George Kennan's vanishment. No more dacha. No more vegetable garden. No more talks *po dusham.* As event tumbled after event, I began to feel that I must prepare for even bigger news. The conventional cable facilities no longer sufficed. My old UP communications instinct broke through the surface and I wrote the *Times* bureau in London to arrange to dictate my late-breaking dispatches by telephone. Clifton Daniel was in charge and he promptly advised me that London had a man on duty every night until 3 A.M., Moscow time, who could, in a pinch, take my dictation. I felt reassured. Whatever was coming, I would be able to handle it. I tried to figure out what lay ahead. Not a new purge—of that I felt pretty certain. "The break with the 'purge' technique," I wrote in my journal, "is, I think, final." The party membership had been fairly well overhauled since the war. Deadwood had been cleared away. What lay ahead, I thought, was not a tempest at the national level but more localized storms, like that in Georgia. I was still watching Georgia closely, still not understanding that the "cleanup" was directed against rather than by Beria. The volume of my transmissions to New York was extraordinary. In the first fifteen days of October, during and after the Nineteenth Party Congress, I spent sixteen thousand rubles—full-value, four-to-the-dollar rubles—on tolls to New York. Ordinarily I didn't spend that much in four months.

I might not yet be seeing Stalin's forest for the trees, but I was understanding, reporting and accurately analyzing most of what happened at the Nineteenth Congress. I perceived that it provided a backdrop for the full emergence of Malenkov as Stalin's designated successor. He was given every opportunity to star, and took it. I also understood quite clearly that the purpose Stalin had in mind in creating the big new Presidium of twenty-five members and eleven candidate members was to dilute the Polituro and, in a sense, unhinge the status of all the old leaders. I understood something else: Stalin himself overshadowed the congress, yet made only one cameo appearance at the very end, a fleeting moment with throwaway lines. It was a gesture of contempt and of total power, as if he was tossing the congress a glove to fight over as a symbol of his dominance.

There was another fact, and I took notice of it in my journal. Malenkov *seemed* to dominate the proceedings, but did he really?

In mid-November I wrote: "People are apt to overlook Khrushchev. I wouldn't do that. After all, he is the Moscow party boss. That is the biggest single boss position in the country and I don't know of a party position where you are more likely to shine—if you really have ability—than Moscow. And Khrushchev obviously still had his finger firmly on the Ukrainian pulse. I think he ranks much higher than he seems to. . . . In general, it is fairly clear that should Stalin die in the present period, Molotov would succeed him as head of state, Malenkov as head of the party, and the actual power would be held in varying degrees by Molotov, Malenkov, Beria, Bulganin, Voroshilov and, quite possibly, Khrushchev."

And at the same time—and for the first time—I began to speculate on the possibility that Beria was dropping from the inner circle. One of the prime devices in analysis of Kremlin politics was the display of the portraits—that is, the order in which they were arrayed around the central figure of Stalin in published photographs and wall displays. For years, the order had been: Stalin, Molotov, Malenkov, Beria. Now, at a stroke, Beria dropped two positions. The displays on November 7 arranged the pictures in this order: Stalin, Molotov, Malenkov, Voroshilov, Bulganin, Beria. As I noted, unless Stalin was merely "exercising his jovial humor," that meant a tip of fortune away from Beria.

Though I toyed with the possibility that this phenomenon was linked in some way with the events in Georgia, I failed to draw what seems to me now the obvious conclusion that Georgia was being taken away from Beria. I hadn't yet pinned down the Abakumov-Ignatiev shift firmly enough to put it into the equation.

But I was tightening my belt for what looked more and more like a new tempo. There were only five American correspondents in Moscow now. No English whatever. We had coalesced into two harshly competitive groups: the AP's Gilmore and Whitney, with whom I aligned myself, plus Andy Steiger, the Reuters stringer, and on the other side, Henry Shapiro of UP, and Jean Noe, stringer for Agence France-Presse. The principal papers, *Pravda* and *Izvestiya*, were delivered to the Metropol at 8 or 9 A.M., and that was when the news agencies customarily had filed their stories. Because 8 A.M. was midnight in New York, too late for the *Times* except for the biggest news, I usually wrote and transmitted my stories in the afternoon or early evening, for use in the next day's paper. This gave me time to evaluate a development and write, I hoped, with more depth and interpretation than the split-second transmissions of the agencies.

Now, due largely to the enterprise of Tom Whitney, we were getting the papers the moment they became available at the *ekspeditsiya*, the special dispatch booths at the newspaper plants. Late papers invariably meant a big story. Each team assigned a man in rotation to be at the Central Telegraph Office a bit after midnight. He would wait until the papers came, then telephone his colleagues if there was big news. If the papers were delayed after 3 A.M., he would phone and we would all come down to be on hand for a big story. There was no problem in picking up *Izvestiya*. Its plant was in the center of town and the *ekspeditsiya* was just off Gorky Street. *Pravda* was another matter and rather scary. The plant was located near the Dynamo metro station, well out (in those days) on the Leningrad chaussée. The *ekspeditsiya* was at the back of the plant, in a compound patrolled at night by soldiers with rifles. As time ran on and tension built up in Moscow, going to the *Pravda* plant at 3 A.M. on a dark winter night with trigger-happy soldiers in an unlighted courtyard did not appeal to me.

But these exercises were important. We got the papers hours ahead of ordinary delivery. It made the difference, so far as I was concerned, between getting my story into the morning paper or losing it to an agency report. There was a seven- or eight-hour time differential (depending on the season) between Moscow and New York. If I got *Pravda* at 4 A.M., it was still only 8 or 9 P.M. in New York—plenty of time to make the second edition if the censor did not delay the story and if the telephone line to London came through promptly. Even if *Pravda* was delayed until 8 A.M., I could with luck catch the final edition in New York. This was meaningless for ordinary stories, but more and more we were dealing with front-page, lead-the-paper news. Night after night, I found myself sitting in the Central Telegraph Office, a big modern building on Gorky Street. The pressroom was located to the rear off a side street, a tiny mezzanine with four telephone booths, a table and a counter behind which worked two women—a telegraph clerk, who accepted our copy and delivered it to a closed rear room, where it was censored, and a telephone operator, who sat at an old-fashioned switchboard with telephone jacks and headphones. She placed our international telephone calls to London, Paris, New York or wherever. Sometimes Mongolian students descended on the cubbyhole to telephone their parents in Ulan Bator—they shouted so loud I thought they hardly needed a telephone line. This bandbox came to be my second home. Tom and I alternated on the watch. There were always two of us there, one from each rival syndicate, often not on speaking terms, stealing sly looks, wondering if the opposition was onto any special bits of information. In this close confrontation I came to realize that there were favors granted by the Press Department, that not all was a matter of equity or enterprise. On more than one occasion, my "opposition" would suddenly appear on the scene, tipped off, presumably by the Press Department, that something was about to happen.

Later if would seem to me that November 1952 was a brooding, oppressive time, a period of hush in which I could hear the rustle of unfamiliar noises in the background, hints of disturbing events. It was quiet, compared to the tensions of October; routine saber-rattling by Marshal Timoshenko on November 7, retrospective rumbling in the press about the evil George Kennan, new men put in to run two ideological journals—nothing dramatic, but an undercurrent of unease produced by the enigmatic Nineteenth Party Congress.

Not until December 1 did my apprehension begin to take a more tangible form. On that day, the Kiev newspaper reported under the simple headline "Chronicle" that a military tribunal had decreed the death by shooting of three individuals, all bearing Jewish names, as "enemies of the people," guilty of "counterrevolutionary wrecking." In my years in Moscow, I had never seen or heard of such an event.

145

The "crime" for which the men were tried was fraud and peculation. Invocation of the death penalty and a military court in a petty commercial case, the phrase "counterrevolutionary wrecking" and the label "enemies of the people" instantly linked the event in every Russian's mind with the 1930s purges. It was as "enemies of the people" that Stalin sent millions of innocent Soviet citizens to the labor camps and it was as "counterrevolutionary wreckers" that he destroyed the Old Bolsheviks and his closest comrades.

The message was unmistakable. I immediately referred back to an address made by "General" Aleksandr Poskrebyshev, Stalin's chef de cabinet, at the party congress, in which he called for vigilance and inveighed against "wreckers." This man bore a reputation as ugly as his name (which contained the root of the vulgar Russian word for afterbirth). He carried out Stalin's most evil bidding. But in the weeks before Stalin's death, he himself was arrested. Later I would meet a woman, Galina Serebryakova, an Old Bolshevik who spent many years in Stalin's camps and lost two famous Bolshevik husbands, successively, Georgi Sokolnikov and G. P. Serebryakov, to Stalin's purges. She met Poskrebyshev in the Kremlin hospital in 1962. He did not die until 1966. He was, she said, not only unrepentant but actually proud of the crimes he had carried out at Stalin's behest. His memory was infallible. He fulfilled every order Stalin gave him without a tremor. Stalin executed Poskrebyshev's wife. He did not blink an eye. He had a story he liked to tell about Beria. He had asked Beria once whether a certain Bolshevik was "sitting" (the Russian phrase for being in prison). No, no, said Beria, he's not sitting any longer; he's lying flat on the floor. Poskrebyshev, telling the story, laughed uproariously. Serebryakova asked about a friend who she knew had died in prison. Had she possibly been poisoned? Poskrebyshev asked the date of the death. It was 1937 or 1938. She must have been shot, he said; "we didn't start using poison until 1940 or thereabouts."

Through December the arrest of persons in the trade networks, many bearing Jewish names, went forward. Many arrests were in the Ukraine. There were more changes in the ideological organs. *Pravda* got a new editor and a new round of crticism broke out on the economic front. My feeling of unease was not relieved when, unexpectedly, Stalin responded to a series of questions cabled to him by Scotty Reston, the *Times* correspondent in Washington. Stalin, responding to Eisenhower's election, seemed to be offering to act as mediator between the U.S. and Korea, and encouraging the idea of a meeting between himself and Ike. Nothing came of either initiative and Reston took some vicious criticism (including, I'm sorry to say, some from top *Times* editors) for having made himself available to "Soviet propaganda."

I met New Year, 1953, with some trepidation. I wanted very much to get back to the United States. I was worried about Mike and Stephan. Mary had finally come to rest in Evanston, Illinois, but reports on the boys were not reassuring and Moscow was becoming a strain. I saw no early end to Stalin and was beginning to wonder whether I could last him out. I had had a fine run of news, my standing with the paper had radically improved, I had published two good articles in the *Times Magazine* at year's end and felt that I had regained the confidence that had been lost by the Korean episode. But I did not know how much longer I could take Moscow, particularly a Moscow which on that cold New Year's midnight, swept by wind, the temperature well below zero, seemed to be acquiring an un-defined aura of menace. I wrote my mother and my sister that I surely hoped to get back in 1953, though I could not yet be certain when. My uncertainty arose from a sense that I had lost track of Russia's direction. I could feel a hand on the tiller, but I did not know from what compass the helmsman was taking his course.

January 13, 1953, was an ordinary winter's morning at the Hotel Metropol. I was still living in Room 393. When I opened *Pravda* at about 8 A.M., I found in the middle of the back page, under the one word "Chronicle," a ten-inch announcement, which even today causes a chill to run up my spine.

It said that a group of nine doctors, all but three of them Jews, had been arrested on a charge of plotting against the lives of high party, government and army leaders. They were linked through Zionist organizations with the U.S. and British intelligence and had carried out their activities by the negligence of Soviet security organs.

Here it was. I did not need one more detail. Here was the sketch for a purge to end all purges. Every Russian citizen who read the "Chronicle" knew exactly what it meant. Now I knew why goose-flesh had crawled on my skin during these winter nights as I tried to figure out what was going on behind the scenes. This announcement gave the whole scenario. I could name the defendants: the doctors, of course (and they were the most distinguished in the country, all

147

connected with the Kremlin hospital, personal physicians to the Politburo); the security chiefs (that meant Beria and Abakumov); Jews (and this meant Lazar M. Kaganovich in the Politburo); members of the trade system, and this meant Anastas Mikoyan, whose Politburo rating had slipped badly; and Aleksei Kosygin, who had slipped even more. What about Nikita Khrushchev, whose ties to the Ukraine were so strong? Many, many arrests were taking place in the Ukraine. And would there not be a spot reserved for "foreign agents," representatives of the U.S. and British intelligence? I could see George Kennan being cast, in absentia, as the mastermind of the plot; he had been portrayed repeatedly since the Nineteenth Party Congress as the director of the international cold war against Moscow. Would it not be convenient to name someone still in Moscow as a link between Kennan and the other plotters—for instance, a foreign correspondent, or even better, two foreign correspondents who set up a "nest" in Saltykovka where Kennan could hatch his evil doings?

It sounds absurd today. In fact, it was absurd. But that did not mean that such ideas did not pass through the mind of the master of the Grand Guignol. There was nothing he was not capable of. He compelled his new son-in-law, Yuri Zhdanov, who had recently married his daughter, Svetlana, to attack ideological weaknesses among scientists. Zhdanov's father, the late Andrei Zhdanov, who had died August 31, 1947, was one of the alleged victims of the "Doctors' Plot."

As days went past, the horizons of the "plot" rapidly broadened. Rumors flew through Moscow. A man named L. D. Gurevich was arrested. I didn't know him, but the other correspondents did. He had worked for Tass, once had wide connections with foreign correspondents, acted, for a time, as kind of a go-between. Now he was "exposed" as an "ex-Trotskyite and intelligence agent." My old friend Palgunov of the Foreign Office and Tass had vanished. Madame Molotov had been arrested, it was gossiped, and banished to Siberia. She was Jewish and had been the best friend of Stalin's wife, Nadezda, who killed herself in 1933. There had been arrests in the universities in Moscow and Leningrad and in the Academy of Sciences. There were rumors about many Soviet diplomats. My old friend Maisky was repeatedly criticized, along with others of long standing, most of them Jewish. Central Committee members had been arrested.

The question was not who was in trouble—but who was not. I could hardly believe my own conclusions as I added up the potential defendants at the show trial to come. Not many members of the Politburo would escape. Could Stalin really be thinking of doing away with everyone—Molotov, Beria, Mikoyan, Kaganovich, possibly Voroshilov? (Khrushchev later revealed that this was exactly what Stalin had in mind.) Certainly Malenkov and Bulganin would not be in the cast—still, there were rumors.

And the Jews. The net was being cast very wide. On February 12, 1953, Moscow broke diplomatic relations with Israel and the long-harassed Israelis left the country.

Three times in February, Stalin went out of his way to meet with foreigners, Argentine Ambassador Bravo, Indian Ambassador Menon and the Indian peace leader Dr. Kitchlew. Each spoke of Stalin's "excellent health," his lively mind, his keen grasp of the issues. Only later did Menon tell me that Stalin had doodled on a pad with a red pencil. He was drawing pictures of wolves, many, many wolves. Stalin spoke of wolves, as well. He said Russian peasants knew how to deal with them—they killed them. Menon had thought the remark curious and I thought it even more curious.

Tom and I talked one day. Would there be a correspondent as a defendant in the upcoming trial? We both believed the chances were good that there would be. Tom thought he was a strong possibility. He was married to a Russian woman; he was close to George Kennan; he had come to Moscow with the OSS, that is, as an intelligence agent, and the Russians knew this. His reasoning was too good for comfort. I thought I was an equally promising candidate. I represented *The New York Times*, which every day was castigated by *Pravda*. I had a long, long record of conflict and hostility with the Russians, going back to World War II days. (Had I known of the Nosenko revelations, I would have considered myself the number one candidate.)

What to do? Should we pick up and ship out? That was easy for me: I knew the *Times* would agree if I told them the situation; I had no entanglements. For my four American colleagues, however, to leave would send their wives straight into concentration camps and maybe the wives would end up as defendants or witnesses at the forthcoming trial.

That was the kind of talk we had, riding in the blue Chevrolet of which Juli was so proud. We didn't want to talk indoors for fear of hidden microphones, nor did we want further to alarm Juli. There was no one at the U.S. embassy to whom we could turn for guidance or comfort. We knew the situation better than they did; there were no Kennans, no Kirks, no Harrimans, no Archie Clark Kerrs on the horizon in the winter of 1953. We were on our own. It was not difficult for me to make up my mind. I was frightened with good reason, I thought. But I would not have left Moscow if Turner Catledge had ordered me to. I was on the verge of the biggest story I had ever heard of. Of course I would stay. That was why I had come. I would take my chances on where I would find myself—in the dock or in the press box.

# Chapter 13

# Stalin

February is the longest month of the Russian calendar, its dark days bereft of sun, with cold winds, gray skies, falling snow day after day, the women in gray quilted jackets and gray shawls sweeping the streets with witches' brooms, the Metropol's corridors dimmer and dimmer, ghosts in the corners—a time when life congeals and hope vanishes. Russian winter sets in by late October. In December and January, the sun rises feebly after nine in the morning and its yellow wafer is fading at two in the afternoon. By February, I would wonder whether I could survive the two long months of winter still ahead. I understood now the peasant rhythms and the northern drunkenness, sleeping on the brick stove winter long, the frenzy of spring, the orgies of the midsummer solstice.

The rhythm of Russian life was compelled by endless winter, savage spring, fierce summer, brief fall, and this rhythm had been imposed on industrial Russia: the factories "storming" to meet their rigid production quotas, the somnolent pace in winter, molasses in spring, more lively in summer and madness as the year neared an end.

February was the low point, and February 1953 was not only low but foreboding. At the end of January, Juli's mother had died after a few days in hospital, a time of total grief and guilt for Juli, who spent every moment at the bedside, listening to the nurses gossip of the Doctors' Plot and whisper their own evil fantasies, the hospital alive with letter writing, denunciations pouring into the Kremlin.

Estella Khokhlovkina was buried in Vvedenie cemetery in a plot off a snow-banked *allée*, obtained by bribing the cemetery adminis-tration. I don't know what Tom paid—one thousand rubles, three thousand rubles, whatever was the going rate. Estella Khokhlovkina, at last at peace, lay briefly on an iron table in her wood coffin in a room with a cement floor in the basement of the Third Moscow *Krematoria*. I suppose a dozen people gathered there—a few relatives whom I did not know, edgy because of the foreigners, and motherly Maria Ivanovna, cook for the Whitneys and later for me. Outside the room, three women squabbled over the dress, the shift, the shoes, the stockings, they removed from the corpse of a friend, which lay on a trolley about to be wheeled to the crematorium furnace.

We rode in a small blue bus to Vvedenie; Tom, myself and two cemetery workers carried the coffin to the graveside. God knows whose bones had been disinterred to make a place for Estella Khokhlovkina. We stood a moment. Juli cast the first handful of frozen earth and the gravediggers began to fill the hole, the temperature at twenty-five degrees below zero, centigrade. Maria Ivanovna had brought a little bottle of vodka so the women could wipe their faces and the tears would not freeze on their cheeks. Then we went back to the apartment. Maria Ivanovna had prepared the traditional funeral *kutiya*, a dish of boiled rice and raisins. One more Russian soul had been laid to rest.

We waited. Slowly the days of February slipped off the calendar. On the streets, the black beetles who are the people of Moscow in winter padded past in their *valenki*, the slap of felt boots slurring into a soft murmur. I sat inside the Metropol and tried to understand what was happening, the ripple of arrests in every paper, the growing silence of the Metropol maids. No longer did they gossip around the desk of the *dezhurnaya*. Now they slithered along the corridors, eyes averted, faces closed. Did they know something? Or was it the fear of working with foreigners, any one of whom might be a *shipon*, a spy, or a *diversant*? Even a maid who cared for a *shipon*'s room might find herself labeled an enemy of the people. The corridors of the Metropol, always so dark, now seemed hardly lighted. I pulled tight the heavy wine-coloured draperies at my windows and tried to shut out Russia, but it seeped in through every crevice. I was afraid. I think all Moscow was afraid.

Toward the end of February, General Sokolovsky, a hero of World War II, replaced General Shtemenko, an obscure timeserver, as chief of the General Staff. It wasn't announced. We found it out when Sokolovsky signed the invitations for the Red Army Day reception. Was this good news or bad? No one knew. Lev Mekhlis, a Jew and an old crony of Stalin's, a man whose intrigues had cost the Red Army heavily in the war, died, as the obituary said, "at his fighting post," whatever that meant. The leading pallbearer was Lazar M. Maganovich, the only Jew in the Politburo. The Jews burying the Jews? Perhaps. Stalin's son Vasily lost his job as commander of the Moscow

Air Force, but the censor would not let me transmit the news. Minister of Health Smirnov lost his job; probably, I thought, he was being tagged in the Doctors' Plot. A brief obituary of General Kosynkin was published on February 17. He suffered an "untimely death." I had never heard of him. He turned out to have been Stalin's Kremlin commandant. These were little pieces of a big mosaic. I didn't know how to put them together.

My mood was touchy. I was nervous. I wrote sarcastic letters.

To Burobin (I had been trying to get an apartment for a year): "Is this a fair example of Soviet efficiency or does it reflect a general absence of adequate housing facilities in Moscow?"

To the Press Department (about Burobin): "Do you suppose there is anything your department can do to cause these Rip Van Winkles to bestir themselves?"

To Chief Censor Omelchenko: "What does a censor do with a cable which he or she passes verbatim after one hour and forty-five minutes—sit staring at it for one hour and forty-five minutes? Or does he or she sit drinking tea and reading light literature until the spirit moves him or her to bother with doing a small amount of work? Yours in some asperity, Harrison E. Salisbury."

I went out to Saltykovka. It was an hour's walk through deep snow from the station to the dacha, which stood peacefully in the grove of tall pines. Straight columns of blue smoke rose from the chimneys of neighboring dachas. I lighted a little fire and huddled over it, warming my frosted hands and ears, then walked back to the station. That night I wrote a friend: "I only wish the world was as quiet and peaceful as the countryside around Moscow now appears. Everything is covered in a deep blanket of white snow. There is a strong frost, close to 30 degrees below, centigrade, and the sky is that pale winter blue. The air is crisp and horses' and humans' mouths are quickly covered with hoarfrost. The countryside is sleeping quietly, the peasants are busy with their winter chores, the youngsters' skates are ringing on the village ponds and the forests stand dark green and silent and a little frightening. It looks and is a simple, comfortable world.

"But, unfortunately, I do not think we can consider this countryside exactly a symbol of the state of affairs in these perilous days."

Tom and I had established a new routine for night duty—one week on, one week off. It was my week on, the week of March 1. I spent the early evening of March 3 monitoring the dictation-speed Tass transmission. Tass sent its news to the small country papers all over Russia by radio dictation, the same thing I had done for UP in my early days at St. Paul, by telephone. The Tass reader, usually a woman, intoned the items slowly, spelling out every name ("*M kak Maria, O kak Olga, S kak Sara, K kak Kostya, V kak Viktor, A kak Andrei—Moskva*"). Once in a while, Tass dictation carried an important item before regular Tass. I listened with half an ear while combing the fifteen or sixteen provincial papers to which I subscribed. I was looking for clues, haunted by what was happening behind Stalin's curtains.

I found nothing in the papers, heard nothing on Tass dictation. I picked up my portable typewriter and made my way to the telegraph office. *Pravda*, upset at our prowling about the back courtyard, was now delivering the paper to the telegraph office. So was *Izvestiya*. I was uneasy as I opened my typewriter and settled down for the usual wait. Thanks to Clifton Daniel, I could dictate my stories to London until 3 A.M. The trouble was that hot Moscow news was breaking more and more often after 3 A.M. After that hour, since London had no one to take my messages, I had to use urgent cable service, urgent in name only. Night after night my stories arrived in New York hours too late. Since early February, I had been urging New York to arrange for all-night dictation. I truly felt there was something apocalyptic in the Moscow atmosphere. I could smell it. I felt it in the metallic taste of fear under my tongue. Somehow I had not been able to convey this feeling to New York. I had in my pocket a cablegram I had just received from Freedman, and it bore his phlegmatic touch: "Salisbury dubious about setting up London Paris dictation posts simply for late breaks Moscow but still awaiting results of cost inquiry. Freedman." Manny had sent that telegram at 12.57 P.M., March 3; I got it at 1 A.M., March 4—about seven hours transmission time.

How could I stir Manny out of his routine, his concern about costs, and make him understand that I was sitting on a charge of dynamite?

As so often in the long hours after midnight, I began to think about Russia. I had been living in Moscow for four years now, plus the better part of a year during the war—five years in all, give or take a few months. Every day I was learning how little I knew about this complicated country.

What was it that we were waiting for—what was it that frightened us so much? Simply that no one knew what the tyrant ruler would do next. "Watch out!" Eddy Gilmore had said. "The old man has reached for the bottle again." That was it. We were waiting for 1934, 1935, 1936, 1937, 1938, for the purges to happen again, the time when the Revolution was turned inside out, when the heroes were declared villains and darkness fell at noon. When Koestler's book first came out, I didn't read it. I could not abide the disputes of the sectarians, the worshipers and the skeptics. To me, they were all of the same pattern. I despised them. I think there was a little xenophobia in that, a feeling, basically, that they were a bunch of foreigners. Not until I came to Moscow in 1949 did I read *Darkness at Noon* and become powerfully moved at Koestler's insight.

These were the kind of thoughts that flowed through my mind as I drowsed at Entrance 11 of the Central Telegraph Office in the hours after midnight on March 4, 1953. I looked at my watch. It was two-thirty. No sign of the papers. The "opposition," Jean Noe, was across the room, his head on the table in the cradle of his arms, fast asleep. A dark, good-looking Frenchman who had come to Moscow as a soccer player and stayed on to coach the Russians, he had wound up as a correspondent for Agence France-Presse. So far as I could see, the only one awake in the telegraph office besides myself was Clerk Vassileva, the woman who took the telegrams, her face just visible through the little opening in the frosted glass.

At three-thirty, the papers still hadn't come, and I telephoned the *Izvestiya ekspeditsiya*. The woman had heard nothing. At four, the papers still had not arrived. I called again. No sign. I began to get jittery. Jean Noe had awakened and called someone. He did not go back to sleep. I called *Izvestiya* again. The woman said the papers were late. Well, that I knew. At five, I called Tass. No, they had heard nothing, but the man spoke in a way that gave me an idea something might be up. Should I call Tom? I decided to wait a few more minutes. Jean Noe was stirring about. He had the same problem as I, but we did not speak. It was not considered appropriate. We spoke when we met, a rather stiff greeting but nothing more. I called the *Izvestiya* woman again. The papers are going to be very late, she said. That was it. Something must be up. A little before six, I called Tom. "Better come down," I said. "The papers are very late. Something must be breaking."

A little before 8 A.M. we got the news. Stalin had suffered a cerebral hemorrhage. He was unconscious and partially paralyzed. His condition was critical. The attack had occurred, the announcement said, Sunday evening, March 1–2, "in his quarters in Moscow," that is, the

Kremlin. It was now Wednesday morning. The news had been held up more than forty-eight hours. It was obvious that the chances of Stalin's surviving the attack were slim. The medical bulletin was signed by ten physicians, headed by the new minister of health, A. F. Tretyakov.

Even now, as I pounded out my bulletins, sending them on at "urgent" rate (the London dictation facilities long since closed), I thought of the Doctors' Plot. Stalin had arrested the men who had looked after his life for so many years; now that life lay in the hands of new and unknown physicians. Was this just an ironic twist?

In this moment, I was filled with relief. The story I had been dreading had been an announcement about the Doctors' Plot, some new and terrifying revelation, an arrest of Politburo members or even of a correspondent, an announcement that the trial was about to open. Something of that kind. Now Stalin himself had been stricken. This had to be good news, although there remained the inescapable thought: Who might be charged with guilt in the death of Stalin?

The next two days run together in my mind. I *knew* Stalin was going to die. I knew that every word, every impression I could record would be part of history. I was in constant motion. I traveled Moscow from Khimki to Sokolniki. I talked to the Americans, the British and the French. I broke my rules and talked to Russians. They were very reserved. They did not know whether Stalin's illness was good or bad, and they were not going to discuss it with a foreigner. Occasional official bulletins were issued. Not very revealing. They showed that Stalin was alive, his condition grave, but little more. I had no more transmission problems. I could dictate anywhere I wanted—London, Paris, New York. Later I got a plaintive letter from Freedman, congratulating me on the coverage, on my insistence on better transmission facilities, apologizing for not setting them up more quickly and wondering how I had got "advance warning" on the big news. I could not bring myself to tell him that all I had had was a hunch based on the stories I had been sending him.

I went to the Central Synagogue and listened with pitying ears as Chief Rabbi Schliffer called on the congregation to pray for "our dear leader and teacher Josef Vissarionovich Stalin." He decreed a day of fasting and prayer. I went to the great Yelikhovsky Cathedral and there the Russian Orthodox patriarch Aleksei led the congregation in solemn prayer for Stalin. "All the Russian people and all people everywhere pray to God for the health of the sick one," he intoned. Acolytes held aloft the Bible in its golden case, and the patriarch, in gown of gold and purple, carrying his golden rod, passed through the multitude of kneeling believers. Hundreds of candles burned before the altars, young men and women joined with their elders in crossing themselves. Shudders ran down my back as I watched the people sink to their knees, chanting prayers for the man who had desecrated Orthodox churches by the hundred and unleashed an anti-Semitic terror second only to Hitler's. Back at the Metropol, I carefully read a volume of Walter Duranty's dispatches for his account of Lenin's last days, in January 1924. This, I felt, would be a guide to the ceremonials of 1953.

As I sat at my desk, my eye caught the carbon copy of a letter I had written a few days earlier, the last of scores to Stalin, small bets on the lottery of Letters to Stalin. Occasionally he responded to these, but never had he replied to one of mine. I had sent this letter the previous Thursday, inquiring if he wished to reply to a declaration by Eisenhower that he was ready "to travel halfway around the world" if a meeting with Stalin would serve the cause of peace and freedom. I had asked Stalin if he was willing to meet Ike, and if so, where. I had given the letter to my chauffeur to put in the Kremlin post box, that is, to hand to the sentry at the Troitsky Gate. At this moment, I thought, my letter lies on Stalin's desk, maybe at the top of the pile. It would have been put there Friday or Saturday. Perhaps he even read it before being stricken and set it aside, intending to return to it on Monday. I decided to write a little story about the letter and Stalin's method of responding to correspondents. I wrote another story, a reminiscence of my trip to Tbilisi in 1951, of Stalin's early literary career, his romantic poems. I quoted my favorite:

> The rosebud is opening
> And all around are bluebells;
> The iris, too, has awakened
> And all nod their heads
> In the breeze.
> The lark flies high in the sky,
> Chirping and singing.
> The nightingale with feeling and quiet voice sings:
> "May my dear country flourish,
> May you wed and be happy, my dear land of Iberia,
> May you wed yourselves to your studies
> And to your youth and your homeland."

Good God, I thought, as I typed the lines. What had happened to this naïve young poet in the years between nineteen and seventy-three; what had turned Dzhugashvili into the Stalin who had made a slaughterhouse of his country; what savage gods had possessed this Georgian youngster with his dark face, burning eyes and romantic spirit?

I typed the words out, picked up my dispatches, went over to the Central Telegraph Office and turned them in for censorship. Neither dispatch was ever cleared.

There were a few signs that Moscow was passing through a moment of high drama. More people than usual clustered around the pasted-up newspapers on the hoardings; queues gathered at the kiosks; the maids at the Metropol talked in little groups, quietly, not a word for foreign ears.

I spent the night at the telegraph office, waiting for the papers, but they had no more news. After two or three hours' sleep, I began my rounds on Thursday, March 5. Stalin had been ill, officially, since Sunday night, three and a half days. The crisis could not go on much longer. I was beginning to think that the measures to save his life were as much to prepare people for his death as to change his condition. Why had there been the long wait from Sunday night, when he was said to have suffered the attack, until 8 A.M. Wednesday, when the public announcement was made? My guess was that Stalin's "closest comrades in arms" were waiting to see how the illness was going to come out. If there was to be even a partial recovery, why say anything? Stalin would not thank his comrades for taking such authority. (I didn't know then that a few months before, he had told them that without him they could not survive. "You are blind like newborn kittens," he had said.) So they had waited, not twenty-four hours, but another twenty-four hours. When they put out that announcement at 8 A.M. Wednesday morning, *they knew what the end would be.* Stalin was dying and they wanted the country to know that and they were not now afraid that he would recover and send them to the Lubyanka cellars.

In the back of my mind was the thought that until this apparently fortuitous event, the Lubyanka cellars were where most of these good comrades had been headed.

All day March 5, I scurried about town—and waited. Members of the diplomatic corps this day went to the Foreign Office to express their sympathy over Stalin's illness. But not Jake Beam, my old friend from London, once Winant's secretary, now chargé d'affaires in Moscow. Charles Bohlen, another old friend, had been nominated as ambassador, filling the vacancy left by George Kennan. Bohlen had been given Soviet *agrément* but had not yet been confirmed by the Senate. In the interim, Beam was in charge. He was unable to join his

158

colleagues because he had no instructions from Washington and did not dare act on his own. It appeared that John Foster Dulles was not certain whether we should act like gentlemen or make a cheap political display by omitting this conventional gesture. Dulles was a great one for meaningless rudeness. A bit later, he demonstratively refused to shake Premier Zhou Enlai's hand at Geneva.

I had my attention fixed on the Kremlin, where I presumed from the communiqués that Stalin lay dying. Not until Khrushchev's "secret speech" in February 1956 was it confirmed that Stalin died not in the Kremlin but at his country villa at Kuntsevo, called Blizhny—"the near one," to distinguish it from other, more distant villas. The fact was that for several years, Stalin had lived at Kuntsevo, commuting to the Kremlin in the swift motor convoys that I so often saw speeding along the Arbat.

We got a bulletin on Stalin Thursday afternoon. His condition was said to be markedly worse. Believing he would die before the night was out, I was determined to get a beat on the story. I decided to establish headquarters in the telegraph office and stay there until Stalin died. These were the days before transistor radios. I had a big Hallicrafters shortwave receiver (once these remarkable machines were the trademarks of CIA station chiefs). Mine was battleship gray (I had got it from a departing naval officer) and was the size and shape of a steel filing drawer. It must have weighed forty pounds. About 7 P.M., I lugged this monster to the telegraph office and set up shop. None of my colleagues had arrived. I was alone and a bit nervous about bringing in my set. No one had done this before. I hadn't been there ten minutes when two uniformed soldiers carrying bayoneted rifles appeared. Oh, Lord, I thought, I'm going to be put under arrest on the night of Stalin's death! They were grim, tough-looking. They demanded to know what kind of a machine I had there. I told them it was a radio receiver. Probably they had been told by my bête noire, Clerk Vassileva, that it was a transmitter. They ordered me to get it out immediately. Radio sets were *vospreshiate*, forbidden. I removed it with alacrity. Fortunately, my car was outside. I gave the set to my chauffeur, Dimitry Grigorievich. He would be my listening post. I tuned the set to Tass dictation speed and told him to listen for news about Stalin. If he heard something, he was to come quietly, I emphasized, quietly, into the office and whisper in my ear. I was not going to risk my scoop for anything.

I went back to the cubicle. My colleagues began to gather. We glared at each other like angry dogs. There was a news bulletin on Stalin at

8:45 P.M. He was sinking rapidly. I got that off to London, then went for a quick auto tour around the Kremlin. There were many cars in the Red Square parking area; lights gleamed from the government buildings. The flag flew at full mast over the dome of the central palace. Lots of bustle. Later I wondered about this; that trip of mine around the Kremlin occurred just twenty minutes before Stalin's official death.

Back at the telegraph office, I wrote dispatches for use in the event of Stalin's death. I listened to the midnight news broadcast. Nothing. Then I drove around the Kremlin again. Some cars were still parked outside. But many offices now were dark. At the telegraph office, I telephoned London with some of my early copy and at 3:30 A.M. I again toured central Moscow. Everything was quiet; one government limousine drove into the Kremlin garage under the Moskva River bridge. There were three long black government limousines parked outside the Moscow City Soviet building, just a block up the street from the telegraph office. I got back to the telegraph office at five minutes to four.

A few seconds after four o'clock, my chauffeur slipped into the office and whispered in my ear. I quietly rose, my prepared cables on Stalin's death in hand, and gave them to the telegraph clerk. I also handed her my code message: "Freedman final expense account mailed last night regards Salisbury."

Before I could get back to my typewriter, bedlam burst loose. The agency men filed their flashes, shouted for telephone connections to London and dashed into telephone booths to await their calls. I had asked the operator to get me both London and Paris, but I was relying on Paris. There were only two lines normally to London and the operator automatically gave priority to the agency men. The shouting and excitement (and my code message) all went for nothing. The censors refused to pass any copy whatever. The telephone operator sat with hands folded, paying no attention to the shouting. Within a few minutes, a sleepy electrician in overalls appeared. As I watched, he ripped off the back of the telephone switchboard and yanked out the main cable. Moscow was broadcasting news of Stalin's death in a score of languages. But the Moscow correspondents could not transmit a word. I slipped outside to a pay telephone booth, put a ten-kopeck piece in the slot and called Jake Beam, waking him up at Spaso House. "He died at 9:50 P.M. last night, Jake," I said. "Thanks," Jake replied, and hung up.

I stood by until 5:30 A.M., then I went out for the fourth time that evening and toured the center of the city. All was normal. The red stars glimmered like jewels in the Kremlin towers, the Spassky bell tower chimed the hours, the traffic police in their warm uniform greatcoats and sheepskin collars stood at their posts under the brilliant lights of the central squares. The lights flashed green-amber-red, green-amber-red. There was no traffic. It was a chilly night. The streets were clean of snow, except for a light dusting earlier in the evening. Just as I returned to the telegraph office, I saw a small convoy of trucks coming down Gorky Street. I wrote more copy, turned it in and sent angry notes to the censor, demanding its release. Nothing happened. The greatest story in the world—we had it in our hands but might as well have been manacled to the cellar walls of the Lubyanka. I almost died of frustration. The other correspondents alternately shouted, faces red, at the impassive women clerks or slumped into despondency.

One more time I walked out of the telegraph office. The golden hands of the clock in the Spassky tower had moved to six o'clock. Moscow was stirring. Buses were running. Traffic was moving. People had begun to appear. I drove down Gorky Street, around the Kremlin and through the big squares. More and more convoys of trucks were entering the heart of Moscow, mustard-green troop trucks, with soldiers sitting cross-armed in rows, twenty-two to a truck, blue-and-red-capped NKVD troops, the special troops of the Ministry of Internal Affairs, whose camps ringed Moscow in the little villages just beyond the city limits. The convoys crisscrossed the central squares. I was momentarily puzzled and wondered if a coup d'etat might be under way. I did not pursue my thought. I was hurrying back to the telegraph office to see whether the censorship was still sitting on the story. Just before eight o'clock, the dam broke, our copy cleared, telephone calls came through. While my colleagues fought over the London lines, Paris came up and I was dictating my dispatches just after midnight in New York. The story moved forward crisply and clearly. I had written in laconic terms. I did not want to give the censor any excuse for holding it up.

By the time I emerged from the telegraph office, the city was bustling. The *dvorniki*, the building porters, were putting up black rosettes and draping the buildings in red, placing black-bordered red flags in the stanchions. At the Hall of Columns, the old Noblemen's Club, workmen were stringing red and black bunting and hoisting into place an enormous gilt-framed portrait of Stalin. Here Stalin's body would lie at rest for the formal mourning, displayed in the beautiful old hall, with its white columns and crystal chandeliers, where the nobility

161

had danced their quadrilles. Here, one by one, Stalin had brought the Old Bolsheviks—Kamenev, Zinoviev, Bukharin, Radek and the rest— put them on trial and then sent them up Lubyanka Hill to meet their end with a bullet from a Nagan pistol in the head. How apt, I thought, that Stalin would lie in rest in this hall. One way or the other, they all met their end in this glittering Romanov souvenir. The Revolution had been in power for thirty-five years and it had not yet created its own settings for the rituals of life and death.

I walked up past the Lenin Museum, once the City Duma, and entered Red Square through the opening left by the destruction of the Iberian Chapel. On the wall was now inscribed: "Religion is the opiate of the masses." I wondered. In Red Square I saw a sight I had never before seen in Moscow. A crowd of two or three thousand people stood in a cigar-shaped body opposite the Spassky Gate. They were waiting for Stalin's body to be brought out, presuming, as I did, that he had died there. Never had I seen a crowd like this collect of its own volition in Russia. In fact, it was against the law. Freedom of assembly was not among the rights guaranteed by the Stalin constitution.

I joined the throng and found it a startling experience, Stalin dead only a few hours and already people assembling on their own—no orders, no agitprop. They stood passively, not speaking, waiting. Here and there an old peasant woman sobbed a bit, the conventional symbol of mourning.

As I waited, I tried to sense the mood of the crowd. Was this a harbinger? I was not prepared to make a judgment. I did not think the people could yet absorb the fact of Stalin's death, of his absence from their life. In this I was right. Many older people went to their graves never having emerged from Stalin's penumbra. He was a true tyrant, and even in death he held the people in his granite grip.

Now the security troops were everywhere. They were moving in from all sides. Gorky Street was thick with them and traffic was trickling to an end. The autobuses halted. Trucks and passenger cars disappeared. Tanks emerged at the head of Gorky Street. I could hear the rumble of their motors. No regular army troops could be seen. Just the blue-and-red-capped security men. I began to see what they were doing. They were placing a collar around the throat of Moscow, gradually moving in closer and closer, shutting off the circulation of traffic and blocking the streets with barricades of trucks and tanks. Now they began to enter Red Square, just a thin line at first, halting people from entering, then slowly but irresistibly—no force, no

162

commands—simply advancing and pressing the crowd back, back out of the square.

I retreated into Sverdlovsk Square, past the metro station, toward the Metropol. I understood now what was happening. Using the operational plan for traditional lying-in-state ceremonies, the NKVD was sealing off the center of the city. I had been through this many times on the occasion of other state funerals. The Metropol was within these lines and from my office I had a view of the Hall of Columns, the Moskva Hotel, past the Lenin Museum and the State Historical Museum toward the Kremlin itself.

My car happened to be within this inner circle, parked beside the Metropol. By dint of brass and patience, I was able to drive from the Metropol through Pushkin Street almost to the back entrance of the telegraph office. I did not have to run back and forth, dodge under trucks and tanks, argue with soldiers and officers, to get through the barricade, one more proof of the rule that if you are resolute, if you act with authority, gall and blarney, you can whisk through almost any security barricade.

Again and again I moved within the heart of the heart of the Moscow security zone. I sauntered into Red Square, the square sealed off, not a person there except a work detail chiseling Stalin's name above the Lenin Mausoleum in preparation for his interment there the next day, guards and soldiers all over the place. I walked up to the tomb as though I was conducting an inspection for the Central Committee, observed what was going on and walked out without a challenge by a guard. It never entered their heads that anyone would dare enter this sanctuary without authority. It was much the same when I left the Metropol early Sunday morning and made my way by foot through one barricade after another, walking with an air of authority past the soldiers huddling around their bonfires, and found that not only were Red Square and the center in the hands of security troops, but the whole inner ring, the "White Stone City," and beyond that the "garden ring" of boulevards. I walked to the Kursk railroad station, intending to take the electric train to Saltikovka and see what was happening in the countryside. I found some angry Muscovites reading a hand-lettered notice. A regular train service was running *out* of Moscow. But no trains were coming *into* Moscow. I knew that tens of thousands of Russians had clambered aboard trains to attend Lenin's funeral. This was not going to be permitted for Stalin's funeral. *No one could enter the city.* Moscow and all access to it was in control of the security forces. It suddenly struck me that Moscow was held by Lavrenti P. Beria. These were his troops, his tanks, his trucks, his guns. He held the Kremlin within his power. I was astonished. No one else knew this, I felt sure, no foreigner, none of the U.S. military attachés who spent so much time assiduously counting telegraph poles on the rail lines. They had not had the gumption or the imagination to get out into Moscow and have a look at what was happening. (When I first gave a detailed report of all this in my articles in the *Times* in the autumn of 1954, after leaving my Moscow post, the State Department and military were amazed and, characteristically, inclined to dismiss my report as of no significance.) Alas, I could find no way of reporting this development. The censors killed every attempt, even when I praised the efficient "traffic" control of the police, the skill with which they avoided jams in the heart of the city and the special measures they had taken to handle the hundreds of thousands of mourners who were moving past Stalin's bier in the Hall of Columns, twelve abreast, day and night, in a column that I estimated would number in the millions. (I did not know then but was not surprised to learn years later from the poet Yevgeny Yevtushenko, who had witnessed it, that in an inner courtyard through which these lines snaked, something went wrong. Before the police could halt the inexorable advance of the column, twenty or thirty people had been crushed, simply squeezed down and trampled to death—not so bad a scandal as that which attended the coronation of Czar Nicholas II, when hundreds died in the throng assembled in Khodinka fields to receive the beer mugs and scarves that were the Czar's coronation gifts to his people, but the same kind of tragedy, the product of careless planning, poor police work and an unconcern for human lives.)

From the first announcement of Stalin's illness, editorials stressed "vigilance," warned against "panic and disarray." I saw no signs of "panic." The theme of vigilance echoed that which had resounded so loudly as the drums beat over the Doctors' Plot. So far as I or anyone knew, the affair of the Kremlin physicians was still on the agenda. The scenario might take a few new turns, but there was no sign it had been junked, and in fact there soon appeared in the kiosks a new red-jacketed pamphlet, called "Vigilance," which cited the Doctors' Plot as the basis for today's need of vigilance.

On the surface, power seemed to have flowed smoothly to the triumvirate of Malenkov, Beria and Molotov. Bulganin and Voroshilov were prominent, Khrushchev in the shadows. One new player turned up—Marshal Georgi K. Zhukov. He emerged from rustication as commander of troops in Odessa. Magically he was back in Moscow, deputy defense minister beside Marshal Vasilevsky, and in one of the pictures at Stalin's bier, Zhukov, Sokolovsky and Timoshenko peered out from behind Malenkov, Beria, Molotov and Company, as though they were the men who were manipulating the whole show. This picture was designed to send a message. The military, and Zhukov in particular, had played a role in the March events and would go on playing a role.

Stalin was buried on the morning of Monday, March 9, in Red Square. Three men spoke—Malenkov, Beria and Molotov. Malenkov, a middle-aged fat boy, was surprisingly appealing. He spoke beautiful, cultured Russian, his words were mild, he seemed to be promising a new, intelligent regime. Beria was ingratiating and condescending to his companions. After all, he held them in the grip of his security troops. Molotov impressed me most. His voice broke repeatedly, his face was white as paper. I jotted in my notebook: "Such sorrow in his voice!" Molotov alone of those present conveyed to me a feeling of loss. His words, as always, were dull metal. There was no poet in Molotov. I knew that his wife was in Stalin's camps. I did not know she had been in prison since 1949, that Molotov since then had been barred from Stalin's inner circle, excluded from the midnight drinking parties at Blizhny. I suspected that Stalin had marked Molotov as a target of his forthcoming phantasmagoria. Molotov knew all that. Yet his voice broke again and again, and he was close to tears as he spoke of his tyrant master— Molotov, whose nickname had been *kameny zad*, stone bottom.

At 11:50 A.M., Molotov concluded. The Red Army band of three hundred struck up Chopin's "Funeral March." The leaders, Malenkov, Beria, Molotov and the rest, descended from atop the mausoleum. The black and red coffin of Stalin rested at the portals of the tomb. There was a moment of silence. Then the hands of the Spassky clock pointed straight up. The tower bells pealed and the steel salute guns of the Kremlin sounded in counterpoint. Malenkov, Molotov, Beria and the others lifted the coffin of Stalin and carried it inside. Every factory whistle in Moscow screamed. The toll of bells halted at twelve, but the guns slammed on to thirty. The factory whistles fell silent. All over Russia, every moving vehicle halted—every train, every tram, every truck. There was total silence. As I watched, a single sparrow left the Kremlin wall and swooped over the mausoleum. Then the voice of General Sinitsin, commander of the Moscow garrison, thundered out, echoing against the gray walls of the still shuttered merchants' arcade across the square. The thousands of troops began to mark time, their leather boots raising a surf of sound. The band struck up Glinka's "Hail to the Czar" (comfortably retitled "Hail to the Russian People"). The red flag over the domed Kremlin palace slowly rose to full mast.

Notebook in hand, red press pass and passport clutched in the other, I slipped out of the stand beside Lenin's tomb, into the square jammed with marching troops, shoulder to shoulder, and running beside and against their stream of movement, I began to race to the Central Telegraph Office. I ran head up, eyes on the alert for any obstacle, moving on the flank of the troops, darting around their officers, past the State Historical Museum, out of the square, across the endless expanse of Manezhny Square, wider than three football fields, past the Moskva Hotel, shouldering my way through denser and denser concentrations of troops, on to the north side of the square, up to the great barricade of trucks that blocked the throat of Gorky Street at the National Hotel, then under the greasy truck bodies, scrambling up and over the next truck barricade, to the startled shouts of the lounging troops, down the far side, plunging like a football back through the knots of soldiers, stumbling now and panting like a hound. I raced up the incline of Gorky Street, past the shuttered vegetable shop, the shuttered antiquarian bookstore, the theater, on toward the telegraph office, encountering a truck barricade nearly three trucks high. I squirmed through and over it and staggered into Entrance 11, up the narrow flight of steps in the now deserted press cubicle, calling to the operator to put me through to London, the line coming up miraculously fast, and still panting, I told London to advise New York instantly: Stalin was buried; release my advance dispatch and new copy was coming. New York was holding the final edition until 6 A.M. for Stalin's funeral.

And so Stalin was buried in the mausoleum beside Lenin. He was dead, his era ended. Something new lay ahead. Next morning as I walked back to the Metropol in the hours before dawn, having filed my last dispatches about Stalin's funeral and the new epoch, I passed the Hall of Columns. Men were up on ladders, working under the ghostly blue of a carbon arc floodlight, taking down the sixty-foot portrait of Stalin. It slipped as it came down, and canted into the street at an oblique angle.

"Careful there," one shouted.

"*Nichevo*," another said. "Never mind. They'll not be needing this one again."

## Chapter 14

# Nikita Sergeevich Khrushchev

There is no way in which I can pin down Nikita Sergeevich Khrushchev on paper. Try as I will, the moment I type the words, he bursts off the pages and plunges into life, hands flying, jaws working, little pig eyes darting, snub nose poking into everything, a bundle of curiosity as insatiable as the Monkey King in the Chinese fairy tale. Khrushchev looked like a butterball on short legs, but I never encountered such compact energy in human form. He was not very tall, probably five feet five. None of the men in Stalin's Politburo were tall, Stalin was short. Tall men made him nervous. Khruschev was fond of referring to himself as a barefoot boy from Kalinovka in the Kursk *gubernia* on the northern fringe of the Ukraine.

I spent an hour sunning myself in the quiet courtyard outside the Presidium offices in the Kremlin on the morning of July 26, 1959, while Richard M. Nixon, then Vice-President, paid a ceremonial call on Khrushchev. It was supposed to last fifteen minutes. When Nixon emerged, he looked pale and shaken. A year passed before I learned what had happened. Khrushchev didn't like Nixon, never had, never would. He was tolerating Nixon's trip to Russia because he wanted to make a return trip to the U.S.A. The meeting had not been very agreeable.

Later I heard Khrushchev in an argument with Spiros Skouras, chief of MGM studios, at a banquet in Los Angeles. Skouras told how he had been a shepherd boy in Greece, so poor he could not even afford shoes. Now he was head of a vast film industry. His studio employed five thousand—or whatever the figure was—workers. He had reached the top.

Khrushchev paid tribute to Skouras, then turned to his own career. Also a barefoot shepherd boy, he had not had to leave his own country. Right there in Russia, he had risen to head a whole nation, with 230,000,000 people.

167

I spent a lot of time with Khrushchev. I got to know him as I did the American politicians I covered in Washington or on presidential campaigns, and in much the same way—on the road, traveling with him, getting up in the morning before he did and sticking to him until he went to bed, at midnight or later. On a campaign you see a man in constantly shifting crises, unexpected encounters. After two or three weeks, you know each other pretty well. Perhaps I got to know Adlai Stevenson or Richard Nixon or Jack Kennedy better than I did Khrushchev. But I am not so sure.

Khrushchev would have been a successful politician in the United States had he been born there, just as Mikoyan would have been a successful businessman. I think Khrushchev would in fact have been a better politician in the United States. He reminded me of Huey Long. When I knew Huey, he was twenty years younger than Khrushchev. Both men had the same shoebutton noses, round faces and ovoid shapes. Both were born rabble-rousers, born actors. Khrushchev mustered tears in the corners of his little eyes when he was denied permission to go to Disneyland, and you could see the fuses of nuclear rockets sparking when he was angered by the mayor of Los Angeles. Put him on the barnyard trail in Iowa and he was unbeatable. He had the common touch. He didn't need media consultants to tell him how to behave in Roswell Garst's corn fields. He was pure corn himself.

I was with Khrushchev on the afternoon when he visited the American exhibition in Sokolniki Park in Moscow in August 1959 as the guest of Richard Nixon. Khrushchev was on guard. When Nixon took him to a TV studio to demonstrate color videotape with instant replay, Khrushchev was sure Nixon wanted to use the tape for some nasty stunt back in the U.S.A. When Donald Kendall, head of Pepsi-Cola, tried to get Khrushchev to taste his product, he refused (although Mikoyan and the rest of the Politburo accepted). When Nixon escorted Khrushchev into the American Home exhibition, Khrushchev was determined to waltz right through, to demonstrate his contempt for American "propaganda." Nixon tried to lure him to the model kitchen, but Khrushchev wasn't buying it. "We've got all that in our kitchens," he said. "I've got everything in my home that you have there." But then his eye caught a glimpse of the shiny new garbage disposal, the food blender, Lord knows what, and he was lost. His legs steered him over for a closer look and the famous "kitchen debate" was on—a debate that almost elected Nixon

168

President in 1960 and made the reputation of Bill Safire, the PR man for the exhibit, who kindly lifted up the rope and let me sit on the kitchen floor at the feet of the champions of American Capitalism and Soviet Communism, enabling me to record almost all they said for posterity. It was a fine scoop and I've been in Safire's debt ever since.

I saw Khrushchev's curiosity lead him into a tour of the beautiful IBM building in San Jose, California, as the guest of Thomas J. Watson, Jr., who had no notion he was doing something revolutionary. The IBM facility was a fine example of a modern technological plant, an endless succession of cinder-block halls, one blending into another on a single level. Khrushchev started at the executive suite and moved into the general office section, along the assembly lines, into the shipping department, the warehouses, all the same building, all the walls pastel greens or pastel purples or pastel blues, all wall-to-wall carpeting, the same gentle piped-over background music, no lines of division, you couldn't tell whether you were in the director's office or the assembly line by the shape, contour and ambience of the structure, the same casually dressed men and women whether they were vice-presidents or on-line workers. Halfway through the tour, I caught a glance exchanged between Khrushchev and one of his aides. *They* knew what Watson was showing them, even if Watson didn't. I knew too, because I had read my Marx. I knew that the great goal of Communism, and hence of the Soviet system, was to abolish the distinction between blue and white collar, between physical and mental labor, to wipe out the historic divisions between the "toiling" class and the "exploiting" class. I had been in hundreds of Soviet factories and knew their grim, back-breaking nature. The distinctions were far from gone in the Soviet Union. A blue-collar family would make any sacrifice to lift its sons and daughters out of the "toiling" ranks and into the white-collar bureaucracy. But here in America, in the citadel of capitalism, the historic distinctions of blue and white collar had been obliterated so completely that there wasn't a person in the IBM plant who knew what they were. No one in the IBM plant or among the Americans accompanying Khrushchev had any notion that they were walking through a chapter in Marx's forecast of the future.

That was the nuance that underlay the quick glance passed between Khrushchev and his aide, and it told me more about the

169

Soviet Union and the distance that separated it from its aspirations than a thousand words could.

Capitalism had achieved Marx's goal and didn't know it; Communism was so far distant from it that Khrushchev didn't dare talk about it.

Khrushchev's boyhood had been as close to poverty as his arguments with Nixon and Skouras suggested. He grew up in and near the mining and steel complex of Yuzovka, a Russification of Hughes, the name of the original Welsh entrepreneurs of this Donbas works. There was lots of foreign capital—English, French, Belgian and German—in the Donbas. Khrushchev, as I often heard him say, got no formal education in his childhood, but he worked for French, Belgian and German firms. Most of his education came after the Revolution, in *rab-fak*, workers' factory classes. He once said sadly that he was the only member of his family who couldn't speak English. As a young man, when he heard people in his boardinghouse talking about ballet, he didn't know, he said, whether it was a fish or a fowl, something to eat or to drink. When he read Zola's *Germinal*, he thought it was set in Yuzovka, the conditions were so similar to those he endured when he was growing up.

He was born in 1894 and from the beginning was tough, earthy, poking his nose into everything in response to his fierce curiosity.

Looking back on Khrushchev, it is difficult for me to see how he survived under Stalin. True, he was canny. He knew how to play the fool, and as he once said, when Stalin told him to dance the *gopak*—a Ukrainian folk dance—he danced the *gopak*. And when Stalin called him a *khokol*, a rude word for "Ukrainian," Khrushchev did not grimace. He jumped to obey Stalin's whim. He played the fool and knew he was playing the fool and knew why he was doing it—to survive. As he was to recall after March 5, 1953: "Sometimes a man goes to see Stalin in the Kremlin and he does not know whether or not he will come home again." Khrushchev always came home.

I saw a good deal of Nina Petrovna Khrushcheva. She accompanied Khrushchev on his American tour, and the more I saw of her, the more I respected this warm, intelligent, shrewd, motherly former schoolteacher. She was the sheet anchor that kept Khrushchev's bark steady.

In the great family crises, it was Nina Petrovna who came to the fore. After Khrushchev was deposed, on October 12, 1964, she was seriously concerned. Khrushchev fell into deep depression. Nothing captured his interest. For weeks he dissolved in pathetic tears. She it was who arranged for the purchase of a German Leica and got him interested in taking pictures. She it was who had a greenhouse constructed and got Nikita Sergeevich to grow hothouse tomatoes and cucumbers, and she it was who managed to win him over to the notion of dictating his memoirs, a task facilitated when the family gave him a German tape recorder. It took Khrushchev some time to start using it. The family plied him with questions and insisted that he dictate the answers. This was how he fell into the habit of sitting on a bench in the garden (the noise of birds and of planes—the villa is not far from Vnukovo airport—is loud and clear on the tapes) and dictating his memories, which eventually were fashioned into two volumes edited by Strobe Talbot, a Time-Life correspondent. No one who knew Khrushchev can listen to those tapes, now at the Columbia University library, without an intense nostalgia. Here is the Khrushchev we knew so well, talking in his familiar style, grumbling that he doesn't feel so well this morning, wondering where he left off in yesterday's dictation, gradually warming up to his task and beginning to talk in the salty, frequently repetitive style to which we became so accustomed during his ascendancy.

The tale of how the tapes reached Time-Life has never been told, but I think I have pieced together most of it. Aleksei Adzhubei, Khrushchev's son-in-law and onetime editor of *Komsomolskaya Pravda* and later of *Izvestiya*, lost his post at the same time as his father-in-law, but he did not lose his connections with Komsomol leaders, some of whom had gone into the security apparatus.

I believe that the Khrushchev family sanitized the tapes, removing materials that would obviously cause state problems. Possibly Khrushchev refused to dictate material on high-level party matters. Certainly no such material is present in the tapes that reached the West. I think the family and Khrushchev wanted the materials to be published. Khrushchev probably had nothing to do with the complicated mechanism by which they were transmitted to the West, but I do not believe he objected to it and I know that the family had no criticism of the channels that were employed.

What was the route? I believe that Adzhubei played the key role. I think he turned the tapes over to one of his old friends in the police apparatus. The police may have made excisions in the tapes (careful examination of them makes it clear that whatever may have been taken out, nothing was added; Khrushchev's voice and manner are clear and unmistakable). The materials were then put into the hands of Victor Louis, a middleman-agent for the KGB who has often been used to convey materials (for profit) from Moscow to the West.

The first time I met Victor Louis, in 1959, he was just beginning his career. He had, I later learned from a friend who had been imprisoned with him, served a term in the camps, where he quickly acquired a cushy job in the commissary. His surname came from a French father who somehow became a Soviet citizen—so he said. When Victor emerged from the camps after Stalin's death, his first job was with the Moscow patriarchy. In 1959, he was a correspondent for the *London Evening News* and he had married a young Englishwoman named Jennifer. He invited me to his apartment in the new Cheryomukha quarter on Moscow's outskirts, very fashionable. Ostensibly, Victor wanted my advice on a motorists' travel guide which he and Jennifer had written after making an auto tour of Russia the previous summer. "You can imagine how many times we were arrested by local police," Victor said solemnly.

After we had talked about the guide, Victor rose with something of a flourish and started his record player. He pulled a fat sheaf of papers from his drawer and asked me in a conspiratorial voice whether I was interested in the transcript of the Writers' Union plenary session that had expelled Pasternak. He was greatly disappointed when I said I wasn't interested (I knew Louis had sold the transcript to *Time* magazine a few days earlier; I wasn't going to buy a secondhand pup). He switched the subject to art. It was a moment when dissident artists had just appeared on the scene. I knew that Victor had introduced Western buyers to the artists (who were then often called in by the police). I didn't show much interest, so he brought out a portfolio of gouaches by an artist named Rabin, who was much in vogue among the diplomatic colony. When I didn't want to buy a Rabin, Louis was stunned. "You must have a Rabin," he said. "Everyone has one. I'll give you one." Hurriedly he shuffled out a half-dozen dreary-looking gouaches. "Here, take your choice." I selected one of the least obnoxious. Louis beamed. "That's a fine one," he said, examining it. Then he hastily pulled it back. "My God!" he said. "He forgot to sign it. You can't have an unsigned

172

Rabin." He took out a pencil stub, wet it with his tongue and put a neat initial "R" in the corner.

Later Louis and I exchanged postcards from exotic parts of the world. He sent me one from Taipei. I sent him one from Lhasa. Once he sent me a series of letters. The first was on stationery imprinted: "On Her Majety's Service: MI6." The next letterhead was boldly embossed: "CIA." The third and last: "KGB." He had picked them up, I deduced, in a novelty shop, perhaps in London's Soho. The letters were not, I was amused to see, mailed from Moscow. Victor had got someone to post them in Helsinki. I fancy he did not feel certain that the KGB would share his sense of humor.

Not all of Louis's gambits were so innocent. He was given a manuscript of Svetlana Alliluyeva's *Twenty Letters to a Friend*, which she had left behind in Moscow. He attempted to sell it in the West in an effort to cut into her royalties. He obtained an album of Svetlana's personal photographs which had also been left behind in Moscow, and sold them in the West. He made similar efforts to sell materials about Aleksandr Solzhenitsyn. He wrote a highly tendentious but revealing book which, in effect, laid out the rationale for a Soviet "liberating" attack on China. To Louis's outrage, the publishers commissioned me to do an introduction that would explain exactly who he was and what he was up to.

The motives of the police in the Alliluyeva, Solzhenitsyn and China cases are obvious. But motivation is not so clear in the case of Khrushchev. If the caper was designed to destroy Khrushchev's reputation in the Soviet Union, it seems redundant. He had already lost his constituency there.

Nina Petrovna's strong hand was revealed in another family crisis. In the summer of 1969, Yelena, the youngest of the Khrushchev daughters, fell ill and the Kremlin physicians pronounced her dying of a medically irreversible disease, a rare form of cancer.

Nina Petrovna refused to accept this verdict. She set in motion an elaborate scheme to obtain for Yelena the best American treatment. A friend of the family who was attending a scientific meeting in Copenhagen took out a précis of the case and passed it to an American colleague, asking him to seek the top American specialist. The American brought the description back to the United States, where a friend put him in touch with Dr. A. McGee Harvey at Johns Hopkins. After two or three mysterious meetings with a first secretary of the Soviet embassy in Washington, Dr. Harvey agreed to go to Moscow. Until the night before he and his wife left New York, Dr. Harvey did not know the identity of his patient. The Harveys were met at Moscow airport by an Intourist representative and a pleasant, quiet, intelligent young scientist wearing Chekhovian steel-rimmed glasses—Sergei Khrushchev, whose identity was not known by the Intourist guide.

The Harveys were put up at the National Hotel. It was the beginning of November, cold and wintry weather. The first two days were spent in sightseeing, Sergei accompanying them despite the protests of the Intourist guide. On the second day, a Sunday, it was arranged to drive to the old Yusupov estate, about fifteen miles from town. There was a heavy snowfall and the guide didn't want to go, but Sergei insisted. They drove over slippery roads, and made a quick tour of the Yusupov palace. Then, leaving the guide, they got into Sergei's car and he drove them to the Khrushchev villa at nearby Petrovo Dalnye. They whizzed past the guards, through a gate in a green-painted fence, believing the guards did not spot them—probably a mistaken impression.

That snowy Sunday was a delight for the Harveys and for the Khrushchevs as well. Nikita and Nina Petrovna greeted the American couple at the door. Khrushchev was seventy-five then, in apparent good health, and in fine spirits. The table was set for dinner. Most of the Khrushchev family, including grandchildren, were present and there was a holiday atmosphere. Nina Petrovna and Nikita Sergeevich took their guests for a tour of the house. Khrushchev proudly displayed the cucumbers and tomatoes that he had raised in his hothouse.

This was to be Khrushchev's last meeting with Americans—and possibly his last with any foreigners. He talked freely and easily, in his old style, of his life and career. He left no doubt of his continuing distaste for Richard Nixon, "a typical middle-class American businessman" (this was, of course, nearly four years before Watergate). He had warm words for Eisenhower, a man for whom he professed deep admiration, and for President Kennedy. He thought Kennedy had been inept at their Vienna confrontation, but believed he was learning fast, and he did not conceal his sorrow at Kennedy's untimely death.

As for his own political career, he dated the beginning of his fall to the shooting down of the American U-2 over Sverdlovsk on May

Day, 1960. Never again, he insisted, did he regain full control over the government; he had to share power with those who believed that "only military force" would enable Moscow to deal with Washington.

Not everyone, myself included, would agree with Khrushchev's personal evaluation of how he lost power. I have spoken with men close to the Politburo, who challenge Khrushchev's analysis. They believe he lost his power because of overconfidence, a tendency to overplay his hand, the consistency with which he denigrated his fellow Politburo members (except for Mikoyan), his misjudgment of the character of men whom he advanced to high office, in particular, Frol Kozlov and KGB chief Semichastny, and his bad relations with the military. The military never forgave him for forcing the retirement of thousands of officers to half-pay pensions, with loss of cars, chauffeurs, aides, and perquisites.

But Khrushchev's version may, after all, be correct. The late Llewellyn Thompson, then U.S. ambassador in Moscow and, in a curious way, a man closer to Khrushchev than even Khrushchev's Politburo associates, once told me that on the day the U-2 incident was announced, he went to the Czech embassy for their national reception. The whole Politburo was there. Khrushchev took him aside and said, "I must talk with you." The two men went to a little side room. Khrushchev told Thompson: "This U-2 thing has put me in a terrible spot. You have to get me off it." Thompson promised that he would do everything he could. They rejoined the reception. Several Soviet marshals came up to Thompson, one after the other, each with the same message: We want to smooth this over. We don't want any war with the U.S.A. Thompson did his best to pour oil on the waters, but when Eisenhower insisted on taking personal responsibility for the overflight, the fate of the Eisenhower-Khrushchev summit in Paris and the Eisenhower visit to Russia was sealed.

The day after his dinner with the Khrushchevs, Dr. Harvey went to the Kremlin hospital. He examined Yelena and met with her doctors. He was, he thought, the first American physician to serve as a consultant in this hospital, reserved for the highest circles in Russia. He concluded that the diagnosis in Yelena's case was incorrect, and that she was suffering from a rare allergy. Nina Petrovna insisted that he write a detailed report on the disease and its treatment so there

175

could be no possible confusion after he left. (In spite of the new regimen recommended by Dr. Harvey, Yelena died about two years later.)

The Harveys spent a week in Moscow. Sergei took them to the Zagorsk monastery, where the patriarch of the Orthodox Church presented them with a lovely icon. Nina Petrovna gave them an old samovar, a family heirloom. Sergei tried to get them tickets to watch the November 7 parade from Red Square, but he was not successful and they viewed it from outside the National Hotel in his company and that of the patriarch's physician.

Hardly had the party returned to their hotel suite than ten plainclothes security agents burst in. Everyone was ordered to remain exactly where he was. A three-hour examination ensued. The tiles from the bathroom were removed, electrical connections examined, walls tapped; the carpet was lifted, plumbing disconnected, furniture pulled apart. Mrs. Harvey was made to strip by two women operatives. Toothpaste was squeezed from tubes, every article of luggage was gone through, pockets were turned out. After three hours, a man whom Sergei identified as a deputy chief of the KGB arrived and the process was repeated for another hour.

The only explanation offered by the security detail was that the Harveys had entered the country for a purpose other than that described on their visas. The security men took away the icon, saying it could not be exported from the country. They also removed eight rolls of exposed color film. They said they would develop them, and if they were merely snapshots, return them. A lengthy "protocol" was written. Dr. Harvey insisted that every detail be put down. Later the film was brought back, except for one roll. At first Dr. Harvey thought it contained the pictures he had taken at the Khrushchev villa, but they were intact and he decided that the missing roll had simply been spoiled in development.

Sergei was mortified. He apologized repeatedly, but had no explanation to offer. Next day at customs, there was another fine-tooth examination, and the samovar was taken away. At length, the Harveys were permitted to board their plane, the last passengers to climb the staircase.

A couple of months later, Dr. Harvey had a call from *Life* magazine. The editors had acquired some photos of the Harveys' visit with the Khrushchevs. Harvey thought the pictures must be from his missing roll of film, but they were black-and-white shots made by one of the Khrushchev family. They had obviously made their way to *Life* by the same route as the tapes of the Khrushchev memoirs which *Life* had acquired earlier.

What Dr. Harvey told me of his adventure reinforced my belief that Khrushchev lived at the center of police intrigue, with more than one faction of KGB operatives active in the shadows around him. The extraordinary actions in the Harveys' hotel suite, conducted in Sergei's presence, seem to have been designed to ferret out any message or manuscript (the uncut version of his memoirs, for example) that Khrushchev might have entrusted to the Harveys to take to the West. They also demonstrated to Sergei the lengths to which the security apparatus was prepared to go to prevent the Khrushchev family from establishing *independent* contact with the West.

The fact that the black-and-white photos of the Harveys' Sunday with Khrushchev turned up in *Life*'s hands demonstrated that someone within the Khrushchev family was doing business-as-usual with the police. I think that individual was Adzhubei.

I believe Nikita Sergeevich Khrushchev was a flawed politician. Any politician growing up under Stalin was bound to be seriously damaged. The important thing about Khrushchev was not his flaws but his virtues. He was a bit like Fiorello La Guardia. He committed terrible blunders. But when he saw what he had done, he had the courage to admit it.

In 1962, he paid a visit to a famous exhibition of works of Moscow's young artists at the Menazhny Gallery, a visit organized by reactionaries to turn him against the young avant-garde by offending his middlebrow taste. A couple of months later, at a meeting of artists and writers, Khrushchev said to the sculptor Ernst Neizvestny, whose shoulders are slightly thickened by war wounds: "Only the grave will correct the hunchback." To which Yevgeny Yevtushenko interjected: "Surely, Nikita Sergeevich, we have come a long way from the time when only the grave straightens out the hunchback. Really, there are other ways." And he spoke of two Cuban partisans, one a constructivist, one a conventional painter, who died side by side fighting for the Revolution. Khrushchev joined those in the hall in applauding Yevtushenko.

After he retired, Khrushchev invited Neizvestny to his dacha, and apologized for his words. Following his death—at his specific wish—

his widow commissioned Neizvestny to design the simple monument that stands at his grave in Novodeviche cemetery.

In his retirement, Khrushchev for the first time had leisure to read. He read everything Mikhail Sholokhov had written. Sholokhov had been his literary hero. When he finished his reading, he told his family: "The son of a bitch! He's written only one novel, *The Quiet Don.*"

When Pasternak's *Doctor Zhivago* appeared in the West and Pasternak was awarded the Nobel Prize, Khrushchev led the attack that resulted in Pasternak's expulsion from the Writers' Union.

Now, in his enforced leisure, Khrushchev read *Doctor Zhivago.* When he had finished, he burst out in a stream of Russian *mat'*, that primitive Russian profanity constructed around the mother oath.

"Damn it," he said (his actual words were more bawdy). "Those bastards simply fooled me. They told me this was a terrible book, an anti-Soviet work, that it befouled our Revolution. They were just lying. There is nothing wrong with *Doctor Zhivago.* Sure, we might have cut out four or five lines—so what? To create an international furor over this book and hold us up to ridicule and denunciation all over the world—it is just impossible."

He blamed himself and his lack of time. "I never should have paid attention to them." His family was kind. No one mentioned that when the Pasternak affair arose in 1956 and 1957, they had urged him to read the book and he had waved them away.

The fact was, of course, that Pasternak, Neizvestny and the rest of the intelligentsia were caught up in a political backlash that followed Khrushchev's attack on Stalin.

One of Khrushchev's strengths was old-fashioned stump oratory. He did not play by the rules. If he lost a vote in the Politburo—and, yes, questions are decided by recorded votes, as I learned from Nikita Sergeevich himself—he would carry the questions to the people. No one, not even Lenin, had acted like this and in the end Khrushchev paid a price for his freewheeling.

Putting the missiles into Cuba was a telltale indicator. His throw of the dice in favor of friendship with Eisenhower and partnership (which was what he really wanted) with the U.S.A. was another. Pulling out in one swoop thousands of Soviet specialists from China was another. Khrushchev thought he could bargain his Cuban missiles for a disarmament deal with the U.S. He thought he could bring China to her knees by pulling out the experts. He thought

Eisenhower and he could divide the world (a peaceful reenactment, if you will, of the deal Hitler and Stalin laid on each other).

None of these gambles paid off. But behind the bravado Khrushchev was prey to a thousand fears. He had never been in a helicopter before Eisenhower invited him up to take a look at Washington as the government closing-hour rush jammed the highways. He was afraid it was a trick; he might crash or be hurled overboard. He wouldn't do it until Ike said he was going too. He was afraid to go to Camp David. What kind of trick did Ike have in store? After he went there, he basked in his intimacy with Eisenhower. When he sailed on the Soviet steamer *Baltika* in September 1960 to attend the United Nations session, he invited the Eastern European heads of state to come with him. Privately he worried that a U.S. submarine might torpedo his ship and sink the whole crew.

Because of the distortions of political life in the Soviet Union, Khrushchev was not always able to gauge practical political matters with accuracy. I watched him on his famous appearance at the United Nations. One day he had signified displeasure by pounding the table with his fists, rub-a-dub-dub. I think he had picked up this touch from what he'd heard about the prerevolutionary Duma, a most unruly parliament, and I think he thought his gesture would appeal to the third world nations. Foreign Minister Gromyko was sitting beside Khrushchev. Gromyko is a very formal man. A flicker of distaste crossed his face when he saw what Khrushchev was doing. But dutifully Gromyko doubled his fists and lightly tapped them on the table. Next day, the two again were sitting together. Khrushchev's fists went rub-a-dub. Gromyko followed his master's example. Then suddenly, hearing a new sound, he saw that Khrushchev had pulled off a shoe and was banging the table with it. Gromyko resolutely went quietly on with his fists. He would not take off his shoe for Khrushchev or anyone else.

Khrushchev's "proletarian" gesture backfired. It amused Americans, but third world politicians, who are nothing if not formal, thought Khrushchev gauche. The Soviet public thought the same thing. Twenty years later, Soviet men and women still cited Khrushchev's shoe-pounding as a vulgar act which brought contumely on the great Soviet state. "He made foreigners laugh at us," they say. He embarrassed the intelligentsia with his bad manners, his scruffy Russian speech, his baggy trousers (and later on, his too-tailored Italian suits). They thought him crude, rude, vulgar, ignor-

179

ant. It was only when he was gone and replaced by Brezhnev and his faceless bureaucrats that they realized what they had lost.

Nothing made Khrushchev more angry than complaints that he and the Soviet Union were anti-Semitic. He was forever citing *numerus clausus* to demonstrate how fair Russia was in giving the Jews their appointed number of places in the university, in the academies, in the Bolshoi Theater Orchestra. But he would never explain why Jews were so rare in the upper ranks of the party, the army, the security service and the Foreign Office.

Even in retirement, when he seriously examined and reexamined his past, he never managed to get straight on the Jewish question. I think Khrushchev was so steeped in the conventional anti-Semitism of the Ukraine that he could not sense the virus in his system.

Khrushchev's strongest characteristic was an openness to new impressions, a willingness to change his mind based on physical observation. Again and again he harried the Russian bureaucrats to get out of their offices and into the streets to see for themselves. He pushed their noses into dirty, disordered, backward local conditions, bad plumbing, poor housing construction, inept planning, shoddy agriculture. He was like a cloud of bees when he descended on a provincial center where party bureaucrats preened themselves in cozy complacency.

Khrushchev respected American reporters. He delighted in banter with them and never missed an opportunity. He admired their open eyes and ready repartee, their frankness, their camaraderie and their hard work.

I spent two or three weeks in the autumn of 1960 at the corner of Park Avenue and Sixty-eighth Street in New York, where the Soviets then had their mission and where Khrushchev lived during his stay for the United Nations session. I was out on the pavement at 6 A.M. and I did not leave until midnight or 1 A.M. As soon as Khrushchev discovered the reporters on his doorstep, he began to perform, emerging on a balcony, ostensibly for a breath of fresh air, actually to banter with us, to speak into the microphones that the TV reporters hoisted up on long poles, and to indulge the whims of the photographers.

Khrushchev was a reporter's dream. All you had to do to get a story was wait. On weekends at Glen Cove, Long Island, where the Soviets had an estate, I would appear at the big iron gate with a dozen other reporters at 8 A.M. Sure as rain, Khrushchev would "accidentally" stroll down to the gate and discover us. He would repeat his "discovery" several times a day. I had the impression he was bored with his bureaucratic entourage and Eastern European companions, and found us better company.

He talked to me one evening as we strolled in the circular driveway at the entrance to the Glen Cove mansion. It was dusk and I could hardly make out his features, but he was very serious. He was talking about diplomacy, statesmanship and politics: the difficulty of politics, the difficulty of being a politician, the hard work. "You have no idea how hard it is," he said, and in the timbre of his voice I heard the echoes of the crises of the past. He had spent his life in Soviet politics. He had survived nearly twenty-five years, moving from the outer fringes of Stalin's clique to its very center. He knew politics at its most dangerous vortex. He knew what it meant when a casual word could cost you your life.

On another occasion, he told me that while he had not agreed with some of my articles, he thought others were objective and could provide a basis for the "peaceful coexistence" of our two countries. "So," he said, "if you were nominated for President, I would vote for you."

The next moment, he was listening to a reporter who suggested that he could have made a success in American politics even though the Communist party was not very strong in the U.S.A. Khrushchev said he might well have been a successful American politician, and had he been elected President, maybe many people would have wanted to join his party.

I like and enjoy politicians and I became fond of Khrushchev, as did most of the reporters. He had a good sense of humor and, what was most important, he was willing to learn and did learn. He did not bear grudges. I do not think he ever got over his inclination for quick fixes. One of his most disreputable moves was his short-lived restoration to favor of Trofim Lysenko, the quack agronomist whose mini-Stalinist purges destroyed Soviet genetics (the generation with which Hermann Muller had worked) and did terrible damage to Soviet science. Khrushchev's children strongly opposed his flirtation with Lysenko but could not halt it. Fortunately, Brezhnev brought a final end to Lysenko's influence. Far better and more wholesome was Khrushchev's friendship and fondness for the pragmatic but scientific farming practices to which he was introduced by the Coon Rapids,

Iowa, farmer Roswell Garst. Garst knew what he was talking about and Khrushchev understood this. Garst brought into Soviet practice hybrid corn and the theory of the Iowa corn-hog economy, use of silage to produce beef and hogs, and mass production of poultry. It was Khrushchev who initiated the slow but certain Soviet transformation from a cereal diet to a meat economy.

On one of the first days of September 1971, Yevgeny Yevtushenko got a telephone call to come to the Khrushchev villa. It was a fine day, with sunshine and the scent of autumn in the air. Zhenya, as he told me, found Nikita Sergeevich, Nina Petrovna, Khrushchev's son Alexei and his daughter Rada there. They sat on benches in the garden and talked almost all day. Khrushchev had been ill and in the hospital, and he felt his end was approaching. He wanted to apologize to Yevtushenko and to the other writers he had criticized. He wanted to explain what had happened. When Yevtushenko had spoken to him in 1962 about the two painters, the conventionalist and the constructivist, who had died side by side, he had known that Yevtushenko was right.

"Then why did you shout at me, Nikita Sergeevich," Yevtushenko asked.

"Because I knew you were right," Khrushchev replied, "and I had to shout. You are very lucky. You are a poet. You can tell the truth. But I was a politician. You don't know what a terrible job it is to be a politician. I had to shout to hold my job."

Khrushchev said that after the 1956 Hungarian uprising, which was touched off by the Petöfi Circle of poets, the middle ranks of the Soviet party wrote many letters to him and to the Central Committee. They said that the Soviet intelligentsia were undisciplined, immoral, not reliable. They were like the Petöfi Circle; they had unbuckled their swords and were ready to strike.

Those bastards, said Khrushchev, referring to the party apparatchiki. The *svolochi!* They did not know what the Revolution was about. "We gave birth to them," said Khrushchev, "and they will kill us."

For hours, Khrushchev spoke with the poet he had once criticized. He went back over the events of his life, the tasks he had carried out for Stalin. Finally, they went inside and had a meal. It was dusk when Yevtushenko left the dacha, tired and drawn, tremendously moved by Khrushchev's talk. It was his *Areopagitica.*

A week later, Yevtushenko's telephone rang. It was Rada, the Khrushchev daughter: "Poppa died." Yevtushenko went to the service at the Kuntsevo funeral home. There were about fifteen members of the Khrushchev family, a few others: Julian Semenov, a writer; Sergo Mikoyan, son of Anastas, who brought a wreath from his father; perhaps twenty persons outside the family. There were one hundred police on hand, another one hundred plainclothesmen. Across the street from the funeral parlor, a hundred curious people stood, women with baby carriages, passersby. There was nothing to keep them from crossing the street. But no one did. Yevtushenko did not go on to the services at the cemetery. He was sick at heart and sick to the stomach. He went home and vomited.

Like Mikoyan, Khrushchev was denied his rightful place of burial in the Kremlin wall. He rests in Novodeviche cemetery under Neizvestny's monument. Each year the number of pilgrims to Nikita Sergeevich's grave grew. Each year more handfuls of flowers appeared on his grave. The pilgrims finally became too much for the Brezhnev administration. Now Russia has a *closed* cemetery along with all the other *closed* institutions—*closed* stores for the upper echelons, *closed* dacha communities for the *nomenclatura, closed* archives for the party priests, *closed* meetings for the party elite.

For five years, Novodeviche has been closed to the public, to visitors who might want to lay a flower on Khrushchev's grave. Only relatives of the dead who are buried there are now permitted.

I liked Nikita Sergeevich with all his faults, all his scary flights of fancy. I think he wanted a decent life for his people. I think he wanted to make a firm peace with Eisenhower. He had staked a lot on Eisenhower's promised trip in 1960. He had even, or so it was said, built a golf course in the Crimea and had taken some lessons himself, hoping to join his distinguished guest in this strange Scottish pastime which has never been played in Russia. There was talk of his building a Russian Disneyland. And I have seen the beautiful guesthouse Khrushchev built high over Lake Baikal, in which Eisenhower was to have spent his last night in Siberia on the eastward flight to Japan.

I am not so naive as to suppose that Eisenhower's trip would have resolved all the differences between the U.S.A. and the U.S.S.R. But I suspect the two men could have laid the basis for an evolving collaboration which by now might have given us two decades of serious investment in resolution of conflict rather than aggravation.

Nikita Sergeevich Khrushchev died at the age of seventy-eight on September 11, 1971, at his home, with his family at his side. The world first learned of the event through Victor Louis, who told foreign correspondents about it that afternoon. Not until two days later, on the morning of the funeral, did *Pravda* publish a brief notice. No official of party or government attended the services. Thousands of police surrounded the Novodeviche cemetery and only members of the family, a few diplomats and correspondents were permitted to be present. His son Sergei spoke over the grave. "An honest and brave man has died," he said. I agree.

## Chapter 15

# A New Day is Coming

I got to Russia too late to meet the writers of the 1920s and 1930s—Babel, Mandelshtam, Tsvetaeva, Mayakovsky. They were all gone, all, in one way or another, victims of Stalin. And I was far too late for Blok, Bely, Ivanov and Merezhkovsky, whom I later learned to admire. I was not too late for Akhmatova, I suppose, but I was too ignorant in 1944 to know about her, and in the late Stalin era she was, of course, inaccessible. In the last years of her life, I felt too naive and too *American* to approach her.

I did catch a glimpse or two of Lila Brik, the woman with whom Mayakovsky was hopelessly infatuated. But it was very late in her life, at a time when the Soviet literary hit squads had taken to bushwhacking her, publishing articles insinuating that she was not Mayakovsky's femme fatale, that he had tossed her over for Tatiana Yakovleva (it was true Mayakovsky had fallen in love with Tatiana in Paris in the last year of his life); that Francine Grey, Tatiana's brilliant daughter, was actually Mayakovsky's daughter (a concoction which Francine repeatedly had to disprove by showing Soviet writers her passport and date of birth). In these times, Lila Brik lay back on the couch of her drawing room, the walls laden with magnificent works by Nikko Pirosmanishvili, the famous Georgian primitive, by Kandinsky, Tatlin and Picasso, and sometimes told how she had never permitted Mayakovsky to make love to her; how she would lock herself in the bedroom with Osip Brik and ignore Mayakovsky, who would bay in anguish, scratching at the door like a dog. She would tell her visitors, tell me, that had she been in Moscow in 1930, when Mayakovsky returned from Paris, "it never would have happened"—that is, Mayakovsky would not have shut himself into that cubicle of a room which he inhabited on Lubyanskaya Pereulok, just a prisoner's moan from the Lubyanka Prison itself, written a last poem to Lila, taken out his pistol and put a bullet through his heart.

A few hours with Lila Brik was not much, but it gave me a whiff of the wild emotions, despairs, delights, and exuberance of Russian life before Stalin put the poets into uniforms of gray and began, in Boris Pasternak's words, to sell Mayakovsky to the people as Catherine the Great had sold the peasants on planting potatoes.

Of the galaxy of poets who witnessed the Revolution, there was only one whose life persisted long enough to touch mine—Pasternak. I went to meet him on Orthodox Easter of 1959, taking the suburban train to Peredelkino on a warm spring day, the train filled with shoppers returning from Moscow. I had no idea where to find Pasternak's dacha and I was certain there would be police sniffing around the station. Pasternak was still the center of international controversy over *Zhivago* and the Nobel Prize.

I had yielded to the entreaties of a young American woman and allowed her to come with me. No question but we would quickly be spotted. I noticed on the train a woman wearing a gray topcoat with a small gold pin. She was, I was certain, a writer or a writer's wife. If she got off at Peredelkino, I would see if she could tell me the way to Pasternak's. At Peredelkino, she rose and I asked her the question. She smiled. "Of course, I'll show you the way. I'm going to Fedin's [the writer Konstantin Fedin], just next door."

We started off and I saw a car beside the road, a man sitting in it. Sure enough, we were being followed, the car crawling along behind and a man ahead of us, casting a look back from time to time. Fortune favored us. We came to a large field and our guide suggested that we cut across it, directly to Pasternak's. By the time we got to the dacha, the *shpiks* had been outflanked.

A pleasant woman, possibly Pasternak's wife, Zinaida, answered my knock. I heard voices; an Easter feast was in progress. I didn't think she was too happy to see us. While we waited, a yellow dog, probably an Irish terrier, hobbled from an outbuilding. There was something wrong with its hindquarters and it brought a sick and fetid odor to the steps where we waited.

A moment later, Pasternak appeared, tall, lean, gaunt, high cheek-bones, scraggly hair, a strong jaw, penetrating blue eyes, his profile more like that of an American Indian than I had imagined. I had brought him a small gift, a letter from Helen Wolff, his American publisher, a sheaf of reviews. We stood talking in the sunny court-yard, his clumsy hands—he was, or so he seemed to me, a clumsy man—encircling my companion's hands and mine. He apologized for not inviting us in. The house was full of guests, his sons and their wives. He was so sad not to receive us. But he had to be very careful.

186

Things were going to be better, but now it was the government's wish that he live quietly.

I apologized for intruding. I said I had felt it was the most appropriate day to come, Easter Day. He smiled and accepted my remark. Pasternak had been born a Jew, but for years had been under the strong influence of the Orthodox faith. He talked a bit about how he worked: two hours in the morning, then he dusted his room, worked a bit in the garden, and back to his desk for two hours. He was deluged by mail. The dog—its name was Mishka—whimpered and the odor seemed to grow stronger. Pasternak stood a moment, then released our hands. We said goodbye and walked to the gate, opened it, glanced back and saw him still standing there. He gave a little wave and went inside.

I came back to Peredelkino on January 7, 1962, Christmas Day, Orthodox Christmas, a snowy day, eighteen months after Pasternak's death. I went to the blue, rose and white chapel of the Church of the Assumption, which lies close to the meadow before Pasternak's house. Hundreds of small candles sparkled at the altars. Believers filled the church as the priests chanted the services. I walked out into the world of snow, the world Pasternak had painted in "Christmas Star," one of the Zhivago poems: "It was winter, the wind blew from the steppes, And it was cold for the child in the cave of the hillside."

The world was white and great snowflakes sifted down from gray skies. Youngsters tumbled off the electric trains from Moscow and crisscrossed the fields on their skis, in costumes of red, yellow and blue. I made my way up to the ridge where Pasternak was buried beneath two great pines, his gravestone hidden in snow so that I could only see the words "Boris Leonidovich Pasternak." A fresh wreath lay there, together with a winter-frosted bouquet of chrysanthemums and a spray of cedar. I was not the first pilgrim of that snowy Christmas.

I can no longer remember when I first met Zhenya Yevtushenko, Andrei Voznesensky and Bella Akhmadulina. I mean the exact circumstances. It must have been in the early sixties, but it seems to me that I have always known them. You could not find three persons more different, three who have been more close, three who have been more at odds, three who have quarreled and loved, and fought and cried and hated and loved again, three poets so poetic, three Russians so Russian, three persons so important to the life of their country for, amazingly, the last twenty-five years! Three heroes, three friends whose friendship embraces me, warms me like a fire in winter and sometimes splashes me with the freezing water of Russian reality.

I cannot and will not in these few pages trace more than a few lines of what I believe Bella and Andrei and Zhenya mean to their country, to me and to the world. If there was anyone in Russia to whom my war-time friends Ilya Ehrenburg and Konstantin Simonov addressed the admonition: "Tell the truth," it was to these three. Oh, yes, I know that these three would have told the truth in any event. You could have frozen Zhenya in the sixty-degree-below-zero mists of his beloved Lake Baikal and he would have told it so long as he could move his frozen jaws. The same for Bella. Even while her teeth are chattering as her imagination conjures up not unrealistic visions of the consequences of her candor, she speaks out the words that are in her heart. "I am not a heroine," she says, shaking her lovely russet head, "I am not brave." But she is the bravest, and God himself could not put a lock on her tongue. And Andrei, so slight, still with his schoolboy's posture, his head cocked to one side, squaring his shoulders and plunging ahead because there is no turning back . . . Three young poets of Russia. Young? Yevtushenko and Voznesensky are turning fifty and Bella is close behind—but they are still Russia's three young poets; younger voices have not appeared. They, with Joseph Brodsky, the Leningrad protégé of Akhmatova, who was compelled to leave Russia (like Solzhenitsyn) and has settled in the United States, constitute Russia's voice today.

What a voice! Any country would be blessed with one of them. It tells us something about Russia *in repression* that Bella, Zhenya and Andrei for all their difficulties (and they are real difficulties and often extreme) go on speaking, have never been silenced. It tells us of their courage and of the curious blend of permission and suppression that has marked Russia's years since 1953.

It has become the fashion in New York literary circles to disparage Yevtushenko. He has been criticized by certain intellectuals as being an instrument of the Soviet state, a propagandist for the regime, a carrier of anti-Semitism, a self-indulgent climber, a publicity hound —Lord knows all the things that have been said of Zhenya. Perhaps they even charge him with cowardice.

All this is spoken from the comfortable security of the barracks of the Upper West Side, from lazy beachheads at Southampton and on the pages of smart literary journals. This is said of the man who wrote "Babi Yar," that eloquent testament to the most savage crime against the Jews committed on Soviet soil, a crime which successive Soviet regimes, beginning with that of Stalin, sought to suppress from public knowledge. It was the "anti-Semite" Yevtushenko who spoke up for the martyrs of Babi Yar and whose poem was published by *Pravda*. When it had become apparent that Nikita Khrushchev was wavering on anti-Semitism, it again was Zhenya who spoke directly to Khrushchev in public and told him his regime was anti-Semitic; and it was he who in the Brezhnev days joined with Dmitri Shostakovich to create the "Babi Yar" symphony, music by Shostakovich, the stark, unlovely words from Yevtushenko's pen.

This poet who has been accused of pandering to the authorities is the man whose poem "Stalin's Heirs" remains the most dramatic warning to Russia, to its leaders and its people, that the danger of Stalin did not die with the old dictator, that Stalinism is alive and flourishing (as it is particularly in these days) and that the tomb of Stalin must be guarded with eternal watchfulness lest his evil spirit again spread over the land.

This is the poet whose lines have roused Russia's younger generation to new horizons, who has sought to give them a new consciousness of the world (not the stale old agitprop world but the contemporary world of rock and blues, the Beatles, the Beat generation and Watergate), never losing his taste for his homeland, Siberia, the Lena, the taiga, the free spirit of the generations that came by étape.

No, I have not lost faith in Zhenya. I know he can make a fool of himself, concocting silly stunts, confusing the Mongols with the Chinese in the xenophobic Russian fashion, taking himself seriously as a politician, not a wandering troubadour.

I have listened to Zhenya talk by the hour. I know his dreams, sometimes adolescent, sometimes soaring. I do not think he is Pushkin (whom he sometimes thinks he is); I don't know whether, as he believes, he has been shot at in Chile, plotted against in Moscow, targeted by the Mafia in New York. But I know he has moved Russia's conscience and sometimes even the conscience of Russia's rulers, and never, so far as I know, for any bad end. I know he has an ego as big as the Pamirs, but that is natural for a poet. I know that he wants the world to survive so that his two sons by his English wife can survive in peace.

I know that Andrei and Bella often criticize Zhenya, and I do too.

But that's not bad. I feel uncomfortable with unanimous opinions. When others criticize Zhenya, you will usually find me at his side. I am glad that Zhenya exists. This is a better world for his living in it.

I know Andrei better than I know Zhenya. Perhaps we are more compatible. Zhenya is bigger than life, is forever dashing off to Alaska or the Congo or Vietnam or the South Seas or rafting down the Lena into the Arctic Ocean. God knows where he will turn up next. Of course, Andrei is no slouch at traveling. He has been to the North Pole and I would not be surprised to find him in outer space or on the moon. Andrei is a more *poetic* poet than Yevtushenko, whose style derives more from Mayakovsky, Russia's model of "civic"— that is, politically oriented—verse. Andrei was a protégé of Pasternak. He showed Pasternak each of his early verses and sat at the feet of that enigmatic man. It is no accident that Andrei has undertaken the burden of bringing Pasternak back into Russia's heritage. In 1980, he finally opened the way, or so I believe, for the publication of *Doctor Zhivago* in Pasternak's homeland. Andrei published in that year a long tribute to Pasternak, speaking as Pasternak's pupil. He succeeded in having included in an important anthology four of the religious poems from *Zhivago*, including "Christmas Star."

I know that I am prejudiced about Andrei. When I read his poetry, I hear his voice reciting from a bare stage in a crowded hall in Moscow or New York. I see him with his writing pad, alone beside a quiet pond in Connecticut. I am with him in a snowstorm in the Moscow countryside or sharing the ecstasy of a performance at the Taganka. I watch his face, like that of an impish child, his long pullover, his Oliver Twist cap, his wry grin, and his voice, extraordinarily and unexpectedly loud and resonant, roaring out the rhythm of "The Architectural Hall Is on Fire!" at a mass meeting of thousands of his Russian admirers. I hear him in the passenger lounge of a ferryboat, Allen Ginsberg beside him to translate, booming out his verses to a five o'clock commuting crowd between Manhattan and Staten Island. I am with him on a mountaintop in Connecticut, eating sandwiches and drinking wine; I am on the staircase at Tatiana Yakovleva Liberman's New York house, listening to Andrei read his new poems. We are drinking together late at night in a Moscow restaurant. Too many images, too many memories, warm, close, comradely. I cannot think of a line of Andrei's poetry with which I would argue.

Bella—well, I simply dissolve in Bella's presence. If Andrei is Pasternak's impish pupil, if Zhenya is Mayakovsky today, Bella is the child of Tsvetaeva and Akhmatova, a bit of one, a bit of the other, and very much Akhmadulina, offspring of hope, elfin, a woman of deep tragedy, carrying her fate in her lovely hands, seeing for herself a tragic end because tragedy awaits every Russian poet. I cannot believe it. I cannot believe that haunt will pursue Bella to the darkest corner of her life, but I see it in her eyes when she is sitting in a crowded room, everyone talking but she silent, her eyes far away, her mind far away, thinking perhaps of Tsvetaeva at Tarusa, thinking perhaps of Akhmatova in the queue with the other women at Kresty Prison, bearing a package for her son, telling her neighbor, yes, I will remember it all, I will remember everything, as she did and then wrote of it in "Poem Without a Hero." Akhmatova survived and remembered. Bella will survive and remember. Nor does she forget even now. Careless of herself, careless of reprisals, she goes into battle like Joan of Arc, but she insists, "I am not brave," "I am very frightened," and her eyes look like those of a doe. She is frightened but she does not halt. She cannot. She is a poet. There is no moderation for a poet; moderation is death; Bella is life.

How blessed, I think, that Russia has these poets; how great they are and how much of their greatness comes from the fact that they must fight to survive and they know what they must fight. The enemy is there, clear, obvious. They knew it even before the word was spelled out to them by the "fathers," the generation ahead of them, the Simonovs and the Ehrenburgs, the Mandelshtams, the Tsvetaevas, the Akhmatovas, all the rest. The poets know their mission. It is to tell the truth. Eternally to tell the truth. To make Russia listen to the truth. No matter how awful. To speak and speak again and to use every talent to make their voices heard. How I envy Russia these poets! How proud Russia will be a hundred years from now of their voices, their bravery, their honesty. No matter their little games, their feuds, their fantasies.

I believe the poets of Russia can tell us more of the future, more of the state of their land, than analysts of think tanks, strategists of security councils, and satellite scans by the CIA's high tech. So I listen to the voices of the Akhmadulinas, the Voznesenskys, the Yevtushenkos, the Brodskys. Above all, I listen to the voice of Aleksandr Isayevich Solzhenitsyn.

Solzhenitsyn once said that a nation which possesses a good writer is a nation which possesses "another government." I do not know whether he was thinking of himself. He well might have been. Aleksandr Isayevich is not merely the foremost writer of Russia, the foremost writer of the world—he is "another government."

So it was, of course, with the giants of the nineteenth century—with Pushkin, Dostoyevsky, Tolstoy, Dickens and Thackeray, Heine, Hugo and Balzac. Perhaps even with Samuel Clemens. But I can think of no one in England, France or the United States today who speaks with a magisterial voice. Solzhenitsyn does. He towers above all. It is not unnatural that he is criticized, harassed, niggled at by poetasters in the salons of London, Paris and New York. But there is one government that does not underestimate the power of his mind and the weight of his pen. That is the Soviet government. (Russia possesses only one intellect of comparable power—that of Andrei Sakharov, and he has been deported into internal exile in the isolated city of Gorky.)

I did not know Aleksandr Isayevich in Russia. I shared in the excitement of his first published work, *One Day in the Life of Ivan Denisovich*—the event of that watershed year in Russia, 1962. In 1967, when I got back to Moscow, Solzhenitsyn had not yet crossed the line of contact with foreigners and correspondents. Not until he emerged from Russia, forcibly compelled to leave by the KGB, did our contacts begin, at first by letter and then, after he came to America, in person, meetings rare and precious.

Long before Solzhenitsyn left Moscow, I had, by chance, become privy to much of the secret side that led to the publication of *The First Circle* and, later, *The Gulag Archipelago*, works that, with *Ivan Denisovich* and *The Cancer Ward*, have changed the landscape, as we perceive it, of Russia and specifically of Russia in the Stalin years. I think no literary talent in the second half of this century has had a force comparable to Solzhenitsyn's. There is the meticulousness of his observation, the dense brushwork with which he fills his canvas, the philosophy that gives his work resonance. And there is his grasp of the character of the Russian man and the Russian world, which matches that of his greatest predecessors. If it can be said that Dostoyevsky changed our notion of the geography of the emotions, that Tolstoy gave us our moral values, then Solzhenitsyn has given new dimension to the architecture of the soul, its corruptibility, its nobility, its inscrutability.

Solzhenitsyn is not a man for the weak of heart. He does not spare himself, nor does he spare anyone. He is dedicated to a single purpose, the overthrow of Bolshevism and the restoration of a Russia faithful to the Orthodox Church and the traditions of the Russian ethos. He is a radical in a world of time servers. His words ring harshly in our ears. He has no mercy for the idolaters in the temple. He expects no mercy from Moscow, but is contemptuous of Moscow's ability to match his Cromwellian zeal. He has laid out his life like a military commander embarking on a long campaign behind enemy lines. He has provisioned himself for hard times, long sieges, unexpected assaults. He has total confidence in victory and in a Russia Redux.

If I make Aleksandr Isayevich sound formidable, even frightening, I have every intention of so doing. He is a man who believes he can bend kingdoms. I am not one to say he is wrong.

His face is familiar to the whole world, the deep-set eyes, wary with the experience of Gulag, fierce in conviction that faith will prevail over the Antichrist that has possessed the Russian spirit. His forehead seems to be marked by a deep scar. It is not. The strong line has been etched by resolution and will. He moves gracefully, like an animal, or, more plausibly, like a hunter slipping through the forest, conscious of every beast in the undergrowth, hardly rustling a leaf, deft as an Indian tracker. His figure is slight but muscular. He does not walk for miles every day, as he used to; he does not cut wood, as he once did; he does not carry heavy burdens on his back. But his muscles have not gone slack. There is a sense of steel in his close-knit frame. His beard is red and his eyes are blue. They see deep into you.

A fearsome man? No, a gentle man, but if he has you within the sights of his rifle, don't expect his shot to miss. He has a steady hand. Aleksandr Isayevich is a military man. I can see him in command of his artillery unit in East Prussia in World War II, following in the trail of his father, who fought over this land in World War I. A superior artillery officer, he is a man who knows his guns, his mathematics, his trigonometry, his discipline, a man whose company is smart, obeys swiftly, acts with precision.

Aleksandr Isayevich has programmed himself like a computer—his daily working schedule, his monthly writing quotas, his years of productive life, his series of historical novels, soon to come on line in a publication sequence that he worked out years earlier, and finally his great project for a new history of Russia to replace the classic

Klyuchevsky and give a foundation on which to rebuild its nobility and respect—all this and more. Alekssandr Isayevich is not only a literary classic, he is a moral and political preceptor for the ages.

We sometimes try to fit Solzhenitsyn into an American iconostasis. It makes no sense. This man is a Russian, first and always. Every word he writes, every breath, every minute, is dedicated to one cause—Russia. If he criticizes American life (and he does), if he finds fault with our mores (and he does), if he is dismayed by our political life (and he is), if our press seems to him unruly and unprincipled (which it often is), if the policy of our Presidents and Congresses seems incomprehensible to him (as it may well to us), the basic and enduring reason is that Aleksandr Isayevich assesses all these from a single perspective—how do they affect his grand design, the resurrection of Russia, free of Communist influence, purged of modern decadence, arising again in the grandeur of ancient Rus, the Pravoslavnye Church and the purity of an earlier social contract.

Unless we understand this truth about Aleksandr Isayevich, we understand nothing.

I am afraid this picture presents the image of a forbidding man, a narrow man, a fanatical man. Nothing is further from reality. I judge a man not solely by his words, his goals, his public personality. I judge him by his private person, his interior life, the milieu he inhabits, the men and women about him, his family, the home he makes for them.

One winter day, Charlotte and I and two close friends visited Aleksandr Isayevich in his sunny, cheerful, invigorating house in the hills of Vermont, far from any city, set in a small forest, the great living room windows looking out on white birches, pines, distant snow-covered meadows, as Russian a vista as any to be found in the Ryazan *gubernia*. Here was a home that radiated life and cheer and *goodness*—that old-fashioned word, but I know no other—the goodness of Russian black bread, of the Russian word, of the bright Russian colors of a woman's dress. Here, in a house and working compound organized with exquisite attention to detail, Aleksandr Isayevich lives and works, with his wife, Natasha, their three blue-eyed, blond-haired Russian boys, Yermolai, then nine, Ignat, seven, and madcap Stepan, six, and his wife's mother, Ekaterina, in an atmosphere so Russian it brought tears to my eyes. Instantly I was transported back to the Russia of the last century, to the *Sovremennik* of Chernyshevsky and Dobrolubov, the bright dreams of the *narodniki,* the familiar pages of that companion of every Russian family of 1890, the illustrated weekly *Niva,* something like the *Harper's Weekly* of my father's youth, to that distant, intellectual, moral Russia which had already begun to disintegrate by 1900, not so much by the desiccation of the monarchy as by the battering rams of the new capitalists, the Morozovs, the Ryabushinskys, the Guchkovs and the others, who were demolishing the old Russian society with their new railroads, steel mills, coal mines and textile plants.

That evening, after a Russian dinner and toasts to those absent in prison and in exile, a toast which Russians have drunk for a hundred years, we seated ourselves in a small "ballroom" and the three boys, with their square-cut hair, their straight backs, their beautiful manners, their perfect English, their perfect Russian, distributed programs of their *konsert.*

Ignat played the piano, announcing his piece, a minuet by Bach, in proper Russian fashion before taking his seat at the Steinway. He played easily, confidently, a bit slowly. Aleksandr Isayevich said with a father's pride that Rostropovich thought the boy had talent. I think that is correct. Yermolai announced his piece, Lermontov's "Otchizna," and spoke the poem's words in confident Russian.

Stepan was next. He recited Mother Goose verses in English—"Fe, fi, fo, fum" and "Eeny, meeny, miney, mo," "Tom Thumb," "Jack and Jill" and "The Cat and the Fiddle," recited in his own rhythm: "Hey-y-y-y-y-y-y-y-y-y-y diddle, diddle."

Each boy stood straight as an arrow, head high, arms at sides, responding to applause with a little bow.

I asked Aleksandr Isayevich which of the boys he had most resembled in childhood. In appearance, he said, Yermolai, but in character, Stepan. I had been certain Aleksandr Isayevich had been bright, indulged by his parents, and in his youth mad for the theater, his ambition to be an actor, but cut off from that when a doctor told him his throat was not strong enough for an acting career. There was, I thought, still something of the actor in Aleksandr Isayevich. He could play the prophet, the thunderer, but the role in which he felt most congenial was that of paterfamilias, the head of a Russian family improbably planted in Vermont, as Russian as rye, as Russian as the Orthodox Church. They had their own little home chapel and icons, a priest who gave the youngsters instruction in religion, music and art. Aleksandr Isayevich taught them mathematics, Russian history and Russian literature, and conduct, and Natasha watched over them with motherly warmth.

Never in Russia had I been in so Russian a household, never in Russia had I met so Russian a family, so Russian a house, such Russian children, such Russian parents, and nothing so exquisitely nineteenth-century Russian as the children's *konsert*. It came from the pages of Chekhov or Turgenev, the shining faces of the boys, the quiet, confident parents. I was plunged back a hundred years in history, when all over Russia families lived like this, the children brought up in a close bond of morality, good literature, good works, companionship and religion.

When good night and *do svdaniye* was said by all and we went out into the star-sprinkled night with fresh snow on the ground, the Vermont hills dusted with diamonds in the distance, I felt that I was leaving the heart of Russia, the warm, beating heart of Russia, remarkably transported to New England. I realized that I had been on a visit not alone to the Russia of the 1880s but to the America of Longfellow and Hawthorne and Emerson.

It was a bracing moment, and as I looked back on it, I could not but share the faith of Aleksandr Isayevich. In truth, whatever their extremes of personality (and I know none of them who would welcome comparison with another), all of those in the company of this chapter share a single goal. They wish to see a better world and a better Russia, and if they differ widely as to how that goal is to be reached, they have one common bond: they believe that, one way or another, in the spirit of Herzen and in the words of Chernyshevsky, "a new day is coming," a day of truth.

And for all the pessimism which sometimes suffuses me, I share that belief and take strength and hope from these men and women of Russian courage.

## Chapter 16

# Damn the Law

The time stamp on my registration card at the Tutwiler Hotel in Birmingham, Alabama, reads 9:53 A.M. April 6, 1960, a Wednesday. I had flown in from Baton Rouge, Louisiana, and a bellhop showed me to Room 1117. I had not yet unpacked my bag when the front desk called: Would I mind changing my room? There had been a mistake. I grumbled a bit, allowed myself to be moved to Room 1060, sat down at the telephone and went to work. It would be sixteen years before I understood why I was moved from Room 1117 to Room 1060.

I thought that by 1960 I had a pretty good grasp of what the United States was about. I had done a lot of political reporting and knew Adlai Stevenson and, improbably, Richard Nixon quite well. I had had a good look at my native Minnesota and the Middle West and been shocked by the abandonment of smaller farms and their consolidation into tracts of 300 to 360 acres and amazed at the corn/hog prosperity in Iowa where, as I reported, every farmer seemed to own a Cadillac—a finding which so enraged the Iowa farmers that they took a full page advertisement in the Des Moines Register-Tribune in protest. I had studied the deep social cleavages in the big cities and come to realise that the United States was not the paradise it had seemed to me during my long Moscow years. I had watched with concern the rise of violence in the South in the wake of *Brown* v. *the Board of Education* and the outburst of intolerance, still largely confined to the South.

But at least, I thought, we were making progress. I had been in Eastern Europe in 1957 at the time of Little Rock. Everywhere I went, I met denunciation of the United States for its "racist" policies.

Finally, in Bucharest, at a dinner given by Romanian journalists, I spoke out. Yes, there was racism, and there was violence. No American condoned that. But the reasons must be understood. The violence was the product of our effort to change the oldest prejudices known to man, prejudices of color, creed, ethnicity, and religion. No nation was so diverse as we, and now we were moving to make our principles of democracy, equality, and freedom more than words enscribed on a piece of parchment. Where else, I asked, had such a Herculean task been undertaken—to change attitudes thousands of years old, dating, perhaps, to the cave men? Certainly there was violence and bloodshed and certainly there would be more, and the task would take a very, very long time. Look around, I said: what is being done in your part of the world? Instead of criticizing Little Rock, I suggested, they should attack their own prejudices as we were attacking ours.

I spoke from my heart, and I think my words got through. I received a standing ovation, and in Bucharest, at least, I heard no more about American racism.

I had not been in the front ranks of *The New York Times* coverage of the South. As far as possible, Turner Catledge placed these stories in the hands of well-trained, courageous reporters of Southern birth, experience, and accent. Not until I returned to New York in late 1954 had I realized what a Southern tradition had been bequeathed to the *Times* by Mr. Ochs. He himself was born in Tennessee, founder of the Chattanooga *Times* (still owned by the family and published by his granddaughter, Ruth Holmberg). Iphigene Sulzberger made two or three trips a year to the city where she spent her earliest years (she was born in Cincinnati because Mr. Ochs didn't trust the Chattanooga doctors). Her Chattanooga-born grandsons, Stephen and Michael Golden, played an important role among the thirteen cousins into whose hands the *Times* ultimately would fall, and were deeply imbued (as were all the cousins) in the Ochs tradition and not too happy with the conservatism of Punch (although happy with his business success) and the ego-trip editorship of A. M. Rosenthal.

Of the paper's four editors in the half-century after 1930, three had been Southerners—Edwin L. James of Virginia, Turner Catledge of Philadelphia, Mississippi, and Clifton Daniel of Zebulon, North Carolina. Rosenthal, the fourth, was born in Canada and raised in New York City; as he said plaintively one night in the spring of 1986, "I think I'm the last Yankee who will edit the *Times*." Not everyone would describe the Canadian-born New York-raised Abe as a Yankee.

Well, Alabama is a long way from my native Minnesota. And I confess I never tried to conceal my Yankee background from Southerners. My grandfather and my great uncles fought for the

Union in the Civil War, most of them in Wisconsin volunteer regiments. But my sentiments bore no resemblance to the caricature drawn by John Temple Graves, editorial columnist of the Birmingham *Herald-Post*, who in April 1960 described my Minnesota as "the most South-hating of the States."

I had been given a minor role in the remarkable survey of Southern sentiment conducted under Turner Catledge's direction in the aftermath of *Brown* v. *the Board of Education* in 1955. Catledge went down to his hometown of Philadelphia, Mississippi, and came back believing that things were working out, that the South would opt for peaceful transition, not violence. He sent a ten-man team into the South to test this assumption. The team was headed by that extraordinary ex-Marine officer (and son of a Marine officer) John Popham, whom Catledge a decade earlier had named *Times* roving correspondent in the South—the first and for many years the only correspondent of a major news organization covering the South. Both Catledge and Popham believed the day of Southern transition was inevitable. The *Times* would be prepared. Iphigene Sulzberger shared that belief and so did her husband, Arthur, who had personally in 1955 desegregated the obituary columns of the Chattanooga *Times*. No longer would black and white deaths be listed separately. The action cost the paper 8,000 in circulation, not regained for years.

The vision of the New South, free of race oppression and hatred, prospering industrially and economically, was an article of faith in the Sulzberger family as it was in the minds of Catledge and of other liberal Southern editors like Ralph McGill of the Atlanta *Constitution*, Harry Ashmore of the Little Rock *Gazette*, and Hodding Carter of the Greenville, Mississippi, *Delta Democrat*. With considerable hesitation I had come to embrace this view.

Popham had been traveling the South since 1946, 50,000 miles a year by road before the days of the Interstate system. There was hardly a cow patch or a shade tree mechanic below the Mason-Dixon line he did not know or a mayor or sheriff who did not know him, his Jim Dandy hat, and his extraordinary Tidewater Virginia accent, which his successor, Claude Sitton of Georgia, once compared to "dollops of sorghum syrup sprayed from a Gatling gun."

I performed only one function in the *Times* survey. I sat at Popham's elbow, as he struggled to synthesize the tens of thousands of words from the reporters, and helped him shape the mass into an overview, in which Popham proclaimed that the country was confronting a profound and inevitable social revolution with which, he believed, the Southern leadership was coming to terms. (But he offered a caveat: There could be vengeance in the deep South against moderate and liberal elements.) I agreed with that conclusion. In fact, I probably put some of those words into Popham's copy.

We all believed and hoped that we were correct. We were not. Years of pain and violence lay ahead.

Within a few months standpat segregationists were beginning to call the tune. Popham was always to blame President Eisenhower, his failure to give clear leadership. Ike left the field to hard-liners, Little Rock and all the rest followed, the cry of "The South Will Rise Again!" echoed over the land, and fiery crosses lit up lawns and hillsides.

As levels of violence rose, Catledge tried to keep *Times* coverage in the hands of reporters with Southern accents. It was much better to depoy Popham with his Tidewater tongue or Claude Sitton and his Georgia drawl than flat-toned Midwesterners like myself or hard-edged Balts like Peter Kihss, who faced down a mob at Tuscaloosa by challenging the whole Alabama student body to fight him, two at a time.

By the winter of 1960 there weren't enough Southern accents to go around. On February 1, 1960, at about three o'clock in the afternoon, four freshmen from the all-black Agricultural and Technical College in Greensboro, North Carolina, walked into Woolworth's, sat down at the counter, and asked for a cup of coffee. The waitress refused them. The students remained seated. Nothing like this had happened in history. Within a week young blacks were doing it throughout the South, walking quietly into drugstores and five-and-dimes, sitting down, politely ordering coffee, and sitting there when service was refused. Johnny Popham had never seen anything like it. Neither had Claude Sitton. Or the white power structure. The sit-ins leaped like crown fire in the forest, spreading headlines and consternation through the South. The young men were *so polite* and so persistent.

I was quickly preempted by the national desk, and a month after Greensboro, on March 1, 1960, found myself in Nashville, Tennessee. No city in the South had developed race relations so sophisticated, smooth, and silky. Nashville had integrated its schools without a hitch. It was proud of a reputation as "the Athens of the South," a city of gracious, tree-lined streets, culture, taste, good manners, colleges (two of the best black colleges in the country), a city where voices were not raised. Its first sit-in came February 13 at the Woolworth, Kress, and McClellan lunch counters, polite young men from Fisk University.

I hurried straight from the airport to the center of town, where I found a crowd milling about a shopping complex—black students, curious passersby, police, and reporters. The lunch counter had been closed, the standard tactic with which proprietors met the sit-ins. A tall, thin, strongly built young man with notebook in hand introduced himself. He was David Halberstam, Harvard 1955. He had gone to Mississippi to learn the mechanics of reporting and now was working on the Nashville *Tennessean*. Within the year he would be off and running on *The New York Times*, first to the wars in the Congo and then to Vietnam with the best of the brightest. On this sunny, soft spring day Halberstam was tremendously excited by the sit-ins and eagerly began to tell me what was happening.

This was my first glimpse of the civil rights movement, which would plunge the country into an almost revolutionary state and take the life of Martin Luther King and all the others, black and white. On this balmy morning no one seemed to know how it had started (the young blacks thought it was their own personal idea). But someone that day, possibly David Halberstam, mentioned the name of Dr. Allen Knight Chalmers of Boston University's Divinity School. As time went on it became clear to me that his teachings about non-violent resistance, patterned after Gandhi, lay near the heart of it all. Chalmers wrote me after Birmingham, saying, "You do a good job," and told me that Martin Luther King was his student. Then Chalmers was off to the Far East and I to West Virginia and the Kennedy-Humphrey primary, and we never did meet.

That morning I had only a taste of sit-ins, but I came back to Nashville a month later and confirmed my suspicion that, given the will, racial progress could be made. Nashville had been hit with the same blitz as other Southern cities, which had met it with bluster, bloat, billyclubs, and bullying. Nashville took it on the cool side. The universities and colleges helped. But most of all it was the city's tradition of civility. A professional man apologized: "I'm sorry for what brings you here." A woman wrote the Nashville *Banner*: "Nashville, the eyes of the country are upon you! Are you proud of what they are seeing? Until now I could look anyone anywhere straight in the eye and say, gladly, 'I'm from Nashville, Tennessee.'"

Imagination, I thought, that was the key—imagination and will. Elsewhere I would discover stereotypes and even stereotypes of stereotypes, spite words, "hollering nigger," the "bloody shirt," the clichés of a century of hate and conflict. I began to feel an echo of the days before and after Appomattox. I had grown up with the last of the *Uncle Tom's Cabin* tent shows, those nifty ones with two Uncle Toms and two Elizas. Uncle Tom was, I thought, a tired old joke. I had snickered when I found Uncle Tom presented at the Children's Theater in Moscow as a realistic slice of today's America, and now in the heat of the sit-in I found John Temple Graves proclaiming in the Birmingham *Herald-Post* that Harriet Beecher Stowe lived again in the prose of Harrison Salisbury.

I was out of the South for a few days, covering a blizzard that left Times Square looking like the North Pole. Then I went to Raleigh, North Carolina, again to a border region which prided itself on civility (these were the days before Jesse Helms) and where the moderation and intelligence of Chapel Hill and Frank Graham and the transplantation of the textile industry were laying the foundation of the New South. So Turner Catledge believed. So Iphigene Sulzberger believed. So, hesitantly, I believed.

In Raleigh for the first time I felt the cold whisper of terror—very faint but unmistakable. The story here was a court case which, it was thought, would go to the U.S. Supreme Court and establish the constitutionality of sit-ins. Jack Greenberg, the smart, aggressive counsel of the National Association for the Advancement of Colored People, was there to mastermind it.

When court adjourned after convicting two black students from Shaw University of trespass, Greenberg, myself and several blacks—decided to have dinner and talk things over. Where to eat? We could not go to the hotel or a white restaurant. That would have provoked an incident. What about a restaurant in the black area? This was not easy either. If a cruising police car spotted whites "segregating together"—in the classic phrase of the late Police Chief Theophilus Eugene (Bull) Connor of Birmingham—we would be arrested.

We went to a black restaurant anyway, carefully selecting a table hard to see from the street. It was an edgy meal. The proprietor was nervous. The blacks were nervous. I was nervous. No one wanted to cause a "mixing" incident and complicate the case of the right of two young black men to walk on the sidewalk of the Cameron Village shopping center. The sit-in movement was heading into uncharted legal waters, and lawyers like Jack Greenberg were improvising as they raced to keep up with it.

We hurried through our ham hocks, turnip greens, black-eyed peas, cornpone, and pumpkin pie and slipped away. I thought I now knew how the young *narodniki* felt in St. Petersburg in the dark days of the 1880s when Lenin's elder brother, Alexander, and his friends were conspiring against the Czar, expecting at any moment that the *shpiki*, the third section plainclothesmen, would pounce.

Next day I was on the road again, deeper into the South, each day the temper, the level of violence on the rise. I entered South Carolina, once the citadel of secession, now a satellite capital of segregation. Edges were more raw. The day before, 350 students at black South Carolina State College had been rounded up with high pressure, knock-down firehoses, arrested, and herded into the courtyard of the Orangeburg jail (the jail had only thirty-nine cells). I had left the New South but not completely. I had a long talk with Governor Ernest F. Hollings, handsome, young, hoping for a national career, trying to split the middle between the old nigger talk of Senator Cotton Ed Smith and the sleek New York idiom of the industrialists being lured by South Carolina's lazy tax laws and cheap labor.

We sat in his bright, airy statehouse office as he pondered his dilemma. Black students, he said, could violate any law they wanted so long as they sang hymns and carried Bibles. What about the police and their Bibles? Public order had to be maintained. He was trying for a balance, but my hunch was that the nightstick would prevail. Yet, in his pleasant office, in his troubled manner, little suggested that South Carolina was taking the first steps toward the terrible day in the Cambodian spring of 1970 when the guns would bark and twice black Orangeburg students would lie dying of bullets fired in the name of "law and order."

Three weeks later it was April 6, and I was checking into the Tutwiler Hotel, first to Room 1117 and then to Room 1060. I was, I confess, a bit leery about Birmingham, very much on guard. It was a rough town. No city had taken a rougher stand on integration. The commissioner of police, Bull Connor, an ex-radio announcer, ran a rough department. He swore segregation would prevail in his lifetime.

I had tried to argue myself out of coming to Birmingham. But there was no way I could not go in. Catledge had been impressed with my sociological reporting on Red Hook, Yonkers, and the City of the Future (reversing Lincoln Steffens, I had said of Los Angeles, "I have seen the Future—and it doesn't work"), and Catledge had liked my trial run in the South with the dispatches from Nashville, Raleigh, and Columbia, South Carolina.

So here I was, cut loose to pick some key Southern cities, analyze what was happening, and try to figure out what was likely to happen. I left New York with four possible cities on my list: Baton Rouge, Louisiana; Birmingham, Alabama; Memphis, Tennessee; and Marshall, Texas. I would make a final decision on the basis of developments. I had gone to Baton Rouge twenty-five years earlier to cover the Huey Long assassination. Now I wanted to see how it had changed and whether Huey's revolution had made a difference in race relations. (It hadn't.) Marshall, Texas, was on my list because race violence had erupted, Memphis was there because of Catledge. He had begun his metropolitan newspaper career there, coming up from Mississippi.

I could not persuade myself that Memphis was as significant as Birmingham. There had been only minor incidents in both cities, but everyone told me that Birmingham was Gibralter, impregnable. It would take an earthquake to roll over Birmingham.

So I came to Birmingham. Claude Sitton told me that Bull Connor didn't like outside newsmen, better just turn up at his office. I didn't take that advice. I telephoned. He wasn't in. I said I would call back later.

Sitton had warned me to be careful in Birmingham, be careful when you are talking to people. That was in my mind as I began to make my calls, and I had another concern. The Alabama press was full of threats and denunciation of *The New York Times*. I had stopped over in Montgomery, the state capital, and found that officials were talking of a libel action because the *Times* had published a full-page advertisement, an appeal for funds for Martin Luther King. The ad was signed by forty or fifty notables, including Eleanor Roosevelt. It quoted from a *Times* editorial of March 19, 1960, on black demonstrations and called on Congress to "heed their rising voices."

Grover Hall, the vinegar-tongued editor of the Montgomery *Advertiser* (who had written me about the "New York student princes"), called the advertisement "Lies, lies, lies—and possibly willful ones." He demanded that the *Times* disassociate itself from the declaration. Alabama officials began to talk of sueing the *Times* for libel. To me this sounded plain nutty, but I took it as a serious reflection of the feverish temperature of the state, a clear warning to watch my step.

I was, I knew, moving across a field sown with hidden mines. The first person I met in Birmingham (twenty-five years later I still don't feel I should mention his name) warned me: "Birmingham is no place for irresponsible reporting."

"Be careful of what you say and whom you mention," he said. "Lives are at stake."

He did not tell me this over the telephone. I was (so I thought) on guard from the beginning about the telephone. I sensed, in the care with which people spoke, that they did not trust the telephone. It was a throwback to my days in Moscow, where I learned not to mention my name, not to mention the name of the person with whom I was talking. If we did not know each other well enough to recognize voices, we shouldn't be talking. I knew the dangers of careless contacts. In Moscow I never called a Russian from Room 393 in the Metropol Hotel. I always found a booth on the street. I thought of doing the same in Birmingham, then dismissed it. This was Birmingham. This was the United States. I would be careful, but I would not be paranoid.

I took a drive around Birmingham. I saw the brooding statue of Vulcan that looks down from atop Red Mountain—a symbol of the steel-and-coal industry that made Birmingham the Pittsburgh of the South. I lunched at The Club, where the bankers and businessmen, the "Big Mules" in their Brooks Brothers suits, talked over a martini or two and a king crab salad. I saw the $100,000 and $200,000 homes of Mountain Brook ablaze with shad, redbud, and the flowers of Birmingham's lush April. I passed through Honeysuckle Hills, the best black residential district (a federal housing project) and toured the one-block remnant of 18th Street, where the characters created by the writer, Octavus Roy Cohen—Florian Slappey and the "Sons and Daughters of I Will Arise"—used to entertain the nation in *The Saturday Evening Post* of my youth. I gazed on the gleaming white of the Birmingham jail of the legendary Judge Abernathy, who, it was said, used to hand a black defendant a pair of dice and invite him to roll the length of his stay in the jailhouse ("C'mon snake eyes!"), and the refrain of the old popular song reverberated in my mind as I looked on a Birmingham past that had almost vanished. (But three years later Martin Luther King was to write his "Letter from Birmingham Jail" as he sat there.) I saw the unpretentious head-quarters of A. G. Gaston, the richest black in Birmingham, an authentic millionaire. It was sited only a stone's throw from the haunts of the fictional Florian Slappey. I drove through Bessemer, grim and sooty, and the great Tennessee Coal & Iron complex, still belching smoke and steam as if the future were forever.

I heard tales of Bull Connor (as he listed himself in the telephone book), and somehow I still couldn't raise him on the phone. I heard his celebrated aphorisms: "Damn the law—down here we make our own law." "White and Negro are not to segregate together." "Only legitimate holdups will be investigated" (in response to allegations that some Birmingham policemen had a hand in local robberies). Once he had been flushed out of a room at the Tutwiler, where he was spending the evening with an attractive young lady. Connor's conviction (and $25 fine) on a morals charge had been overturned by the Alabama Supreme Court, and he had squeaked out an electoral victory, the voters ignoring the finding of the Jefferson County grand jury that Connor was "a hard taskmaster, explosive and vindictive." Connor had publicly proclaimed to the blacks of Birmingham that "as long as you live and as long as Connor lives, there will be segregation in Birmingham and the South."

The more I saw and the more I heard, the more I knew that I was treading dark and bloody ground.

## Chapter 17

# Fear and Hatred

Full dark had fallen before my cab pulled up at a pleasant house in the Canabaw Heights section of Birmingham. The Reverend Robert Hughes's home was set back on a wide lawn beside a big field where a tall pine rose, stately and brooding. One night not long before, a cross had been set afire beside the gloomy tree. The next morning Bob's little girl went out to play. After a while she came in and told her father: "Daddy, we had a visitor last night. Jesus Christ was here."

"Why do you say that?" Bob asked.

"I found his cross on our lawn."

Bob, a slim, boyish man, swiftly answered my ring and admitted me, after peering to see if any car had followed me. He carefully closed the door and led me to his study, where a row of green filing cabinets ranged beside the wall. The shades were pulled and curtains drawn. I think Hughes had expected I would be driving myself rather than taking a cab from the Tutwiler.

Bob Hughes was a Methodist minister who had accepted the post of director of the Alabama Council on Human Relations, which dedicated itself to fighting the conditions which had caused one black to say that Birmingham had become "the Johannesburg of America." No one knew better than Hughes what was happening in and around Birmingham, the dangers, the tensions.

All that evening he talked in his soft, almost apologetic voice, telling me the Birmingham story: of the black mother and daughter who with their own bodies protected a teenage son from hooded men armed with iron pipes, clubs, and leather blackjacks into which razor blades had been set; of a middle-aged white man who flogged a black high school girl with a bullwhip in the open street when she had an argument with a white teenager; of a black working man who stood by as white men raped his wife ("I have to work here. I'm not filing any complaint"); of wiretapping; of letters he mailed that never arrived; of after-midnight telephone threats; of a young divinity student arrested because he visited a black friend; of murder; of the pusillanimity of some fellow clergy; of businessmen afraid to lift their voices for fear their stores would be ruined; of the Ku Klux Klan; of Bull Connor; of Bull's police; of the racist politicians, the intimidated power structure. No one was brave enough to speak out, the penalties were so extreme.

We talked until midnight. He drove me back to the hotel, swiftly scrutinizing the street and the neighborhood. He said he never knew what he might find outside his house.

That was the night I began to understand how different Birmingham was from my idealized image of an American city. The next morning I visited a rabbi, who led me carefully into his study, locking the door behind us. He had installed floodlights around the synagogue and hired a night watchman, after dynamite had been found in the parking lot. Bombings and threats had been reported at other synagogues. The same violence-prone individuals who beat up the blacks were perpetrating anti-Semitic attacks. I talked with the civil rights lawyer, Charles Morgan, on the telephone and listened to his Aesopian language, the veiled double-talk I had heard in Moscow from Soviet dissidents fearful of the KGB. (Morgan's support of civil rights defendants cost him his political career in Alabama.)

Back in Room 1060 at the Tutwiler I assembled my notes and began to write my story. Before I left Birmingham, I dictated most of it to New York—from the airport telephone.

My story began:

From Red Mountain where a cast-iron Vulcan looks down 500 feet to the sprawling city, Birmingham seems veiled in the poisonous fumes of distant battle . . . . More than a few citizens, both white and Negro, harbor growing fear that the hour will strike when the smoke of civil strife will mingle with that of the hearths and forges . . . .

The *Times* editors headlined my dispatch: "Fear and Hatred Grips Birmingham."

The story was published on page 1, April 12, 1960. Only one change was made.

Fairly high up I had written:

To one long accustomed to the sickening atmosphere of Moscow in the Stalin days the aura of the community which once prided itself as the "Magic City" of the South is only too familiar. To one who knew Hitler's storm trooper Germany it would seem even more familiar.

The national desk of the *Times* thought that was a bit strong and deleted it. I did not object. I too thought I was laying it on a bit thick.

All hell broke loose. The editor of the Birmingham *News*, E. L. Holland, chanced to be at Princeton for a conference on the New South. He read *The New York Times* and next day in an editorial column Holland wrote: "That headline in the *Times* says words: 'Fear and Hatred Grip Birmingham.' This is the big lie. Perhaps the biggest of all. Salisbury has done his damage. Moscow please copy." On the following day Birmingham read the story. Both papers reproduced it. The headline in the Birmingham *News* was "N.Y. Times Slanders Our City—Can This be Birmingham?"

Birmingham raged. My mail was filled with hate letters. The city demanded retraction. It asked Turner Catledge to send another reporter down to check up on my stories and expose their falsity. Turner Catledge turned them down. No retreat. He had confidence in his correspondent. He did publish a statement put together by William F. Engel, a Birmingham civic leader, and Clarence B. Hanson, Jr., publisher of the Birmingham *News*. But Birmingham didn't think much of the statement. Even Mr. Hanson's own paper denounced it. It didn't go far enough. "The city of Birmingham," said the *News*, "is a lovely city. It is a city in which fear does not abide." It called on citizens not to "demean [our] pride by resorting to the angry retort, the hot word, the blind retaliation."

The idyllic picture painted by the *News* was not shared by black citizens in Birmingham and a few others, but this did not deter the Birmingham city commissioners. Three weeks after my report was published, Bull Connor and the two other city commissioners filed a $1.5 million libel action against me and a $1.5 million suit against the *Times*. The three commissioners of Bessemer, Alabama, weighed in soon, each asking $500,000. That brought the total to $3 million for me, $3 million for the *Times*. Then a Birmingham city detective sued for another $150,000. The numbers added up. Governor John Patterson and the Mongomery city officials joined in a similar libel action against the *Times* for publication of the advertisement "Heed Their Rising Voices." They wanted another $3 million. That brought the total in Alabama to nearly $10 million and set the pattern for a new Southern Strategy, designed to chill, control, and, if possible, suppress reportage of the civil rights movement. Before the Supreme Court brought this game to an end with the landmark *Sullivan* v. *The*

*New York Times* decision, nearly $300 million in libel actions were outstanding against the media. Coverage had been chilled. I could not return to Alabama for four years. Few *New York Times* reporters went into the state, and news gathering was inhibited all over the South. In fact, to this day, despite the Supreme Court, a plague of libel suits has infested exercise of First Amendment rights, caused newspapers and electronic media millions in legal fees, and often dampened press enthusiasm for hard-hitting reporting.

I was quickly placed in double jeopardy. A grand jury was convened in Bessemer, Jefferson County, Birmingham's steel mill adjunct, and I was indicted on forty-two counts of criminal libel. I was subject to instant arrest if I set foot in Alabama. If I went to Birmingham to defend myself in Federal court on the civil libel, I would be clapped into jail in Bessemer in the criminal case for which I might be subjected to several hundred years of consecutive sentences. No one could remember anyone in modern times having been indicted in Alabama for criminal libel.

This was no joke. But it was trivial compared to what happened to the people with whom I talked in Birmingham. I thought I had taken precautions. I hadn't. Robert Hughes was served with a subpoena to appear before the Bessemer grand jury and bring all his records—that is, the names of everyone who gave money, everyone who contacted him for help, and all his sources of information. He refused and went to jail for thirty-six hours before Charles Morgan, the civil rights lawyer, got him out.

Morgan might have suffered the same fate, but I had not talked to him from the Tutwiler. The hotel records were subpoenaed. Everyone I called was brought before the grand jury, even Clark Stallworth, reporter for the *Post-Herald*. There was no way Clark could wriggle out. He had interviewed me ("Nikita Could be Elected Governor of Alabama, N.Y. Times Writer Says"). There it was under his byline with a photo of me reading the *Literaturnaya Gazeta*, which I had tucked into my briefcase to while away those long dull airline flights.

Stallworth's career was blunted for several years, "guilt by association." The North Alabama Council of the Methodist Church unfrocked Hughes, expelling him from the ministry, but gave him his reversed collar back on a promise to go to Africa as a missionary. He spent years in Southern Rhodesia. Two black clergymen with whom I spoke—Fred Shuttlesworth and J. Herbert Oliver—already were

210

targets of Bull Connor. Shuttlesworth had been arrested more times than he could remember. He continued to be. Oliver once had been arrested and dragged off in his nightclothes. Now he was even more harassed. Ultimately he and his wife moved to Brooklyn and threw their energy into the northern slum of Bedford-Stuyvesant. (Shuttlesworth moved to Cincinnati.) Dr. Henry Stanford, president of Birmingham Southern College, was subjected to a vicious whispering campaign. His talk with me cost his college at least $1.5 million in promised contributions. Rabbi Grafman was called before the grand jury and browbeaten. One man whom I telephoned repeatedly (but never seemed to reach) was Bull Connor. He suffered no ill consequences. He was not called before the Bessemer grand jury.

To this day I cannot forgive myself for exposing honest, courageous citizens to the hazards of wrecked careers, physical danger, and changed lives. I simply was not as careful as I would have been in Moscow, but I did not believe—in fact, I still find it hard to believe—that Moscow conditions could prevail in a great modern city of my own country. This was naïveté. By 1960 I should have known better.

Times were tense in Birmingham. They were tense at 229 West 43rd Street as well. When the Birmingham and Montgomery cases arose, *Times* counsel, the venerable firm of Lord, Day and Lord whose partner Louis Loeb had handled *The New York Times* for many years, routinely contacted its correspondent firm in Birmingham, the best and most prestigious in Alabama. Sorry, the firm replied, they could not handle the *Times*, there was a conflict of interest. Loeb tried the No. 2 firm in Birmingham. Same answer. And so it went with the third. Lord, Day and Lord, got the message. No one in Alabama wanted any association with the *Times*. The *Times* was appalled. So was Lord, Day and Lord. "Nothing had ever arisen that was more worrisome," Loeb told me. "Nothing scared me more than this litigation." Finally, Lord, Day and Lord found a small litigating firm in Birmingham. As Cecil Roberts, a bright, taut-tongued Birmingham lady, put it, "They were the kind of lawyers who took black clients and got them life sentences instead of the death penalty." Beddow, Embry & Beddow, was indeed willing to take the *Times*. They were used to defending unpopular cases and doing it very well. A few years later Eric Embry, who handled my case, was elevated to the Alabama Supreme Court, a far more capable man, I am sure, than his colleagues in the blue ribbon firms.

I was not frightened by Birmingham. I had total confidence in the *Times* and its counsel. I had total confidence in my reporting. I knew I had the story right. I agreed totally with a man in Birmingham who told me privately: "Birmingham is going to blow—and I don't want to be around here when it does." I smiled to myself in January 1961 when David Lowe, working with Edward R. Murrow on a CBS documentary on Birmingham, told me he had found a grave defect in my Birmingham coverage: Conditions were much worse than I had reported.

Murrow said he had seen nothing to compare with it since Berlin under Adolf Hitler. People had been unwilling to meet publicly or talk over hotel telephones. Murrow met people at night, in shadowy park corners, obscure lunch counters. No one would come to the hotel. Nor did people want to meet in their own homes. Stocks of arms were being accumulated. Each side was now armed with machine guns. The working title for their CBS documentary was "The Johannesburg of America."

On Sunday, May 14, 1961, Birmingham did blow. The Monday morning headline in the Birmingham *News* proclaimed: "Mob Terror Hits City on Mother's Day." Thugs had attacked a group of Freedom Riders at the Birmingham bus station with fists and iron pipes and blackjacks. A giant of a man, reported the Birmingham *News*, beat whites and blacks against the cement floor, until his fists ran red with their blood. Connor's headquarters was two blocks away, but no policeman showed his face.

That Monday morning across the eight-columns of page 1, the Birmingham *News* asked:

Where were the police? The City of Birmingham is normally a peaceful orderly place in which people are safe.

Harrison Salisbury of *The New York Times* last year came to Birmingham and wrote two stories about us which said, in substance, that fear and hatred "stalked our streets." The Birmingham *News* and others promptly challenged this assertion. The *News* knows Birmingham people as others know them and they didn't fit that definition.

But yesterday, Sunday, May 14, was a day which ought to be burned into Birmingham's conscience.

Fear and hatred did stalk Birmingham's streets yesterday....

The News asks when will the people demand that fear and hatred be driven from the streets of Birmingham.

Next morning I found on my desk in the big city room at 229 West 43rd Street a copy of the Birmingham *News* with its ugly black headlines. Attached to it was a memo:

> To Mr. Salisbury
> Vindication!
> ECD [Clifton Daniel]

Well, it was, and it wasn't. I had not written the Birmingham story in order to be vindicated. I had written it in hope that my words might change the course of events, that "fear and hatred" might be driven from the streets of Birmingham. I knew from private talks that my report did bring the city up short, that the reaction was not all bluster and bloat. There were people in Birmingham, including many who were angered by my reports, who felt them unfair, sensationalized, and biased, who now began to think more deeply about their city and what could be done. This did not cause a change in the tide of events—not immediately and not for a long time. The momentum was too great, the forces of intolerance too powerful.

My reports did not change Birmingham. Neither did the savage attack on the Freedom Riders nor the indignation of Birmingham over the event. More than headlines was needed, and, in fact, worse was yet to come—the terrible year of 1963, the year Martin Luther King was jailed in Birmingham and wrote from Birmingham jail of "the dark clouds of racial prejudice" and "the damp fog of misunderstanding." Two months later to the day, civil rights leader Medgar Evers was shot and killed outside his home in Jackson, Mississippi; five months and three days later, a bomb killed four black children at Sunday school services of the Sixteenth Street Baptist Church in Birmingham. On November 22, 1963, President John F. Kennedy was shot dead in Dallas, and five years later Martin Luther King was to die, shot to death in Memphis, Tennessee.

It was still a long, long way home for Birmingham. Not until March of 1964 did the U.S. Supreme Court hand down its historic ruling in the Montgomery, Alabama, case of *Sullivan* v *The New York Times* (the case about the Martin Luther King advertisement).

This decision broadly affirmed the right of the press to criticize and report on activities and conduct of public officials. The principles of the Montgomery decision supported my right to report, as I had, on Birmingham. I came back to Birmingham for the first time in September of 1964, to appear in the U.S. District Court before Judge Grooms in the Birmingham libel case. Quickly the other plaintiffs were thrown out and only Bull Connor remained, a bulky man with an ovoid Roman head, incurably the politician, greeting my lawyers and myself as we came to court each morning with classic Southern affability, small talk about the weather, little jokes. For years now he had been teasing correspondents about what he would do when he took over *The New York Times*. Claude Sitton fell in with this hee-haw humour and asked Bull for a raise.

The trial lasted for a week. The *Times* lawyers and I stayed at the Tutwiler. I didn't bother to notice my room number. Nothing seemed to have changed in Birmingham. The lawyers had rooms on either side of me. We came to breakfast together, we walked over to court together, lunched together, dined together, and spent the evening in each others' company. A lot of togetherness.

The moment Judge Grooms announced the verdict [we lost], Louis Loeb and Tom Daly of Lord, Day and Lord and I jumped into a taxi and sped to the airport. After we boarded the plane, Loeb and Tom ordered drinks, settled back, and Louis wiped his brow with a handkerchief.

"You're perspiring, Louis," I said.

"You would, too, if you knew what has been happening," he said.

Federal court officers and the sheriff's office in Bessemer had made an agreement safeguarding me from arrest or interference during the trial. All seemed peaceful until three days into the trial. Then U.S. marshals received word that a posse of sheriff's deputies was on its way from Bessemer (just outside the Birmingham city limits) to arrest me and hustle me off to the Bessemer jail. Judge Grooms called a recess in court proceedings, directed the chief marshal to assemble his men, and repel the deputies by force if they attempted to storm the courthouse. He then got on the telephone and warned Bessemer that if their deputies appeared in his courthouse, his marshals would throw them into jail on charges of contempt of court. There was a little argument and hard breathing, but a few minutes later word came that the Bessemer posse had turned back.

From then on everyone was on the alert. The lawyers never let me out of their sight. Judge Grooms had put his marshals on twenty-four-hour alert to protect me if any new move was made to spirit me away from Birmingham.

Of none of this had I been aware. I had just thought that Loeb and Daly had been unusually solicitous.

"We didn't want to alarm you," they said. "We were afraid it might throw you off stride when you got on the stand."

A year later the U.S. Circuit Court of Appeals gave us a sweeping victory. Costs of $3,220.25 were awarded to the *Times* as well as vindication of my Birmingham reporting. I still cherish a photocopy of the check.

So, I thought, Birmingham had come to an end. It had begun, I hoped, the long, slow struggle of throwing off the evil past and trying to enter the New South which so many of us had envisaged. Of course the violence had not ended. It rose and fell all around the perimeter of Birmingham, it ebbed and flowed in Alabama and Mississippi. But, it seemed to me, the tide was beginning to turn because of the strong stand taken by the Kennedys and Lyndon Johnson. Bull Connor's image was waning. He suffered a stroke, got around for a while in a wheelchair as state utilities commissioner, and finally died.

Birmingham was no longer center stage. Neither was the south. Gradually the focus had shifted away from civil rights in the South to the North and to the whole country. It was Vietnam that rang the alarm bells now.

Long since I had forgotten that morning of April 6 when I checked into the Tutwiler Hotel and had been shifted from Room 1117 to Room 1060.

In 1977 the city of Birmingham decided to remodel a disused, decaying firehouse. The second floor of the building had been used as a dumping ground for old documents. Robert Corley, and J. R. Marvin of the Birmingham Public Library, were sent to see if any of the papers were worth saving. They climbed the dirty staircase and found the roof had leaked and papers in fiberboard containers were strewn in all directions. They pawed into the mess and discovered—fortuitously protected by the papers heaped above them—a treasure trove of civil rights history, seven years of secret archives of the Birmingham Police Department.

Here were tape recordings, transcriptions of listening devices,

215

detailed reports by surveillance agents, taped telephone conversations, police records of surveillance of anyone thought connected with civil rights in Birmingham in the years 1957–63. Here was evidence of arrangements by the police for hotel and motel clerks to advise them if reporters or activists checked in, reports of undercover operatives who attended meetings of civil rights or black organisations. As a whole it constituted one of the most valuable and complete archives of the civil rights movement in the South.

Bull Connor had been dead several years by now. The era symbolized by his name was long since gone. Now he had inadvertently bequeathed to history a rare source of documentary materials. It was not complete. No record of my visit to Birmingham was uncovered. But the explanation for my shift in hotel rooms from 1117 to 1060 seemed clear. By mistake, I had been placed in a room without a bug. The desk clerk remedied that by shifting me to 1060.

Why weren't the tapes and surveillance notes on me found in the old fire station? We will never know, but I would guess that Bull kept them personally. Perhaps they were destroyed along with other caches of secret and sensitive information before he died.

This is not and cannot be a history of civil rights and Birmingham. Rather it is a chapter in the education of myself, in my never-ending struggle to understand my own country and our society so that I could better report and interpret it.

If you had asked me in 1960 or 1964 where to look for future progress of the races, for the elimination of the deepest abuses of humanity, I might have said Nashville or Charlotte, North Carolina, or even Greenville, Mississippi. Birmingham? Never! The imprint of Bull Connor was too deep. And I would have been wrong. It would have been reasoning with what passes for a logical, rational mind. But human beings do not move with computerized precision.

On the twenty-first anniversary of "Fear and Hatred" I was invited to return to Birmingham. Vulcan still brooded on Red Mountain but not much of my Birmingham was still there. Steeltown was dwindling. No longer was Birmingham raw and redneck. Now it was dominated by education and medicine, the greatest medical complex in the South in downtown Birmingham, 17,000 students. The old city, the wastes of cheap bars, vacant warehouses, the haunts of the Klan and the remnants of Florian Slappey's day—gone. Gone, of course, was Bull Connor, his name only a myth to a bright-eyed, black-and-white generation keyed to upward mobility, high-tech education, ignorant of the "dark clouds" and "damp fog" of which Martin Luther King wrote. Gone was the ancient Tutwiler, its giant brass cuspidors and seedy lobby. Gleaming glass-box skyscrapers caught the eye, and on the top floor of the biggest of these, the First National-Southern Natural Gas building, a luxurious auditorium had been turned over for a retrial of the case of Harrison E. Salisbury versus Birmingham.

It was hot, lush springtime, the temperature 89. Birmingham was a mass of azaleas, white and pink and lavender blossoms everywhere. The room was filled with button-down-collar young men and women, black and white, curious to hear the stories of a world they could hardly imagine. When films flashed on the screen showing Connor's attack dogs leaping at black crowds ("four flea-bitten old police dogs," as Arthur Hanes, once Birmingham's mayor, insisted on calling them), the young men and women, could not believe their eyes. "*That* happened in Birmingham?" a handsome black woman exclaimed. "Really? I can't believe it. Not here in *our* Birmingham."

I was glad that Arthur Hanes was there. His was the only authentic voice of the old Birmingham. I needed him to remind me that the Birmingham I had written about really existed.

On my flight back from Birmingham to New York I jotted down a few notes, just as I had when I flew back in 1960:

"My principal task was to convey to these young people the reality of what Birmingham had been. They simply do not know and cannot get it. This is the most striking measure of the distance Birmingham has traveled. And the young people, too."

Not that Birmingham was home and free. I heard talk of "survivalists" up in the red clay hills, training camps in racism and sadism. The Klan was not dead. Birmingham had a black mayor but (at that moment) no public transportation, previously used almost entirely by blacks.

No, I thought, Birmingham is not home free. But how many, many miles the city has traveled! Once again I was filled with hope for my country. Where else in the world could people come through such a caldron of hate and fear and emerge to this bright and sunny plateau?

# Chapter 18

# Death in the Family

I was never a Kennedy idolator. Idolatry is not my style. Among the Presidential possibilities of my day I placed Wendell Willkie and Adlai Stevenson ahead of any of those who actually held the office, with Alf Landon not far behind. I don't know whether they would have made good Presidents, but they had a human touch that was lacking in so many who won the White House.

I got to know Jack Kennedy in the Presidential campaign of 1960. I covered both Kennedy and Nixon in that year, and I was not wild about either. I often spoke of Kennedy as a "lace curtain Nixon," by which I meant I did not think there was much difference, if any, in their ideology. That was not true, but there was, I think, a nubbin of truth in my remark. Nixon was shabby in character but had a better grasp of the world. He had seen more of it and thought more. Kennedy had style; there were not many reporters he didn't charm, but he was lazy. I think that had he not been martyred, his Presidential rating would be much lower.

Most newsmen thought Kennedy loved them. That was not true. I have observed every President since Calvin Coolidge. None of them loved the press. FDR, Kennedy, and Reagan were the best at conning the reporters, Hoover and Carter the worst. One of Harry Truman's most amiable traits was his honest dislike of reporters. He put up with the marriage of his beloved Margaret to Clifton Daniel, but it was a bitter pill that Clifton was a newspaperman.

Jack Kennedy gave me a lift one evening from West Virginia, where he was campaigning against Hubert Humphrey. He was on his way to Washington. The plane was a puddle-jumper, and only the two of us were aboard. He spent the brief ride cursing "those sons-a-bitches," the newspapermen. He had a big envelope of clips which he pawed through and tossed away. Most of them seemed to be pieces about his father Joseph, and most of them, Jack felt, went out of their way to dig up the old Joe Kennedy scandals—his borderline bank manipulations, his speculative deals in Wall Street, the maneuvers that got him the Scotch whiskey franchises and the great Chicago Merchandise Mart (where in prohibition days, the building almost empty, a huge speakeasy with a 100-foot bar was the liveliest activity under its roof—I often ate my lunch there), and his role as a spokesman for America First and appeasement before FDR yanked him out of London as the U.S. ambassador. "Bastards," gritted Kennedy as he leafed through the reports. "Just a bunch of lies. They never tell the truth. Bunch of bastards." I didn't talk up the case for newspapering. It was his father, and he was a true member of the clan—the Kennedys against the world and, in this case, against the newsmen. But I had been given an insight into the true Kennedy feeling about the press. One thing was certain about the Kennedys. You were with them or against them. Totally. The press was on the other side.

I don't want to suggest that Nixon had any more love for the press. I think the feeling of the two men was mutual in this regard. But Kennedy could put on a bravado act, make a half dozen important Washington correspondents believe they were real friends (inside the clan). Nixon was a poor actor. His lies stuck out like cold sores. He was forever wrapping his anger at the press in a sleazy tangle of "I know what your problems are," or "Of course you have your job to do," "I don't mean to include you personally," and then out would come the hurt and anger. I guess you could say that, in his way, Nixon was the more honest man. Jack rarely let his distaste show in public.

I got to know Bobby Kennedy long before I met Jack. Bobby was assigned in 1956 to ride shotgun with Stevenson as "liaison" with the Kennedy politicians in big cities and particularly with the Catholics (often the same thing). Stevenson was vulnerable to the Catholic vote; he was a divorced man. Not infrequently Adlai coerced one of his sulky sons to campaign with him to show that he was a family man. Bobby was supposed to work the Catholic power brokers. Actually he did nothing of the kind. I never saw him lift a finger for Stevenson. The Kennedys did little to conceal their contempt for Stevenson. They thought he was a wimp and a loser. Bobby went along for the ride—to learn what not to do when his brother ran in 1960—and he didn't bother to conceal his feelings.

By 1956 the Kennedy machine was already in place, just waiting for Adlai's defeat to take off and start running for 1960. (Within days of Adlai's defeat the Arthur Schlesinger, Jr.s and John Kenneth

Galbraiths were jumping on the Kennedy wagon. I thought this was bad taste. They could have waited a few weeks.)

I remember one warm October evening in Ohio or Indiana, sitting on the railroad track with Bobby, one of those whistlestop tours that candidates used to inflict on themselves and their entourages. I had dictated my story to the *Times*, and Bobby and I sat talking, he plucking tough yellowing straws from the grass growing through the tracks and talking about the bumbles of the Stevenson campaign, Adlai's nit-picking at his speech text until he got up to speak, no rapport with the local machines (at least in part, Bobby's fault), the lousy advance work (poor crowds, lost luggage).

"We'll change all that," Bobby said, the elements of the 1960 campaign shaping up in his mind.

I didn't like Bobby. I resented his cynicism. I thought he and his brother should make a college try for Adlai. "What's the point?" Bobby said. "He hasn't got a prayer against Eisenhower." That was true, but I didn't like the arrogance. Nor did I like the arrogance of Bobby and his brother after President Kennedy named Bobby attorney-general.

I modified my opinion as I watched the brothers handle the confrontations in the South. They did not blink, and I gave them credit. Later, when JFK was killed in Dallas November 22, 1963, I watched Bobby mature in a way that I would not have thought possible. He shed the preppy touch-football image of Hyannis. We had a long talk on a ride up the Hudson River—a steamboat ride to spur the conservationist fight to save Storm King from the power people. I saw Bobby's eyes that day—the tragic shadows, the emotion as he spoke of Vietnam, his determination to bring an end to LBJ's escalation. The gung-ho days of his partnership with General Maxwell Taylor had gone. This was a man, not the Kennedy brat with whom I sat on the track on an October evening in 1956, chewing straw and spitting out the seeds....

By the time Jack Kennedy was shot to death in Dallas at 12:30 P.M. of November 22, 1963, a lot had changed for me. Reluctantly I had bowed to Turner Catledge's insistence and taken on the post of national editor of *The New York Times*. (Catledge coined the title "Director of National Correspondence" so as not to hurt the feelings of Ray O'Neill, who held the title "National Editor.")

Catledge's proposal had reached me in Kabul, Afghanistan, where I was trying to persuade the authorities to let me go through the Khyber Pass. A small war was in progress. I never did get to the Khyber, going to Tashkent, Bokhara and Mongolia instead. I had to accept Catledge's proposal—much as I preferred reporting. He had twice tried to make me an editor, and I knew I couldn't say no a third time. But I did get his pledge that once or twice a year I could abandon my desk and go off on a reporting trip. The promise was meticulously kept by Catledge and Punch Sulzberger, even after I set up the op-ed page and became an associate editor of the *Times*.

I had concluded before going to work for the *Times* in 1949 that the essence of journalism was reporting and writing. I wanted to find things out—particularly things which no one else had managed to dig out—and let people have the best possible evidence on which to make up their minds about policy. It was essentially a gloss on the old Scripps slogan: "Give Light and the People Will Find Their Way." I have never ceased to believe in it.

One day in November 1963 I was sitting at the long table in the third floor dining room of the Century Club, waiting for my lunch.

At that moment, just on one o'clock, the waiter having brought my purée mongole, Alfred De Liagre, the theatrical producer, elegant as always in English tweeds, rounded into the room, raised his voice over the cheerful hum of Century conversation, and said, a bit theatrically: "Gentlemen, I am sorry to interrupt, but the President has just been shot in the head . . . in Dallas." I dropped my napkin, leaped down the stairs, and ran the two and a half blocks west on 43rd Street to 229, up on the elevator, and to my national news desk just south of my old spot, the Hagerty desk, which I had occupied for nine years. There I would remain almost continuously for the next several days.

I was used to violence in the South, violence in the country as a whole. It seemed to me that I had inhabited a violent world since I had come back from the deceptive quiet of the Moscow streets—violence in the slums of Brooklyn and Manhattan, a nationwide uprooting of populations, technological revolution in the farm belt, the bondage of the great cities in straitjackets of steel and concrete freeways, and now rising terror in the South.

Dallas . . . Kennedy . . . violence . . . it seemed an almost inevitable pattern, and my mind leaped instantly to the passion in Dallas that had raged since before Kennedy's election. Dallas had seemed like another country, ranting against *everything*. I knew of the threats and the hate ads that spewed out before the Kennedy visit. I had hardly gotten on the telephone to order staff to Dallas—everyone I could reach who could fly in by nightfall—than my mind spun with thoughts of a conspiracy by the radical right or even—I hardly dared formulate the thought—by some in the diehard LBJ camp who so hated the Kennedys. What it might be I did not know. But plots, conspiracy, coups raced through my head. From the vicious anti-Kennedy propaganda, there seemed to me but one short step to a conspiracy to assassinate the President.

The arrest of Oswald before the afternoon was over blew the gas out of my conspiracy balloon. In the supercharged Dallas atmosphere the raging Dallas billionaires might have created the atmosphere in which the Oswalds of the world were born and thrived. But that was another thing. I *knew* Oswald. I don't mean I knew this Oswald, but I had known other Oswalds in earlier years. I knew their fantasies, the paranoia, the tawdry sense of self-power. I had *met* Oswald in a dozen forms in the depression years. I had met him in the public library in Minneapolis, reading in the newspaper room (he never had money for newspapers), poring over texts by Ignatius Donnelly or Henry George, the single taxer, furiously taking notes, digging his way through volumes of shabby theorists seeking the true villain of the age, the one who must be destroyed if his vision of a new day was to be fulfilled. I had talked with Oswald in 1932 in a ratty late-night bookstore on North Clark Street in Chicago, a gaunt young man with the deep-set eyes of a fanatic, holding a moldy volume in his hand and spouting about the conspiracy of the Morgans and the Jews against the gentiles; I had listened to him shout from a soapbox, a real soapbox, in Union Square, New York, in 1934, shouting: "Down with Capitalism!" He was sometimes old, sometimes young, always on the thin edge of survival, eyes fixed on an image no one but he could see, mind dusty with fragments of political theory, broken bits of philosophy.

Yes, I knew Oswald as soon as we got to his background, and I gave my reporters assignments consistent with the Oswald whom I knew, the universal Oswald. I told them to check the public libraries in New Orleans near where he had lived, visit secondhand book-stores, look at the squares where cranks hang out and harangue, do the same in Dallas. He would be a bus person. Check the bus routes from New Orleans and Dallas and Mexico.

The pattern paid off. He was precisely the Oswald I had met in the bitter days of depression, his haunts the same, his confusions the same—one moment stalking General Walker, the next Nixon, the next Kennedy; pro-Cuba, anti-Cuba; pro-Soviet, anti-Soviet. Could this confused Oswald be the man in a conspiracy? Never—no matter how many shots had been fired from the grassy knoll, no matter how many men were seen at the window of the Texas Book Depository. Nor was his trail hard to follow. It was broad, obvious, blazed wherever he went by his paranoid inability to accomplish anything— except shoot the President of the United States. When he took out a card in the branch library near his Magazine Street flat in New Orleans, the first book he checked out was a biography of Mao Zedong. Ten days later he borrowed a Kennedy biography and another on the Huey Long assassination. *Perfect.* Oswald could, of course, have been used—as suspicion long suggested the Czar's *Okhrana* gave the drifter Bogrov a chance to enter the Kiev opera house in 1911, knowing he would assassinate Prime Minister Stolypin, or as Stalin's OGPU let the young Nikolayev slip into Smolny and kill Leningrad's Party leader, Sergei Kirov. Certainly Oswald could have been a cat's-paw, but I saw no trace of such a cunning trick. Oswald hardly differed from the classic American assassin of Presidents. After the assassination of Martin Luther King and Robert Kennedy, President Johnson named a commission to investigate violence in the United States. The authors noted the frequency with which the "lone killer" had struck at the White House, Guiteau at McKinley, Czolgosz at Garfield, Zangara at FDR, John Schrank at Theodore Roosevelt.

In an introduction to the LBJ report I wrote: "The notion that violence and assassination is something new, something 'un-American,' a peculiar product of the present day, is demonstrably and remarkably mistaken. Violence has marked every step of the creation and building of American society.... Violence may not be 'as American as apple pie,' but it has been synonymous with the American experience from the earliest days."

That understanding has hardly been accepted by Americans. The notion that John F. Kennedy was killed by a single morbid drifter, his head stuffed with unbaked philosophy and tawdry phobias, is rejected everywhere. I think I understand this. On November 27, 1963, five days after Kennedy was killed, the first moment I had time and strength to put down what I felt, I wrote a memorandum to myself. I said that in the year 2000 the Kennedy assassination would still be a matter of debate, new theories being evolved how and why it happened. The lone, crazed killer would not then—or ever—be accepted. It offended nature. For the Sun King to be struck down by a vagrant with bulging eyes—no, the concept was repugnant to our very being. For a man so noble the cause of death must lie in high conspiracy, the most powerful courtiers, the great barons, the captains of the earth.

As a young reporter in Chicago, each year when the anniversary of Lincoln's death approached, I prepared for the annual ritual—the revelation of the "true story" of what had happened—an interview with a dying ancient in a log house in southern Illinois whose father had told him of the haunted, bearded, gaunt-cheeked man who had lived on into the 1880s, appearing suddenly in the village and living a life of solitude. "It was Lincoln," the dying man gasped. "My father knew him well." Or the legend of the grave, a hardy perennial. Loncoln's tomb had been secretly opened. *There was no body in it.* Or the tangled tale of conspiracy. It was not John Wilkes Booth—he was a fall guy for the man who engineered the plot, Lincoln's secretary of war, Stanton. There was always a new legend because with Lincoln too we could not accept the simple facts. They were not grand enough. They did not satisfy our sense of Homeric drama.

As I said in my memorandum to myself:

"I am sure that the echo of this killing will resound down the corridors of our history for years and years and years. It is so strange, so bizarre, so incredible, so susceptible to legend making.... It matches Lincoln's assassination."

I added—"We are running down every single item of Oswald's background that can be found. Strange story though it is, there is not one fact thus far which essentially changes the public story—or makes it any more understandable."

It was no surprise to me that the Warren Commission report did not halt the "revelations," the rumors, the legend making of the conspiracy theorists, now grown to a kind of carrion industry.

I did not think the Warren Commission had dug out any essential fact that the *Times* had not found in its intense coverage in the days and weeks after the assassination. The coverage had begun with classic reportage—Tom Wicker's on-the-scenes eye-witness. It could not be beat. Tom was the only *Times* man in Dallas that day. I made one contribution to Tom's beautiful story. At 5 P.M. I ordered him—

no, *command* is the word—to halt reporting and start writing. No interruptions. Any new details we could put into the piece, if necessary, after it went into type about 8:30 P.M. that night. Just write every single thing you have seen and heard. Period. He did. No more magnificent piece of journalistic writing has been published in the *Times*. Through Tom's eye we lived through each minute of that fatal Friday, the terror, the pain, the horror, the mindless tragedy, elegant, bloodchilling prose.

To this day not one material fact has been added to *The New York Times* account of the assassination and the events that followed it. This record would be enhanced had it not been for Vietnam and my trip to Hanoi in December 1966.

Catledge and Daniel, now executive editor and managing editor respectively of the *Time*, decided to reinvestigate the whole affair because of the torrent of conspiracy yarns, challenges to the Warren Commission report and general hysteria about the assassination.

The decision was made in autumn 1966. Once again I was placed in charge of the Kennedy story. The veterans of 1963 were assembled, Peter Kihss, at their head. We listed every point that had been challenged by the conspiracy buffs and reinvestigated them. The work was nearing completion. Peter Kihss had roughed out the whole story by early December 1966. Then came the telegram telling me that a Hanoi visa awaited me in Paris.

"We'll just put it on the shelf until you get back from Vietnam," Clifton Daniel told me. By the time I returned from Hanoi the furor about Kennedy had died down—it had had a regular sequence of heights and depths. Daniel decided to let the inquiry stay where it was until interest rose again. That moment never seemed to return. The massive inquiry remains on the shelf, unfinished, unpublished. I will say only one thing: nothing in our new investigation undercut, contradicted, or undermined in any fashion the basic conclusions of our original work or that of the Warren Commission. The work is all there, solid as Gibraltar, and as I suggested in my memo of November 27, 1963, there will still be questions raised, again and again, well after the year 2000.

A footnote. I was filling in as national editor once again on June 4, 1968. Robert F. Kennedy was speaking in Los Angeles, and that night I stayed in the office until the Kennedy rally was concluded and Bobby's speech finished. I then said good night, slipped away, and

225

took a taxi from 43rd Street to East 84th Street. As I entered the house, the telephone was ringing: Bobby had been shot. In ten minutes I was back in the office and stayed the night.

It was worse than his brother's assassination. Bobby was so young, so vigorous, he had come on so straight, he had grown up so real, the act was so senseless, the repetition so banal, the plain blunt facts of it no mystery, no chance for the mind to ponder possibilities. Just the brutal act. The bullet. I sat at my desk, talking with the reporters on the telephone, running through the copy as it poured in, my mind numb, unbelieving, almost in shock. A bit after 2 A.M. my phone rang. It was Jacqueline Kennedy. I did not know her. She did not know whom she was talking to. She just wanted some word. There was none to give. Bobby was alive. But I knew he would not live very long. I could not tell her that. She seemed on the edge of the world. I could not imagine what she was passing through, her voice vague as a child's, the image in my mind of her in the car in Dallas, dress drenched with blood, her husband's shattered head in her lap. Now this. About 3:30 A.M. she called again. There was nothing I could do but talk, hoping perhaps my droning, flat, Midwestern voice would somehow disconnect her from tragedy too deep for any soul to endure. She hung up. I did not see her for years and, of course, never spoke of the conversations, which probably existed for her in some plane where reality could not penetrate. After a while Bobby was dead, and there was nothing more to do at the office. I went home and told Charlotte and held her in my arms and cried. I had not cried for Jack, but I could not keep the tears back for Bobby. He was, I thought then and now, America's best and brightest future, and he was dead.

226

# Chapter 19

# Behind the Iron Curtain

I did not think, as I sat talking about Milovan Djilas with his wife Stefica in their Spartan apartment in central Belgrade, a Singer sewing machine in one corner, a rubber tree in another, that I was about to take my first step in a journey that would place me behind the American lines in Hanoi nine years later. I had gone to Yugoslavia in that pleasant summer of 1957 to fill in while Elie Abel, later to be dean of the Columbia Journalism School, went home on leave.

I spent my days poking about Yugoslavia, talking with Mrs. Djilas, her china-blue eyes sparkling like a child's, and with other Yugoslav intellectuals. That was the summer the name of Milovan Djilas was on all lips. *The New Class* had just been published in the United States, and Djilas was serving a three-year term in the Sremska Mitrovica prison (in the same cell he had spent 1933–36 as a revolutionary) because of his heretic conclusion that Marxism had given birth to a new class, an elite bourgeoisie comprising the ruling hierarchy of the Party.

Djilas' ideas had stirred a storm in Eastern Europe. "Milovan has talked enough politics in this flat to last a lifetime," his wife told me with a puckish smile. She was not worried about her husband— except for the cold. The prison at Sremska Mitrovica was not heated during the icy Serbian winter. This was the summer I met Vlado Dedijer, a craggy man with deep-set eyes, Tito's close companion and biographer, as controversial as Djilas. We talked to the early hours of morning, Vlado complaining that his head still ached from the bullet lodged there in a mountain firefight during World War II. He was still talking all night and complaining of the bullet thirty years later.

With a long lazy summer ahead, I decided to try my hand at penetrating the forbidden Balkan kingdoms of Communism that surrounded Yugoslavia. I had been banned by Moscow since the 1954 publication of my exposé of Stalin's years, and it was a delicious experience to breathe the air of a Communist country which delighted in doing everything just the opposite of the Russian way.

Yugoslavia was surrounded by countries which had closed their doors against Americans. I decided to try the toughest one first—Albania. There hadn't been an American reporter in Albania since World War II, no U.S. relations since Mussolini invaded Albania in the 1930s. I sent wireless messages to the Albanian leaders, Enver Hoxha and President Mehmet Shehu, but I did not hold my breath for an answer. I traveled around Yugoslavia, got a big blister on my toe walking Belgrade's cobblestones, and, coming back from the trip, found to my astonishment that the Albanians were trying to reach me: I had a visa. I went around to the Albanian embassy. It looked like a fortress, heavy doors, steel shuttered windows. I had the feeling—maybe my imagination—that there were machine-gun nests in the recessed windows.

I rang the bell. A long wait. I rang again. Finally a small slot, something like a Russian *fortochka*, opened and a scowling face confronted me. I said: "Salisbury. American. Visa." No response. I said it three times, and the *fortochka* slammed shut. Long wait. I rang some more. The window opened again, the face peered at me. "Salisbury, American, visa." The door opened, and I was led into a central hall with a staircase to a second floor balcony fitted with four doors on each side and another at the rear. As I entered, eight doors opened, and eight small men, each dressed in a dark suit, emerged and exited through the door at the rear. The doors closed. Suddenly the rear door opened, and the eight men emerged. Each went into his office and closed the door. It was like a scene from a ballet by Meyerhold.

Finally a ninth little man emerged, motioned me to a chair, filled out a visa form on a piece of paper, sneering at U.S. passport restrictions. (My passport carried a prohibition against travel to Albania; when I got back to the U.S.A. the State Department lectured me for going to a forbidden country.) As I got up to leave, I heard a whispered sigh from the balcony. I did not turn back, but I imagined the eight little men tiptoeing out again through the doors to their eight little rooms.

I booked a ticket for Tirana. There were two planes a week, Wednesdays and Fridays. An Albanian plane in Tirana and a Yugoslav plane in Belgrade took off simultaneously and landed simultaneously. No trust.

I took off for Tirana on Wednesday, August 21, 1957, in a low mood. As I wrote in my journal: "Never have I started a journey in poorer heart, more despondent, less enthusiastic. I do not know what *chërt* (devil) it is that draws me into such crummy parts of the world. I am half-afraid of them. They upset and annoy me. My tolerance for police and bureaucracy grows less and less." (In November, 1985, as Charlotte and I flew out of Sheremetevo airport in Moscow, I said to her: "I just can't stand the police and the bureaucracy. This is my last trip to Russia." "That's what you said the last time," she told me with a grin. Six months later I was back in Russia.)

The first thing I saw as the plane set down in Tirana was three soldiers in dirty uniforms at the end of the runway, lolling in the grass with bayoneted rifles, watching the landing with shifty eyes.

Each night I spent in Albania I heard the chatter of machine guns in the mountains and an occasional mortar shell. For practical purposes Albania was more or less in a state of war with her neighbors, Yugoslavia and Greece. God knows what was going on in the hills. I began to understand the paranoia. My visit was the first and last by an American correspondent until the summer of 1986, when a Boston *Herald* man was allowed to attend a family wedding and write a few pieces.

Not only was Albania at war with her neighbors; she was, as I was assured by Petrit Aliu, the dark-haired, brown-eyed young man who served as my guide and interpreter, the No. 1 target of the CIA, which was trying to put King Zog back on the throne. I expressed astonishment that King Zog was still alive. The only interest Zog had ever stirred in the United States, I said, had been in the 1930s when it was reported in the tabloids that he smoked 300 cigarettes a day.

Petrit was infuriated. I had insulted him by not taking Albania's security threat seriously. He was certain the United States was devoting great time and resources to the Albanian question. (He probably had been told that I was a dangerous CIA agent.)

I retorted that most Americans didn't even know where Albania was. "The whole thing is ridiculous," I said. Actually, it was not ridiculous at all, as I came later to understand. Albania in 1948 had been the target of the first big CIA plot to overthrow a Communist government. We had been helped by the British, and it had been a disaster. Later the Russians tried the same thing. They bought up a clique of officers in Albania's gunboat-and-destroyer navy but failed as badly as the CIA. Hoxha and Shehu took the excuse to slaughter hundreds of fellow Albanians and broke connections with every country but Italy and Communist China. Beijing seemed far enough away not to be a threat. (But when Deng Xiaoping denounced Mao Zedong, Albania cut her ties with China as well.)

I met with Mehmet Shehu and tried to coax him into speaking English. He only essayed a few sentences (excellent American accent). I knew he had been educated in an American school in Tirana founded by the Junior Red Cross in 1921. When I got back to New York, I got ahold of *Laboremus*, the school magazine to which Shehu had been a frequent contributor in the early thirties.

Shehu, it turned out, had been a devout Sunday school pupil. In one long poem he concluded:

> It is not of our religion
> That God will ask:
> It is our behavior
> And how we did the task

He contributed an essay on "My Summer Vacation," work on the school farm, operating a tractor. He and his companions, he wrote, "Worked from sunrise to sunset with one hour out at midday. We ate with peasant farmers and slept on the straw, enjoying the beauty of moon and stars."

I would have given a good deal to have had Shehu's poetry and essays with me when I interviewed him in the presidential palace. For many years I sent him Christmas cards, I also sent cards to Petrit Aliu, my young Albanian translator. After four or five years Petrit Aliu's cards came back stamped: "*Destintaire inconnu*," "inexistant." It took Shehu a bit longer to become "inexistant." He committed suicide, it was said, in 1984. Since then his name has vanished from the Albanian press.

Next stop, Bulgaria. I found it a rather tedious market-gardening Communist country. Its principal export was attar of roses.

In Bucharest I stayed at the venerable Athenee Palace hotel, still luxurious in a seedy Balkan way, and swam in Bucharest's great outdoor pool with its artificial waves. I went to Ploesti where so many American airmen had died in the longest (out-of-range of their bases) raid of World War II on the oilfields. As far as I could see, the U.S. deaths had caused only a few nicks in the vast oil refinery.

I got to know the backwaters of Communism, these little Communist kingdoms, differing one from the other, but all shabby, all lackluster all trading on misery not hope, distinguished by heavy-handed police and a heavy-labor proletariat. Was this what Lenin and comrades had in mind when they carried out their coup in Petrograd on November 7, 1917?

As I noted in my journal:

"They believed that Europe and the whole western world stood on the brink of the apocalypse, which was to mark the end of man's subjugation by man. When the guns of the cruiser *Aurora* rattled the windows of the Winter Palace, the Communists believed they had fired a signal which would bring an echoing cannonade from Berlin, from Vienna, from Paris, from London and perhaps even from New York."

What had they gotten? Only poor, backward Russia until the Red Army in 1944 and 1945 marched into Bucharest and Budapest and Belgrade and Prague and the rest. The specter which Marx said "haunted Europe" now haunted the Communist world. Nowhere did I feel that haunting quality as in Budapest, still scarred and dazed from 1956, Americans not very popular.

In Prague I feasted on *keks garazh*, a nine-layer chocolate cake, and attended services at the 400-year-old synagogue. I arrived in Warsaw at 6 P.M. October 5, 1957, to roaring shouts in the streets: *"Ges-ta-PO! Ges-ta-PO!"* The streets were lined with thousands of university students (and thousands who weren't university students). They chanted: "Ges-ta-PO!" to the thousands of police who confronted them. Sometimes they shouted: "MVD ... MVD ... MVD" (the initials of the internal security police).

Police rumbled through the Place of the Republic, a paved plaza big as Red Square, in olive-drab trucks, troop carriers, jeeps, command cars. The streets echoed with the blast of concussion bombs. I didn't know what was happening. But it seemed like a revolution. Tear gas grenades discharged clouds of mustard-scented mist.

It was, Sydney Gruson, the *Times* Warsaw correspondent, told me, a student manifestation, a protest against restrictions on the universities, the closing of the student paper, *Po Prostu*. But it was more than that. How much more remained to be seen. Sydney took me to the Journalists Club, jammed with people, and we sat at a table with his wife, Flora Lewis, and his assistant and friend, Tommy Atkins. It was pandemonium.

231

Was it a dress rehearsal like that of 1905 in Russia? People hurried up, whispered to Sydney and Flora, ran out again. Tommy Atkins came and went. His name was actually Seweryn Ben Izrael. He was a Polish Jew born in Łódź who got the name Tommy Atkins in the British army in England during World War II. He wore heavy horn-rimmed glasses. Years later he told me: "People thought I was a spy because I looked like a spy." He still looked like a spy after twenty years as a professor at Baruch College. We all looked like *The Third Man*—Sydney, blond, nordic, Irish as a shamrock, a Jew born in Dublin; Flora, auburn hair, sharp face, typecast ace reporter (which she was) and myself, long nose, trenchcoat, snap-brim hat, wandering in from the set of *The Front Page*.

My mind was awhirl. In my journal I noted: "This rioting has a curious sense of unreality. What do the crowds want? Probably they themselves don't know." My nose prickled with the scent of tear gas, the streets littered with half-bricks, Gomulka, it was said, meeting continuously with the Politburo in secret session—about what? Within half an hour Sydney Gruson was cabling to New York the topic of Gomulka's discussions—an absolute cap on further talks with foreign correspondents, no more leaks, a crackdown on the press.

All evening I was asking questions. Atkins had few answers.

This was the Polish world Sydney and Flora had inhabited for eighteen months. I had arrived almost on the anniversary of the "Polish October" of 1956 when Khrushchev sent his tanks up to the gates of Warsaw. Gomulka, prison pallor still on his face, told him the Poles would fight if the tanks came further.

In those days Sydney Gruson had filed the most remarkable dispatches I have ever seen from the Communist world, documenting hour-by-hour, almost minute-by-minute, the inside story of the crisis: what Gomulka was doing; what the Polish military were doing; what they were telling the Russians; what the Russians were telling them. Sydney and Flora were Warsaw's lifeline to the West, the channel through which Gomulka could raise the alarm if Khrushchev and Marshal Zhukov tried to crush Poland as later they did Budapest. Khrushchev blinked, and the Gomulka experiment began. Now a year later Poland again stood at the brink—or did it? No one, not Sydney, not Flora, not Tommy Atkins not anyone in that hubbub could say.

I spent a week in Warsaw, had an interview with Premier Cyrankiewicz, then I was on my way back to New York, my Balkan summer at an end.

Those months engrained deep in my consciousness the diversity of Communism. Albania was not Poland; Hungary was not Bulgaria; Poland was, had been, and always would be, Poland. On Sunday, October 13, 1957, I went to the Warsaw airport and boarded an SAS plane for Copenhagen. With me was Sydney Gruson, his marvelous Irish color faded to a pasty white, as nervous a man as I have ever seen. Tommy Atkins, he told me, had been arrested. Sydney had excellent information. His turn, he had been told, would be next.

The chant of "Ges-ta-PO ... Ges-ta-PO ..." will, I think, echo in my brain for the rest of my life. In autumn 1957 I had not yet experienced the Japanese film *Rashomon*, the dramatization of the classic enigma of truth, the inescapable, ordained contradictions, life distorted to infinity in its own mirror. I knew in Warsaw as I walked through the October events that I was walking in a hall of facets, but I could not measure the angles of refraction, nor can I thirty years later be certain what was real and what was imagined.

It is this realization which has caused me to return to *Rashomon* again and again to study this metaphor of life and remind myself that there is no truth. There are many truths, some valid for one, some for another. *Things are not what they seem.* We suppose we learn this lesson in kindergarten the first time a magician projects a rabbit's ears on the wall with the shadow of his hands. But it is a lesson we must learn and relearn because always we keep searching for certainty, and certainty does not exist.

Was the Polish government about to collapse that October of 1957? Surely it does not seem so today. Yet on those evenings when the cries of "Ges-ta-PO!" reverberated outside the iron gates of Warsaw's university and echoed in the narrow alleys of the Old City it *could* have been true. Certainly as that troubled man, Gomulka, met hour after hour with his associates wondering if the security police could contain the rising violence, worrying whether troops would have to be summoned, worrying whether the uniformed forces would joint the multitude as they had in Petrograd in 1917, worrying whether Khrushchev's tanks would rumble out of their camps and clank again down the autostrada toward Warsaw, worrying how many Poles would stand by the students and their suppressed paper,

*Po Prostu*, and how many would stand with Gomulka and the "old Party"—yes, it is easy to see that when Gomulka stared past the Brussels lace curtains at the windows of the Central Committee, there was more than one Warsaw within his field of vision.

And this was true in the smoky dining-room of the Journalists Club. Who were these people? Sydney Gruson and Flora Lewis I knew. Tommy Atkins I knew through them. But I did not know what was happening, nor as it turned out, did Sydney or Flora or Tommy. Neither they nor I could have imagined, sitting in the clutter of uneaten cucumber pickles, fragments of herring, plates that once contained eel in dill sauce, half-consumed bowls of borscht, cut-glass *ryumki* of Polish vodka, goblets of resin-heavy Polish wine, brandy spilled on the white tablecloth, ashtrays heaped in cigarette butts, that something was occurring that would affect all our lives.

Sydney and I sat side by side in the plane all the way from Warsaw to Copenhagen. I told him again and again that it could not be as bad as he thought; the Poles were not going to forget what Gruson had done for them in October 1956.

How could I convince Sydney his information was false? If there was anyone who knew Poland, it was Gruson. He and Flora had agreed: best for Sydney to slip out of the country with me. After all I was leaving directly from an interview with Prime Minister Cyrankiewicz. Certainly they would not arrrest Sydney in my company.

Gruson had done the best reporting of the decade from behind the Iron Curtain, but that did not win him a Pulitzer prize. Not because the Pulitzer judges did not understand he deserved it. He did not win because on the heels of Poland's October outburst came the Hungarian Revolution. The judges could not give the prize to Poland, because Hungary was a bigger show. So the prize went to Russell Jones of United Press International.

Next year the Pulitzer judges almost compounded the injustice to Gruson. For 1957 the *Times* submitted my Balkan dispatches, the scoops from Albania, Bulgaria, and all the rest. They also nominated Gruson again and several other foreign correspondents. The jury picked me as the winner. Fortunately there was reconsideration, and the award went to *The New York Times* for the overall excellence of its foreign reporting; the further slight to Gruson was averted.

Tommy was in jail. It was not the same, and it was not going to be

234

the same. I knew Sydney was finished in Poland and I told that to Turner Catledge and Emanual Freedman, the foreign editor.

"This unfortunate situation," I said in a memo, "arises directly out of Sydney's magnificent coverage and his unequaled contacts and knowledge of what is happening in Poland. I think it can be fairly said that for the last eighteen months no one in Poland, either in the Government, the diplomatic colony, or the press corps, has had as full a picture as Gruson."

But Gruson had become an embarrassment. There was no way the Polish government was going to permit Gruson's intimate and informed reporting to continue. A replacement, I told Catledge, was going to be needed.

Abe Rosenthal was in India while this was going on. He had been there for four years with Ann and his boys (Andy, the youngest, born in India in 1956). He and I were not really close, but we were part of the fraternity of foreign correspondents, the network; we wrote often, exchanged gossip, shared our aspirations, kept in touch. I loved Abe's India coverage and told him so. He liked my New York reportage—and my stories from behind the Iron Curtain—and told me so.

By the winter of 1958, Abe's discontent with India had boiled over. He had accepted—with many qualms—an offer by Freedman to succeed Gruson in Warsaw. He made no secret that Warsaw was not his heart's desire. To me he wrote of his concerns over the constraints in covering news from a Communist country and the *smallness* of Poland. Years later he said he really didn't like Poland, and once he told Dan Schorr he accepted the assignment with reluctance. He really didn't like Poland. "I didn't speak Polish," he remembered. "I was very disturbed. I could imagine them talking about me."

Gruson had said: "I like Poland and my Polish friends." Rosenthal responded: "You aren't talking about Poland; you are talking about six Jewish revisionists." Gruson extolled the freedom of speech in Poland. "It's not freedom of speech," Abe snapped. "It's freedom of conversation. You can't get up on a platform and say what you think."

In August Abe was still very, very tentative about Poland—even as he was writing what I thought was his finest story, a report of a visit to Auschwitz, which had moved him as few things in his life had moved him. How could he write of Auschwitz, he thought, everyone had done it years before. Tommy Atkins urged him to write. "How can I?" he said. "There's nothing to write. Just that awful silence." "Write that," Tommy urged.

Abe couldn't get over the feeling of being hemmed in. He traveled to Prague, he visited Romania, he went to Yugoslavia. It didn't help much. In February 1959 he was writing me: "I don't feel a great deal of zest and scope in being part of a three-man team covering a second-rate story in the suburbs.

"There," he said, "I've said it."

By this time Tommy Atkins was again in the hands of the Polish police. Looking back on it, the arrests of Tommy Atkins seem almost inevitable. The first time he was arrested he had been held five months and fourteen days—the maximum he could be held without formal charges—while they tried to squeeze some kind of case out against Gruson. When Tommy was arrested in December 1958, they tried to squeeze out a case against Rosenthal. Neither time did they succeed. Tommy wouldn't talk.

There was a difference in Tommy's two prison interrogations. The Gruson period centered on Gruson, bureau finances, currency dealing, people with whom Gruson met. The Rosenthal period covered these points but there were new twists. Tommy was questioned intensively about a murder case—the murder of the son of Boleslaw Piasecki, leader of a Polish Catholic group. Piasecki had been active in right-wing politics in Poland before World War II and in the right-wing Polish partisans. In postwar Communist Poland he headed Pax, a quasi-political organization, obviously cleared by the Soviets. His son was a student at Warsaw University. In March 1957 the son was lured into a car (by a trumped-up story of an accident to his father), kidnapped by two unknown men, shot, and his body dumped on the edge of town. This line of inquiry was soon dropped. At the time of the murder Tommy was in Japan.

The police also questioned Tommy about the Pavel Monat case. Monat was a Polish military attaché who had defected to the United states in the summer of 1959. This event happened while Tommy had already been in prison for seven months.

The effort to link Tommy with Monat had—although Tommy had no knowledge of this—considerable significance.

Poland seemed more drab, more dreary to Abe in the autumn of

1959. There was no joy or laughter. The second anniversary of the Polish October came and went. The days were very short at that time of year, lights turned on by two in the afternoon, dark clouds, cold, snow.

Rosenthal had never met the lonely, tough-minded, individualistic, prison-hardened Gomulka. Now in these darkest autumn days, Abe began to write about Gomulka and what was on Gomulka's mind, sensitive, revealing stories, etching an unforgettable portrait of the isolated leader, his insoluble problems, his growing touchiness, his outbursts at his associates (really his outburst against the Polish fate).

They were remarkable vignettes, and no one who read them could fail to see Gomulka pacing his office, nervously smoking cigarette after cigarette, crushing hand to bony skull, suffused in frustration over problems for which there was no solution.

Rosenthal's pieces were too much for the Poles. His wife Ann, shopping in Vienna, got a telegram. "Come back to Warsaw at once." Abe had been expelled.

Four months later Abe won the Pulitzer for his Warsaw coverage (the one I always thought really belonged to Gruson—although Abe had earned it fair and square). Out of his dead-end beat in "the suburbs," as he had called it, he was catapulted to fame.

Tommy Atkins lingered in jail. He was told nothing of Rosenthal's expulsion. He stayed in prison until the spring of 1960. Years later Tommy told me about the fifth man at the table on the Warsaw night in October 1957, the propelling force of this particular Rashomon. The man had come and sat at our table for a long time. To me he was just a gray blur. I vaguely recalled someone sitting down with us. I could recall nothing of the conversation. Nor did Sydney remember him. But Tommy did, because he alone realized that something unusual was going on. I had been peppering Tommy with questions about what was happening. Tommy had answered some, ducked others. Many of my inquiries had sharp political edges, much sharper than I realized. Then this man, a Warsaw newspaperman with excellent connections, came up, introduced himself, and pulled a fifth chair up to the littered table. I asked more questions.

"And he answered them." Tommy recollected as we sat in a quiet Gramercy Park restaurant nearly thirty years later. "He answered all your questions. I knew something dangerous was going on. He should not have been so outspoken—his answers were remarkably complete and accurate. My jaw dropped. I did not know what he was up to."

What the Fifth Man was up to was very simple. He was acting as a stand-in for Tommy. When Tommy was arrested, he was accused of giving to me the answers the Fifth Man had offered. No denial by Tommy was accepted. They pretended that the Fifth Man was not there. No, they said, it was you, Seweryn Pomerancz (Tommy's name of record), who gave this dangerous foreign intelligence operative this intimate Party information.

The Fifth Man had come, done his job, left the table, and no trace of what he had said or even his presence remained in my mind.

# Chapter 20

# A Time of Change

I came back to New York with the feeling that it was time to give more shape to the random pattern of my life. I had become a kind of journalistic soldier of fortune, moved from Brooklyn to Budapest, from Garbage to Gomulka, by Frank Adams, Emanuel Freedman, and Turner Catledge. I loved living like the Three Musketeers, always plunging into a new adventure—but where did it lead?

I was a year shy of fifty. I had long been divorced. My two boys were growing up in the Midwest. I saw them occasionally, but I was leading a bachelor existence in New York (or wherever), still under the trauma of my failed marriage. Perhaps, I thought, I'm just not cut out for a permanent relationship, perhaps it demands more than I have the ability to give.

Now, at least, I must try to organize my professional life. I had gone to the *Times* because it *was* the *Times* and because I knew I wanted to be a correspondent and not an editor. I didn't want to make marks on papers or push them around. I belonged on the scene where I felt challenged, excited, at home. I loved to write, and I came back from Eastern Europe with a new sense of how important it was to see with my own eyes, hear with my own ears, touch with my own hands, before making a judgment.

But there was a problem. My speciality was the Soviet Union. I knew the territory (I thought) better than anyone in the business. I would match my judgment about Moscow against anyone's, in or out of government, American, European, or Asian. In fact I would match it against that of most Russians. But the Soviet bureaucracy would not let me set foot on Holy Russian soil. I had been banned since 1954. I felt like Antaeus, I had to touch the *chernozëm*, the black earth, regularly or I could not interpret Russia accurately. I did not believe (and I do not now) in the armchair "expert," the scholarly dilettante who examines dry bones of Marxist dialectic and proclaims eternal truths about the Politburo. To analyse you have to have a fresh eye, draw a little blood, and possess seat-of-the-pants luck.

Now, out of Warsaw, out of Budapest, out of Tirana, I began to sketch for myself a broader horizon—the whole of the Communist world from the Elbe to the Bering Strait. If I could score a hat trick in Eastern Europe, why not in Asia, China, Mongolia, Korea, Indochina (just beginning to emerge from the distant thunder of Dien Bien Phu)? And somehow I would have to squirm between the barbed war and get back inside Russia.

This, I thought, made sense. Side by side I would continue a healthy diet of grassroots America. You could not, I had become convinced, write from Kabul, Vientiane, Pyongyang, or Sofia with understanding unless you knew what was playing on Broadway and the price of wheat in North Dakota. If the cry "Yankee Go Home!" arose in Berlin, you had to know why they were chanting "Yankee Go Home!" in Tuscaloosa, Alabama.

It was—like it or not, and I did not pretend to like it very much— one world.

I had learned in this summer of 1957 that the Iron Curtain was as leaky as a tin roof, that the Kremlin's sway ran just as far as the writ of the Red Army, no further, that the "Communist Gibraltar" was just a lot of grubby little dictatorships. More and more I began to wonder whether it was the reality of Communist power that frightened us or a nightmare conjured up by our overheated imagination.

I could not believe that this ramshackle structure would endure. One day it would topple down like Humpty Dumpty. I had invested five years waiting for Stalin's death and the extraordinary story that followed. If I took the whole Communist world as my oyster, I could be the man to report on the inevitable collapse of the century's colossus. That was worth a lifetime.

I don't want to give the impression that all of this, dovetailed neatly, tied down in logical propositions, filed away in tan folders in a green filing cabinet, was spelled out in my mind. I don't function that way. I am a disorderly, instinctive kind of person. But even I could see the parameters of this future and how I should position myself.

My Balkan summer had moved me into a new and different orbit. Henceforth the *Times* (and I, too) would begin to think of Salisbury as the man who could pick the lock and get behind the Iron Curtain and, who knows, perhaps the Bamboo Curtain and other curtains not quite so visible. As time went on, this would dominate my life.

240

I can't say that anything spectacular happened as a result of my musings, not for a time. Then Isaac Asimov gave my life a twist. Stephan, my eleven-year-old, spent Thanksgiving with me in 1958. My old friend of Moscow days, Tom Whitney, and I had bought a rundown farmhouse in Connecticut. The day after I had carved the turkey, I took Stephan for a ride through the autumnal countryside.

Stephan had fallen under the spell of Asimov, and he wanted to get a copy of the master's latest work. We were driving up Route 7 in the white TR-3, which I had proudly acquired a year earlier, hyperventilated in England's best tradition, a darling in the New England snowdrifts. When we got to Salisbury, Connecticut, I spotted Maurice Firuski's rare book shop, and we hopped out. A marvelous young woman, clear blue eyes, head and shoulders high, the walk of a rather mortal goddess (or at least that of a one-time Powers model) asked if she could help. It was Charlotte. We had not met for nearly four years, but her image was clear in my mind as the crisp November light. Stephan bought his book, and I knew that one way or another I had to see Charlotte again (if possible, again and again).

Charlotte was married, had several children (four as I found out), and, so far as I knew, was living a happy life. It was silly of me to think about her, but I did. Some months later I dropped by the shop again, and this time she invited me to tea in the cozy house where I had stayed the first time I came to Salisbury for a lecture in January 1955. We talked. I have no idea what we talked about, but I left with a feeling that we were going to meet again and that somehow, perhaps, it was not so hopeless a case as I had thought. Nor was it. Unknown to me Charlotte was in the process of moving out of her marriage. Before too long she and her son, Curtis, eight, would go off to Florence, to stay in Italy for some months, to live and work at Villa Mercedi, an American girls' school. I hoped to get to Florence to see her but didn't. Visits to Moscow, Nikita Khrushchev, his trips to the U.S.A., interfered. Somehow this didn't make much difference. We were very cautious, both of us. We didn't want to make any mistake. And we didn't.

I feel shy about writing of happiness, unexpected, miraculous, but that is what the years have brought since that April day of our marriage in 1964. We have become a team, not only living together, sharing our six children, four of hers, two of mine, our great brood of grandchildren, our extended family, our almost Victorian kind of existence (except, of course, no "below stairs" staff), a life of intense

241

intimacy and warmth such as neither of us could have dreamed. First we reclaimed an old Bohemian rooming house in Yorkville, of twenty-seven crib-sized rooms, restoring it to the splendor of 1880. After a decade we moved into a rambling house at the very corner of Connecticut, New York, and Massachusetts, under the shadow of the Berkshires, snowy, clean and white in winter, shimmering green in summer. Charlotte's cool realism, her excruciating honesty ("I'm just a flat-footed Boston woman"), keeps me from flight into Cloud-Cuckoo-Land, and, I hope, my defiant optimism lightens the dark pessimism with which she faces the world, expecting the worst and preparing to meet it.

I cannot tell how many hundreds of thousands (maybe millions) of miles we have traveled together since 1964. We started out with a trip to Atlantic City, by bus, for the dreadful Democratic national convention at which LBJ humiliated Hubert Humphrey by dragging him like a slobbering hound around and around the convention hall before finally, with an offhand gesture, anointing him as No. 2 on the 1964 ticket, an omen of worse to come.

Again and again Charlotte and I would travel to distant corners of the earth, never for pleasure except that of each other's company, always on the trail of news and new barriers to surmount—Russia's farthest reaches, odd corners of Siberia (we love Siberia), the Gobi, the Himalayas, Mongolia (again and again, Mongolia), Sihanouk's doomed delicate Cambodia, Ne Win's eccentric Burma, Hope Cooke's Sikkim, Madame Gandhi's India, Korea, and, of course, China—first, all around its circumference during the mad days of the Cultural Revolution, then into China, dinners with Zhou Enlai, Soong Chingling, and Hu Yaobang, explorations of the Soviet frontiers, north and west, the stone trail from Lhasa in Tibet to Katmandu in Nepal and in 1984 the climactic retracing of the Long March, Mao's Red Army retreat of 1934–35, 7,400 miles into the most remote mountains and deserts. No better comrade than my Charlotte to be found in all the world.

Charlotte changed my life in an epoch in which change was the order of the day. The sixties would leave deep marks on America. We had entered an age of unannounced revolution in political, economic, social, and personal relations—civil rights, race rebellion, women's rights, gay rights, Indian rights, student rebellion, an upheaval in morals and technology as had not been seen since the Industrial

242

Revolution. It was a time of change everywhere and no less at the *Times*, an old order rapidly, painfully, erratically, and even hysterically giving place to new.

For me the changes within the *Times* began in 1962 with the cable from Turner Catledge that caught me in Kabul, asking me to take the job of national editor. I felt I couldn't turn him down, but first I went to Ulan Bator, the capital of Outer Mongolia, the farthest out capital in the world. It was winter—60 degree-below-zero winter. I stopped off at Irkutsk in eastern Siberia, cloaked in steam-frost from Lake Baikal, the world's largest body of fresh water, still unfrozen in the minus 60-degree frost. In a five-minute walk in icy sunshine, I froze my ears iron-white, worse than in a childhood of sledding in 30-degree-below Minnesota.

I put Mongolia ahead of the national desk, because I had found it to be a primary fault line in world politics. Here an earthquake could be detected quicker than anywhere. Two years earlier when I talked my way into Mongolia, I hadn't known what I would find except yaks, yurts and yogurt. To my astonishment it had produced spectacular news. Mongolia, the distant, nomadic ward of Moscow, lacked modern skills, the heirs of Genghis Khan lived by horses and horsemanship. There were no better riders in the world, but they couldn't tell a hammer from a handsaw. Thousands of Chinese workers and Soviet soldiers were building roads, dams, bridges, factories and housing for Mongolia.

Russia and China were staunch allies then, bound in eternal friendship and defense against the world, especially the U.S.A. But, as I discovered, they weren't speaking to one another. There was no friendship, no cooperation, just hostility. I went to the Mongolian national holiday, *Nadam*, and found the reception hall divided into two grim camps, Russians on one side, Chinese on the other. A beefy Russian general drank toasts to American-Soviet friendship, then put a pudgy arm around my shoulder and whispered confidentially; "Tell me, Mr. Salisbury, don't you feel more comfortable on *our* side of the room." Well, as a matter of fact, I did, because not one Chinese in Mongolia had been willing to say a word to me. They turned their backs and walked away on finding out I was an American. I was no more popular than the Russians.

This was not a charade out of Emily Post's *Etiquette*. These were symptoms of a profound split in Mr. Dulles' "monolithic" world of Communism, which he was sure had its headquarters in the Kremlin.

I could hardly wait to file my dispatch. Of course, the State Department tagged me once again as a naif: "Everyone knows there can't be a real split." But my information was solid as the Pamirs. Angry polemics in 1960 made it all hang out, and Nikita Khrushchev underlined this by pulling 14,000 Soviet aid experts from China.

By the time I got back to Mongolia in 1961–62, the Chinese-Russian cross fire was hot and heavy. Still, there were those (and some exist even today in 1989) who slyly sidled up to me and asked whether I didn't *really* think it was all just "disinformation" to fool the trusting American people. I said, no, I don't think so.

No one had been there since my 1959 expedition, and I needed an update. Many young Mongols had sided with China then. I wondered if they still did and whether the Russians had made the Mongols send the Chinese workers home.

I did not meet the pro-Chinese Mongols of 1959. They had lost their jobs. Some had lost their lives. Moscow wasn't playing beanbag. Most of the Chinese work teams had gone home. I talked to Party Secretary Tsedenbal, a moon-faced man who looked a little like one of Chekhov's schoolteachers. I had first met him in Tirana, and I had seen him in 1959 in Ulan Bator when he talked earnestly about establishing U.S.-Mongol diplomatic relations. (Not until 1987 after more than twenty-five years were they established.) I would see him on all subsequent visits. Tsedenbal had been educated at Moscow University, was married to a Russian woman, spoke perfect Russian, and sometimes made speeches in Russian. No doubt where he stood—and yet . . . I hadn't met a Mongol who really didn't want a Greater Mongolia, dominated by neither Russia nor China. They had let the Russians in before 1911 to drive the Chinese out. Once the Russians got in (the Communists just picked up the Czarist Russian policy), the Mongols began to lean toward the Chinese. Mongols were split into three packages—Outer Mongolia under Russian influence; Inner Mongolia, part of China and rapidly filling with Chinese, and small Mongol enclaves in the Soviet Union called autonomous regions. The Mongols wanted to put the jigsaw together. There wasn't a chance either great power would cooperate. On my 1961–62 findings, I calculated it would be a long, long time before the Sino-Soviet alliance was revived—if ever. Naturally, the State Department did not agree.

When I got back to New York in the winter of 1962, I didn't know what I was walking into nor could anyone have foreseen what lay ahead. The city room seemed as cozy and shabby as ever, cherubic Frank Adams still city editor, slipping off to a back corner at the end of day for a rubber or two of bridge, passing through the aisles in his patriarchical progress to give the reporters "Good night." Solemn, serious Manny Freedman presided over the foreign correspondents. Ted Bernstein, the iron-willed nervous boss of the bullpen, dictated the front page as imperiously as ever. Catledge with his Southern politician's soft-shoe, easy Mississippi accent pulled invisible wires from his cubbyhole office, and my old friend of London days, Clifton Daniel, training to succeed Catledge, seemed more busy, more active, more up-front than I recalled. Something suggested transition, and I took my appointment as national editor as the first move on a complicated chessboard that would lead Daniel to the top editor's chair.

I was right, but neither I nor anyone was ready for what was to come. Orvil Dryfoos, polite, patient, proper, was now publisher, succeeding his ailing father-in-law. Dryfoos had brought in a "corporate management team" to run the paper. I hadn't seen much of "corporate managers," but they made me nervous. I thought they masked ignorance with self-assurance, multicolored flow charts, and slide presentations. Their bureaucratese obscured their lack of know-how. Not that the business management of Arthur Hays Sulzberger and his wife's cousin, General Adler, had been brilliant. Still they had kept the *Times* ahead of the competition (principally the *Herald-Tribune*) in the troubled New York field. Now the New York newspaper business was put to a terrible test—the "long strike," 114-days of idleness in 1962–63. I sat that out in the empty city room, as drear an episode as I can remember, wondering who was going to pay the price. Everyone, as it turned out. The strike ravaged New York, only three papers survived in the end—the *Times*, the *News*, and the *Post*.

A few weeks after the strike, Dryfoos died of a heart attack.

No successor waited in the wings. A couple of years before, in an advance obituary which I had prepared of Arthur Hays Sulzberger, I had noted how careful the *Times* was to train successors—Orvil Dryfoos to succeed Sulzberger, and Punch (Arthur Ochs Sulzberger, Dryfoos' brother-in-law) to succeed him—if necessary.

Catledge read the obit and called me in. "Who told you that?" he asked.

"No one," I said. "It's just obvious."

It had not been obvious to Turner. He thought I was on to something—which I wasn't. Catledge was the only one at 229 West 43rd Street who had paid any attention to Punch. He had been relegated to menial chores, no training for a major executive post. One day in 1957 or 1958 I came into the city room and found Punch with two men, unknown to me, standing by my desk, "Jim Hagerty's desk," looking out at the room. I liked Punch. I thought he had a hard row to hoe. He was pleasant and unassuming. We sometimes indulged in casual chatter. He often shared a drink with Catledge at day's end, and I sometimes joined the Catledge group.

"What are you up to?" I asked. Punch said they were going to replace the old oak desks and chairs with new formica-top steel furniture. I was appalled. I *loved* Mr. Hagerty's desk and all the desks. They were *perfect*, perfect for typing, for editing.

"I'm sorry about that," I said. "I've never had such a good desk."

Punch shrugged his shoulders in a what-can-I-do? gesture. "Saves a lot of time and labor for the cleaning ladies," he said. And probably because I looked forlorn, he crinkled his eyes and added, "Sorry." He was, too. And I was sorry for him. It just couldn't have been easy, the son of the publisher, in charge of housekeeping, painting, and cleaning at 229 West 43rd Street. Everyone liked Punch, everyone in his family, and almost everyone he met. But they didn't think he had much ability. The only one in the establishment who had a warm man-to-man relationship with him was Catledge. Both were divorced. They had evenings on their hands. I was divorced, too, and I had an affinity with Punch. Not that I thought he would make a great publisher. I was stunned when he was named, still with no preparatory training, to succeed Dryfoos, and yet some small voice told me none of us really knew this man, not Catledge, not his parents, not his sisters, and certainly not me. In a showdown, as time would tell, no matter how many bumbles Punch made, he came down with the right answer, the right man (often after firing two or three bad ones), the right policy after some wild goose chases. He had, I concluded, an instinct for decisions—if left to himself. But how many, many times those who thought they knew better politicked him into wrong choices which he ultimately had to correct.

In the beginning Punch had some very able men to help him. He relied enormously on Turner Catledge and, to a lesser extent, on James Reston, both outstanding, rivals for years but this had not limited their effectiveness. On the business side Punch had a far worse time. Not until he had worked through the whole legacy of the Dryfoos "management team" did he emerge with the solid, uncharismatic, pragmatic, and brilliant Walter Mattson, and the two piloted the *Times* to extraordinary heights of financial success, leaving in their wake an unbelievable train of systems men, corporate symposia, executive psychiatrists, consultants, and medicine men. These men taught Punch a lesson. He was seeking a magic button, a "way" to run the *Times*, a fail-safe system. It took a long time before this rather slight, dark, handsome, exquisitely soft-shoe man had to concede that there was no yellow brick road to the Emerald City.

I had been in place at the national desk about eighteen months when Abe Rosenthal came blazing back from Tokyo. I think "blazing" is a just word. He was like a Roman candle, shooting his sparks in every direction, no aim, no ear for the hubbub around him, as much a young man in a hurry as ever climbed up from the mean streets of the Bronx, from the rough poverty of an emigrant family out of Russia's Pale of Settlement, survivor of brutal illness, eyes like caramel candy (except when afire with anger), once so thin his schoolteacher said, "If you close one eye, you'll be a needle" (filled out now; later a tendency to pudginess).

I was delighted Abe was back. He was much more to my taste than the genial Frank Adams. My delight did not last. Somehow this was not the Abe I had known for twenty years. I had looked forward to working together, helping him to know New York again. No way. Abe was off and running on his own, suspicious of me and of almost all his colleagues. I had not been privy to the negotiations that brought Abe back. I did not know he had written Clifton from Tokyo, expressing great concern over rumors he said he had heard that "there is going to be trouble in the city room" (Clifton sharply rebuked Abe: "I think your conclusion is 100 percent wrong"). Years later Arthur Gelb told me how Abe persuaded him to become the other half of "Abe'n'Artie." "We can do anything. We'll create it all and do everything we want. We are going to make enemies."

They did. They did, indeed. They made enemies, they roughed up fine correspondents, they broke the spirit of bright young reporters, they drove talented men and women away until the third floor of 229 West 43rd Street reeked of envy, greed, jealousy, ambition, snideness, savagery, hypocrisy, and tawdriness. But they produced stories! Nothing stopped them. Not libel suits. Not complaints from the highest. They never quit. Sure, a lot of it was junk, including the famous thirty-nine witnesses who didn't stir to help a girl who was being murdered. But it was lively, readable, fresh, original, feisty, impudent, irresistible, and sometimes even important. The bottom line was that what Rosenthal-Gelb produced put the *Times* back in business. It wasn't the Ochs' *Times*. It wasn't Van Anda's *Times*. It wasn't Catledge's *Times* or Iphigene Sulzberger's. Sometimes it wasn't even the *Times*. Abe did not, although he was fond of saying it, "keep the paper straight," whatever on earth he meant by that. (No *Times* editor in history had ever felt it necessary to say anything like that.) In fact, Rosenthal's *Times* was often a good deal more like Pulitzer's *World* or Mr. Hearst's *Journal*. It rode hobby horses, to put it politely, and did not neglect private quirks. But, my, oh my, how it was read.

What I didn't know in the early sixties and found hard to believe in the late sixties was that the *Times* was on the line. It was softly settling closer and closer to the red ink. The New York newspaper field had been devastated, and inside the big old building on 43rd Street blood ran in the corridors. The question really seemed genuine: Could *The New York Times* survive? Or would it join the *World*, the *Herald*, the *Sun*, all those giants, that now were only ink-stained nostalgia?

I couldn't believe what my mind told me. But by the end of the 1960s, the *Times* was in terrible trouble. All the newspapers were in terrible trouble. And at the *Times* the tiller was in the hands of a young, untrained, untried publisher, and bulling his way to the top was the most hyperthyroid, emotional, brilliant, remarkable man who had ever headed the paper. Could the *Times* be saved? There were many in New York who thought not. By this time there were many in the *Times*, casualties of the infighting, who almost hoped the *Times* would go under and take the piratical new crew with it. I was not one of these.

*Chapter 21*

# Nightmare in Sikkim

I awoke at 4 A.M. in a sweat, wide awake, feeling that the nightmare which had roused me was totally true, a premonition of events to come. I thought I knew its meaning precisely. The date was June 30, 1966, and the room in which I lay beside Charlotte, she peacefully sleeping, her breath smooth and regular, was the guest chamber of the palace in Gangtok, capital of the mountain-top kingdom of Sikkim in the Himalayas.

We had come there, Charlotte and I, as guests of King, or *Chogyal*, Thondup, and Queen, or *Gyalmo*, the former Hope Cooke, with whom Ellen, Charlotte's daughter, had gone to Sarah Lawrence College. The bedroom was big and airy on the top floor of the modest Edwardian country house which served as the palace. On a staircase landing just outside was a massive white enamel urinal which flushed every five minutes, night and day—Old Faithful, Thondup called it when he came up, wrench in hand, to tighten a washer and slow down the burblings.

We were two months into a journey of 25,000 miles that was to take us around the rim of China. This had been Clifton Daniel's idea. No one had ever done it—and I don't suppose anyone has since. I had been trying unsuccessfully to get to Beijing. This expedition would give me a look at China through her neighbors' eyes. We would see the Forbidden Kingdom over the wall, and I would try my magic at getting into China and other sealed-off lands. Our passports were cleared for travel to Communist China, North Vietnam, and North Korea.

Now we had arrived at the high Himalayas, twenty miles as the falcon flies, from China (actually Tibet). For days the roads south to India had been closed by avalanches. This was the monsoon season, and I could hear the rain pelting on the tin roof as it had for a week. I had to get out. Somehow we had to get over those rock slides and out of Sikkim, down to India, and on our way. There wasn't a moment to lose. We had not received our visas for Russia. There had been delay after delay. I had applied in Washington. Nothing but smiles. No action. We left the U.S.A. without them. They will catch up with you, the pleasant Russian in Washington said. We had been two months without word. We had to get out of the Himalayas. We had visas for Mongolia, but they were about to expire. They must be extended. And now this nightmare.

It was vivid as life. I had walked into the city room on 43rd Street, coming back from my orbit of China. The room was filled with people, typewriters hammering away, copyboys rushing back and forth. Not one person looked up. No one took notice of me. I glanced over the room. There was not a person in that indoor acre from 43rd Street to 44th Street whom I knew. No one looked up, and when they did they looked right through me.

I lay on my back, listening to the even murmur of Charlotte's breath, the patter of rain, the rhythmic gurgle of Old Faithful. I knew what the dream meant. There flashed into my mind a telephone call from Reston a couple of days before we left on the long flight to Hong Kong. We gossiped a bit, and then Scotty said, "What are you going to be doing when you come back?" Nothing new, I replied, back to my job. There was a pause. "Oh," he said. "I see. Well, I guess Abe is sitting in for you." "That's right", I said, "Clifton asked if he could sit at my desk and fill in while I'm nosing my way around China". Another microscopic pause, then Reston: "Well, good luck on the trip. See you when you come back."

I had not given Reston another thought. I was enchanted with the grand circuit, enchanted to be off in Asia with Charlotte, our first big trip, and I was sure that it would lead us into China—if not immediately, then before very long. And there just might be a chance for Hanoi. I had been working on China since 1949 and on Vietnam for nearly two years. As for North Korea, I would be entirely happy if I never went to Pyongyang.

It was not just these three closed kingdoms. There were others on the periphery of China—Cambodia, locked tight against Americans by Prince Sihanouk because he thought (correctly) that the CIA was plotting his downfall (he'd gotten a birthday package which blew up when servants opened it); Burma, the doors sealed by Ne Win to all foreigners, particularly Americans; and not many got to Sikkim and Mongolia.

It would be a grand coup, and I was glad to get away from New York. The atmosphere had changed. Too much pettiness. Sharp edges. Unaccountable happenings. Clifton Daniel had made me assistant managing editor when he became managing editor in 1964. "We'll do all kinds of things," he said. "Things no one will know about. We'll often be here working, late at night, working on secret stuff. It's going to be exciting." But he added an admonition: I would not be his successor. We were too much of an age (I was three years older than Clifton). When his term was up, the prize would go to a younger man. That suited me fine. I insisted that I continue to do two or three big reporting assignments a year. He gave his OK.

Later on, the inner power structure of The *Times* was radically altered. Catledge, supported by Daniel and Rosenthal, sought to grasp control of the quasi-independent Washington bureau headed by Reston. The maneuver failed in a dramatic sequence of events chronicled in detail by Gay Talese in *The Kingdom and the Power* and in my own *Without Fear or Favor*. Catledge, in effect, was kicked upstairs. Reston came to New York briefly as executive editor. Daniel fell into disfavor with Punch Sulzberger and Rosenthal, although a prime figure in the failed endeavor, won Sulzberger's favor. After a short interlude Reston gave up his New York post and returned to Washington to concentrate on his column. The field was thus cleared for Rosenthal to rise to the top as chief news executive of the *Times*.

In all these shennanigans I was only an observer, a very interested one but on the sidelines. I knew all the participants intimately; they were my friends and there was very little that went on that I did not learn, sooner or later. But I was not a player in the Big Casino.

What my dream in the palace bedchamber told me was the depth of my hidden fear of being dealt out in the fast-moving intrigue and the strength of my own emotions, which I had not understood until this moment. Now I saw clearly that I was at peril. Scotty, I thought, as I lay listening to the ceaseless tropical downpour, was right. Absolutely right. I was being shuffled off center stage in a most elegant manner, and Clifton had to know that this was going on. (Never under my most persistent questioning in later years would he admit what seemed so obvious to me. It hadn't been, he insisted, a maneuver to open up my spot for Abe.) But, of course, I thought, that was exactly what was going on. Rosenthal was sitting in my chair—not, thank God, Mr. Hagerty's chair. That was long since gone, and when I got back to New York, there might or might not be a chair for me.

251

I had to get out of Gangtok as fast as possible, avalanches or no avalanches. Let them get a helicopter. I had to hit the road. I had to complete my perimeter journey, and I had to make it ring bells. I had to make this trip the foundation for future successes. Otherwise, my dream was going to come true.

I looked at Charlotte, quiet beside me, and told myself there can be not one word of this to her. This was our first great expedition. We had been thrilled to be together, looking up at the stars, lying on our backs on the teakwood deck of the Toppings' junk in the Hong Kong waters, riding elephants like tourists at Angkor Wat, dissolving in the beauty of the royal Cambodian dancers against the stone frieze of their ancestors as the moon rose over the jungle ruins, watching the great peak of Kanchenjunga flash pink and gold in the 5 A.M. sun, sleeping in each other's arms high above the Pacific. But now I was on the line. We had to get out of Gangtok. The Mongolian visas were expiring. They could only be renewed in Moscow, and we had no Moscow visa. Catch-22.

We left Gangtok in fog and rain at 8 A.M. and by noon we had come back to Gangtok. The rain poured, the road was blocked by pyramids of boulders, all telegraph and telephone lines were cut, no one knew if planes were flying. Certainly nothing could get into Gangkok. There wasn't even a landing strip. The amiable, gin-drinking Chogyal, a kind of Himalayan Jack Kennedy, and Hope, the whispering Queen, looking like a girl out of a Sarah Lawrence fairy tale in her handsome *kuo* and carmine makeup, thought we should wait. Why hurry? Sometimes Gangtok was cut off for a week or more. My nightmare burned a hole in my mind. I was sorry. We *had* to get out. We had to. That evening a plan was made. We would take a very roundabout route. We would start at 4:30 A.M. If we were lucky, we might get through. Then in late evening the Indian Army general in charge of roads came in with a new plan. We would take the shorter road. There were blockages, but we would walk across them, and jeeps would pick us up on the other side. He seemed sure we could make our 1:30 P.M. plane to Calcutta.

It was murky when we started, our luggage with us in one jeep, an army colonel and two Indian soldiers in a jeep ahead. Rain came and went, fog seeped into the valleys and crept down to our ankles, water roared from the high mountains, and a tributary of the Brahmaputra leaped and surged beside the road. Gangs of soldiers worked to clear the debris. There was blockage after blockage.

252

We skirted rock falls, inching along the edge of 2,000-foot drops, shifting our weight toward the mountain side. Mile-by-mile we made progress, but my mind was filled with gloomy thoughts. Then we arrived at a mammoth slide. The whole mountain top had fallen in on the road where it skirted a cliff. Scores of workers, men, women and children, pawed at the mass with picks, shovels, and bare hands. We got out of our jeep, took shelter behind small trees, and they blasted away with dynamite charges, rock flying through the air like shrapnel. It would take days to clear the slide.

Our Indian officer conferred with the captain in charge, half a dozen skirted Sikkimese shouldered our luggage, and we were off over the treacherous rock like billy goats, the smell of cordite heavy in our nostrils, the officer in spotless uniform picking his way in the shattered stone, the fallen trees, the tumbled debris as though escorting us to the races. Miraculously, we got over, across the pile, still smoking from the dynamite blasts. How Charlotte managed I can't imagine. On the far side another jeep awaited, and we set off again, slithering down the mountains, halted time and again, waiting for smaller slides to be cleared and yawning holes to be filled.

Finally we were off the mountain and racing across flat country toward the airport. I relaxed. Then the motor sputtered, coughed, and died. Out of gas. Ten minutes to plane time. My heart sank. A Red Cross jeep came down the road, our escort flagged it, hopped in, and soon returned with a couple of gallons of gas. He poured it in, but the engine wouldn't start. Again and again he depressed the starter. Not a cough from the engine. Out we leaped. The luggage was transferred to the Red Cross jeep, and we hurried on. Plane time came and went. We were covered with mud, tearing down a flat dusty road at sixty miles an hour. God save us, I thought, if we hit a cow (sacred in India). We hit no cow, but we did slam to a halt a mile from the airport. The gate was down at a railroad grade crossing. No train in sight. No gatekeeper in sight. This was an old Pearl White serial. Our colonel got out, serenely strolled across the tracks and disappeared. We stood in desolation. I had run out of encouraging things to say or think. We had lost another day and probably would spend the night in some hovel. Finally, our colonel came back, smiling. All was well. The plane hadn't arrived yet. Wouldn't get in for half-an-hour, maybe longer. Plenty of time to wash up and have a decent lunch before taking off for Calcutta. Miraculously, the gate

253

went up, we chugged across the tracks (no train ever appeared), and all was well. We had a pleasant lunch and were on our way.

Back in Delhi that evening, July 2, I took myself in hand. I had been too gloomy. The dream didn't mean anything. It was just the product of my worry over the blocked roads, the monsoon, the long, complicated arrangements, the lack of Russian visas. Now we were in Delhi, there was time to spare, everything would work out. It didn't.

Tony Lukas, the *Times* correspondent, just beginning his spectacular writing career, greeted us. There was even a handful of mail. Letters from the children in New York. We devoured them. There was also a letter from Turner Catledge. I opened it warily. The last time I had received a message from Catledge while abroad had been in Kabul, proposing that I become national editor. I scanned the letter, and my heart sank. My dream had been on target. Scotty had been right. Turner was asking, just asking, mind you, whether I would be interested in giving up my news job and taking over the *Times*'s fledgling (and ailing) book publishing division. I had so many contacts in the publishing world. He thought I would be just the man for this.

So there it was. My premonition had been correct. What to do? The travel agent who was getting our visas for Moscow had not received them. What to do? I concealed my thoughts as best I could. I was in as tough a bind as I had ever been. Yes, I told myself, the publishing division might be fun and profitable—if that was what I wanted. But it was really just a Catledge gimmick to get me out of the city room and leave that chair and desk open. And, I told myself, if this trip flopped, if I could not get into Russia, if I could not get into Mongolia, if I had to cancel the sprawl of the vast frontiers of Russia and Mongolia with China, the most sensitive, hottest segment of all, the whole thing would fall to the ground. True it would have been a great travelogue. Sure, I had got into Cambodia. Sure I had made it into Laos. I had astonished everyone by breaking into Ne Win's Burma, thanks to an assist from Jim Linen, the *Time* executive, and a personal telephone call from New York to Ne Win. But what did it add up to? Yes, Charlotte and I had been guests of Himalayan royalty. We had had fun. An adventure. We had our thrills and excitement, but when I got back to New York and walked into the city room, no one would notice.

First things first. I spent the night tossing and turning. Fortunately, Charlotte was exhausted. I did not wake her. I made my plan of action. I would cable Catledge and tell him I would explore the publishing project the moment I got back. That would put it on hold until I saw how the wind was blowing in New York and whether my apprehensions were correct (I was 100 percent convinced they were). Abe was a young man in a hurry. He had been expected to spend six months learning the ropes of the city room. Frank Adams, his friend from United Nations days, was delighted to have his protégé back. He looked forward to working with Abe. But in three weeks Frank Adams was gone, kicked up to the tenth floor to write editorials. Abe couldn't stand having to sit beside the plodding Adams. Abe knew what he wanted to do. He had recruited Arthur Gelb. He had looked over the young reporters. He had picked those he wanted to work with. Turner arranged for Frank Adams' immediate departure, hardly time for a farewell handshake. Adams left the city room a bitter man. His consumption of midday martinis at Goughs went up.

Next morning I checked with the Indian travel agent about Moscow. The agent was very handsome, very suave, very certain the visa would come through. No problem. I thought there was a big problem and went to the Soviet embassy myself. The embassy was equally benign. Not to worry. The visa would be ready. I was not reassured. Not for a minute. Our Mongolian visas were valid until July 7. It was already July 3. We had to get the Mongol visas extended in Moscow. No way to do it in Delhi. I had dealt with the Mongols and knew that even this small clerical detail could not be solved instantly. My relations with Ulan Bator were fine. But no one was more bureaucratic than the Mongols. We had to have a couple of days in Moscow to attend to the Mongolian visas.

That must have been the day I went to the Soviet embassy again. The morning mail had brought a letter from Abe. He was full of admiration for my Asian stories, particularly those from Burma. He had known I would fall in love with India. (I hadn't.) He put in a trifle or two of office gossip and added: "It's been fun for me, keeping your chair warm."

Everything will be fine, said the Russians that afternoon. If the visas don't come through, you can get them at the airport in Moscow. New regulations. They will issue the transit visas at the airport. A two or three-day stopover is automatic. I hoped that was true. My, how I hoped. But I only half-believed the men. Nothing so convenient had ever happened to me in Moscow. I believed the consul, because I had to believe him. The alternative was to abandon everything and go back to New York and the book business. The

255

worst part was not to let Charlotte catch my worries. Charlotte is a great worrier. There were enough day-to-day worries on the trip without adding this kind of complication.

We took off from Delhi July 8. Our visas to Mongolia had expired the day before. We had no visas for Russia. It was as risky a gamble as I had ever taken. I did not know how it would work out. But I would *make* it work. I told Charlotte that, if worse came to worse, we would go to London and have a ball. I didn't tell her that the chances were 10 to 1 that we would go to London and not to Ulan Bator. I didn't tell her about the book business.

As she wrote in those days in her diary:

"I like to know where I am, what I am supposed to do, why and what is coming next. . . . We are always getting into cars, driving off to unknown places with people we can't communicate with, trusting everything to strangers and somehow or other it works out one way or another."

If she had only known.

It is a long, long haul from New Delhi to Moscow. We left in early morning and, even with the time difference, got into Moscow at midafternoon. Peter Grose, the *Times* correspondent, and Sara Shaikevich, my old secretary, met us. But there were no Soviet transit visas. We were confined to the transit lounge. It was Saturday afternoon. No way to contact the Mongol embassy. No explanation, no argument would change the minds of the airport officials. We had telephoned Foy Kohler, the American ambassador. Foy was an old, old friend. Couldn't someone telephone the Foreign Office? He laughed unpleasantly. "This is Russia, Salisbury, you know that as well as I do." Never have I been so frustrated. Charlotte was worn out—and we faced another twelve-hour flight to Ulan Bator. Nothing for it. At midevening we took off. What lay ahead I hated to think.

At the Irkutsk airport, we bumped into Bernie Reisman, just in from Ulan Bator where he had gone to do a documentary for ABC. He thought all his arrangements were OK. He had visas. Permits. Everything. The Mongols hadn't allowed him out of the airport and had shipped him back to Irkutsk. He had 16 mm cameras, not 35 as the documents provided.

Charlotte was exhausted. So was I. I assured her nothing like that would happen to us. No way. I had friends in Mongolia. (Privately I feared we would not be allowed out of the airport. We would be shipped back to Russia on the same plane. The Russians would not allow us out of the Irkutsk airport. Where they would ship us I had no idea.)

We flew down to Ulan Bator over the mountains and the flat steppes. It was a brief, even a pleasant flight. A nice woman in a blue Mongolian *del* served weak apple juice and Russian chocolates. We set down at the Ulan Bator airport in early afternoon. Everyone was pleasant. The Mongols got off the plane. Pleasant chattering Mongols met them. The Russians got off the plane. Pleasant Russians met them. Gradually people left the tiny airport, and we were alone. No one met us. No one paid any attention. We sat with our bags, and I wondered what to do. Finally a young Mongol, a student returning from Sofia, came to our rescue. He telephoned the tourist bureau and presently a polite tourist representative arrived, apologized, swept us up, passed us through customs, brought us into town, put us up in a big suite at the Ulan Bator Hotel on Suke Bator Square in the center of town. Our troubles were over. I could not believe it. The hotel manager waited on us. Everyone was solicitous. The load dropped from my shoulders. My God, I thought, we're in! Incredible! We had won the 10 to 1 bet. Either they haven't noticed the date on our visas or didn't care. We relaxed in exhaustion, slept twelve hours, awoke, had a good breakfast, bumped into Owen Lattimore, the old Sinologist and Mongologist, McCarthyite target and Russian target (his picture was still on the wall of the Mongolian Historical Museum, identified as a CIA agent, along with that of Roy Chapman Andrews), met the British and French ambassadors, both staying in the hotel. I lost so much tension I thought my knees would buckle.

Back at our room we found the hotel manager and an interpreter. The manager was very polite but firm. We had entered Mongolia illegally. Our visas had expired. It was a most serious crime. We would have to remain in the hotel until the proper officials could be notified. Today was Sunday. No one was available. Tomorrow was the national holiday, *Nadam*, July 11. There would be a three-day celebration. Whether anyone could be located until after the holiday, he did not know. He was very sorry. Very correct. Listened earnestly to my explanation. Rules were rules. We had to stay inside.

Gloom settled down again, but somehow I thought there was a glimmer of hope. I did not believe they would expel us. I consulted the British and French. They didn't think so either. We relaxed a bit. We needed the rest. The next day, *Nadam*, Monday July 11, it rained. It rained all day, a monsoon on this barren desert land. We stood at our window. The great *Nadam* parade, all of Mongolia, it seemed, passed before our eyes, wet, sodden, banners drooping but singing in the rain. It was not an unpleasant front seat. Charlotte knitted. I tried to persuade myself that we would overcome. We had gotten this far. We would not be thrown out.

Next morning after a rather formal talk at the Foreign Office, a vast apology by myself, all was forgiven. We got new visas. Charlotte had a sinking spell. Never in her life (as she said) had she been confined or restrained by any kind of governent. The moment passed. We went for a walk in the great square with Lattimore. The rain was still pouring down. The Mongol national games—horse racing, wrestling, archery—were postponed. The rain came down and down and down.

The Tola River, normally as dry as the Los Angeles River, runs through the heart of Ulan Bator. Now it surged over its banks, several feet over its banks, factories flooded, apartment houses collapsed, hundreds of people homeless, many drowned. Army helicopters came to the rescue. Vast Suke Bator Square was turned into a refugee encampment. The power station was knocked out. No electricity. No telephones. No lights. No water. The hotel kitchen out of service. The plumbing out of service. Army generators tried to provide power. Army field kitchens set up outside the hotel, which was filled with "distinguished guests," delegations from Communist and Asian countries to the Nadam festival. Lives had been lost, bridges swept away, highways cut, the airport closed. Never had Mongolia experienced such floods. Thousands lost their homes. Suke Bator Square blossomed with yurts, soup kitchens, bedraggled people.

The flood disrupted the whole country. I filed a dispatch and got a good scoop. I didn't say what the foreign guests were telling me— that the Mongols were having such a good time at the big national day reception they paid no attention to reports of the rising Tola and danger to the city.

Travel was impossible, and after a week we took off for the Soviet Union, this time with proper visas (no problem at the Soviet embassy in Ulan Bator), flew to Irkutsk, went to Lake Baikal, took off for Khabarovsk but ended up in Vladivostok (strictly off limits to foreigners, especially Americans). A savage electrical storm prevented us from landing at Khabarovsk so we flew along the Sino-Soviet border, lightning flashing about us as I have never seen it, my nose to the window expecting at any moment to see Chinese antiaircraft batteries open up. They didn't, and we had several hours with the commandant of the Vladivostok airport, the colonel toasting us in glass after glass of vodka, *do adna*, bottoms up. We flew back to Khabarovsk, boarded the Trans-Siberian, down to the big port of Nakhodka, took a cheery Soviet steamer to Yokohama and on to Tokyo. We had completed the 25,000-mile itinerary just as I had planned, despite floods, avalanches, monsoons, Communist bureaucrats, nightmares—harvesting splendid stories, a splendid series, giving me a broader dimension of Communism and Asia, I felt, than anyone in the world yet had. I was not modest about this. It had been a perilous trip. A lot was at stake. But we had come through.

We arrived back in New York. No longer was I under the chilling spell of my Sikkim nightmare. I walked into the third floor of the *Times*, went to my desk (vacated by Abe), caught my breath, and went to work. I knew how I would handle the publishing assignment. The *Times* should get into the publishing field. I believed in that, but only in a first-class way. No half-measures. No fiddling around. The way to do it was to buy a good publishing firm, one compatible in character and objectives with the *Times*, one with good management in place. Nothing sick, broken down, or second-rate. Nothing cheap. The *Times* could take over the firm, give it *Times* backing, *Times* funding, let it grow and prosper. I knew exactly which company I wanted the *Times* to buy, and I knew the company wanted and needed the *Times*. A perfect fit. (My recommendation was for Harper & Row. I knew it well. Knew its executives and particularly Cass Canfield, its chief.) If Punch Sulzberger and Ivan Veit, the vice president in charge of the operation, liked my idea and were willing to go forward with it—fine. I would—for an appropriate (generous) sum—be glad to take it in hand for a fixed period, just long enough to be sure everything was going well. Then back to my own trade—reporting and writing.

I discussed the idea thoroughly with Cass Canfield. It appealed strongly to him. It came at a time when Harper & Row needed access to capital which we believed the *Times* could provide. Cass met with me and several *Times* executives very privately (I don't believe word ever got out about these talks). Cass was insistent that if Harper & Row were to be sold that it go to an institution compatible with its philosophy. He thought the *Times* was just right.

Unfortunately this was too big a deal for the *Times*. It was still in the process of becoming a public company. The purchase would involve a big exchange of stock as well as cash. Veit and Sulzberger were afraid to take such a big bite. They elected to buy a small company and "learn by doing." I don't know how much they really learned. In the end this and other publishing experiments cost the *Times* so many millions I don't dare put the figures down. Thankfully, I had no part in this; it was not my bag. Nor should it have been that of the *Times*.

There was something else on my mind, something more important. I hadn't got into China but now I thought that with the contacts I had made and the broader understanding I possessed of China, I had a good chance of breaking down the barriers. I hadn't gotten to Hanoi either. I might never make it, but I had reason to believe that I would. I had a secret promise that I would get to Vietnam before the year was out.

My Sikkim nightmare had not been all bad. Without it I might have given up in Delhi, taken the easy way out, booked passage for London, had a fine stay with Charlotte at the Savoy, shown her my favorite city, London, and my favorite countryside, England, and come home to empty out my desk and turn the keys over to Abe.

# Chapter 22

# The War Next Door

Vietnam . . . Vietnam . . . No one called it Nam in those days, and actually many people in Southeast Asia still thought of it as Indochina. But no longer in the United States. By now it was Vietnam to all of us, and more and more our lives, our thoughts, and increasingly our politics had begun to center on these two syllables, Viet Nam— the Land of the South as the Chinese call it.

Charlotte and I had not gotten to Hanoi on our 25,000-mile orbit of China, but we had gotten close enough to hear and feel the war a few miles away. I had applied for visas in Phnom Penh, and soon, I was sure, I, at least, would be behind the enemy lines. I was not eager to take Charlotte with me, and the North Vietnamese were not eager for a woman visitor.

On one Cambodian evening we sat down to a banquet in the palace of the governor general of Svay Rieng, a pleasant man in his thirties with a round soft-featured face who reminded me of Prince Sihanouk. Svay Rieng was a provincial capital on Highway No. 10, a half a dozen miles from the Vietnam border.

All day we had been plunging in and out of the jungle along the Caiboc River in our Land Rovers, inspecting villages which had been bombed in what the U.S. Military called Operation Birmingham. I had seen my share of the dark and bloody ground of Birmingham, Alabama, but I could find no reference points to Bull Connor in the ruin of thatched-hut villages, leveled by stray (were they stray?) American bombs, the random rubble left by artillery shelling, burned-out vehicles, black and rusty, in talking to confused villagers who told us their confused stories, running with them for shelter (there wasn't any) at the sound of throbbing airplane motors, sighing with them in relief when the sound faded into the distance. We were not in Vietnam, but this was part of war Zone C, as it was called by Big Red One, the American division assigned to this location during Operation Birmingham.

This was no-man's-land where Viet Cong moved in stealth and

Americans moved after them, the border being the meandering Caiboc River, twenty yards wide at one place, thirty at another, lush with water hyacinths, a faint brown streak from the air. The jungle was identical and unbroken on either side, and there was hardly a sign as to whether you were on Cambodian soil or Vietnamese soil: heavy, heavy vegetation, the thatch of the villages blending into the jungle, trails losing themselves in the forest, bunkers and trenches here and there (whether for Cambodian defense or Vietcong offense, who could say?). People with weapons kept appearing and disappearing, all looking the same, small and bronze, tattered cotton shirts and trousers, no way a careful American commander could know whether they were neutral or hostile. This was the war that had come to preoccupy America, this was its uncertain face, and this was what I was determined to examine from the inside. What *were* we doing? Did anyone know?

That day we had twelve hours of rugged travel, in and out of our vehicles, over what was said to be a trail along the border. Not until midevening did we return to Svay Rieng to see the palace, a fairyland of lanterns, red and green and blue, swaying from the mango trees. Within the palace, ceiling fans slowly stirred the turgid air, moving the fat flies from room to room. We had drinks from frosty glasses, a quick shower, and then seated ourselves at a mahogany table strewn with ivory camellias and exotic lilies, the perfume heavy in our nostrils, the table laid with fine silver, cut glass and Limoges, the wine from France, of course, waiters in white jackets, the governor general's lady, svelte, under thirty (Charlotte swore), pregnant with her tenth child, chic in black silk *sampot*, white embroidered blouse, and fine rubies, everyone cool, sophisticated, speaking French.

As we dined, I heard a distant rumble. Sometimes the table trembled, and the crystal lightly tinkled against the silver. Bombs were falling just down Highway No. 10 on the other side of the line. Oh yes, our host said. It starts almost every evening about this time, about ten o'clock. It's been going on for a year or so. Sometimes, he said, I'm afraid the bombs may fall on us. It was a fear I heard many times in Cambodia, a fear that the war would spread across the vague frontiers into Sihanouk's peaceful kingdom.

Cambodia was still, as Sihanouk proclaimed, "an island of tranquillity" in the sea of war. One day we visited the State Museum in Phnom Penh. A Cambodian girl, gentle and young, led us through the antiquities, stopping now and then to caress the polished figures, passing her slender hands over their curves, so subtle, so sensuous. The image of that young woman is as clear in my mind today as it was in the time of Pol Pot when I closed my eyes and saw Pot's teenagers, no older than the Red Hook Cobras I had described in *The Shook-Up Generation*, glance at those lovely Cambodian hands without a callus, put a bullet through her head, and straggle on as the blood spread over the palace tiles.

All around China we had skirted the edges of war: warnings in Hong Kong that China would intervene; warnings in Bangkok that Thailand would change sides and go with China if we pulled out; warnings in Russia that the United States was out of control; warnings in Mongolia that China had gone out of control; warnings in Tokyo that nuclear war was too close for words.

It was against these warnings that I had come back to New York with a private guarantee, one which I shared only with Clifton Daniel. In Phnom Penh I had put my case to the North Vietnamese. I had prepared my way with care. I had tried to win the backing of every person who might have influence in Hanoi. There were quite a few. Early one morning I was sitting in the big city room of the *Times* when a slight young man in chinos, a tan open-collar sports shirt, and dirty white sneakers wandered in, looking for Scotty Reston. Scotty wasn't there, and I had a talk with him. He was Tom Hayden, the SDS leader, his publicity-prone career and Jane Fonda distantly ahead of him, just back from Hanoi. We talked for a time, and when I was launching my campaign to get into Vietnam, I enlisted his help. I did the same with Staughton Lynd, son of the *Middletown* Lynds, sociologist and visitor to Hanoi. I talked to David Dellinger, and I wrote to Wilfred Burchett, the Australian journalist deeply engaged in long-running, long-range combat with his Australian critics. In 1961 I had lunched with Burchett in Moscow and knew more than most about his relations with Communist movements—the Russians, the Chinese, the Koreans, and especially the Vietnamese. Burchett, I found, was already trying to assist my *Times* colleague Seymour Topping (whose father-in-law, the Canadian diplomat Chester Ronning, was in close touch with Hanoi) to get into Vietnam. But Burchett agreed to help me, too.

I had, of course, bombarded Ho Chi Minh and Premier Pham Van Dong with cables and letters. I had sought the help of James Cameron, the English correspondent who had been in Hanoi about a year before.

I had solicited several French correspondents, diplomats, and even two or three Soviet colleagues in Moscow.

As the years have passed, it has become clear to me that, if there was any single voice which spoke for me in tones which penetrated the minds and hearts of the Vietnamese, it was that of Anne Morrison.

Not many today may remember the name of Norman Morrison, an American Quaker who gave his life for peace. This was the period when yellow-robed Buddhist monks immolated themselves in the public squares of Saigon, sitting cross-legged on the pavement, calmly drenching their bodies with gasoline, touching a match and burning to death, passive and immobile as the flames leaped up.

Morrison, as devout in his belief in peace as a man could be, seated himself cross-legged outside the Pentagon one day, poured gasoline over himself and lighted a match in the manner of the Buddhist martyrs.

No American of that time was so venerated in Hanoi. Norman Morrison, as I found when I arrived in Hanoi, was regarded as a saint, an object of almost holy worship. I did not know Morrison nor did I know his widow. But John Corry, a warm and sympathetic *Times* reporter (his later emergence as waspish electronics scourge then unthinkable), knew Anne Morrison. Through Corry's good graces, she wrote a letter supporting my hopes for reporting from Vietnam. She vouched for me.

"As a Quaker pacifist," Anne Morrison wrote, "it is my belief that truth itself contains power to evoke change." She expressed her trust that *The New York Times* would bring my stories "unedited to the American people." Anne's words, I am certain, won my entry into Hanoi.

In Phnom Penh the Vietnamese had received me with politeness and even warmth. They could give me no immediate answer, but they felt my chances were good; perhaps I could come up to Hanoi almost immediately, within a few days. They would communicate with the Foreign Ministry and let me know. Charlotte and I spent ten days traveling about Cambodia but finally were told that we could not go to Hanoi then—a more favorable occasion would have to be awaited.

I now began to experience what might be called the Rashomon of the Vietnam war. Nothing in the news as published gave me a clue why this was not a "favorable" opportunity to come to the Vietnamese capital. Only later did I learn what was secretly going on. Chester Ronning, the Canadian, had just brought to Hanoi new American proposals for a halt in U.S. bombing in return for a halt in

North Vietnamese operations in the south. As I waited in Cambodia, this proposal came to nothing amid bitter rhetoric, and on June 27 and 29 American bombers went into action, bombing Haiphong and the Hanoi area for the first time. Thus it was that Hanoi conveyed to me word that a more appropriate occasion for a visit would have to be found later on. As I would learn, this was not the first time nor would it be the last when peace missions touched off new bombings, new escalations by LBJ. It became almost a fixed pattern.

As for my visit Hanoi passed down the message: "It will occur before the end of the year."

I was too experienced to take those words at face value. I might or might not get into Hanoi in the next few months. It would depend on events over which I had no control and probably no knowledge and the decisions would be made by men whom I did not know and who did not know me. I was disappointed. I wanted to go when the iron was hot. Now it would cool down, and the moment would vanish.

Back in New York I did not neglect Vietnam. I resumed my rain of letters and telegrams. I hunted up more persons who might be helpful. The promise of a trip before New Year's was in my pocket but I was not going to let anyone in Hanoi forget it. I said nothing to my associates at the *Times* (except for Daniel). I am superstitious, and I do not believe in arousing exaggerated expectations. Time enough for others to know when and if a telegram came through. While waiting on Hanoi, I headed up a team of a dozen *Times* correspondents who—if Moscow permitted—would go to Russia and size up the Bolshevik regime after fifty years. And I was heading a small group which was taking a new look at the Kennedy assassination, the Warren Commission report, and the cloud of "conspiracy" chatter that was spewing into the public media.

But most of all in that autumn of 1966 I was quietly pursuing Hanoi. This was the autumn when Vietnam began to overwhelm America, when it began to dominate television in the evening, to fill front pages and bring people to the streets and campuses to turmoil. Vietnam was hot, and it was getting hotter as Mr. Johnson and his generals sought to pour on the pressure and bring a fateful war to a victorious conclusion.

To me Hanoi had become a sphinx. Not one sign, not one message, not one hint. Nothing. I wrote my letters and sent my cables. I read the news reports, day to day, in the *Times*. I kept my ears peeled for gossip. I took to reading the *National Guardian*, which printed the reports from Wilfred Burchett. I thought there might be some clue in what he was writing, sometimes from Phnom Penh, sometimes from Hanoi, sometimes from unknown points in Vietcong territory. I subscribed to *Le Monde*. I read England's *Guardian* and the *Times* of London. I don't think I was any the wiser.

I was as ignorant as almost all Americans as to what was happening in Vietnam. I picked up through the grapevine word of Chester Ronning's failed mission to Hanoi in June 1966, but I had never heard of earlier efforts by the Canadian Blair Seaborn in 1965. The words "Mayflower," "XYZ," "Rangoon," "Marigold," "Sunflower"—the whole series of flower-coded negotiating endeavors—were meaningless to my ears (as to almost all Americans). I would have been amazed to learn that at that moment a complicated but futile sequence was being played out in Rangoon under the sponsorship of U.N. Secretary-General U Thant.

And certainly I did not know of the mirror-image dealings called Marigold, a complex bit of hugger-mugger, the full outlines of which are not entirely known even today. This had many players—American, Polish, Russian, Italian, French (probably), and, of course, Vietnamese. In some ways it seemed to insiders to be the most serious of all the secret peace initiatives. (So many were now under way, LBJ named Averell Harriman to coordinate them.) But in the end Marigold was shot down, a sunburst of recriminations coming to a head in early December 1966. I knew nothing about this during those long, puzzling autumn days. Nor do I know whether or how it may have affected my trip to Hanoi. But I have finally concluded that all missions to Hanoi, journalistic, diplomatic, or otherwise, in some mysterious and unseen manner were linked, if not in the minds of Ho Chi Minh and Pham Van Dong, then in the minds of LBJ and his diplomats, generals, and bureaucrats.

So far as the war was concerned, the combat, the commitment of American troops, the concentration of American warships and naval aircraft, the steady increase in participation of our great B-52 bombers went on with routine ferocity. No one—least of all myself, as the dreary 1966 autumn ran down from November into December —could see any sign that the cluster of men around Lyndon Johnson had doubts about what they were doing, any suspicion that all was not going well: that, indeed, there was no light at the end of the tunnel, that the daily body counts, the plastic statistics of the Five

O'Clock Follies at Pentagon East in Saigon did not tell the story of a strong, unified leadership carefully quantifying the precise levels of napalm, high explosive, and artillery which in Lyndon's immortal words, would "make 'em holler uncle" and "bring home the coonskin." All was well in this most technological of wars. So it seemed.

One of the war's architects was Robert S. McNamara. For more than six months, unknown to the public, he had harbored deep doubts about the war and the prospect that it could be won. McNamara's views were as secret from me as from the country—and indeed from McNamara's closest aides—but the brightest of the brightest, the whiz among the "whiz kids" who brought Henry Ford's Motor Company back from disaster after World War II, the man John F. Kennedy picked to usher the American military establishment into the new technological age, had turned against the war.

Who can say precisely what is a turning point in so vital and so vast a case? Robert McNamara could not pinpoint that moment in talking to me in 1985. But he did remember, as did his closest aide, General Robert F. Pursley, his rising concern over ever vaster and non-effective employment of air power. Specifically Pursley remembered a time in the summer of 1966—July 4, to be precise. That day McNamara, with a broken foot hobbled into his office, holiday or no holiday. Pursley was there too, in a state of shock at the sudden death of his mother. That was the day McNamara asked Pursley to determine what intelligence lay behind the June 27 and 29 U.S. bombings of Haiphong and the Hanoi environs. Pursley asked Defense Intelligence. They had none. McNamara went to Richard Helms, head of CIA, and asked for CIA intelligence on the problem. This was, as later would be seen, McNamara's first positive act, which would lead to his order for the compilation of the Pentagon Papers (exploring the reasons for the Vietnam war; its conduct and its failures—to instruct future generations how to avoid the pitfalls of the present), to his open break with LBJ; it was the first crack within Johnson's iron framework, which ultimately led LBJ to his bombing halt of March 1968 and withdrawal from the 1968 Presidential race.

McNamara's action of July 4, 1966, was in response to the very American bombing that marked the breakdown of the Chester Ronning mission in June 1966, the bombing that blocked Charlotte and me from going on to North Vietnam from Phnom Penh. It triggered the reaction that turned Robert McNamara from a hawk to a dove.

For eighteen years I would not know this curious intersection in the lives of McNamara and my own. Not until we talked in 1985, trying to fit together the known and the unknown, the war as it seemed and the war as it existed below that mirrored surface, the war which I and millions of other Americans thought we were fighting, and the war as it came to be seen by those who were directing it.

This was the first of the separating images which, as time went on, showed me that in war, as in the simplest things in life, truth is multifaceted, a crystal that refracts light in many forms and many shapes, the quicksilver of the mind.

For all my talk and all my thought, I did not understand this in November and December of 1966. I still—against all probability—believed that the truth could somehow be quantified. Somehow as a reporter I could venture out into the field, even into the acrid jungles of Vietnam, torn by high explosive, roots fed by the blood of many men and women, many wars in a long and complex history, and bring back the truth; I would go into the country of Rashomon and tell my people what was its color and its nature. I was, I know now, very naive but so were the American people and, when you come to think of it, the human race.

I did not then know—nor would I for many, many years, not until I began to retrieve my FBI files under the Freedom of Information Act—that I had acquired a small tail.

General Ne Win and his wife, Katie, were coming to the United States and LBJ had invited them to dinner in late August. The White House decided to invite Charlotte and myself to the State dinner, probably because we had spent time with Ne Win and Katie in Rangoon. First there must be a security check. Mrs. Mildred Stegall, LBJ's liaison for security matters, sent our names over to J. Edgar Hoover. J. Edgar promptly replied to Marvin Watson, LBJ's special assistant. I don't know what his reply was—two thirds of it was blacked out in the copy I received—but we were not invited.

A small cloud in the sky, invisible to us, but soon there would be more, and they would not be so small.

# Chapter 23

# A Walk Down
# Pho Nguyen Thiep Street

We sat at one of those big round tables with heavy black leather chairs to the rear of the Oak Room at the Plaza, Clifton Daniel and his wife, Margaret Truman, Charlotte and myself. It was Sunday night before Christmas, December 19, 1966, and the room was very crowded. Everyone from Jersey and the Island had come to New York that weekend to walk down Fifth Avenue, ogle the glitter in the Saks windows, watch the skaters at Rockefeller Plaza, and throw dollar bills into the iron pots of the Volunteers of America to the electronic sound of "It Came upon a Midnight Clear."

We talked about everything but what was on our minds—my departure on Monday for Hanoi. Clifton talked of the duchesses he'd known in London and Margaret complained of Washington. She hadn't liked it in White House days, and she liked it less now. Charlotte and I hardly spoke. Too much on our minds.

I was going off into the enemy territory, shooting territory, behind the Vietnam lines. I had worked my heart out to get permission, but the reality didn't seem so dashing. Yes, it would be the scoop of my life and a great feather in the cap of Clifton as managing editor of the *Times*. Yes, as Charlotte and I tried to convince each other, it might bring peace a step or two closer, but it was dangerous. It was not an expedition to be undertaken lightly. And I was leaving great burdens on Charlotte's shoulders—my son Michael was getting married on New Year's Eve, and we (that is, in my absence, Charlotte) were putting on the wedding. My younger son, Stephan, at Columbia, was going through a midschool crisis. Whether he would still be enrolled by the time I got back, I could not guess. I was miserable and full of guilt.

These thoughts were swirling around in my mind when I heard Clifton say: "You know, we don't go in at the *Times* for much in the way of promotion. But I think this trip to Hanoi is something special.

When you actually get to Phnom Penh and board that plane for Hanoi, send me a cable. I think it would be worthwhile to raise a little fuss about this—we could run some spots on WQXR [the *Times*-owned fine music station] and maybe even put a few ads in the paper.

"It isn't every day that we get a man into Hanoi," he went on. "I think we could brag a bit."

I thought that was a fine idea. Time and again, it seemed to me, the *Times* had pulled off great scoops, and no one quite understood this because the *Times* played them sotto voce.

Clifton and I could not have been more naïve. If there was ever a story that needed no advertisement it was Hanoi. When it broke on Christmas morning, December 25, 1966, it broke on every front page of every newspaper around the world. It led the Vatican *L'Osservatore Romano*, it led BBC, it led every TV and radio newscast.

I got to Paris in the gray chill morning of Tuesday the twentieth. I spent the day shoving through the traffic between the Vietnamese and Cambodian embassies for my visas. That evening I dined with Henry Tanner and Dick Mooney of the *Times'* Paris bureau in Les Halles at the Pharamond. No one knew what I was doing in Paris. No one knew where I was going. Only six people on the *Times* knew, no one outside the paper. But of course all the Paris bureau had guessed. We drank mysterious toasts to the "success of your mission," then I caught a few hours sleep at my favorite Paris hotel, the Louvois on the Rue Richelieu (alas, no longer extant). Early in the morning, making my way through serpentines of school children at Orly, viewing the crèches (some looked like Picasso, some like medieval Florence). I boarded the plane for Phnom Penh. Not many passengers that morning.

It was Thursday noon before we touched down in tropical 100-degree Phnom Penh. Little Christmas spirit but the same mildewed Graham Greene atmosphere at the Hotel Le Royale as when Charlotte and I stayed there in June.

I had crossed beyond the threshold of my imagination. In the long flight across the Atlantic, in sleepless hours in the Louvois waiting for dawn, in the endless progress from Paris to Tirana, to Cairo, to Karachi, and finally Phnom Penh I had amused myself making up stories about the impeccably blond French stewardesses, the band of Albanian clowns and tenors flying out to Shanghai, the seedy Frenchman who slunk off the plane at Cairo and disappeared through immigration before I had a clear view of his dark skin and jet moustache; the too obvious English diplomat, six feet eight inches, who reminded me of Sir Hughe Montgomery Knatchbull-Hugessen, the World War II ambassador to Turkey who was so thoroughly flummoxed by his valet, Cicero, an agent of German intelligence.

Now relaxing over a Coca Cola on the terrace of Le Royale, watching a luminous young Thai goddess slowly kicking herself in a back stroke from one end of the pool to another, I was descended upon by the real spies and agents, men and women, who flourished in Phnom Penh.

If airtight security about my mission to Hanoi had been observed in New York, if my colleagues in Paris had nothing but intelligent guesses to go on, if no one in Washington had yet caught on (I had had my passport cleared for Vietnam months previously), there was absolutely no mystery in Phnom Penh as to who I was and what I was doing.

I don't know how many persons came up, shook my hand and congratulated me. They knew I was leaving on the International Control Commission plane the next day, Friday the twenty-third, for Hanoi. The ICC plane was one of the great phenomena of the Vietnam war. From start to finish it provided service between Saigon and Hanoi with stops at Phnom Penh and Vientiane. It was neutral. The commission had been set up under the protocols of the 1954 Geneva Convention. Originally it possessed two silvery four-engined Constellations and four Bell helicopters. One Constellation had been shot down a few months previously and the helicopters were grounded for lack of pilots.

The single Constellation lumbered along. It made three round-trips Saigon–Hanoi–Saigon each fortnight. The Control Commission was run by India, Poland, and Canada. It carried a passenger from Phnom Penh to Hanoi for $235 and, except for a dilatory service from China via Canton and Nanking, it was the only way to get to Hanoi. There had been an Air Cambodge service when Charlotte and I visited Phnom Penh in June, but Prince Sihanouk suspended it after American fighters warned it off Hanoi during a bombing raid.

Le Royale was full of pleasant Poles, jolly Canadians, and mysterious individuals of unknown nationality. They all seemed to know more about me than I did myself. And they all connected my presence with a letter our United Nations representative, Arthur Goldberg, had sent to U Thant, supporting his peace efforts. I didn't know such a letter had been sent. None of them paid heed to my protests of ignorance. They winked and looked at me slyly. Naturally I would deny it. But those simple denials just confirmed their suspicions. I was, in their minds, an unofficial messenger from LBJ to Ho Chi Minh. Not a doubt of it, and they wished me well.

I was, I confess, embarrassed. We had gone out of our way to make certain that the administration would not be compromised by my presence in Hanoi. I had spoken to no one in the State Department or the White House. Even Scotty Reston had not breathed a word to Dean Rusk or Walt Rostow. In no way would I be acting in Hanoi as a spokesman, unofficial or otherwise, for Washington.

Try to make the Poles or the Canadians or the Indians or the French believe that. I finally laughed and shrugged my shoulders. What else was there to do? I could think of nothing more unlikely and more irritating to LBJ than to find me in the role of his official emissary. I had never met LBJ beyond a formal handshake. He had put on a great campaign in his first days in office to win over the *Times*, telephone calls to the publisher, Punch Sulzberger, to Turner Catledge, two or three a day to Reston, so many phone calls that the *Times* people were embarrassed. Then, LBJ, realizing that he was getting nowhere, cut off the calls and entered the name of the *Times* and its editors in his ever-expanding black book.

That night I lay on the great brass bed of my room at the Royale and wondered what might lie ahead. In this decaying yet pleasant French colonial city, I had the impression that for all my research, my contacts, the expertise I thought I had acquired, I was, in a sense, a naïf. I seemed to have wandered into a chamber of mirrors in which little was what it seemed. There was *our* war in Vietnam, the one which, officially, we were fighting, the war reported every day in the *Times*; there was another war in Vietnam which, somewhere below the level of information and communiqués, seemed to be going on; there was the war the Vietnamese believed they were fighting; there were the versions which the Europeans perceived—East Europeans, West Europeans, and French—especially the French.

And then there were the Chinese. In the U.S.A. I heard nothing about the Chinese. Oh, yes, occasionally in Washington someone would warn that "if we go up to the north, if we invade North Vietnam, if we begin to bomb along the Chinese frontier, Peking will come in."

But in Phnom Penh that was not the China on the lips of the Poles and the French and the Cambodians. Sihanouk had designated China as Cambodia's best friend. But the question troubling these cynical, weary men, in their sweat-stained linen suits, their woven Panama hats, was a different one. What, after all, is happening in China and how will it affect Vietnam? Their question related to the turbulence which had boiled up in China just a year ago and, as of this date (late December 1966), showed every sign of escalating and escalating again. Where was it headed? Every one in Phnom Penh knew, as few in Washington yet recognized, that China was out of control, that China had halted Soviet shipments to Vietnam and threatened to do it again, that China had halted its own shipments to Vietnam and threatened to do it again, that China was implacably hostile to *any* contact or diplomatic initiatives to halt the U.S.-Vietnam hostilities.

"Wait till you get to Hanoi," one of the Poles told me, eyes sparkling (a good Pole, he loved diplomatic intrigue). "Wait till you get there. It has taken a lot of guts for Hanoi to invite you. I am sure the Chinese have told them to send you packing." (Frankly this thought had never entered my head.)

China, I quickly understood, was the hottest story in Hanoi. Not the China Washington had conjured up from Korean experience— not a China which was getting ready to send 1 million men into Vietnam if we got too close to the passes.

Not at all. This was the China which sat in judgment over Hanoi and Ho Chi Minh, the China which sat in judgment over Nikita Khrushchev and Leonid Brezhnev in Moscow, the China which had decreed that Khrushchev had abandoned Marxism and embarked on a capitalist program, the China which was tearing itself apart in the Cultural Revolution, the China which was denouncing its leaders Liu Shaoqi and Deng Xiaoping as "capitalist roaders," the China that was convulsed by a chaotic Marxism which viewed any hint of negotiations between Hanoi and Washington as treason.

This was not a China which I knew or understood. Nor was I alone. The Great Proletarian Cultural Revolution had started in Shanghai in November 1965. It had ripped China end to end. Not even in Communist Vietnam so close to China and so intimately associated with China was it really understood. So I came to believe.

I did not understand it but still distant from Hanoi's boundaries, I was wondering if this might not be the most important development which I might uncover.

I had hardly slept for forty-eight hours but even in the comfort of the Le Royale I was fitful as a cat. I pulled out of my briefcase a copy of *Le Monde* which I had picked up in Paris. My eyes bulged. Here was a dispatch from *Le Monde*'s special correspondent, Jacques DeCornoy, just back from Hanoi, an excellent dispatch. He told of the damage inflicted on areas near Hanoi by American bombing: a textile center named Nam Dinh, south of Hanoi, which had been badly damaged; a railroad town nearby called Phuly had been destroyed—he had followed the railroad south from Hanoi, had seen segments ripped up by American bombs. Within a few hours they were back in operation. He had a lot of good detail. I hoped he had not taken the edge off what I would report.

The ICC plane was late the next day, Friday, December 23. As I waited, a Canadian sergeant talked of incidents in which ICC planes had been involved. The danger of attack was so great that they did not fly into Hanoi until darkness had fallen. We took off a bit after noon and got to Vientiane about 2:30, to wait until dusk so that, we hoped, we would not be shot down. The Poles invited everyone to their embassy for cold drinks or good French coffee and pastry. More talk of China. More talk of the danger of being shot down. Everyone, it was said, in Laos and Vietnam, carried a gun and shot at anything they saw in the sky.

I thought of giving U.S. Ambassador Bill Sullivan a ring. I had had a long talk with him when I was in Vientiane the previous June, but I didn't like to call him from the Polish embassy. By the time I got back to the airport, the Air America pilots were beginning to pull in from the day's run—whatever it had been. In those days there was no nonsense about Air America. It was a CIA "proprietary." The planes were coming in, and a long row of Mercedes had pulled up to meet the pilots and take them home to their wives or their mistresses, to their sleek white villas, and the moment to call Bill was lost. Well, I thought, he'll find out soon enough that I've passed this way.

He did, indeed. There was, as I discovered years later through FOIA documents, a convenient arrangement whereby Bill was advised (presumably by a clerk in Laotian passport control) of any one passing through Vientiane on the ICC plane. At 6:36 A.M. the morning of Saturday December 24, Bill dispatched a cable to Washington reporting I had transited Vientiane, apparently en route to Hanoi. The cable was received in Washington (because of the time differential) at 1:18 A.M. December 24 and sent on to the White House and the U.S. Information Agency.

This was Saturday, the eve of Christmas. LBJ had abandoned the Capital for his Texas ranch. There were only duty staffs at the Executive Mansion and the State Department. On no other day of the year was Washington more closed down. There is no evidence that the Sullivan telegram was relayed beyond receiving clerks, no indication that anyone picked up a telephone. The President slept soundly at his ranch and headed happily into his traditional round of Christmas festivities. In Washington the operational agencies closed at noon on Saturday (and they had hardly turned a wheel since noon on Friday).

All was quiet on the Potomac. By the time the Sullivan cable was tossed into "in" baskets on the bleary Monday morning after Christmas, I had been roaming North Vietnam for three days, having checked in at the fine old colonial hotel, the Metropole (now called the Thong Nhat [Reunification]) at midevening Friday night, December 23.

When I flew into London in early February 1943, the first walk I took was down Fleet Street to St. Paul's and to the city to see the bomb damage. When I went to Russia in 1944, the first thing I observed was the obliteration of Stalingrad—by bombs and artillery shells. When I went to Leningrad, I walked down Nevsky Prospekt to see the bomb damage (much damage but not very visible). Not much bomb damage in Moscow, but the rest of Russia was carpeted with rubble, every city—Kiev, Kharkov, Minsk, Sevastopol. When I got to Warsaw, I walked down the first morning to see what bombs had done to the ghetto. When I got to Berlin, I walked in the bomb-shattered Wilhelmstrasse and looked at the ruins. Bombs, I sometimes think, are as familiar to me as apple pie.

My first walk in Hanoi was down Pho Nguyen Thiep Street—to see the bomb damage. It wasn't much by my World War II standards. A few houses, a handful of people killed, I was told, at Nos. 44, 46, 48, and 50. Very unimpressive. All in all thirteen houses knocked down, thirty-nine families made homeless, five killed, eleven injured. It wouldn't have made a communiqué in Leningrad or Warsaw, nor in London during the Blitz.

Those cities had been bombed by the Nazi Luftwaffe in World War II. This was Hanoi, 1966, and the people had been killed and the houses destroyed, so the Vietnamese said, at about 3 P.M. on December 13 by American bombers.

I had been living, it seemed to me, for twenty years in a world in which somewhere bombs were dropping. From a military standpoint, the incident on Pho Nguyen Thiep Street was not worth recording. Except . . . except that these were, so it was said, *American* bombs— *American* bombs falling in an area which our Defense Department said we had not bombed (for a while the Pentagon spokesman insisted it must have been the North Vietnamese who hit themselves with a misfiring SAM antiaircraft missile); moreover, as President Johnson had insisted time and time and again, our bombing was so accurate that all we hit was steel and concrete.

I did not believe the houses on Pho Nguyen Thiep Street had self-destructed; I did not believe they had been knocked down by a North Vietnamese SAM; did not believe that we were so accurate we hit only steel and concrete. I was, I am afraid, too old a hand on bombing. I had been very close to the U.S. Eighth Air Force during World War II. I knew the commanding generals, and I knew their public claims for the Norden bombsight. Hitting a target, they swore, was "like shooting fish in a rain barrel." But I knew, too, that pilots sometimes hit the wrong city, occasionally even the wrong country. I sympathized. It was not an easy business to fly deep into enemy territory through clouds of shrapnel, hundreds of guns firing to bring you down. It took courage, determination, great skill, and luck—lots of luck. But I never knew a pilot who seriously pretended he could bomb targets in or near a city or populated area without hitting nonmilitary targets and killing civilians.

It was not possible. I don't know whether LBJ understood this or not. He may well have convinced himself that U.S. bombs hit only steel and concrete and North Vietnamese in full uniform. He was capable of such an extension of belief. I was not. I saw nothing to surprise me on Pho Nguyen Thiep Street. Nor on any of the other streets in Hanoi, nor in the bomb-leveled villages and towns I saw in North Vietnam. Bombing is bombing, and war is war. It is not a neat or pleasant business and there is no way that adjectives and patriotic words can paint it pretty. There is nothing heroic about a corpse that has lain a few days in the sun, no matter what uniform tries to contain it.

I wrote about the incident on Pho Nguyen Thiep Street in my first dispatch to the *Times*, which was printed in the paper of Christmas day. I didn't put any spin on it. I wrote a Christmas story, the great crowds at the Cathedral of St. Joseph, the strings of Christmas lights—blue and yellow and green and red—the masses of flowers and the little Vietnamese flags with their golden stars on a field of red. I wrote about the young Hanoi wives sitting sidesaddle on the bicycles their husbands pedaled, bringing them back from countryside evacuation for the holiday. I wrote of the mood of the city, which seemed to me to be sturdy and purposeful, of the concrete manhole air raid shelters that lined the streets, of the broad French boulevards of Hanoi and the Christmas parties in the Metropole Hotel. Only after nine descriptive paragraphs about Hanoi, a city at war, did I present a vignette of Pho Nguyen Thiep Street and a quiet view of other bomb damage which I inspected—a freight yard, a small and shabby truck park, and some damage to the Chinese embassy, the Romanian embassy and a few other embassies in the diplomatic quarter. (A Canadian had picked up a hot fragment which came through his window and sent it back to his friends in Saigon with a note: "Look here, chaps, this is going a bit far.")

It didn't add up to much by military standards, by the air war standards with which I and my fellow correspondents had measured the bombardments of the last two decades. It was thin gruel. The ugly truth is that war is thin gruel. It is repetitious. Again and again the same thing—death and destruction. Only the geography changes, the terrible process of man's self-degradation which Ernie Pyle once put into three words. Sitting on the edge of a bed, a mosquito-netting enfolding a colleague who was suffering from dysentery in the Aletti hotel in Algiers, Pyle, just back from America and facing another combat tour, said he could hardly bear it, could hardly bear going back to the GIs. I just can't take it any more, he said, I can't take them. I can't take war. I can't listen to them. Every other word is fuck or shit. The other day one of them said, over and over: "Fuck my shit. Fuck my shit." That's the bottom. The end.

So here I was on Pho Nguyen Thiep Street. It could have been Threadneedle Street, London. Or Unter den Linden in Berlin or Admiralty Square in Leningrad. After Ernie Pyle, what was there to say? I wrote my dispatch, went through agonies of bureaucratic negotiation to get it transmitted to Paris for relay to New York, got a photo I had taken on Pho Nguyen Thiep Street developed and printed and wirephotoed to AP for transmission to *The New York Times*.

277

(By an unpleasant mistake AP distributed it as a Vietnamese propaganda photo; it took several days to clear up the error.)

When my chores were done, I went to a party being given by the Vietnamese for the small band of foreigners who found themselves on Christmas eve in the Metropole Hotel.

I have in my file a description of that party written by a German Communist correspondent whose name and visage have long since vanished from memory. He writes of "a mysterious man in his midfifties, a mixture of English lord and German schoolmaster; posture very erect, carefully trimmed gray-blond mustache, serious and cool, inquiring eyes behind rimless glasses."

In the gathering, he notes, are a Hungarian writer named Molnar, a Cuban poet, Felix Rodriguez, an Italian Communist correspondent, Trumbadori, the Australian Wilfred Burchett, and some Vietnamese officials. The German is atingle at finding himself in this room with "the man of the management of one of the largest American newspapers." What, he asks himself, can I be thinking when one of the Vietnamese blurts out an attack on the "American pirates who bring death and destruction to our country." He watches in fascination as I listen "calm, serious, without moving a muscle." What are my thoughts? How will I react? The Vietnamese finishes. There is a moment of suspense, then I rise, the German recalls, and utter a single sentence: "I'd like to drink to true friendship between the Vietnamese and American people."

A Communist sympathizer in the ranks of *The New York Times*? the German asks. No, "only a journalist who was influenced by what he had seen."

Well, perhaps the German didn't get it all right. I don't think he could have understood Ernie Pyle's words; I don't think he could have understood how nauseated I was to witness again this banal newsreel which history had played over and over in my lifetime now being put into reruns by men who did not understand the meaning of its banality or did not care.

It was late that night before I went to sleep. I could not get Ernie Pyle's words out of my mind. I still can't.

# Chapter 24

# Noël

At 4:30 of Christmas morning, December 25, 1966, I came down to the lobby of the Metropole Hotel and looked around for the guide who was to escort me on a trip south to a city called Nam Dinh.

I was not in a Christmas mood. This was the hour when I had awakened as a child at 107 Royalston Avenue in Minneapolis, slipped out of bed in my cold room, and stolen a peek at the tree in the parlor. The smell of those spruce needles was still in my nostrils.

On this morning there was no one in the Metropole's tile-floored lobby. A little earlier four American peace ladies had left for I didn't know where, and now I sat alone staring at a green Chinese urn in which a tropical pine had been planted and decorated with twists of red and white cellophane, probably stripped off cigarette packs. The only light came from a milky neon tube that flickered on and off around the ceiling.

It was a low. I never find Christmas easy, and I was missing Charlotte and the boys and the whole of our big family. And I could not get yesterday out of my mind. Not the little girl with the broken arm whose mother had been killed when her house was hit by a bomb. Nor the slightly older girl whose body was covered with black, green, and purple bruises from, it was said, the impact of ball bearings from one of our lazy-dog bombs. Not even the young woman whose eyes were glazed and whose mind was hazy, survivor of a family of five, the others, including her baby, having been killed by a direct hit. No, it was not the living horrors, painful as they were. It was the Revolutionary Museum where I spent an hour being shown the artifacts of the wars which, it seemed, had constituted the tapestry of Vietnamese history for hundreds of years—wars with the Thais, the Cambodians, and the Chinese. The French and we were tacked onto the saga as a tailpiece.

The weapons which the Vietnamese had devised over the centuries were ingenious and deadly. They killed slowly, cruelly with much pain, and they were so simple that any child could make them, sitting

279

in the dust beside a thatched hut. A woman could construct an arsenal, hardly moving from the pot where the family's rice was cooking—long needlelike thorns tipped with poison and set upright in a wooden board to be concealed in a depression in the trail. The thorns penetrated the tough soles of barefoot Chinese or the leather boots of GIs, inflicting festering, crippling, often fatal wounds. There were invisible garrotes of silk or fiber, to be dangled from the limbs of trees to break the neck or sever the windpipe of a careless passerby on the trail. There were arrowheads, fashioned of fire-hardened wood, copper (going back to 310 B.C.) and flint, with sawtooth edges which ripped the flesh and muscles when the victim tried to pull them out (American Indians used the same technique), and elongated wire bird cages, decked with fishhooks—a leg plunging into this trap was hacked into morsels of meat when the victim sought to struggle free. Simple, deadly, dreadful. No electronics, no high tech, no military-industrial complex, no bottom line, no commissions. The Viets could not construct a lazy dog or a bullpup missile, but the thorns and nooses and cages were effective killers—at a cost-efficiency ratio McNamara would have admired.

I could not get these weapons out of my mind as I sat alone in the hotel lobby on this chilly morning. I had learned a lot about Vietnam in an hour's visit to the Revolutionary Museum. Why hadn't I known before of the hundreds of years of war between the Chinese and the Viets—wars always won (according to the museum) by Vietnam. But I saw from the map that the Viets had once occupied the Canton area—now they were hundreds of miles to the south.

I wondered what William Westmoreland knew of this history and McNamara and Rusk. I didn't have to ask myself about Lyndon Johnson. The only history he knew was the history of Texas. Perhaps he knew the history of Texas too well.

In 1969 James C. Thomson, Jr., one of LBJ's young China experts, chaired a seminar at the Council on Foreign Relations on how Vietnam decisions were made. The participants were a dozen bright junior aides to the top players of Kennedy-Johnson. Not one could recollect a time when such questions were brought into the decision-making process. The facts about Vietnam did not come up. Why? I asked, in astonishment. They looked at me with that condescension which the young display for an older person who really isn't with it. Why? Well, it wasn't considered necessary, they said. The U.S.

possessed such overwhelming military power there was no need to take local peculiarities into account. The power could be applied in any manner the United States desired in order to achieve its goals. Whatever capabilities Vietnam might possess, whether Vietnam was a warrior nation (as it was), whether it had historically displayed iron resistance to an enemy (as Vietnam had for hundreds of years) did not signify. That history had *always* pitted Vietnam against a superior opponent made no difference. All of these factors could be answered by American firepower (95 percent air power). French experience in Vietnam? Forget it. The French were never consulted, never considered. They were losers. Why talk to them after Dien Bien Phu? What was there for Americans to learn? Nothing but sour grapes.

I wondered whether it would have made a difference had the McNamaras, the Johnsons, the Rusks, the Westmorelands, and the Rostows visited the Revolutionary Museum in Hanoi—would the lessons have penetrated their cast-iron convictions? I doubt it. American power threw such a shadow over the consciousness of these men, they believed they could impose the American will anywhere, anytime, anyway. It was supreme. To doubt it was to doubt God. Or their own existence.

It was still dark when we started down Route National No. 1, straight south for a destination that was as murky in my mind as the weather. All I knew was that Nam Dinh lay sixty miles to the southeast of Hanoi, eighteen miles inland from the Gulf of Tonkin, and southwest of Haiphong. It was, I was told, the third largest city in the North, a textile town with a population of perhaps 93,000, much bombed.

I knew that the Vietnamese were early risers, and it seemed to me that traffic had been continuous, day and night, since I had arrived. Now I found the highway jammed, Christmas day or no Christmas day—food, arms, ammunition, all kinds of mysterious cargo secured under olive-drab tarpaulins and festooned with leafy branches as camouflage, an endless stream of sturdy Soviet-made two and a half ton trucks. As the day wore on, I saw wagons, horse-drawn carts, man-drawn carts, woman-drawn carts, donkey-drawn carts, and bicycles—my God, there were bicycles! Fitted with balancing poles and struts, they could carry equal loads of 300 pounds or more on either side. And, of course, men and women with great burdens on their backs.

As the sky lightened, I perceived that we were passing through a panorama of war—houses and buildings blasted and burned, craters along the road, endless destruction, the everyday visage of the twentieth century. Our jeep joined the slow procession of vehicles.

We passed through a half dozen bombed-out villages. A railroad paralleled the highway (which ultimately arrives in Saigon) for long distances. It had been heavily bombed but not very accurately. The same was true of the highway. "In the general vicinity" seemed to be good enough for the military. Little woodburning locomotives chugged along, hauling toy trains. They didn't add much to the huge tonnage on the move.

The day was dark and drizzling and stayed that way as we drew into Nam Dinh, a factory town—plain, no fuss, no fancy, no furbelows, a duplicate of a hundred industrial towns in northern France, no architectural flourishes, plain brick factories, plain brick flats, plain brick dormatories. Beside the factories lay the embankment and dikes holding back the River Dao, perhaps ten feet above the town's street level. The Dao was no more impressive than the town. It was used for small shipping and transhipping, boat-to-truck, truck-to-boat.

The mayor of Nam Dinh was a woman, a petite dynamic lady named Tran Tri Doan. She had worked in the textile factories, a good-sized cotton textile mill and a small silk mill. There was also, she said, a rice mill but no military objectives. She was very firm about that, rejecting the thesis later advanced by the Pentagon that Nam Dinh was full of targets—petroleum storage facilities, the railroad, transshipment depots, and, of course, antiaircraft sites.

Hesitating a bit, I finally asked her age. She snapped, "Forty." I would have guessed closer to twenty-five.

Madame Tran impressed me. She knew her town. She was a font of statistics—population, production, housing, industry, schools, hospitals, kindergartens, births and deaths. She had everything about Nam Dinh at her fingertips, and she was ready with her figures on U.S. bombing: dates and numbers of raids, damage and casualties. We walked through the town, visiting half a dozen areas. Each looked much like the other. As I jotted in my notebook: "We walked through the desert atmosphere of Nam Dinh." Most attacks on the town, the mayor said, had been made by aircraft of the Seventh Fleet, which lay offshore in the nearby Gulf. She reeled off designations of

U.S. planes and military ordinance like an operations chief. The aircraft and their armaments, I quickly discovered, represented a new generation to me, but the destruction looked like Coventry or Rotterdam. No change.

I could believe that the obliteration of Nam Dinh had not been the intention of the Americans (although it would have been hard to convince the mayor of that), but, like it or not, Nam Dinh had been destroyed.

Later on there was to be a great deal of argument about Nam Dinh, and our air people stressed that we had to destroy the antiaircraft weapons which had been sited in built-up areas. If they had been put out in the open, people would not have been killed. I thought there was a circularity about this argument, a little like asking which comes first, the chicken or the egg. You are being attacked. To defend yourself you bring in ack-ack guns. Then the attacker comes back twice as hard, because, he says, he has to destroy the antiaircraft batteries. In this argument I found a faint echo later on of the rueful remarks of the American lieutenant who said, in remorse, "In order to save the town we had to destroy it."

While I was standing outside Nam Dinh's city hall talking with the mayor, an air alert sounded. We went down into the bunker, and she continued her talk. She said it was the third alert of the day and that there had been one on Christmas Eve. I heard no ack-ack nor did I catch sight of a plane. Probably, I deduced, the alarm had been touched off by one of our reconnaissance drones, not a real plane.

I saw few people in Nam Dinh. The mayor said most of them had been evacuated as well as a good deal of the industry. Part of the textile mill had been moved. The rest was a shambles. Madame Tran insisted it was still in production, but I saw little sign of that. The silk mill was a skeleton but the rice mill was working, if slowly. That was it in Nam Dinh so far as I could see.

Late on Christmas afternoon, I got back to Hanoi and wrote up Nam Dinh, my second big story from Vietnam. I told about the mayor and the bomb damage in her city and reported the figures she had given me—fifty-one raids up to Friday before Christmas, none of which, she thought, had been reported in the West. She put the casualty toll at eighty-nine killed and 405 wounded, a small figure considering the number of raids and the devastation I had seen. I wrote of walking through the streets and of my conversation in the bunker with Mayor Tran. My presence in the city and my observation of the damage was, I thought, clear to the reader. I didn't underline this, however. The *Times* had a long-standing rule that the reporter was to keep himself out of the story. "We don't want to read about the adventures of the reporter," Turner Catledge had said many times. "Just report the news."

Sometimes, of course, as in the case of Hanoi, the news and the reporter's experiences were intertwined.

After I had done up Nam Dinh, I put a fresh sheet of paper in my typewriter and wrote a letter to Charlotte, a little formal because I knew many eyes would be reading it. I told her how strange Christmas had been and how I had spent the day "looking at our American handiwork" which struck me as "about as senseless an outrage as you could imagine." That was how I felt about Nam Dinh on Christmas night, 1966, and that is how I feel about it today, twenty years later. More so, perhaps, now that I understand so much better what Nam Dinh was all about.

No dispatch from Hanoi appeared in the *Times* on Monday December 26; probably the Nam Dinh story was delayed by the holiday. Then on Tuesday, December 27, there was a double header on page 1—Nam Dinh and a parallel dispatch about our bombing on Route National No. 1. Both conveyed a negative impression of the results of our air offensive—civilian damage in Nam Dinh and failure of bombing to halt movement of supplies down the highway and railroad. I suggested that the basic flaw in the bombing seemed to be "failure to take into account the nature of the country and the people to which it is being applied." Had we been bombing the Pennsylvania Railroad and the major New York–Washington, D.C., highway, it would have been different. That would have caused enormous disruption and the "military consequences in wartime would be grave."

This was a judgmental conclusion, and it probably went a bit beyond the customary *Times* dispatch. But it was a correct judgment and an assessment which, although vigorously challenged by Air Force men, was held, as I would find out much later, by far more informed observers than myself. It was a very important finding in terms of how we were conducting the war and the results we were achieving. It was the kind of observation which an alert administration should have found priceless.

Each evening when I got back to the Metropole Hotel, having toured the country and carried out my interviews, I pulled out my

little Sony shortwave and tried to get an idea of what was going on in
the world. From Christmas day onward, I heard plenty about Hanoi,
about my reports, about worldwide reaction but not very much from
Washington. I attributed that to the Christmas lull.

On Wednesday morning I got a cable from Clifton Daniel, a low-
key message cautioning me to be careful to give a source for any
"controversial" casualty figures and avoid expressions which "readers
might consider editorial" since the *Times* had frequently been accused
of shaping news coverage to fit its editorial policies. "Stuff looks
good," Clifton added.

The next day, Thursday, December 29, I received a message citing
Washington denials of a couple of points in my Nam Dinh dispatch—
my reports of bombed dikes and Mayor Tran's claim that Nam Dinh
was a favorite Seventh Fleet target. There was also a word of praise for
my "outstanding reporting." Next day, Arthur Hays Sulzberger, the
publisher who had hired me for the *Times* (now retired), cabled that he
had read all my Hanoi material and wanted to congratulate me. "I am
sure they are having a profound effect," he added. "You are a lucky
guy."

Lucky guy or not, my shorthand reading of this (coupled with some
barbs I had picked up on the shortwave) was that critics were circling
the wagon train; the *Times* was standing by me, but please be *very
careful*. My reading, I soon found, was 100 percent accurate. I (and, to
an extraordinary extent, the *Times*) was about to be subjected to a test
by fire.

There was no way in which a *New York Times* correspondent could go
to Hanoi in the midst of the controversial war without raising a storm.
That was obvious to Daniel and me before I left New York, although,
as I have suggested, we didn't understand how much turmoil my trip
would generate.

We were naïve in that, as I have said, but there were special
circumstances which contributed to the firestorm, some of them
accidental, some deeply concealed secrets which only a few in
government knew.

It was, for instance, an accident that I arrived in Hanoi in the
backwash of the U.S. bombings of December. As I discovered once I
got to Hanoi, the Vietnamese Foreign Office had been trying to reach
me for several weeks.

A Foreign Office man told me over lunch, "We are delighted

that you have come. We had thought you had lost interest in Vietnam."

"Whatever gave you that idea?" I asked.

"Well," he said, "we cabled you, and you did not reply."

I was shocked. I had replied instantly to the first cable I received, which was on December 15. Now it turned out that that wasn't the first telegram. The first had been sent in late November, but it had been dispatched to the business office of the international edition of the *Times*, then published in Paris. No trace of that message was ever found. Presumably a clerk, accustomed to handling advertisements and subscriptions, could make nothing of it and tossed it away. (This curious bit of information acquired momentary importance when, later on, some Washington officials contended that Hanoi had invited me in specifically to view the damage done in Hanoi by the U.S. raids of December and make propaganda.) In fact, the decision to let me come had been made well before the raids, and at a time, in fact, when there was good reason to believe that when I arrived, Hanoi and the U.S.A. would be sitting down in Warsaw for direct talks on ending the war. The coincidence of the bombing and my arrival in Hanoi and my reports on its results was bound to cause a dustup.

Another factor: When my stories began to come back from Hanoi, no one was minding the store in Washington. LBJ was on his ranch in Texas. He had had a row with his press secretary and protégé, Bill Moyers, over the war and other things. Moyers had not yet left the White House premises but was packing up, and his successor, George Christian, had become White House spokesman. Christian was an old hand with LBJ and the press but foreign policy was not his strong point. Within ten days, largely as a result of George's ineptness in responding to my Hanoi reports, LBJ was consulting Walt Rostow about getting Christian expert support (so I discovered via the FOIA process).

By coincidence, the Pentagon was in a similar situation. McNamara was in Europe for a NATO conference and his press chief, Arthur Sylvester, was with him. Sylvester, like Moyers, had resigned and was preparing to turn his duties over to his able deputy, Phil Goulding. Neither the White House nor the Pentagon press shops were in shape to handle a major crisis.

I did not know Goulding, but Sylvester was an old, old friend. We had sat side by side on the press bus for hundreds of miles in the Stevenson and Nixon Presidential campaigns, he for the Newark

*News,* I for *The New York Times,* usually occupying the first right-hand seat in the bus, for quick takeoffs to the side of the candidate and elbow room in which to unlimber our portables and write the story as we bowled along. Sylvester was a blue-eyed, red-cheeked middle-aged man, an old pro. We didn't stumble over each other's feet, and we didn't speak to each other when we were writing. Sylvester had a flair for arrogance, but we got on well. He had taken the Pentagon job, I believe, because the Newark *News* was getting shaky, and he didn't want to go down with the ship.

I don't think Art was a particularly good Pentagon press secretary. He made a speech in Chicago proclaiming the right of the government to lie to the press (and the people) in times of national emergency. I think he meant the danger of nuclear war, but his quotation inevitably lost its qualifications and was usually quoted as "the right of the government to lie." This hardly helped his credibility or that of the Johnson administration in the heat of Vietnam.

This disarray produced a hesitant, defensive, apologetic initial response quite atypical of LBJ. This was followed by massive overkill, feeding the fires of controversy as the administration tried to repair its self-inflicted damage. This was bound to make a difficult situation worse. I could sense from what I heard on BBC and VOA that LBJ was seething. I couldn't tell about McNamara. He was never mentioned. When I asked him about it nineteen years after the event, he could not remember my dispatches with clarity and expressed genuine amazement that anyone could have seriously questioned what seemed to him perfectly obvious.

McNamara's latter-day reaction was hardly that of the Pentagon at the time. Phil Goulding, some five years after the event in a book which he called *Play It in Low Key,* described my Hanoi trip as "a national disaster," a credibility disaster for the government, "the biggest public affairs mistake" of the Kennedy-Johnson period. He believed my Hanoi reports had undermined public trust in government declarations of policy on Vietnam and led to distrust of government in general.

"Additional lack of trust in the word of the Government was the dominant part of that reaction," Goulding concluded, but another part was deep disenchantment with the war itself. "The impact of the Salisbury stories was to present the United States Government before the world as a liar and deceiver. That in my view was tragic."

Goulding took upon himself much of the blame for this "disaster."

He had known or feared that LBJ's policy of contending that the U.S. hit only military targets, "steel and concrete," was bound to backfire; he knew that we hit a lot besides steel and concrete, that you could not bomb without killing civilians and destroying nonmilitary targets. This should have been said and said repeatedly so that the public would understand the reality of war. The mistake, he felt, was one of public relations—to permit the people to believe that this war was different, that we did not burn down peasant huts and city flats. Some might properly have blamed LBJ for wanting to have it both ways—to wage war and pretend that war was pretty. Goulding did not take this easy way out. He was the Pentagon's public relations specialist. It was up to him to persuade LBJ to adopt a public relations policy which would not blow up in his face. Whether it was morally wrong for the government to lie, Phil Goulding did not say. He looked at the question from the narrow perspective of nuts and bolts. What to do after the horse has been stolen from the barn? What to do? Goulding was pragmatic. He would fight fire with fire. If Salisbury's dispatches had undermined LBJ's credibility, he would undermine Salisbury's. Tit for tat. The option of saying yes, we were wrong, yes, we lied, yes, we misled the public never occurred to him. Nor did it occur to Lyndon Baines Johnson. The fact that it did occur to Robert McNamara was carefully concealed for many years. That part of the story appears only on these pages.

# Chapter 25

# The First Casualty

When I went to Hanoi, I was not a cub reporter. I was fifty-eight years old. I had had my lumps. I knew something about controversy. I had been involved in it since college days when I was thrown out of the University of Minnesota, because as a student editor, I challenged the power structure, the president and the board of regents. I had nearly lost my job with the United Press because of a piece on how the 1930s depression was affecting Minneapolis. The Minneapolis *Journal* took the position that the depression was somewhere else.

When I went to Moscow for United Press in 1944, I was almost thrown out by Stalin in my first weeks—because I didn't present a proper apology for a story our London bureau filed about Stalin and his generals. When I went back to Moscow for *The New York Times*, my life turned into a gauntlet of tomahawk wielders in the U.S.A., who said I was a Bolshevik (the Russians, of course, took the position that I was an American spy). And then there was Birmingham.

No, I should have been hardened to the row over Hanoi. But I wasn't. I knew that Senator Hiram Johnson of California had said during the World War I debate: "The first casualty when war comes is truth." And I knew that Winston Churchill, reversing the metaphor, had declared that in war "truth must be protected by a bodyguard of lies."

I knew that Hitler had succeeded by the Big Lie and that Lao-tzu, the famous Chinese philosopher of war, had preached that deception was the cornerstone of military success. I was well aware that disinformation was not invented by the CIA.

I had seen the lie used so often by governments and politicians I should have felt no sense of shock when it was turned against me during the Hanoi episode. Still I confess that Washington's performance amazed me and still does, although not so much now that I understand better what I walked in on.

Phil Goulding has given a vivid picture of the Pentagon's panic as it hunted for a way to discredit my Hanoi dispatches. He deployed

289

twenty or thirty experts, who went over my materials word-by-word and line-by-line, looking for something—anything—that could be used against me. It was, Goulding admits, hard going. His men checked out my reports on the Hanoi bombings. Not much ammunition there. They checked Nam Dinh—same thing. My dispatch on the paltry results of bombing Route National No. 1? Peashooter stuff.

Finally they hit pay dirt. Not in my reports but with a document which had been sent back in November 1966 by the U.S. military attaché in Moscow. It was a Hanoi propaganda release headed: Report of U.S. War Crimes Against Nam Dinh City." Someone noticed that the figures in the pamphlet were identical with those I got from Mayor Tran Tri Doan. Eureka! Reporters were hastily called in, including, I am sorry to say, two men from the Washington *Post* whom I knew and respected. They were handed copies of the pamphlet. Here it is, they were told, here is where Salisbury got it all, a Commie propaganda sheet. The figures in his story and the pamphlet are identical. He's not a reporter, he's just a conduit for red propaganda the way he was in Moscow. (It was many years before my FOIA inquiries turned up the fact that White House press advisers were pushing this line and that the FBI had started a vacuum cleaner operation to see what dirt it could find on me.)

The gambit worked. Within twenty-four hours the Washington *Post*, the Washington *Star*, and some other papers were saying that Salisbury's stories were Communist propaganda. Clifton Daniel mildly commented, What kind of figures would Salisbury find in Hanoi but Communist figures? Never mind. The Pentagon had hit a live nerve, the old McCarthyite one. To this day in some dark corners, the legend persists that I never went to Nam Dinh, I never saw the bombing, I never collected information on my own—just copied it out of the old Moscow leaflet.

Soon Art Sylvester was making speeches about Harrison Appallsbury of *The New Hanoi Times*. And *The New Yorker* responded with a cartoon of an Army mess sergeant shouting to his cook: "It's direct from the Pentagon—scratch Salisbury steak until further notice."

Of course, none of this got the Pentagon off the spot, but it did not play badly in Peoria, and it gave supporters of the war something to shout about. It turned some eyes away from the sorry images I presented, even though no one could read my stories and be in doubt that I was there on the spot. I had not larded my paragraphs with attributions—"Tran Tri Doan said," "a North Vietnamese official said," the tag we learn in journalism kindergarten. Some critics called this "careless journalism." Others called it "treason." Tempers, it must be remembered, were pretty hair-trigger in those times.

For sixteen years the matter rested, forgotten by everyone but a few Vietnam controversialists and myself. There it would still rest had it not been for the vigilance of Charles Mohr of *The New York Times*, an old Vietnam hand. Poring through thousands of pages of CIA documents declassified for use in the libel action brought by General Westmoreland against CBS, Mohr found a CIA report on Nam Dinh, a special study made coincident with (possibly triggered by) my trip to Hanoi. The study was finally completed on May 23, 1967. It was classified Top Secret and "No foreign dissemination." Had it not been for the CBS–Westmoreland case, it would still be gathering dust in the CIA files.

I could hardly believe my eyes when I read this document. Not only did it support my observations but the CIA's principal evidence was "Report on the U.S. War Crimes in Nam Dinh City," the very one the Pentagon had labeled "Commie propaganda." In the words of the CIA, Nam Dinh had been picked for their study because the statistics in the pamphlet, the casualty figures, the civilian damage, the air strikes "seem to be accurate when measured against detailed studies made on the basis of poststrike photography." "Casualties claimed by the North Vitnamese were also consistent with independent casualty estimates made by this agency, using Nam Dinh as a pilot study."

I had, in a word, been dead on target with Nam Dinh. And, as the agency made clear, the Nam Dinh situation had been known before I went there. The Pentagon declarations about the "accuracy" of its bombing of Nam Dinh, its claim that it was nothing more than "propaganda" that civilians had been killed, the astonishment of naval pilots that their bombs could have missed "military targets," the reconnaissance photos which the Pentagon showed to me in New York after my return to demonstrate that Nam Dinh could not have been bombed as I reported—the whole package put together to undercut my reports was eyewash. And some in the government (but not necessarily Goulding) knew it was from the start.

No wonder McNamara was amazed when I reminded him that

there had been an attack on my credibility. These CIA reports were the very ones he had ordered up July 4, 1966, when he began to feel uncomfortable with the assessments by his own National Defense Intelligence Agency and their use to support "the Rostow line" for more and more bombing.

The CIA had used Nam Dinh as a pilot study, factoring in the aerial photos made by our pilots and our drones, the Hanoi "Report on War Crimes," and information from a Polish member of the International Control Commission. All fitted together, all mortised with my conclusions.

Among the CIA findings was a calculation as of January 1967 that our bombings in the North in 1965–66 caused 36,000 casualties of which 29,000 were civilians. Later the CIA refined this to total 31,300 civilians and 16,900 military in 1965–66 and the first quarter of 1967.

The CIA seemed to be reporting a different war from that of Goulding and the Pentagon. Goulding claimed, "We had taken the greatest possible precautions to avoid civilian casualties . . . never before in wartime had pilots operated under such tight bombing restrictions." The fact was we were killing twice as many civilians as soldiers.

"We did not then," he insisted, "and when I left the government still did not have a reasonable reading on the accuracy of the North Vietnam figures [on civilian casualties]. But one could certainly assume that the enemy was not understating his casualties in a propaganda sheet [the Nam Dinh war crimes pamphlet]."

Did the Pentagon have access to the CIA report? In the hall of mirrors which the U.S. Government had become, it is possible that Goulding knew no more of the CIA's study than I did. But he had access to the reconnaissance photography which the CIA used and which confirmed my reports.

The CIA had a totally different approach to Nam Dinh from that of the Pentagon. It said the textile plant had been "unintentionally" bombed in a U.S. air strike in July 1965 and that its operations had been dispersed to sites fifty to 100 miles away.

The CIA found that, in general, the "success of the U.S. bombing program was limited." Bombing had had no decisive effect on the North Vietnamese economy. It had not influenced the regime's attitude toward the war nor propelled it toward the bargaining table. "In fact, Vietnamese operations were now exceeding the results they had achieved before the Rolling Thunder [The U.S. bombing] program." And, said the CIA, the "outlook for success in meeting current U.S. bombing program objectives is not bright.

"The twenty-seven months of U.S. bombing of North Vietnam have had remarkably little effect on Hanoi's overall strategy . . . or on its confident view of long-term Communist prospects and on its political tactics regarding negotiation."

Indeed, said the agency (in terms very similar to mine), the bombing had not shaken the Vietnam conviction that "they will withstand the bombing and outlast the United States and South Vietnam. Nor has it caused them to waver in their belief that this test of will and endurance will be determined primarily by the course of the conflict on the ground in the South not by the air war in the North."

The CIA concluded that

- The air strikes had had no effect on Hanoi's ability and intention of maintaining "at least a rough military stalemate" in the South.
- There was no evidence that the bombing had impaired the morale of the Hanoi regime or the population.
- Despite the bombing Hanoi had improved its supply position because of an increase in deliveries by Russia and China and better organization.
- Strikes on oil storage tanks had not bothered Hanoi significantly; they simply received their oil and petrol in metal barrels, which they strewed along the roads and in the fields where U.S. planes couldn't find them.

When I read the calm, cool, calculated CIA analysis and matched it against my field reports, the match was about 95 percent. I didn't give Hanoi so much credit for building up its battle capacity under the rain of U.S. bombs as did the CIA.

The secret U.S. assessment of the war fitted mine like a glove fits a hand. But it bore little relationship to the fandango staged by Arthur Sylvester and Phil Goulding.

What was going on here?

Behind the scenes, as I now know, hidden from me, hidden from the American public, hidden from Congress, hidden from almost everyone in the Pentagon, the State Department, and the White House, a huge gap had opened up over the Vietnam war.

293

As I pieced it together years later from the revelations of the Pentagon Papers and documents from the State Department and White House, released under the Freedom of Information Act, two violently opposed views had emerged.

On October 14, 1966 (as the Pentagon Papers would reveal), McNamara had submitted a secret memorandum to LBJ etched in dark pessimism. Things were going badly in the South. The "pacification" program was running backward. Rolling Thunder bombing had neither significantly affected the infiltration of North Viet units to the South nor cracked the morale of Hanoi. "The enemy almost completely controls the night." McNamara proposed a bombing standstill and consideration of a total halt on bombing the North. Instead, he suggested bombing the neck of Vietnam on the chance that this would interdict supply and troop movements. Then, he said, we must give some credibility to our peace moves. In plain words he wanted to end the war.

McNamara no longer believed in the air war; he no longer believed Hanoi could be bombed to the peace table.

The Joint Chiefs exploded. They opposed every point made by McNamara. They wanted more troops, more bombing, more everything. Total victory.

A month later, November 17, almost on the eve of my departure for Hanoi, McNamara returned to the fray. He sent LBJ a memo that challenged the kill ratio the Army was reporting, suggesting the figures were vastly overstated, that four out of every five Vietnamese soldiers whom the Army said it was killing were not soldiers but noncombatants—porters, laborers, bystanders and the like.

He argued that "I believe our bombing is yielding very small marginal returns, not worth the cost in pilot lives and aircraft." He estimated that the program was costing $250 million a month, and he saw no evidence that it was really hampering North Vietnam and the Viet Cong. McNamara, always quick with figures, estimated the total economic and military damage inflicted by bombing on North Vietnam to that point in the war at $233 million, considerably less than the cost to the U.S. *per month*.

McNamara did not convince Mr. Johnson. Walt Rostow and Robert Komer, the President's aides, opposed McNamara. So, of course, did the Joint Chiefs. LBJ did not cut back. Instead he increased the massive B-52 sorties from sixty to 800 a month as of February 1967.

It was into this stormy atmosphere that I charged with my Hanoi dispatches, laying them down, I'm afraid, with the deceptively easy roll of the lazy-dog bomb, so harmless in appearance, like a great basketball, then suddenly erupting into a hundred exploding baseballs, each packed with steel barbs and ball bearings, plastering the landscape in a crazy quilt of death.

No wonder Goulding and the Pentagon went into shock. Chance had timed the Salisbury missive for maximum impact.

But not I nor anyone outside the charmed circle had any notion that our high leaders and their generals were locked in so epic a conflict, one which would determine whether the Vietnam war would be pressed forward full throttle or be gentled down to give diplomacy a chance.

To this day McNamara's actual role, as an opponent of air war and escalation and as a supporter of negotiated peace, has not been accurately evaluated because of classification of key documents. David Halberstam in *The Best and The Brightest* correctly faulted McNamara for his role in the buildup and support of the Vietnam war but, writing before the publication of The Pentagon Papers and without access to the FOIA documents that I obtained, he missed the early start and strength of McNamara's turn against the war. McNamara's role is a subject well worth a close study in itself.

As I sat in my cold bedroom at the Metropole Hotel in Hanoi (I had left my trench coat on the ICC plane, and it kept shuttling back and forth between Saigon and Hanoi), nothing would have been less believable to me than the scenario I have finally managed to put together. Not a hint of a crack in the imposing facade of the U.S. establishment was visible. I knew that my reports had stung LBJ, but I saw no sign that, as the Pentagon Papers were to reveal, they had generated "an explosive debate about the bombing."

I did not know nor did the country that on November 17, 1966, Robert McNamara had told LBJ: "The increased [bomb] damage to targets is not producing noticeable results. No serious shortage of POL [petroleum products] in North Vietnam is evident, and stocks on hand with recent imports have been adequate to sustain necessary operations.

"No serious transport problem in the movement of supplies to or within North Vietnam is evident; most transportation routes appear to be open, and there has recently been a major logistical buildup in the area of the DMZ.

"The raids have disrupted the civil populace and caused isolated food shortages but have not significantly weakened popular morale . . . .

"The increasing amounts of physical damage sustained by the North Vietnamese are in large measure compensated in aid received from other Communist countries."

Nothing in my reports equaled in blunt skepticism McNamara's quiet words about the failure of the air war and the military stalemate on the ground. But McNamara's words were secret. They were rebutted by the Joint Chiefs and argued down by men like Walt Rostow and Dean Rusk. My words were public. The Pentagon did its best, but it simply could not destroy the inherent credibility and consistency of my reports. They fit together. A detail might be wrong, an emphasis distorted, but they far understated the administration's own secret, chilling, negative assessment. For all the rhetoric which the Pentagon unleashed, it was not possible for Mr. Johnson's propaganda to damage the impact of my stories.

LBJ was far too astute a politician not to understand that he was deeply vulnerable on the question of bombing, especially on the civilian casualties. Hardly had the President returned from Texas, than he launched an effort to shore up his position.

But he had a continuing problem with McNamara. McNamara was deeply upset (as the FOIA information reveals) over the bombing issue.

Alone among the men around LBJ, McNamara wanted the public to know the truth about U.S. bombing. He proposed that the administration make public the information which it already possessed (the fact that two years of bombing had caused 36,000 Vietnamese casualties of which about 29,000 were civilians).

McNamara wanted the whole record on U.S. bombing—results, costs, casualties—the works—made public, together with reconnaissance photographs which would disclose that most of the civilian damage was done in proximity to military targets. He submitted a draft of his proposed statement.

This wasn't palatable to LBJ. It was anathema to Rostow and to Komer, strong backers of bombing.

Rostow with the support of Clark Clifford shot down another McNamara proposal, that the President set up an ad hoc committee or group of "wise men" to examine the effects of the bombing and evaluate the whole U.S. bombing policy.

Clifford, as quoted by Rostow, said this would make LBJ look weak and uncertain. Clifford could see no political gain from the idea. Rostow convinced the President that if any bombing data was made public "no matter how the thing is packaged, *The New York Times* would tend to play it for the high figure." As for photographs "The *Times* would use it for its own purposes." Also, he was very much afraid the photographs would "show a lot of misses."

If for some unlikely reason LBJ decided to make casualty figures public, Rostow pointed out that two thirds of the civilians killed and wounded were, as he put it, "males engaged in war-related activity."

Rostow had a point about "a lot of misses." State Department cables sent to guide embassies in handling bombing inquiries conceded that there had been a great many misses.

A secret, no-foreign-dissemination report by Thomas L. Hughes, State Department's intelligence chief, to Secretary Dean Rusk December 30, 1966, reported that in the December 13 attack on the Yen Vien railroad yards in Hanoi, reconnaissance photos showed only three craters within the freight yards and forty outside the target area. In the December 14 raid American planes had jettisoned twenty-three 750-pound bombs when MIG fighters appeared. Hughes said that it "seems quite possible" that these bombs caused damage to the houses at the end of Doumier Bridge—that is, the houses which I had found destroyed on Pho Nguyen Thiep Street, the ones which the Pentagon claimed had been destroyed by Hanoi's own SAM missiles.

The Hughes report that I obtained through FOIA was never published. It was not contained in the Pentagon Papers. It never saw the light of day. There *were* two wars: the one which the White House, the State Department, the Pentagon, carried on in public, and the second, quite different, conducted in secrecy and deceit.

At the end of World War II, the United States commissioned its famous Strategic Bombing Survey to evaluate the effect of American bombing on the war and the collapse of Germany. It pulled no punches. It demonstrated that until the last Germany managed to maintain its war effort, actually increasing production of key war materials, carrying on its remarkable transportation network, despite the rain of U.S. (and RAF) bombings, the firestorms which destroyed Dresden, Hamburg, and much of Berlin. The report was a landmark in military intelligence. It was designed to enable future generations to evaluate air power in the harsh light of reality and not in the capricious glow of publicity and propaganda.

McNamara left a similar testament to the American people in the Pentagon Papers, which he intended to guide us in future military-foreign policy, revealing our successes and our errors, giving us a realistic appraisal of what went wrong and what went right in Vietnam, the actual results of air power, the failures of our diplomacy, our errors of omission and commission.

It is all there—well, not quite all, as this account drawing on documents from the State Department and White House (not included in the Pentagon Papers) discloses.

I have conducted this examination of what was going on inside the administration—what was really known as contrasted with what was given to the public, the discrepancy between what the highest echelons of the Pentagon and White House knew and what they said publicly—using my newspaperman's observations on the scene in Vietnam as a kind of baseline to mark the deviations between public and private, between official and nonofficial reporting.

The contrast between my reports of bombing in Hanoi, Nam Dinh, and elsewhere in North Vietnam and the public declarations of the Pentagon and the White House is great. When the lid is lifted upon what was really known, what was really going on in the war, the discrepancy vanishes—or almost so. My reports were more optimistic about the American cause than were the private evaluation of our intelligence agencies and of McNamara, who was, as a civilian, President Johnson's deputy for the conduct of the war. I do not have access to the intimate realities as seen by the Joint Chiefs. We know their public positions in support of war and ever more war. But if their personal diaries should be made public—indeed, if they kept personal diaries—I should be surprised if their evaluations of Vietnam differed so much from those of Robert McNamara—no matter how they opposed him in public.

I received over 300 letters about my Hanoi coverage, three to one favorable. The *Times* received 1000 more in about the same ratio of pro and con. Normally there is a high preponderance of negative mail. Those who have a complaint are quicker to write than those who have a compliment.

When the Pulitzer Committee met in April 1967, the jury picked my Hanoi stories for the award in international reporting. This decision was overturned by a 6–5 vote of the judges (in which Turner Catledge, the *Times* representative did not participate). One judge, Ralph Pulitzer, Jr., raised the question in the board of trustees of Columbia the next day. The trustees voted 6 to 5 to support the verdict of the judges. Arthur (Punch) Sulzberger of the *Times*, a trustee, did not participate in the vote.

I was asked to comment. I said that I held the judgment of my colleagues at the *Times* above that of anyone else, and I had won that.

Brooks Atkinson wrote to say the Pulitzers "are awarded by timid men indifferently informed about what they are doing." I think Brooks was wrong. The judges knew what they were doing. They were voting their support of LBJ and the Vietnam war.

On the plane flying out of Hanoi I jotted down a few impressions. I felt, I said, a certain nostalgia about leaving. "It brings an end to a period in which I have had a special sense of history, of actually moving and influencing events. The only other time I have had this sense was at the time of Stalin's death in 1953. I think the sense has more basis now."

What to make of the Vietnamese? I asked myself.

"They have heart," as Smokey [one of the Shook-ups in Red Hook] would say. Great heart. They fight with nothing. They have spunk and the devil, and they will go down to defeat rather than budge if you try to shove them.

"They are suffering. No doubt but they can take a lot of that. Can we negotiate? Yes, but only with care and prudence. I don't know if we possess that. . . . "

I exaggerated the effect of my dispatches. They played a role, but a small one, in bringing the country to a more realistic view of the war. It would be a long time before the war would end.

I was wrong about many things. A Vietnamese official told me the war would ruin the United States as it had France—exhausting gold reserves, setting off inflation, dividing the people, poisoning politics. I laughed. He didn't understand. We were so big, so rich. We could fight Vietnam and still have LBJ's Great Society.

I was wrong in the beginning to believe—and the belief was strengthened by the Pentagon Papers publication, the CIA exposés, the strong antiwar movement, Watergate and Nixon's resignation— that a new force had emerged in American life, a combination of investigative reporting and populist action which could turn the country around.

Twenty years after Hanoi I am not so sure. The words of the country's great investigative reporter, Sy Hersh, who exposed My Lai, haunt me. No one has done more to uncover the lies of war and peace, to bring reality to the public, to shoulder the responsibilities which the First Amendment to the Constitution places on the press, to live the journalistic creed of Adolph S. Ochs, founder of the modern *New York Times*, to "give the news without fear or favor."

Could, Hersh was asked at a Vietnam symposium in 1984, it happen again? Could we be led down the fateful path to disaster despite what had seemed to some, including me, the new courage and frankness of the press?

Yes, said Hersh. It could happen again and probably would. How? The government would lie, just as it had so often. It would just lie.

I'm afraid that the poet, Robert Bly, my fellow Minnesotan, got it right when he wrote:

The Chief Executive Enters, the Press Conference begins: The President lies ... the ministers lie, the professors lie, the television lies, the priests lie ... the attorney general lies ....

# Chapter 26

# An Inscrutable Mark

The first talk I had with Richard Milhous Nixon was on the cutting floor of the Degtyarsk copper mine in the Urals, 800 feet below the surface of the earth. The date was July 30, 1959, a hot day. The temperature on the surface was a humid 80 degrees; at the cutting face we were damp and chilly in our miners' clothes. I had watched Mr. Nixon take off his dark-blue summer-worsted business suit, his white Ban-Lon shirt and his black oxfords and don two-piece cotton longies with drawstrings at the ankles, heavy wool shirt, wool miner's breeches, knee-length rubber boots, mustard-colored jacket and miner's helmet with lamp and neckcloth. I was dressed the same. So were the thirty or forty officials, Secret Service and Soviet security men.

We plunged down in the elevator cage to the 800-foot level and sloshed a half-mile to the face. "This may be the shortest way to California," Nixon said gloomily. It didn't sound like a joke.

At the pit face two miners shut off their screaming air drills and asked Nixon questions about nuclear arms. They had been put up to it, but the Vice President didn't mind. He cheered up, had a good chat, and started briskly on the long walk back.

"These men are fine fellows," he exclaimed. He meant it. "Boy, I'm telling you this is hard work. These miners earn their pay." He went on in a thoughtful tone (I was the pool reporter for the mine trip.) He had met Nikita Khrushchev in Moscow a few days earlier. Khrushchev had been a miner in the Donbas. He had grown up working in British and French-owned mines, had been treated badly, with twelve-hour workdays. That had an effect on a man's character, Nixon said. It made him tough and determined—but not necessarily a Communist. A man had to be tough to survive, and you must keep this in mind when you were dealing with someone like Khrushchev. We got into the electric lift and were whizzed back up. Nixon blinked in the sunlight, glanced about, and said: "We look like men from Mars." Then he headed for the changing room.

I had never seen Nixon before I met him in Moscow in July 1959. I had been abroad during his trademark moments—the Checkers speech, the Alger Hiss affair, Helen Gahagan Douglas. I didn't expect to like Nixon, but he was not the banal red-baiter I had expected.

It would be seven years before I understood what lay behind Nixon's ruminations about Khrushchev's toughness and hard work as a miner. The morning after he got to Moscow, Nixon went to the Kremlin for a courtesy call on Khrushchev. Two or three other reporters and I waited outside on the marble stoop of the Great Kremlin Palace for nearly an hour before he emerged. If I had known him, perhaps I could have guessed from his clenched lips, dark and stormy face, that something unusual (and newsworthy) had happened.

It was December 1966 before I heard the story. No Russian in 1959 was prepared to think anything good of Nixon, and Khrushchev was not an exception. He opened up by telling Nixon that he knew all about him—he was the enemy of the Soviet Union, the enemy of Communism, the white knight of Capitalism.

Nixon conceded that he didn't like Communism but as for Capitalism, well, he had grown up a poor boy, working in a small orchard, doing all the chores. Khrushchev snorted. He, Khrushchev, had grown up the poorest of the poor. He had walked barefoot. He had had no shoes. He had shoveled shit to earn a few kopeks. Nixon shot back that he'd been poor and barefoot, too—and had shoveled shit.

What kind of shit? Khrushchev demanded. Horseshit, Nixon said. That's nothing Khrushchev replied. He had shoveled cow shit— loose, runny, stinking cow dung. It got between your toes. I too shoveled cow shit, Nixon said tightly.

Well, Khrushchev grumbled, maybe Nixon had shoveled cow shit once or twice, but he, Khrushchev, had shoveled human shit. That was the worst. Nixon couldn't top that. He came out of the Kremlin in an angry trance. If this was the way Khrushchev started, how would he finish the visit?

That afternoon Nixon escorted Khrushchev through the opening of the first American exhibition in Moscow and engaged him in the famous Kitchen Debate. Later this was portrayed as an angry, chest-thumping confrontation. Actually it was a remarkably able presentation by each man of his viewpoint. I was probably the only American reporter who heard it all. I spoke and understood Russian (so I got everything Khrushchev said), and Bill Safire, who was the

PR man for the kitchen display, lifted a velvet rope so I could slip into the kitchen and sit on the floor at the feet of the great men while they argued their cases for Capitalism and Communism.

I was surprised at how well Nixon handled himself and more surprised years later to hear that he went home with American Ambassador Llewelyn Thompson, whose guest he was at Spaso House, and got sloshed because he thought he had been a bust. Actually, he almost beat John F. Kennedy in 1960 with the face-to-face picture showing him punching a forefinger in Khrushchev's face to drive home a point. It became the icon of the Nixon age.

Soon I got to know Nixon quite well. Political figures have always fascinated me. No one is compelled to lead his life so publicly. Who else but Nixon would get down to his skivvies with a bunch of reporters hanging around, taking in every detail? Or like Lyndon Johnson waving his visitors into the bathroom with him as he squatted on the john? Or, like Huey Long, carrying on an interview as he toweled his rosy pot belly, stepping out of a shower? There's not much the observant reporter doesn't note about the pol he is covering. We are such magpies, our eyes darting to the frayed collar, the missing button, the hole in the shoe, a guilty look, flushes of anger, Freudian slips. If you cover a Presidential candidate day and night, you know him as an English valet knew his master, maybe better. You know his turn of speech, his inflections.

By a perverse fortune I came to know Nixon as I knew no other president, not all at once, but bit by bit and year by year, out of office, in office, the glory, the disgrace. On this Russian trip I gave him high marks. Khrushchev was not a patsy, and Nixon held his own, toe to toe. Nixon was a hit with the Russians. I came to think, as time went by, that Khrushchev could have been a successful politician in Iowa (after his visit there). Nixon could have won plenty of votes in Russia (if they had free elections). He is so nice, he is so handsome, he is so young, he is so American, he has such a marvelous smile. Nixon didn't get these raves in the U.S.A., but I heard all these remarks in the crowds that turned out for him from Moscow to Sverdlovsk. Those crowds bothered Khrushchev's cronies, especially the police. They sent goons out to heckle Nixon with unpleasant questions. At first Nixon was embarrassed, but he quickly sensed that the people were with him. They tried to shush the interrogators. "Why are you so rude?" "Shut up, he is our guest." "Give him a chance." So Nixon began to respond: "I'm glad you asked that question." And was off to the races. The police pulled the goons off after a couple of days. Nixon was scoring all the points.

When I traveled with Nixon on his 1960 campaign, I found he was a lot better in Russia than in the U.S.A. At home the crowds tensed him up. I watched him ball his fists, set his jaw, and hurl himself stiff-legged to the barriers at the airports and begin shaking hands. He was wound up like a watch spring, steeling himself for the ordeal. No ease. But in Russia he was self-confident, cool, enjoying himself and his audience.

Very curious. But there were a lot of curious things about Nixon. As time went by, I became convinced that he was the most interesting President of my time—puzzling, enigmatic, conflictive. I could spend a lifetime and not understand him.

In the spring of 1960, I bumped into a man at a dinner party, a Wall Street man, who told me that he had served with Nixon in New Caledonia in the South Pacific, where, as I knew, Nixon was attached to a naval base. "Nick ran a twenty-four hour poker game there," the man said. He was the only one I ever met who called Nixon "Nick." Nixon, he said, was a hell of a good poker player, but made his money running the all-night game, taking a cut out of every pot. A very smart fellow, the Wall Streeter said.

"Say," he said, suddenly, "is Nick still seeing that shrink of his in New York?" I hadn't a clue. Had never heard of a shrink. Much later, after Nixon entered the White House, I learned that for many years he had been seeing Dr. Arnold A. Hutsnecker, an internist by specialty but a doctor who numbered a good many high-tension men among his patients, men who possessed emotional and psychological problems.

At the moment of our talks, said the Wall Street man, "Nick has gone into his shell," and people were trying to get him out of it. Nixon, I gathered, had severe ups and downs, and it was not easy to pull him up when he fell into depression.

During his fall campaign against Kennedy, Nixon suddenly left the trail, came into New York, holed up in the Waldorf, and we didn't see him for a week. Perhaps, I thought, he had "gone into his shell."

I learned a great deal about Nixon when I found myself in 1983 holding the Richard M. Nixon chair at his alma mater, Whittier College, a small Quaker institution landlocked in East Los Angeles—

an island of the 1900s where Nixon got his degree, where he met Pat, his wife, and where he began to display those traits which were to mark his adult career. Whittier doesn't change much—the same buildings, the same stores, the same sunbaked bungalows under the palms, survivors who knew Nixon in his campus years. There were still cousins and aunts around, and I talked with them. Some remembered and cherished the poor Quaker Nixon boy, with a determined mother, a ne'er-do-well father, and a brother who died of TB, money scarce as hen's teeth. Nixon worked hard. He was ambitious, and his mother was ambitious for him. He didn't like his father, probably he hated him. He adored his mother (he broke into tears when he mentioned her in his farewell speech to the White House staff as he left to go back to San Clemente).

Whittier had a small collection of Nixon memorabilia, which had been shipped out when the Nixons left the White House. It was kept in a locked room in the fourth floor of the library. You had to have permission and be admitted with a special key to see it. I saw it. Not much there—leftover gifts made to the Nixons by Arab sheikhs and African presidents. Hard to see why it had been sent. Not so hard to understand why it was locked up. Not everyone in Whittier was proud of Nixon, and the administration thought it better not to have the things on public display.

It seemed to me then (and now) that Whittier was the place for the Nixon Library (just as I thought Johnson's should be at San Marcos). Whittier had a real place in Nixon's life, both the college and the town. He had lived there and started his law practice there. It was small and reflected the aura of his early years, so poor, so ambitious, so envious of those more fortunate. On the campaign trail, I heard him tell, over and over, the story of his brother who had died of TB. His brother had always wanted a pony and died with his wish unfulfilled. Some richer kids were lucky. They had ponies. It was clear he was thinking of Jack Kennedy. It was also clear that Richard Nixon had coveted a pony and still felt cheated. I could understand the pony bit. I don't know how many contests I entered as a kid, hoping to win a pony. I never did.

I tried to persuade Whittier (and Nixon) that his library should go there. I found reluctance on both sides. To put a Presidential library in the tiny college would change it beyond recognition, and Nixon, a bit like Johnson, didn't think Whittier was grand enough. Yes, there was a good place for the library up on the hill—but what about parking? And could the money be raised for Whittier? Nixon seemed to doubt it. He mentioned the University of Southern California and Stanford. Both wanted it. I was sure he favored a bigger institution or his own site, his own place (San Clemente). I argued that Whittier had emotional and personal associations, a setting that would allow the visitor to understand what Nixon was about and where he came from. That didn't move him, and later I wondered whether the real objection to Whittier was that it told too much about Nixon, just as, perhaps, San Marcos told too much about Johnson.

Nixon had forgotten that FDR's library was at Hyde Park—a perfect place, he said. Where was Jack Kennedy's? Ah, Boston, well, that was right for Jack. I believe he still didn't think he could match the Kennedys, just as I believe he had felt he couldn't beat Jack in 1960. I remember talking with him after the first debates. He told how they had roiled his being, both before and after, so disturbing. "Of course, it's not that way for Jack," he said. A moment later he caught the implication of what he had said and lamely tried to cover it. He couldn't. Jack had put the whammy on him, and I think that made the difference in their close election, in which a switch of 20,000 or 30,000 votes would have changed the outcome.

Years later, I asked John Ehrlichman what could have put Nixon onto the path that led to the Plumbers, the Ellsberg affair, Gemstone, the Watergate break-in, the whole escalating mess.

"It was the Kennedy fixation," John said. "He never got over Jack and Bobby, and he was sure Teddy would do him in in 1972." There was something about Nixon and the Kennedys. Not rational.

Not rational. That, I came to understand, was the key. This was not unusual in politicians of intensity. Lyndon Johnson had displayed similar traits. There is a strain of paranoia in most ambitious men, and no one is more ambitious than a Presidential candidate. Lyndon possessed it, even Carter. (Reagan seems to be an exception, so possibly was Truman.)

I saw nothing of Nixon in his White House years. The line was drawn very strictly against press, old or new. I did, however, make the aquaintance of a man who knew him well and had observed him with insight since the Checkers days or even before. There was, he felt, something unusual about Nixon, a Dr. Jekyll and Mr. Hyde quality. On personal terms he often was very warm, very sensitive, very thoughtful. People who worked for him liked him. He had a good mind, and he knew the world better than any President since FDR. He had an instinct for politics and what would appeal to the country. That was the good Nixon.

But there was a bad Nixon, almost like the Herblock cartoons in *The Washington Post*. Nixon once told me he kept the paper out of the house so his girls wouldn't see Herblock. This was the Nixon who turned on reporters on the morning of his defeat for the California governorship and shouted: "You won't have Nixon to kick around any more." This was the Nixon of the dark Watergate stories, the man of obscenities that demeaned himself and his office, of the trip to the Capitol before dawn with his valet, Manuel, asking him to address the empty chamber and commenting, "I don't think that got over very well," the Nixon who pulled Kissinger to his knees in the Lincoln study of the White House to pray with him, who roved the White House at 3 A.M., talking to the portraits on the walls, and, quite possibly, the Nixon of the murderous Cambodian "incursion" and the Christmas bombing of Hanoi. Nixon's old associate suggested to me that Cambodia and the Christmas bombing might have been triggered by a compulsive need to prove his manhood.

But the President was also a man of privacy, a very private man, not at all like a Johnson or a Roosevelt who lived "by pressing the flesh" of supporters, men who like Antaeus lost their strength when cut off from their roots. Nor was Nixon like Kennedy or Nelson Rockefeller or Warren G. Harding or so many political men, possessed of a sex drive that propelled them from one bed to another. Nixon was not like that at all. He abhorred the arm-around-the-shoulder gesture (when he did it for campaign pictures he looked stiff as cardboard). He was no good at a Latino abrazo or the garlicky kiss of a French politician. Pictures of Dick and Pat in hugs or kisses are rare.

I came to share my friend's conviction that the Nixon mood swings were rooted in childhood adoration of his mother and rejection of his father. He spurred himself to achievement to meet his mother's goals. He underlined his father's failures with his successes. But his methods! He liked to tell how hard he worked to help his mother make ends meet. But he never spoke of running away with a carnival to Prescott, Arizona, to be a barker at the Slippery Gulch Rodeo for a wheel of chance—*gambling*. Nor did he talk of his poker games in the South Pacific. *Gambling*. Nor of the tricks and trades and deals of politics. *Lying*. He rose in the world of politics. But he rose by methods that violated the morals of the hard-rock Quaker faith of his mother. She was not a pacifist Quaker, nor was her son. These were "fighting Quakes," transplanted from Indiana to Southern California about the turn of the century. But—and this was the point—these were very moral Quakers. They did not *gamble*. They did not *lie*. They did not *cheat*. They did not *drink*. They did not *swear*. They were honorable men and women in a world of sin.

From the day I met Nixon (and long before) he was a man laden with guilt. When I heard the good Quakers of Whittier talk about his mother, I understood a lot about him. There was hardly one of his mother's principles which he had not violated time and again. Did he tell his mother how he was earning a dollar an hour at the Slippery Gulch Rodeo? Did he tell her about the twenty-four hour poker game? Did he tell her of the cheats by which he won and held political office? Had there ever been so hopeless a conflict? Was it a wonder that he blurted out in Watergate days: "I'm not a crook!" But, of course, he was arguing with the shadow of his mother, an argument he could never win. No wonder he roved the corridors of the White House after midnight, seeking the support of the glossily varnished, dark-painted Presidents on the walls. No wonder he kept his tapes. The quick answer had been that he hoped to make a lot of bucks with tax write-offs when he turned the tapes over to the Nixon Library. I think the answer was very complex. In some twisted way he thought of them as his ultimate justification. If only his mother could listen, she would understand.

Oh, I suppose that sounds like windy sentimentalism, but it is not all sentiment, and I think it explains, in part, at least, the inexplicable —how so shrewd, intelligent, crafty a man could so entrap himself, make it certain that he would be punished, spin a web with devilish care, as only he could have done, a web beyond the capability of Ehrlichman and Haldeman, John Mitchell, and his adoringly faithful Rose Wood. Only Nixon could contrive it—the ultimate revenge of Mr. Hyde on Dr. Jekyll, or perhaps the other way around.

Late in 1974 after Nixon had retired to San Clemente, after the furor of Watergate had begun to die away, Nixon fell ill, desperately ill, close to death. His old friends believed Nixon wanted to die. The mood shift had occurred. Now he was "in the shell" of despondency. He understood what he had wrought; he saw no way out, nothing for which to live; guilt filled his veins like poison; he had betrayed the mother whom he idolized; he had failed her worse than his father. It was a tragedy from the Greeks.

But unlike Aeschylus, the Nixon tragedy did not end on a neat emotionally fulfilling note. Nixon did not die. Gradually, nourished by the faith of his wife and his daughters, he fought his way back. It was not easy. His loyal friends in Southern California, and their number included Ronald Reagan then governor, did their best to help. They had him to dinner. They invited him out of his den of despond. They tried to lessen his dependence on alcohol (a problem before, during, and after Watergate).

It took time. But it worked. Once again the Nixons pulled up stakes. They came east to New York. Bought a town house on 65th Street, back to back with Arthur Schlesinger, Jr., on 64th. Bought an estate at Saddle River, New Jersey. I began to see him after a ten-year break. Our last talk had been on an airplane flying from Indianapolis to Cleveland, September 13, 1968. The campaign against Hubert Humphrey was at cruising altitude, Nixon's election was certain.

It was an easy, reflective, relaxed Nixon who invited me up front to chat about foreign policy. He wanted to share his thoughts on Russia and China and match his views against mine. Prague had just happened—the Soviet tanks bringing to an end the brief Czech "spring." He was sorry about Czechoslovakia. He had hoped to get to Moscow before the campaign—if he had gone in August maybe this wouldn't have occurred. Anyway, Prague or no Prague, we had to negotiate. No question about that in his mind, but there must be consistency and better State Department planning. It should be done at State, not the White House, and Defense had to be in on it.

When he took office (he had no doubt that he would, nor did I), the first task was to end the war in Vietnam. Otherwise it would paralyze him on foreign and domestic policy. It would become "Nixon's war" as Mel Laird, Nixon's defense secretary-designate, told me in January 1969. The war had to be ended, or it would hang over everything else and damage the whole Nixon program.

The Middle East was *the* danger spot—much worse than Vietnam —the only place where surrogates might drag the U.S. and U.S.S.R. into war against their will.

To negotiate with the Russians, we had to have all the strength we could muster. First, he would go to Europe and get De Gaulle, England and Germany back on line. LBJ had neglected them. The alliance was a shambles. Next, China. He knew exactly how dangerous the Russo-Chinese situation was. He would move on China as soon as possible. He would make the China opening as soon as he had taken care of a few other things—like Vietnam.

Nixon followed that plan—except for Vietnam. Why did it take him five years to sign a peace with Hanoi? I don't know. There is no clue in Nixon's memoirs or those of Kissinger. None in the studies I have seen.

When Nixon told me of his program, he had never laid eyes on Kissinger. That would not come until after the November election when John Mitchell, responding to a suggestion by Nelson Rockefeller (for whom Kissinger was a consultant), met Henry and introduced him to Nixon. The foreign policy was Nixon's, not Kissinger's as so many came to believe.

Did Henry persuade Nixon to go slow on Vietnam, urge delaying tactics, which ultimately strung out to 1973, the Cambodia incursion, and the Christmas bombing? I do not know, and I have not been able to find out. I do know that Kissinger in October-November 1972 negotiated in Paris a good settlement with Hanoi—indeed, the identical, almost word-for-word, settlement we agreed to in the winter of 1973. That autumn Ehrlichman and Haldeman were trying to destroy Kissinger, end his White House influence. They torpedoed the Vietnam settlement and opened the tragic path to the Christmas bombing. But who delayed the process in 1969, 1970, 1971, and 1972? Was it Kissinger or did Nixon for reasons not known (the Dr. Jekyll and Mr. Hyde effect?) scuttle his sensible intentions outlined on the plane September 13, 1968? When all Nixon's tapes are at long last placed in the public domain, we may find the answer—but somehow I doubt it will ever all be spelled out.

In the talks which I began with Nixon a decade after his airplane tour de horizon of 1968, the President exhibited the same perceptive, knowledgeable understanding which had characterized his early talks. Over the years he had written repeatedly on world affairs. He had continued to travel to critical areas, especially China, and to meet with important leaders.

He was—and would be always—properly proud of the opening to China and détente with Russia. While often cloaking his statements in vulgar language (profanity in private), he displayed a keen sense of world power. He wrote a book called *Real War* and matched it with one called *Real Peace*, admitting for possibly the first time that "it's the Quaker in me—but that's not a bad thing."

He was campaigning almost self-consciously for the role of American elder statesman. He wanted Watergate off his neck. His greatest disappointment was inflicted by Ronald Reagan and his men, who made plain they did not want or need his advice. He was compelled to stand by while the White House worked to dismantle the system of Great Power balance Nixon had, with Kissinger's help, even in the worst Watergate days, put into place.

The real irony came when Reagan, entrapped in the Iran-Contra scam, telephoned Nixon for advice. Reagan had succeeded in making Watergate look like a teenage prank.

China—that was Nixon's pride. When he spoke of China, I could not drive from my mind the memory of the Joe McCarthyite lynchings, which destroyed the lives and careers of our extraordinary corps of Old China Hands and of Nixon's role in it.

Now Nixon and Kissinger called on the survivors for aid. They sought out Edgar Snow, who had written *Red Star over China*. The wheel took a full turn but, alas, Ed Snow was to die of cancer in Switzerland on the eve of Nixon's takeoff for his meeting with Mao Zedong and Zhou Enlai.

There was irony, indeed. But, out of it all came what Nixon properly considered the great monument to his Presidency—a new era in U.S.-China relations.

In 1984 I dined with Hu Yaobang, then general secretary of China's Communist Party, in his residence in the Zhongnanhai compound of the Forbidden City. We talked of Nixon. Hu was an admirer, thought him the best of our post-World War II Presidents. Hu and Nixon corresponded regularly, and Nixon sent Hu his books as they appeared. Hu had them translated, read them, wrote Nixon his comments. It was an extraordinary circumstance—Hu Yaobang, heading the world's largest Communist Party, a regular correspondent of Richard Nixon, the staunchest foe of Communism in the United States.

But, to me, it did not seem strange. It seemed natural. Nixon knew what he was talking about in China. Years before I had chided the late Premier Zhou Enlai a bit about China's relationship with Nixon. Not all Americans, I told him, were fond of Mr. Nixon. Zhou reproved me. "I don't care what he has done in the United States domestically," said Zhou. "We value him. He has been right about China."

311

And so he had. But still the questions trailed across my mind, not least now that Hu Yaobang, Nixon's Chinese correspondent, was no longer general secretary but had, like Nixon, been retired from his office before his term. Did the two men still write back and forth between New York and Beijing? I wondered. I wondered, too, what each man really thought of the other and of the world on which each has left a somewhat inscrutable mark.

# Chapter 27

# "The Meanest Queen"

When at long last in 1972 I arrived in China, Premier Zhou Enlai offered me an apology. "I'm sorry that we could not receive you earlier," he said, "but you are known as such a leading anti-Soviet champion, we were afraid it might upset our relations with Moscow."

I thanked him, but I knew that this was persiflage from a very sophisticated diplomat, the most skilled of our time, so thought Henry Kissinger. I agreed.

There was a nub of truth in what Zhou Enlai said, but he had no way of knowing that by my own reckoning I was more than forty years behind in getting to China. The delays (until the last years) had all been on my side, not the Chinese.

Two months after Black Friday in October, 1929, having no notion of what lay ahead, I wrote a Christmas letter to my Aunt Sue in New York, December 20, 1929, in which I informed her that, when I graduated from Minnesota in June, "I'm pretty much sold on the idea of getting a China or Japan job." Whatever happened, I added, "I won't be sticking around in Minneapolis."

I had China on my mind and had had since childhood. As a seven- or eight-year-old, hand in my mother's, I walked up Royalston Avenue, the Victorian street on which we lived, around past the livery stable with its smell of horses, over the small railroad bridge beside the red-brick firehouse my grandfather had built, and turned into Western Avenue at the Home Trade Shoe Store (I still have the well-oiled English hiking boots my father bought me there as a high school graduation gift), and up Western to the Chinaman's shop. I was a little afraid of the shop but I was afraid to say I was afraid. It was a hole in the wall, the window filled with curious objects, jute-covered boxes, marked with bold black-painted Chinese characters, reddish fruits I had never seen before (litchi nuts), tin canisters splashed with labels in red and green (tea), festoons of garlic and long black strands which I believed were dried rat tails, tied end to end.

The store exuded scents that overwhelmed my adenoidal nostrils—tea, sandalwood, incense, spices. To the rear under a dangling naked bulb sat three Chinese, old, wrinkled, yellow, eyes narrow, heavy-lidded, on small stools around a low teakwood table playing fan-tan. They smoked long pipes. Opium, I was sure. Skeins of noodles draped from the beams. There were stacks of blue porcelain bowls, huge Sinbad jars, and bundles of chopsticks.

A bell tinkled faintly when we entered, and a man put down his cards and shuffled up behind the counter, his slippers going slap, slap, slap. I can still hear the shuffle of slippers on the scuffed floor. He came up opposite my mother, a flowery hat on her head, hands in white kid gloves, carrying a small petit-point purse.

For my childhood years the Chinaman's shop *was* China, a place of mystery, romance, excitement—exotic, a world which drew me like a magnet, so different from plain flat Minnesota. I had to see it.

At the Chinaman's shop mother bought candied ginger (too hot for my small tongue—my father loved it), candied kumquats in small blue-green earthenware pots tied with rattan, shredded coconut, bleached almonds, crystalized lilac and violet blossoms (only pinches, they were so expensive). Mother loved the dainty sugared blossoms. I could not wait for the next visit to the shop, but when I entered, timorous as a foal, I could hardly keep from running back into the sunshine.

There was another bit of China in the attic of 107 Royalston in my father's curio case—a bamboo opium pipe with silver mouthpiece, a pair of tiny red-and-green embroidered shoes (for a long time I thought they were the shoes of a Chinese lady whose feet had been bound), and a small cabinet of ebony and mother-of-pearl with tiny drawers and secret compartments. For years I hoped I might find a pigeon-blood ruby or a rare pearl in a hidden compartment, but I never did. This was the China of my youth, and my imagination grazed over it endlessly, so endlessly that when I entered the writing seminar at the university, my first sketch was about the Chinaman and his shop.

A man called Jefferson Jones on the old *Minneapolis Journal*, where I began to work as a cub reporter in 1927, steered my China dream into more practical channels. He had traveled in the Orient and was a good friend of J. V. Fleisher, publisher of the *Japan Advertiser* of Tokyo. In the 1920s and early 1930s there were English language papers scattered up and down the Pacific rim, one or more in every city—Tientsin, Peking, Shanghai, Canton, Hankow, Swatow, Hong Kong, Kobe, Tokyo. Each year Fleisher, a graduate of the University of Missouri, came back to the United States to pick out a Missouri journalism graduate for his paper and to come to Minnesota for a checkup at the Mayo Clinic and a visit with his friend, Jeff Jones.

Jones promised that, when Fleisher made his trip in the spring of 1930, he would try to get him to pick me for Tokyo. I was in seventh heaven. My best friend, Gordon Roth, had just come back from the China coast. He had ridden the rods to Seattle, worked his passage to China on a freighter, jumped ship, spent half a year in Shanghai, and returned to the girl whom he had secretly married before leaving. Very romantic. I was ready to follow him to the far Pacific (I had no secret bride to return to).

It didn't work out. In 1930, probably because of the depression, Fleisher didn't come back. I had been tossed out of school for being an uppity student editor and was hard at work as a full-time reporter for United Press. Jobs were too precious to abandon for a gamble on the China coast. I told myself not to worry. I'd get to China with UP. The United Press was run by an elegant man called Karl Bickel, the first I ever knew who wore spats (pearl-gray), fawn-coloured pigskin gloves, and a homburg. He carried a malacca stick, and there were twenties and fifties in his alligator wallet. I don't believe I had ever seen a fifty-dollar bill before.

Bickel was much at home in countries like Russia and China. He knew Karl Radek and possibly Bukharin in Moscow and Chiang Kai-shek, Madame Chiang, T. V. Soong, the editor J. B. Powell and the warlord Chang Tso-lin in China. I told Bickel I wanted to go to the Far East, and he promised I would get there. As a starter he sent me to Banff, Alberta, in the summer of 1933 to cover a meeting of the Institute of Pacific Relations. There I met Hu Shih, China's leading poet, the first to write in the vernacular, a supporter of Dr. Sun Yat-sen and later Chiang's ambassador to Washington, and Henry Luce, a very young Henry Luce, with his young first wife (not yet married to Clare Booth), their toddling son (today he is Henry Luce II and middle-aged), and Henry Luce's father, the China missionary. I had long talks with the elder Luce. He knew everything about China, I thought. Hu Shih gave me a slim thin-paper, blue-covered collection of poems. It is still on my shelf. Later Senator Joe McCarthy was to attack the institute as a nest of Communists, but in those days it was

315

all establishment. Newton D. Baker, Woodrow Wilson's secretary of war and general counsel of Scripps-Howard, which owned UP, was elected its president at Banff. Hu Shih and Henry Luce fired my imagination. But Bickel didn't get me to China. In a few months UP had sent me to Washington, and World War II took me to London, North Africa, the Middle East, and Moscow. I was as far away from China as I had been in Minneapolis.

China was my destination, but I seemed to have taken a very slow boat. Finally, Earl Johnson, UP news chief, decided to dispatch me from Moscow to Chongqing. Even that didn't work. As I waited in Calcutta to fly the Hump to China, Johnson ordered me back to New York to become UP's foreign editor.

In Moscow I had met Edgar Snow, author of *Red Star over China*, and we became good friends. I had read *Red Star*, and it had given shape to my ambition to go to China, of which I knew very little. I had taken the only course at Minnesota which touched on China (no language instruction in those days)—Far Eastern Diplomacy. It dealt with John Hay, the Open Door Policy, Commodore Perry, and Japan, not with contemporary China. I knew nothing of the Chinese Communist movement until I read Snow. There I heard for the first time of Mao Zedong, Zhou Enlai, Zhu De; there I heard for the first time of the Long March of China's Red Army, an event that would make a mark on my distant future.

Ed and I and Archibald Clark Kerr, the British ambassador who had come to Moscow from Chongqing, talked a lot. They believed Chongqing a more exciting place than Moscow. I accepted their opinion.

One hot July afternoon in 1944 I returned to Moscow from a long trip to Siberia and Central Asia and found the British correspondent, Alec Werth, giving a party for two new arrivals, Ella Winter, the English widow of Lincoln Steffens (she had married him very late in his life and very early in hers) and Anna Louise Strong.

I had heard of Anna Louise for years, a formidable figure, well over six feet tall, sturdily built, strong shoulders, great bosom, tower of gray hair piled up and up, piercing blue eyes, and a gruff voice that carried long distances in the open and resonated within walls. She talked like a drillmaster and possessed many of the human traits I most disliked. She was opinionated, domineering, a nonstop talker,

316

had only the faintest interest in what others said, scorned inferiors (she placed most of the world in that category), dogmatic, what I called a "shouting Marxist" (she knew nothing of Marxist theory), anti-American, pro-Soviet, pro-Chinese, hostile to "capitalist journalists" like myself.

For some perverse reason I liked her instantly. Perhaps she reminded me of an equally statuesque woman, Dr. Anna Von Helmholtz Phelan, who conducted my writing seminar at Minnesota. They were of a size. In each I detected behind an awesome exterior a vulnerable little girl. Anna Louise was a very big little girl, who lived her life in a world of Titans. Her total naïveté came close to destroying her and, I fear, many friends and associates, including her old, close, and loyal friend, Mikhail Borodin.

On that hot July day in Werth's big room, I had no premonition of what might lie ahead for Anna Louise and her friend Borodin. My romantic image of them and many others whom I would come to know—or know about—was drawn from the pages of Vincent Sheean's *Personal History*, which I had gulped down (like tens of thousands of Americans) when it appeared in 1935. There I read of the failed 1927 Chinese Revolution, there I read of Anna Louise and Borodin, the Russian agent sent by Moscow to superintend the Chinese Revolution; of Soong Ching-ling, widow of Sun Yat-sen; her beautiful sister, Soong Mei-ling, wife of Chiang Kai-shek; of Eugene Chen, the Trinidad-born English barrister who became Dr. Sun's foreign minister although he spoke not a word of Chinese; of Eugene Chen's sons, Percy and Jack; and, of course, of Rayna Prohme, with whom Sheean fell hopelessly in love; and of her husband, Bill, later to die in some mysterious underground revolutionary way in Manila. As I read Sheean's star-crossed pages, I ached with emotion. If only I had been in Shanghai in 1927! I did not meet "Jimmy" Sheean, as he was called, until the last dog-eared days of his life—the romance replaced by gin, sad relic of an era, his revolutionary friends long dead, their revolutions dim in memory, and he, the Beau Geste of his time, having to be introduced and identified to young people for whom the name of Rayna Prohme meant less than that of some faded Hollywood star.

I met Borodin in Moscow, tall (so he seemed to me; the police blotter gave his height as 5 feet 8 inches), gaunt, silent, sad eyes that seemed to look past me to some distant horizon which only he could see. I did not know on the evening when we met, during an interlude at the Supreme Soviet meeting in the Kremlin in January 1944, that Borodin's favorite phrase in China had been "we must take the long view" (especially when all was going wrong—Chiang Kai-shek turning on the Communists, the Shanghai Slaughter, all the other horrors).

I can see him now with those deep-set, hawkish eyes, grim, nothing genial, nothing warm about him, no small talk, no desire to be sociable with an ignorant young American correspondent whose only contribution to the conversation was hero worship. He was then editor of the Moscow *News*, a clerk's job, and had a post with the Sovinformburo, a wartime propaganda agency. Even then he was a survivor, a man who had narrowly edged past danger after danger but would not, quite possibly because of the naïveté and loud tongue of Anna Louise, make it past the next.

I never saw Borodin again. When I returned to Moscow in 1949, he was gone. I had heard on shipboard, en route to my new post as *New York Times* correspondent, of the arrest, February 7, 1949, of Anna Louise by the KGB in Moscow as an agent of the CIA. I said to myself: My God! If Anna Louise is being arrested as an American spy, there isn't much chance for me! When I arrived in Moscow, I found that Borodin and the entire staff of the *Moscow News* had also been arrested.

Borodin was not as fortunate as Anna Louise. Not long after Stalin's death, March 5, 1953, Ralph Parker, correspondent of the *London Daily Worker*, whispered to me in a shadowy corridor of the Metropol: "Don't you think Mikhail Borodin deserves an obituary in *The New York Times*?"

"Of course," said I. I filed a brief dispatch, and to my surprise, the censors passed it. A bit later on a Siberian trip, I saw the wooden stockade and watchtowers, the barbed wire and the tommy gunners guarding the prison camp in Yakutsk where, it was said, Borodin died, May 29, 1951.

There were rumors that the Chinese intervened when Borodin was arrested in February 1949, and that this had saved his life (for a time). I am not certain this is true. The Chinese, as I came to know, did not—or at least Mao and his supporters did not—have a high opinion of Borodin. They blamed his tactics for the failure of the 1927 revolution. But here, I think, they were being too casuistic, because Borodin was, in fact, the agent of Stalin to the revolution. Lenin had agreed to send someone to help Dr. Sun Yat-sen, but Lenin was incapacitated before he could do so. Stalin was the man who picked and sent Borodin to China.

It was Stalin's strategy and Stalin's tactics that Borodin carried out. It was true, as Mao and the others declared, that these tactics led to failure. (Borodin at Stalin's insistence supported Chiang Kai-shek long after Chiang had turned on the Communists.) And it was this which led directly to the debacle at Shanghai, the murderous assault of Chiang and his gangster allies on the Communists and workers, the split in the Nationalist movement, the ultimate collapse of the left wing-Communist government at Hankow, and the emergence of Chiang Kai-shek as heir to Dr. Sun Yat-sen's revolution. Stalin's motive for this suicidal (for the Chinese Communists) strategy? To avoid letting his rival Trotsky expose him as a rotten revolutionary, who had backed the wrong horse (Chiang Kai-shek) in China.

Naturally, I knew nothing of this when I met Borodin and none of it when I met Anna Louise. The Chinese Revolution, like all revolutions, is a puzzle box, and not even the participants necessarily know at all times what is true and what is not true.

When I arrived in Moscow in the winter of 1949 and began cautiously nosing around for information about Anna Louise, I did not realize that my curiosity would forge a link with this revolutionary Juno which would play a role in my long-standing ambition to get to China. Nor that, as I learned more and more of her dramatic and contradictory career, this would open for me long vistas into the world of revolutions, that of Russia and more particularly that of China.

The arrest of Anna Louise was too fresh in people's minds and the atmosphere of Moscow too tense for anyone to discuss freely what had happened.

I had assumed that Anna Louise felt at home in Moscow. She had lived there for a long, long time, had been in and out of Russia for three decades, she had a Russian husband (I didn't know he had died in World War II, almost certainly in a Stalinist camp) and quite a few in-laws in Moscow. I knew that she made many friends in Moscow, and I knew her as a true child of the romantic American revolutionary mood which had flourished before and during World War I. That was about all I really knew. As time went on, I put more pieces together.

319

She was the daughter of a well-known American clergyman, a widower who managed to interfere with and distort Anna Louise's relations with men, including a violent love affair with Roger Baldwin, then a handsome young man out of Harvard, later dean of American civil liberties. I knew Anna Louise had played a passionate (whatever she did was passionate) role in the turbulent IWW battles of Seattle before and during World War I.

Anna Louise had come to Russia in the 1920s because Lincoln Steffens had said: "I have been over into the future and it works." (That was a good many years before Ella Winter married Steffens.) Steffens told Anna Louise to go to Moscow, and she did. Anna Louise knew Louise Bryant and John Reed. She was of the generation that came out of the Wobblies, Harvard, and Greenwich Village. There was not a revolutionary cause which this statuesque and beautiful (in those years) woman did not grace.

From Moscow Anna Louise had gone to China. After the fall of Red Hankow and Chiang's violence against Communists and Russians, she made her escape in 1927 with Borodin across north China, into Mongolia and finally on to Russia.

I heard the story much, much later from Percy Chen, then a distinguished man in his upper seventies living out his years in Hong Kong. Percy was the oldest son of Eugene Chen, and he drove Borodin out of China and over the Gobi. As he remembered, Anna Louise swooned over Borodin, then a handsome bold revolutionary (once a Chicago schoolteacher). She sang "Nearer My God to Thee," to Borodin, beside a desert campfire until he dissolved her into tears by shouting: "For God's sake, woman, why don't you sing the Internationale!"

Anna Louise came back to Moscow, settled down in the Metropol along with the Chens, with Borodin, with Madame Soong Chingling and the others. Sooner or later all went their ways, but Anna Louise stayed, joining Borodin in founding the *Moscow News*, writing sloppy books about Red Russia and Red China, coming back to the U.S.A. every year for lecture tours, praising Communism, living on with blinded eyes and (possibly) clenched teeth as her friends vanished in Stalin's purges. Her books are filled with the names of those who would die. She took a trip to the Pamirs in 1930, and almost everyone she mentioned would soon be dead—her friend Dubenko, a leader in the Bolshevik uprising of November 7, 1917 (shot with Marshal Tukhachevsky in 1937), the geneticist Vavilov

320

(arrested in 1940, died in prison, 1943), Bill Shatov the burly and the ebullient American IWW who helped build the Turk-Sib railroad. She sat with Bill Shatov in his private railroad car in 1930, listening to him play on the Victrola his latest record from Tin Pan Alley:

> "She's the meanest Queen
> I've ever seen
> Josephine."

Shatov died seven years later before one of Stalin's execution squads.

There was no way Anna Louise could not have known this.

Anna Louise went to Yan'an in 1946 to sit at the feet of Mao, where she transcribed the essence of Mao's philosophy, his characterization of the atom bomb as a "paper tiger," and his definition of "Chinese Marxism." She put it all in a book called originally *The Thought of Mao Zedong*.

It was the only important book Anna Louise ever wrote, and I suspect she knew it. It declared the independence of Mao and the Chinese Communists from Stalin and his Party line. It was quickly published in the United States and China, and taken for publication in Eastern Europe—but not in Moscow.

She arrived in Moscow in October 1948, en route back to China. She hoped to be in Beijing to witness the Communist takeover.

She told her Moscow friends, as I learned, that it was ridiculous that the Russian and Yugoslav Communists were not getting on, that Stalin should make up with Tito. She said she preferred the Chinese Communists to the Russians. Her friends clapped their hands to their ears. They didn't even want to hear this dangerous heresy. She met Borodin a time or two. He tried tactfully to make her realize that she was treading on dangerous ground. She did not listen. Her exit permit to China did not come through. She proclaimed that she was going to see Stalin and tell him a thing or two. Some petty bureaucrats, she thought, had taken important affairs into their hands.

How she could not have noticed the fear in Moscow in late 1948 and early 1949 I cannot imagine. Everyone I knew had his or her head down. The "anticosmopolitan" campaign (against Jews) was at its peak—Jews being publicly denounced, dismissed from jobs, arrested, imprisoned, sent to Siberia, and executed. The "Leningrad affair" was in progress—the top leadership of Russia's second city (Politburo members among them) arrested, secretly tried and shot. The Jewish anti-Fascist case was underway—twenty-five leading Jews, World War II heroes, writers, scientists arrested, tried and shot. Preparations for driving Tito out of Yugoslavia had reached a climax. Arrests of foreign Communists were beginning again. What else might have been going on at that time, I cannot recapitulate. I can testify, however, that Moscow was more sinister than I ever saw it—except for the period just before Stalin's death.

It was into this Moscow that Anna Louise projected herself. Small wonder that people literally fled (as some whispered to me) from the sound of her powerful voice; small wonder old friends shunned her; small wonder only a few brave souls (including Borodin) tried quietly to shut her up. To no avail. She persisted against all caution.

Some god smiled down on her. She was arrested. She was held only a few days. Her room at the Lubyanka was as comfortable as a room at the Metropol Hotel. She was not tortured. She underwent no midnight interrogation. She did not have to don prison garb. On February 19, 1949, the Kremlin announced she was being expelled from the Soviet Union as an American spy and an agent of the CIA. She was flown to the Polish border and tottered across.

True, she had to make her own way back. True, the Poles wouldn't help her. True, her world was shattered. She was branded in such a way that not one of her Communist and pro-Communist associates —not even the Chinese—would have anything to do with her. True, the *New York Daily Worker* interrupted serialization of her *Thought of Mao Zedong* in midthought.

But she would find her way back to Los Angeles, find herself befriended by kindly people, and live a not entirely unpleasant existence for the next six years—a pariah, it is true, from those whose association she valued, but physically secure. She would even do a bit of quite profitable speculation.

Not until I returned to the United States in late 1954 and wrote my series in the *Times*, called "Russia Re-Viewed," telling what I then knew about Borodin, the *Moscow News*, and Anna Louise, would she begin to cope with what had happened.

In public Anna Louise had consistently claimed that her expulsion must have been carried out by underlings without Stalin's knowledge —a preposterous theory but one only too familiar to me. Again and again during the Great Purges of the 1930s so carefully orchestrated by Stalin, old Bolsheviks had gone to their deaths with the phrase "If Stalin only knew!" on their lips. They tried to smuggle letters to tell him that the system had gone out of control. Even in prison camp, again and again, as Aleksandr Solzhenitsyn has recorded, Party members clung to their cri de coeur "if Stalin only knew."

Now with the publication of my article telling of the arrest of Borodin and the *Moscow News* people, simultaneous with her own arrest, Anna Louise directed a pathetic letter to me. It was the first word she had had of "my old friend Borodin and the fact that his arrest took place February 1949." She had, she said, never known "any reason for my arrest—which destroyed my worldwide career." She begged if I had any more information to forward it and asked how certain was my knowledge about Borodin. Regretfully I had to tell her there was no longer a shadow of a doubt. Borodin had been arrested and died in concentration camp, precisely as I had reported.

Did she then grasp that she had played a role in Borodin's death? I do not believe she did, and it is just as well.

It was March 4, 1955, two years almost to the day after the death of Stalin, before *Pravda* finally and, as it seemed to me, reluctantly, announced that the case of Anna Louise Strong had been reviewed, and the charges found groundless.

Another year passed before I had from Anna Louise (in response to one of mine about Nikita Khrushchev's revelations of Stalin's crimes) a long closely reasoned letter, in which she for the first time conceded that she had, indeed, over a period of time noticed telltale signs (which she had faithfully suppressed) of poor relations between the Russians and the Chinese: the fact that the Russians did not turn over the arms and matériel they had seized in Manchuria in 1945 to the Communist Chinese (they kept it themselves or let the Nationalists have it); the fact that the Soviet ambassador had followed Chiang Kai-shek from Nanjing to Canton in 1949; that the Chinese consular officers in Siberia in 1949 were still Chiang Kai-shek's men; a Soviet proposal to Chiang Kai-shek just before Nanjing's fall in 1949 for a coalition Nationalist-Communist government.

She still tried, a bit wearily, to suggest that "what happened to me" had been "just a blunder of lower officials" but conceded that, if Stalin was behind it, then it undoubtedly was because she was boosting Mao all over the map "before Stalin recognized him and gave a green light." "I really did a job on Mao," she said, particularly with her *The Thought of Mao Zedong*. It had been published in America, in India, in China (in 1948 and 1949), and the Czechs were preparing to publish it in their official ideological journal; she had also addressed the important Varga Institute in Moscow in late 1948 on the economic theories of Mao. She had been, she admitted, "invading the realm of upper Communist theory."

She recalled that then, at a time when her works were appearing all over the world, when she had had requests from East European countries for everything she had written about China, in 1948 and early 1949 the Russians were paying little public heed to the Chinese Communists.

And, she admitted, there had been more personal indications of trouble—Borodin's fears concerning the attitude of Soviet officials. All of this was enough—or should have been enough—to put her on her guard.

There was one more thing, she revealed. Mao himself had given her a warning in 1946 against going to Moscow again, but, she said, it was put in so oblique a fashion—just a hint as it were—that when she came to make her plans to return to China in 1948, Mao's words did not really leap into her mind.

"I assumed that Mao's warning had not really been a warning, or at least applied only to a brief time," she wrote me. But, she admitted, she now had to realize that "there must have been some competition between the two great leaders of world Communism; and that I stuck my head in the way."

She had indeed. Although she never in correspondence with me was to return to this theme, I think any doubts as to what was going on were finally removed from her mind when, after a fight to get back her passport, she finally returned to China, September 22, 1958. She was bubbling over, and her enthusiasm poured out in long letters in which she, for a time, seemed to think that she might win permission for me to come very shortly to Beijing. She was wrong about that as, alas, she was about so many things.

Anna Louise would stay in China for the rest of her life—an indefatigable propagandist for Mao, as prone to the suspension of common sense as ever. She fawned on Mao Zedong and Zhou Enlai, but once flared up madly at a dirty tablecloth in the Great Hall of the People and compelled waiters to change it in the midst of a state dinner—not quite as imperious as on the occasion in Yan'an when she broke into a meeting of the State Military Council to demand that Zhou Enlai come play bridge in her cave. Zhou gently led her out of the room, telling her he had played bridge with her the night before and that she must not interfere with the business of the State Council. Anna Louise wandered back to her jeep in bemusement, saying over and over like a reprimanded schoolgirl: "Why, Zhou Enlai was really angry with me. He was *really* angry. He told me to go away." She repeated it like a litany.

She spent a fair amount of time playing the stock market, directing her transactions improbably through an offshore account. She was quite successful, as she had been in her operations in Los Angeles real estate. She fought a long war with Soviet authorities, trying to get them to transfer balances in her Moscow bank accounts to Beijing. They insisted she had to come to Moscow to make the transfer. Finally she proudly announced she had thwarted Moscow. She had ordered them to transfer her money to a fund for Vietnam war relief. They had bent at last to her will.

I wrote her long, chatty letters full of American political gossip and my notions of why I should be permitted to come to China. After a time her replies came at greater and greater intervals, but when I reached Beijing at long last in 1972, I found that I was famous in the small court of foreigners that had gathered around Anna Louise. She read the letters aloud as they were received, and there were long discussions of the significance of my observations. If I had known, I would have written more often.

Once I had a letter from Anna Louise containing a special request. Could I obtain a dozen pairs of nylon hose for her (I can't remember the size or color) and, so help me, a corset cover, at least, that is what I think it was, an article of apparel so lost in the mists of Victorian femininity that it must have been a companion to the ruffles that Boston ladies once put around the naked "limbs" of their grand pianos. My secretary couldn't find a New York store that carried one.

In China Anna Louise found her heaven. She had long since turned her back on America. She had turned her back on Russia in 1949. Now she had China. She was content, exhilarated, passionate. She threw herself into China, writing, writing, writing.

Then in 1966 China began to change. Anna Louise did not understand it. She plunged into the Cultural Revolution, naïve as a novitiate. She even wore the scarf of the Red Guards and appeared at Tiananmen. She tried in every way to pour what was left of her stock of gilt over the ever-widening cracks in the portrait of Chinese perfection she had painted in her propaganda.

It was not enough. China turned on her in ways too terrible and complex to expound here. Those she trusted went down in the flames of the holocaust, which came close to destroying her along with the whole structure. Anna Louise did not taste prison again, but she did taste betrayal. In the end, bewildered, disillusioned, beset by doubts, fears and pain, she began to try to return to America. Oh, just for a last trip, she said. But she knew that if she went, she would not come back. Had it not been for the stupid bureaucracy of the American consul-general in Hong Kong, she would have left her last Revolution and come back to the land of her birth.

She was, for practical purposes, a prisoner in her own house, breakfasting each morning on the porch of No. 1 Tai Ji Chang, the lovely house in the courtyard of the old Italian embassy. Rewi Alley, her old New Zealand friend, lived in the apartment just above her— two old friends, who had dedicated their lives to China, trying to understand how it could have happened, what was this madness raging over their chosen land, two old revolutionaries trying to perceive what genie had been let out of the bottle and who had done it, not wanting to confess (or fearful of admitting) that they knew the answer.

Anna Louise was still hoping to go home when she fell ill. Her condition rapidly worsened. One day Zhou Enlai, beset with the worry of the Cultural Revolution, discovered to his horror that she was dying, dying alone without proper treatment. He himself went to the hospital. He lost his temper, roared to the hospital to do everything possible for Anna Louise, roared to his aides to find her nephew, who he knew was somewhere on the East Asian coast (Zhou's own foreign office had denied him a visa to visit his ailing aunt). In vain Zhou tried to hold back the gray shadow until at least one familiar face was beside the bed of Anna Louise. But it was too late. She died March 28, 1969, her great-nephew John Strong not yet arrived from travels in Indonesia. Zhou attended the funeral, his face a mask of weariness, tears falling down his cheeks.

Anna Louise had amassed a comfortable sum from her Los Angeles real estate and her market speculation from Beijing. In her will she left various bequests and the instruction to her executor, the American exile, Frank Coe, that the remainder, a sum of a few hundred dollars, be used "to further the cause of the American revolution." How Coe carried out his instructions, I cannot guess. What I can say is that for all her tantrums, loud shouts, vanity, and childlike naïveté Anna Louise taught me much—about men and women, about life and about the people we call revolutionaries, who try somehow to speed up and change the course of human progress. Anna Louise was the product of a deeply religious, deeply idealistic American faith. Her life was spent in what she perceived to be a great moral struggle to make better the lot of man on earth. If she failed, it was not for lack of passion, and if in many ways she was a foolish woman, at least she tried to leave behind a better world than that into which she was born.

## Chapter 28

# Blindfolded in Room 393

I once boasted that you could blindfold me, put me down anywhere in the Hotel Metropol in Moscow, and I could tell you where I was—which corridor, which floor, which room—by using nothing more than my nose.

In the spring of 1949 when I came back to Russia for *The New York Times*, I didn't have to close my eyes to know that the smell in the Metropol was the smell of fear. The Metropol was peopled by ghosts of Bolsheviks past and present, the victims of Stalin's waves of terror. Especially the ghosts of Stalin's Grand Guignol of China and the Chinese Revolution.

As I sat at the great fumed oak desk in Room 393—the room, now mine, which once had been occupied by Alexander Werth—and thumbed over *Pravda* each morning, a curious sensation ran down my spine. It had been difficult for me to believe that China was the connecting link between Anna Louise Strong, the disappearance of Borodin, and the closing of the *Moscow News*, but the coincidence was too strong to dismiss.

Now as I read *Pravda*, a new realization came over me and this was what sent a tremor down my spine. The Peoples Liberation Army was conquering China. Day by day it was driving Chiang Kai-hek from the field, victory after victory. It had swept down from the northwest, occupied North China, seized Manchuria, marched into Beijing. It was preparing to move south on Nanjing and across the Yangtze into South China. It was the greatest revolutionary triumph since the Bolsheviks seized Petrograd in 1917. *And Pravda was not reporting it.*

Oh, yes, as I went through the papers each day with the help of an interpreter (I was just beginning to learn Russian), there would be the occasional item tucked away on an inside page, the report of a battle here or there, three or four paragraphs. But no reader of *Pravda* could be aware that Mao Zedong, Zhu De, Peng Dehuai and all the others were winning triumph after triumph. The events which were bannered in headlines in *The New York Times*, in London, in Paris and Tokyo did not engage the interest of *Pravda*. Tiny stories, no commentary, no editorials, nothing to excite the Kremlin or the Russian people.

I am by nature a contrarian. I tend to challenge common assumptions. But I had not until the spring of 1949, studying *Pravda* in that cavernous room, supposed that there might be fundamental differences between Communist China and the Soviet Union. Policy differences, yes. But deep hostility—it had never entered my mind. Of course I did not know the inner history of Mao and Stalin; I did not understand that there had been, since the 1920s, a basic quarrel (sometimes latent, sometimes open) between the two men. I had read Harold Isaacs *The Tragedy of the Chinese Revolution*, but I had paid more attention to his dramatic account of the slaughter of the Communists in Shanghai in 1927 than to his political analysis, and I am afraid I had discounted it as being a Trotskyite distortion.

So regardless of the ghosts of Borodin, of the Chens, of Soong Ching-ling, of Anna Louise, of Rayna and Bill Prohme (all of whom had once lived on the very floor I now inhabited at the Metropol), I found it hard to digest the evidence of what *Pravda* was not printing, but like Sherlock Holmes and the dog that did not bark, I could not ignore it.

I had been brought up with a cliché dinned into my head by my friend Reuben, whose father had been a Bundist radical in Russia. Reuben used to repeat, again and again, in our arguments: "There is a reason for everything." I am sure he got the phrase from his father, who in turn picked it up in the endless discussions of the Russian radicals. I didn't like the phrase, but it haunted me. If *Pravda* was not playing up the Chinese Revolution, there had to be a reason—an important reason, probably a sinister reason.

A month after I arrived in Moscow, I noted in my journal, April 4, 1949:

> From all I can gather the Kremlin still is very unsure of the situation in China. It gets very scanty reference in the press.
>
> ... My opinion is that the Kremlin has its fingers crossed about its Chinese friends and will keep them that way for some time.

A month later I was writing (privately) about the "touchy relations" of Moscow and the Chinese. I tried to convey some hint of this to

American readers, but the censors killed my reference to the fact that Moscow was maintaining scrupulously correct relations with Chiang Kai-shek and would do so until he actually left the mainland, the Russian ambassador, unlike the American, following him from Nanjing to the water's edge.

I don't want to overstate my prescience about the antagonisms between China and the Soviets. Yes, I spotted the signs, but because of the Soviet censorship my analysis did not reach the public. My observations were hacked out of my copy. True, a sharp-eyed editor could spot that something was wrong by what I was *not* saying. This is the way Russians had learned to read *Pravda*—not for what was printed, but for what *was not*. But Americans are not skilled in this art. I did circulate copies of the materials killed by the censors to the editors of the *Times* and to my friend, Cyrus L. Sulzberger, chief European correspondent of the *Times*. But I did not make any real mark on their minds.

I do not think this is accidental. All eyes were turned in the opposite direction. The State Department's famous White Paper issued on July 30, 1949 (approved, if not drafted, by Dean Acheson), said:

> The heart of China is in Communist hands. The Communist leaders have foresworn their Chinese heritage and have publicly announced *their subservience to a foreign power, Russia* [my italics]. . . . The Communist regime serves not their [Chinese] interests but those of Soviet Russia . . . .

By March 30, 1950, Senator Joseph McCarthy was saying: "it was not Chinese democracy under Mao that conquered China as Acheson, [Owen] Lattimore, and [Philip] Jesseup contended. *Soviet Russia conquered China* [my italics] and an important ally of this conqueror was the small left-wing element in our Department of State."

Or, as Dean Rusk put it in May 1951:

> We do not recognize the authority in Peiping [sic] for what they pretend to be. The Peiping regime may be a colonial Russian government—a Slavic Manchukuo [sic] on a larger scale. It is not the Government of China. It does not pass the first test. It is not Chinese.

Or as Captain Joseph Alsop, then serving with General Claire Chennault, put it simply and plainly in 1945: "We are childish to assume the Chinese Communists are anything but an appendage of the Soviet Union."

It is tragic that there was no difference in view among McCarthy, Acheson, Rusk, and Alsop (Alsop later changed his mind). As years passed, there would be a powerful effort to slip the brass ring on McCarthy's porcine pinky, but he was just a flabby Wisconsin pol, the others were classy, educated men who could have known better but, instead, arranged a well-designed stage on which McCarthy could present his rubbishy performance.

The thin grapeshot of my highly censored dispatches didn't pock the seamless surface of post-war American know-nothingism.

Of course, I did not then perceive how deep the divisions were between Russia and China, Moscow and Beijing, Stalin and Mao. But if I, a non-expert in Chinese affairs, possessing scant knowledge of Russia, not one word of the Chinese language, sitting alone, virtually blindfolded in that heavily draped, shuttered, dim-lighted Moscow hotel room could discern enough to suspect that something was rotten between the two big Communist countries is it not reasonable to expect that the President of the United States, his Secretary of State and all the other secretaries, intelligence analysts, members of the Senate, members of the House and assorted wise men would scent a faint clue? Should we not expect that amongst them there would be one who spoke out for reason and common sense; who had the primitive instinct if not expert knowledge to realize that Russia and China were two great nations neither of which would kowtow to the other? In those days, 1949, the CIA was new; we were only spending hundreds of millions not today's tens of billions on intelligence—but what were we getting for our money? (Of course, I know the same question can be raised today). Should we not expect that a man from Missouri like Harry Truman, so savvy in ordinary walks of life, would have said to them: Show Me!

I once met the famous biologist, A. J. Carlson, at the University of Chicago. He was the man who fed patent bleached flour to rats. They died of vitamin deficiency. Our cosmetic milling of wheat had produced a beauteous snowy powder. Unfortunately there wasn't too much nutrition in it.

This commonsensical scientist gave all of his students a test. He commanded them to bring a test tube of urine to class. Then he stood in front with his own test tube: "Watch closely and do exactly as I do." The test, he said, would demonstrate the basic principles of the scientific method. He held his test tube to the light: "It looks like urine, but that is just the first test." Next, he put the tube to his nostrils. Yes, it smelled like urine, but we must not leap to conclusions. Does it taste like urine? He dipped a finger into the tube and put it to his lips. Yes, he said, it is urine. The scholars dutifully followed his example.

"Now," said Carlson, "you have all failed the test. Watch me closely."

He went through it again—held the test tube to the light, smelled it, dipped a finger into the liquid. This time he moved slowly so all could see that the finger he put to his lips was not the one that had been immersed in urine.

"You see?" he explained. "The basis of the scientific method is close observation. You were misled by my words. You must watch closely. That is the scientific method."

No one in Washington—as is so often the case—was watching the test tubes. There can be no doubt that the logic of Acheson, McCarthy, and Rusk did not pass, in Rusk's word, the first test. None had put China to Carlson's test. They may have listened to propagandistic words; they had not paid heed to the deeds.

I have, over years, seen political leaders—American and others—make many mistakes. None, I think, can match the colossal error of the United States on China. It should be clear, forty years after the event, that this was not McCarthy's fault. McCarthy was only a spear carrier. The men whom he counted his enemies (and who saw him as their enemy) were as like as two pumpkins in the blind infantilism of their opinions.

That was not a point of view I could prove in 1949. But it was not long before evidence came in that the relationship between China and Moscow was of a most special nature.

In June 1949, at a time when Mao had taken over Beijing—but had not yet proclaimed the People's Republic—a delegation headed by the important Chinese Communist leader, Gao Gan, came to Moscow, was received by Stalin, and signed an agreement for economic cooperation between the Soviet and the "Manchurian Peoples Democratic authorities."

This struck me as a fish out of water. The "Manchurian Peoples Democratic authorities" did not exist as a government, so far as I knew. Was this a gimmick to establish relations between Communist-occupied Manchuria and the Soviet Union without violating existing diplomatic relations between Moscow and Chiang Kai-shek? Or was it something more mysterious? The censor would not let me speculate. Later, after Stalin's death in 1953 and the arrest and execution of his chief of secret police, Lavrenti P. Beria, the Chinese arrested Gao Gan and some of his associates. They were said to have plotted to detach Manchuria from China and set up an "independent kingdom."

I don't know exactly what went on, but it struck me in 1955 (when I learned of Gao Gan's arrest) that Stalin and Beria had been plotting with Gao Gan against Mao. I think this was the case. The Chinese were very angry in 1955, because instead of standing trial, being sentenced to death, and shot, Gao Gan committed suicide. That, said Beijing, was the act of a traitor.

I think that Stalin and Beria promised Gao Gan his own "independent kingdom" in Manchuria if he went with them. Not exactly the conduct of warm, friendly allies but conduct which went unnoticed by American minds transfixed with the notion of the "Communist monolith." Our specialists were so bemused by McCarthyism they didn't bother to analyze the significance of the Gao Gan affair.

On October 1, 1949, Mao proclaimed the Peoples Republic from Tiananmin Square and finally *Pravda* gave the Chinese a big sendoff. Next day Moscow transferred diplomatic recognition from Chiang to Mao and sent its ambassador scurrying up to Beijing to represent Russia at the court of Communism.

It seemed a curious performance. I didn't even know of the last minute haggling between Chiang and Moscow over the transfer of Xinjiang province to Russia as a protectorate. It still seems strange today. Of course, trying to puzzle things out in Room 393, I could not perceive the long, consistent tendency of Stalin to favor Chiang over Mao. Nor did I know until I learned it in 1984, while interviewing China's leaders about *The Long March*, that just before the PLA moved across the Yangtze in 1949, Stalin sent Anastas Mikoyan to make a last-ditch effort to keep Mao from crossing the river—to leave Chiang in power in south China—warning that otherwise the United States might intervene. Mao refused. He moved south. He crossed the Yangtze. The U.S. did not intervene.

Later Stalin confessed to the Chinese that he had been mistaken.

He had thought Chiang Kai-shek was too strong and that the Communists could not conquer him. He had been wrong.

Whether Stalin really was sorry is something else. I don't think he ever trusted Mao. I don't think he ever wanted Mao to win. I don't think he wanted a strong China. I think he backed Chiang because he thought he could manipulate Chiang, and he didn't think he could manipulate Mao. I think Stalin was right about Chiang and Mao, but I was far from thinking that as the dreary Moscow autumn of 1949 moved into winter.

I had heard rumors that Mao was coming to Moscow—natural enough in the circumstances. Lots for him and Stalin to talk about. On December 16, Mao arrived by train with a full entourage, accompanied by Soviet Ambassador N. V. Roshchin. Mao had come, it was said, to pay tribute to Stalin on his seventieth birthday, December 21, and for diplomatic negotiations.

Mao graced Stalin's birthday party at the Bolshoi Theater, where an old chestnut, *The Red Poppy*, had been refurbished for Mao's entertainment—a clodhopper ballet about Russian sailors helping the Chinese make their revolution, a blend of canned chauvinism and poor music, which I don't believe Mao enjoyed. Probably that was why Stalin ordered it performed.

After a few ceremonial exchanges, Mao vanished from the pages of *Pravda*. I knew the protocol of state visits. It never varied. The ceremonial greeting. The trip to the Kremlin. The talk with Stalin. The laying of a wreath at Lenin's tomb. The pro forma negotiations by underlings (the real business, of course, transacted before the guest's arrival). The evening at the Bolshoi. The visit to a factory (usually the Trigornaya Textile plant), the trip to a model collective farm near Moscow. A quick trip to Leningrad. Back to the Kremlin to sign the treaty, a Kremlin banquet, an exchange of toasts, farewell at the airport. Home after five days.

Not so for Mao. He simply vanished. There was a vague suggestion he was sightseeing in the countryside. No communiqués. No reports. *Pravda* was silent. Days passed. Finally I went out to the big Chinese embassy to see what I could find out. Nothing. The Chinese were very polite but when they found out I was an American, it was "So sorry." I left a personal letter to Mao, a request to visit the People's Republic. I went on sending letters and telegrams for twenty-three years until I got to Beijing in 1972.

Mao's visit lasted two months. One night he came to the Metropol for a formal reception, which the Chinese gave for Stalin in the grand dining room. I didn't even catch a glimpse of Mao. Negotiations went on and on. After Stalin died, Nikita Khrushchev revealed that Mao had gotten so angry because Stalin treated him like a petty petitioner that he would have broken with Russia and gone over to the American side, had it not been for our ostentatious hostility. Knowing what I know now about relations between the men since 1927, I am inclined to accept Khrushchev's story.

A treaty of friendship and mutual defense was announced St. Valentine's day, February 14, 1950, but not until after Mao had been joined on January 21, 1950, by Zhou Enlai and a complement of Chinese that included the mysterious (to me) Gao Gan. It took three weeks more to hammer out a treaty. Never before, or since, had a diplomatic visit to Russia lasted so long. I didn't know what the delay was about, but I didn't think it could reflect anything but disagreement. When the terms were announced, I was sure I was right. The treaty only slightly broadened the provisions of the existing Sino-Soviet treaty of 1945 (signed by Stalin and Chiang Kai-shek). It preserved almost all of the old Russian Imperial privileges in Manchuria—the treaty ports and the Russian-operated railroads, the colonial treaties giving Russia control of minerals and air rights (51 percent owned by the Soviets). The defense clauses were slightly broadened to become operative not only against Japanese aggression but by powers allied with Japan. A niggardly $60 million a year for five years was promised in economic aid, about what the U.S. gave each year to second-rate Latin American countries.

I put my negative comment as strongly as the censors would permit and stated them much more strongly in private letters to my colleagues, but my version was buried under a sensational report by Cyrus L. Sulzberger that "secret clauses" gave Moscow command over all Chinese armed forces and control of strategic facilities in China, and reduced Beijing to a puppet state. There was not one word of truth in Cy's report. Whether or not it was CIA disinformation, I never found out.

My view was that the agreement displayed "extreme chinchyness" by Stalin and that Mao, far from proving a Moscow puppet or Soviet agent, demonstrated that he was a head of state and his own man.

Once again I found myself in disagreement with the establishment. I was far from understanding the basics of the Stalin-Mao relationship, but I stood even further from the Acheson-Rusk-McCarthy assessment that China was Moscow's pawn.

England and France had recognized the People's Republic. We were moving in that direction, I knew, from conversations with Admiral Alan G. Kirk, our ambassador in Moscow. Acheson had polled him and other ambassadors on recognition. Kirk and most of the others favored it. I strongly agreed; delay could only push China into dependence on Stalin. I was sure the China card was ours to play if we would only play it. But Truman decided to delay until he could get a few important bills through Congress. He knew the Republicans, already toying with the war cry "The Democrats Lost China," would raise a row. It was a fatal, disastrous delay.

I went off to the United States in May 1950 on a brief leave. I was at Pyramid Lake Ranch, about sixty miles from Reno, Nevada (for the usual reason), in late June when the news came of the attack on South Korea by North Korea.

The attack was a total surprise to me and I suspect our response, Truman's decision to defend South Korea, was a surprise to Stalin. He obviously knew (although I had not noticed) Acheson's declaration at the National Press Club in Washington, D.C., January 12 and again at San Francisco March 15 that the American defense line in the Pacific ran from the Aleutians to Japan to the Ryukyus to the Philippines. He omitted any mention of Korea (or Taiwan). He did this first before Stalin signed his pact with China and repeated it after Stalin signed the pact. The inference seemed obvious: Korea is not included in the area of our defense.

I hadn't even heard of the Acheson declarations nor had anyone in Washington whom I knew. It seems to me that no one had been watching the store but Stalin.

I hurried back to Moscow as fast as I could. It was obvious that a world crisis was at hand.

I have studied the Korean episode for many years and I have evolved a theory which I cannot prove but I believe it is correct. I believe that Stalin started the Korean war to put Mao in a military nutcracker. Russia already held North Korea for practical purposes. It circled North China from its positions in Siberia and the Maritime provinces. North China and Beijing were almost in Stalin's hands. By making the deal with Gao Gan he had Mao almost surrounded.

If Stalin could put the whole Korean peninsula in Soviet control, he could squeeze Mao out like the pip from an apple.

Most Americans assumed—especially after China sent 1 million men into the war—that it was touched off by a Korean-Chinese conspiracy. I disagreed. I thought it was Stalin's doing and that his target was China, not the United States. I think he believed Acheson's twice-stated declaration putting Korea outside our defense perimeter. If Acheson was stating U.S. policy, why shouldn't Stalin take advantage of it and use North Korea as a cat's-paw to strengthen his stranglehold on China?

When, contrary to American declarations and Stalin's expectations, Truman rushed American forces to Korea, Stalin played his Machiavellian hole card—he involved China. He knew, as Americans seemed to have forgotten, that Mao had long favored close relations with the U.S.A. Stalin knew, as we didn't seem to understand, that Mao was his stubborn, implacable antagonist. What better than to inveigle China into war with the United States?

I have found much evidence to support my Korean hypothesis. The strongest has come from the Chinese. Once I got to Beijing and began to talk to high-ranking Chinese, I found that contrary to Washington commentators and my skeptical State Department friends, the Chinese were most comfortable with my thesis. They had, they said, come to the same conclusion themselves. For many reasons, they had not thought it tactful to publish their suspicions.

A Russian friend once said he thought sometimes America acted like a blindfold giant. I don't think this is entirely true, but in the case of China we went even further—we figuratively put out the eyes of our best China specialists just as, according to legend, Ivan the Terrible put out the eyes of the architects who designed St. Basil's in Red Square (so that they might not design a church so beautiful for anyone else). We blinded ourselves and by so doing stumbled into two terrible wars—Korea and Vietnam—neither of which need have been fought. We were led out of the paranoid world we created only by that most unlikely of Pied Pipers, Richard Nixon, who with the aid of Henry Kissinger, managed to get to Beijing in 1972 and put us on the right track at last.

# Chapter 29

# Who Lost China?

When Borodin returned from the failed Chinese Revolution, he was not summoned into Stalin's presence, denounced and summarily shot. He was not arrested and sent to the dread isolator at Vladimir or the Arctic Solovetsky islands from which no one returned.

He was given a sumptuous two-room suite on the third floor of the Metropol Hotel, which he occupied with his wife and two sons (one of whom was killed in World War II and one of whom joined the secret police). He sat in his suite for two years, writing and rewriting reports, waiting for Stalin to decide his fate.

It was a tricky decision for Stalin. Half the people in Moscow were calling Borodin a Trotskyite and/or a Menshevik. In a later period, Stalin would have had Borodin shot without notice. But he was a little new at the terror game, and Borodin was so much the instrument of Stalin's China policy that he decided against execution. He let Borodin sit and sit. After two years Borodin was denounced—as a fool, not as a counter revolutionary. That saved his life. He was shunted into small jobs, never again to handle anything Chinese. He was forbidden to speak of China or meet with his old China friends.

But if Borodin's career was ended in 1927, he was most fortunate. His fellow *sovetniks* (as Russia's China hands were called) began to fall by the wayside; some were arrested; even before 1930 a few were shot. It was Stalin's first tentative purge of his China men. Soon he would make Joseph McCarthy look like a pantywaist.

As I ultimately discovered, Stalin purged his China experts three times (and there was a post-Stalin purge in the early 1960s). Why should Stalin do this? Because Russia, thanks to its perfidious experts, had "lost China" three times. Let me repeat for emphasis: Russia had "lost" China three times, and Stalin put the blame on the China hands.

But wait a minute. Something must be wrong. We Americans "lost China." That was what McCarthyism was all about. Didn't Joseph McCarthy present a list of "Communists" in the State Department?

Didn't he blame them and the wimpy Democrats like Truman and Acheson for losing China to Russia? Wasn't that it?

What was going on here—Russia was losing China to whom? To us, of course. And we were losing China to whom? To Russia, of course.

If only I had known what I now know, what I uncovered not in China, not in Russia, but by scratching my fingernails to the bone, digging through old documents, American and Soviet—obscure references in long forgotten or unread Soviet scholarly journals, tracking down the biographies of Soviet men and women who worked in China with Borodin in the 1920s, seeking out the fate of those (many of them survivors of 1927) who were sent back by Stalin in the mid-1930s to help Chiang Kai-shek. (Stalin had a stunning respect for the Generalissimo who had killed so many Chinese Communists—was that one reason?) And then ferreting out the survivors of the 1930s, the ones who lived to be executed or exiled or imprisoned in the 1940s.

When earlier I called Stalin's China policy a Grand Guignol, that was an understatment. It was Lewis Carroll's *Through the Looking Glass*, the mirror image effect. We saw Russia doing what Russia saw us doing. Rashomon? Yes, in a sense but a Rashomon viewed through a prism.

We destroyed our incomparable corps of Old China Hands, men and women, most of them of China background, born there, sons and daughters of missionaries or Standard Oil families, scholars with the Chinese language and decades of firsthand experience, military men who knew the China battlefields, the Chinese generals, and the Chinese fighting men. It was a savage loss. We drove them out of government (in legal battles, many over the years got back their posts): careers and families were wrecked; there were suicides; a handful sought refuge abroad; character and work was vilified. But no American victim of McCarthy suffered as badly as did Anna Louise at the hands of Stalin. No American was imprisoned or sent to a labor camp for the "loss of China"; no American was shot or died under circumstances still unknown.

I do not suggest that Stalin's conduct should be seen as a standard against which to match our own venal and self-damaging idiocy. But when Stalin purged, it was permanent. No wasting time on legal niceties. No appeals.

339

Physical reprisals in Russia after the 1927 failure were not great. A handful of Red Army men were cashiered and a few were shot, probably on charges of being Trotskyites. Among civilians the damage was greater. Borodin was not the only expert to be detached from China. There was a vast shake-up among Far Eastern specialists of the Comintern. This had much to do with Stalin's feud with Trotsky. Trotsky men had run the University of Toilers of the East, where Chinese and Russian specialists were trained. There was a wholesale purge. None of the Comintern's Far Eastern team survived. All were replaced at the direction of a young Ukranian hothead named Pavel Mif, Stalin's new point man for China, taking over Borodin's responsibilites. Out of this shake-up came the naïve "twenty-six and a half Bolsheviks," the young Moscow-trained Chinese (the "half" was for a very small young man) who were sent back to wrest the Party from the hands of Mao. They came close to destroying the whole movement.

As far as I have been able to establish, the Chinese revolutionaries, while grateful, in general, for Russian help, never thought of themselves, as Stalin and McCarthy did, as "belonging to Moscow."

Russia's second "loss of China" was vicious. It accompanied Stalin's violent purges of the late 1930s. Down went a forest of major figures: Marshal Vasily K. Blyukher, Borodin's military counterpart, by then Soviet Far Eastern commander, General A. I. Cherepanov, General Albert Ivanovich Lapin, Blyukher's deputy, Vitovt K. Putna, later Soviet military attaché in London. Colonel Georgy B. Skalov (Sinani), an early victim, was shot in 1935. The list goes on and on and on. In 1938 Stalin purged his whole Far East command, taking the lives of Generals Shtern and Yegorov and scores of officers who had served in China. Many of the officers were two termers. They had been sent out in the early 1920s to help the Communists and were brought home after 1927. Then, with the united front against Japan of 1936–37, Stalin sent back to Chiang Kai-shek the survivors of the first tour and many more.

This second wave suffered severely. Just as Stalin wiped out most of the officers and advisers he sent to the Spanish Loyalists, so he took the lives of the military men who knew (and in many cases loved) China.

Of course, he did not halt with the military. He wiped out the whole cadre of early Bolsheviks connected with China, diplomats and Comintern men: Lev Karakhan, one-time Soviet foreign minister who preceded Borodin to China, Grigory Voitinsky (he preserved his life but not his responsibilities), Sergei Tretyakov whose crime was to write the famous revolutionary play *Roar China*, N. V. Kuibyshev, chief Soviet adviser for all of South China and brother of the Soviet President, V. V. Kuibyshev, and, improbably, Mira Sakhnovskaya, the only woman graduate of the Frunze Military Academy, who bore two children during her China service. Even Pavel Mif, Stalin's fair-haired China expert, went down the drain.

There is no need to reel off name after name. Most can now be found in the memoirs of Madame Vishnaykova-Akimova, whose husband was a military adviser, she a twenty-year-old interpreter; they were married in China. She wrote of her colleagues: "Few of them survived the repressions of 1937–38. The war finished off the others."

Russia's greatest loss was in expertise. McCarthy put a chill on American China studies (academics warned young students against specializing in China; the odds of harassment were too high). Stalin went further. He obliterated not only the China Hands but China itself. I mean he literally stamped out the word "China." The blackout on news of the Chinese Red Army's triumphant progress across China was typical. For years *everything* about China was suppressed. Nothing appeared in the newspapers. Books dried up. Scientific articles disappeared. Scholarly work vanished.

A surviving Soviet Sinologist G. Y. Efimov recalled that political conditions in the 1930s became "so unfavourable" that not one doctor's dissertation in Chinese history was defended until 1953 (the year of Stalin's death). Scholarly studies were simply adjourned. Not one study on Chinese history (ancient or contemporary) was published between 1941 and 1948. Many works completed in the 1930s and early 1940s did not see print until the late 1950s and early 1960s, long after their authors had died in prison or concentration camps. China vanished from Stalin's world. If "China" was uttered aloud or put on paper, the act could be punished by imprisonment or exile.

During Stalin's confrontation with Yugoslavia in 1948, he had exclaimed: "I can snap my finger, and Tito will disappear!" Tito did not vanish. He outlived Stalin by many years. His was the first Communist country to declare its independence from Moscow. Nor could Stalin make China vanish from the globe. But he could make it vanish from the Soviet Union just as he had "vanished" Mao from *Pravda* during his two-month stay in December 1949–February 1950.

I have examined a bibliography of Soviet scholarly works on China, compiled by N. V. Nikoferov. It lists 982 books, articles, and monographs published on what he calls "China problems" in the Soviet era. Eliminating works by Marx, Engels, and Lenin and those published before 1920 I counted these totals:

| | |
|---|---|
| 1920–29 | 303 |
| 1930–39 | 177 |
| 1940–49 | 73 |
| 1950–59 | 92 |
| 1960–69 | 183 |

If you break down the decade of the 1930s you find that almost all the articles appeared in the four prepurge years. For 1937, 1938, 1939 only nineteen articles appeared. Materials on contemporary Chinese affairs vanished. Nothing on the Chinese Party or the Chinese Red Army. Not one scholarly article appeared betweeen 1944 and 1949.

Twenty years after Stalin's death, serious Soviet studies in the China field still limped badly. To compile the extraordinary necrology presented by Madame Vishnayakova-Akimova, her memorial to the lost generation of Soviet Sinologists, required the effort of most of the handful of surviving Soviet experts.

Why did we not see what was happening? How could we have been so negligent and, let's be honest, so stupid?

In part we had inflicted comparable wounds on ourselves. When the State Department finally accepted my findings of 1959, the Sino-Soviet split, based on my observations in Outer Mongolia followed by the open polemics between China and the Soviet Union, Kruschchev's withdrawal of experts from China, and the rest, it decided to inventory its resources, to see how many specialists were competent in both Soviet and Chinese affairs. The survey didn't take long. It produced three names. Two were middle-ranking officers whom I knew, both were basically China experts (ex-missionary brats). Both had been posted to Moscow to get them out of the line of fire, to protect them from McCarthy's offensive against China Hands. Both had learned Russian in Moscow. Neither was now serving in the Russia or China fields. The other man was a beginner. He'd had a duty tour in Moscow and now was studying Chinese at the University of Washington.

I thought to myself, when one of my State Department friends told me of this, How can any government with an atom of concern for national security, with even a primitive notion of responsibility, permit such dangerous ignorance? If one gunboat in the Navy went out of commission, the admirals would clank into Congress and demand six replacements. Here we were, sailing blindfold in a world so tiny that the slightest twinge in Eurasia could mean life or death—and we were careering grandly down the path of simpering idiocy—the President didn't know and didn't care, the Congress hadn't a clue, and the public was glued to the tube, anchored to the Superbowl and beer. Well . . . what can I add?

I know that in these pages I sound like a know-it-all, a Cassandra forever finding things out, making shrewd deductions, breaking the secret enigmas, exposing the daze and laze of the Government. I know that there are fine minds in the State Department, in the Pentagon, and in the analytic sections of the CIA, particularly on the Soviet Union (I am not so impressed with their China work).

For years the U.S. consul-general at Hong Kong comprised the best group of China analysts in the world. True, when Charlotte and I paused in Hong Kong in the spring of 1966 on our orbit of China, the Cultural Revolution already underway for four or five months, the specialists still had not figured it out. They knew it was big, but they had no coherent idea what was going on. I condone that. They were working like spit, but half of the jigsaw was missing. I met many Chinese in the years that followed who were just as baffled.

But on the question of relations between China and Russia, between the two great Communist empires, it seems to me that we continually and habitually lag behind our necessity.

One reason is that the Kremlinologist approaches the problem with a Soviet bias. No, he does not take the Soviet view, but he comes close to taking the "Russian" side. The Sinologist comes in with his Chinese bias. They can't get their heads on right.

That's one reason why I have kept hammering away on the Sino-Soviet question. I spent two or three years collecting the information on "Stalin's loss of China" before I finally published my conclusions in 1971. The symmetry of Stalin's and McCarthy's "loss of China" was so delicious, the ignorance so colossal, the implications so profound I still can hardly believe it.

But I am not so naïve as to suppose that my single article in *The*

*New York Times* jolted American public opinion or the think tanks, governmental and academic, which try to monitor such questions.

As for Presidents and secretaries of state—forget it! They are too busy and/or too ignorant even to understand when they don't know something or to evaluate the quality of information their staffs feed them.

Not much has changed since George Kennan's classic study in *Russia Leaves the War*, his analysis of how the United States reacted to the Bolshevik takeover in Russia in 1917 and the Brest-Litovsk treaty by which Lenin and Trotsky took Russia out of World War I. Kennan demonstrated that not one American decision was based on real knowledge of the situation by Woodrow Wilson or his secretary of state, Robert Lansing. Every American act flowed from some seat-of-the-pants intuition unsupported by accurate information; every dispatch the U.S. received from Minister Francis in Petrograd, a genial St. Louis businessman who relied on his intelligent black valet for 95 percent of what he knew of the Russian Revolution (the valet got it from fellow valets and cooks) was baseless, distorted rumor, gossip or nonsense. Wilson and Lansing paid little heed to the reports and did what they thought was best, acting out of personal ignorance and prejudice.

Kennan's work is based on high precision research. No doubt in my mind that similar research would find that most major decisions today are based on the same flimsy foundations, no matter how many billions we spend for NSA, CIA, DIA, and other secret alphabetical agencies, and—as I hope these pages reveal—this did not start with Ronald Reagan, his "evil empire," and the Contras. It went forward under Eisenhower, Kennedy, Johnson and Nixon. What a President thinks he knows when he enters the White House has always taken priority over the real world.

I don't believe that kind of government is good enough. It is terrifying in an age when communications are measured in millionths of a second, when satellites bring to us any part of the world live and in color, and electronic gear lets us hear a click when a cat knocks Gorbachev's telephone off the hook, a click when a Soviet sergeant enters his missile silo, a click when the oxygen tank is turned on at the bedside of a dying statesman, a click when a Middle Eastern general phones his mistress.

But politicians are too lazy or ignorant or prejudiced, and the public doesn't know what it doesn't know. Or what its President doesn't know. No number of exposés seems to drive the lesson home.

As I have said, I figured out that there was bad trouble between Russia and China sitting in my bugged interior courtyard Room 393 at the Metropol. I put together the intricate history of Stalin's effort to wipe the name of China off the Russian map, sitting in my study in Taconic, Connecticut. If I could do this, I think our intelligence community could do it better, do it quicker, comprehend it more deeply and even—this is the hard part—get the message over to the White House.

Why could reality about Russia and China sail past us in the 1940s, 1950s, and 1960s? Part of the answer can be found on our side of the mirror image. Stalin had put out his China eyes and waved China out of existence. We had not gone that far, but if you calculate that we turned our backs on John Carter Vincent, John S. Service, John Paton Davies, Jr., O. Edmund Clubb, John Melby, Colonel David Barrett (a classic case: denied his brigadier's star because of his magnificent reports on Communist China, branded a spy and vilified by the Communists, refused permission to retire to Taiwan by the Nationalists—a three-way loser, but not so big a loser as his own country, deprived of his unique insights), John Emmerson (perhaps the only Foreign Service officer with credentials to China, Russia, Japan), Ray Ludden, Arthur Ringwalt. No need to mention all the names. You cannot fire your first team, obliterate your second team, and forbid the formation of a third string without paying a price.

We paid that price, venting our anger on the men who brought (what some in the U.S. considered to be) the bad news. As the Luddites of nineteenth century England smashed the new steam engines with their hammers and crowbars to halt the advance of the machine age, so we destroyed the men who stood on the tall hills, spied out the land, and told us years in advance that Mao Zedong and his Red China was coming. By destroying our Old China Hands we did not halt for one day the advance of Mao and Communist China. Nor did Stalin halt the creation of the People's Republic by wiping the word "China" out of the Russian language.

One reason why we were so blind to the reality of Russia and China was that, like Stalin, we put out the eyes and ripped out the tongues of the men who could have raised the alarm. Stalin achieved the silence of the graveyard. We stuffed our fingers in our ears and put gags over the mouths of the men who told the truth.

When I returned to New York from my first trip to China in 1972, my telephone rang almost immediately. A Soviet diplomat wanted to lunch with me. He was, I discovered, a survivor, one of Moscow's China hands. He had been posted to Beijing for several years, knew the Chinese language and had served in China during the Cultural Revolution.

I was not entirely surprised at the call. I knew the Russians were famished for information about China. They had, by the legacy of Stalin's dementia, found themselves in the 1960s with virtually no experts on China, no decent research, no means of knowing what was happening inside the country which had begun to loom more real than Stalin could have imagined.

The Soviets had nothing like the China studies at Harvard, Columbia, Yale, California, and Stanford, which had survived McCarthy's worst and gradually begun a recovery. Nor had Moscow created anything like the Hong Kong consulate-general and its remarkable research and intelligence potential.

What to do? As I had long known, the Russians were barred from Hong Kong. The British, with an eye to the great mainland just behind them, did not permit Soviet citizens entry. In this critical situation Soviet freighters began to "break down" just off Hong Kong Harbor. They were, of course, permitted to enter for emergency repairs. When they dropped anchor, a crew member or two—who "by chance" happened to be Soviet specialists on China—slipped off for shore leave and contacted every China watcher they could find. In the few hours they were permitted ashore, they bought Chinese-language newspapers (both Nationalist and Communist), talked to as many experts as they could, then boarded launches back to the freighters and were off.

With the Nixon opening to China, Soviet China specialists turned up on the roster of the U.N. mission in New York and the Washington embassy. They pumped every American correspondent and traveler back from China. They began to invite American scholars to lecture in Moscow. The hunger for information about China was insatiable.

It was heightened, as I learned, by a new minipurge. When Sino-Soviet relations got worse in the 1960s a security drive, once again, was launched against China specialists and scholarly institutes. Once again the institutes were closed. Professors no longer were permitted access to current literature. Periodicals were not even delivered. The whole academic apparatus was put on hold. No physical reprisals this time, no one, as far as I could learn, put under house arrest, but research on China ground to a halt.

Some academics, famished for the bread of their trade, made visits to Prague and Warsaw to use their libraries (not affected by the minipurge).

The security campaign relaxed after a few months. Someone in the Kremlin suddenly realized that, in a time of crisis, more—not less—information was needed about China. Gradually with the slowness characteristic of a creaky bureaucracy, the institutes got going again, word was circulated to the specialists to collect every scrap of data possible. Teams of experts began to seek invitations to meet with their counterparts in the West.

But the minipurge was a significant event. It told me again what I had long understood—in time of crisis, a bureaucracy reacts in panic; it puts blinkers on its eyes when it should be reaching for a telescope. The first instinct is against those who know most about the potential enemy. They are seen not as resources, but as a nest of possible spies.

In 1972, Stalin had been dead for nineteen years, but his spirit lived on in the headquarters of the Party on Tsentralnaya Ploshchad and up the hill in the Lubyanka, where the secret police still have their headquarters. Their first instinctive move was against the men who might once again "lose China." Only after that could the Kremlin turn to the problem of how to cope with its great rival to the East. It was in the idiom of a great Russian scientist a true Pavlovian response.

## Chapter 30

# War Between Russia and China

I was brought up in the tradition of the scoop. The scoop was dinned into my head by my first city editors, Leslie M. Harkness and Bill Mason, an old Hearst man, on the *Minneapolis Journal*. The scoop was exhalted into a cult by the United Press. First was not only best, it was everything. UP was built on this philosophy: first on the story; first, if even by seconds or minutes, but first.

This was an absolute, and it was the only way the United Press, a shirt-sleeve news agency fighting the mighty Associated Press, could survive. UP didn't have money, didn't have experience, didn't have manpower. What it had was a corps of excitable, underfed, underpaid, lean youngsters who could run faster, think quicker, and write more speedily than anyone. No time for second thoughts. No depth. Just get the story onto the wire a hair's breadth ahead of the stuffy AP, and write it in machine-gun bursts of bullet words—a one-sentence lead paragraph and no sentence over ten words. We were trained to be the toughest, fastest competitors. No money but quick warm praise, a band of brothers.

Our obsession with First was just shrewd commercial instinct. If UP's teletype chattered out the story first, the chances were a newspaper's telegraph editor would send it to the composing room, and it would be on its way into type before AP waddled in.

Of course, being first is a cliché of reporting. Its roots go back to the Pony Express and before. The first messenger to bring the news of Napoleon's defeat carried the power of wealth or bankruptcy in his pouch. The first great news agency was founded by Julius von Reuter to transmit commercial information by pigeon post between Aachen and Verviers, Belgium. The House of Rothschild prospered because its network of informers was bigger and swifter than its competitors'.

There was no way I could enjoy missing a First on China. I had, I thought, positioned myself well to beat the field. True, I was not an

Old China Hand. I did not have the advantage of long close connections, which so many correspondents had woven before World War II and during the war in the caves of Yan'an and the bomb shelters of Chongqing. I did not have the Chinese language. I was, let's face it, a Johnny-come-lately.

But I had built up assets in the long years when China was closed as an oyster to the West, when China was a forgotten story and no one was paying attention. I had worked like a coolie, studying the country from the outside, developing my contacts and establishing a presence for myself. By 1971 I had spent twelve years working on China from that moment of Nadam, July 11, 1959, when I climbed the staircase of the Government Palace in Ulan Bator and found the Russians lined up on one side, the Chinese on the other. From that time forward, I had carried on my campaign month by month, year in, year out, with as much originality and perseverance as I could muster.

All this reached a crescendo in 1969. That was the year Charlotte and I made our second trip to Mongolia (the fourth for me). That was the year Soviet-Chinese tensions hit a peak, and this, of course, was why we were visiting Ulan Bator again. Why the United States had not established diplomatic relations with Mongolia I did not understand and do not to this day. I had strongly raised the question with the State Department in 1959. It seemed so obviously in our interest, and there were those in the department who agreed that Ulan Bator was a listening post par excellence on the Sino-Soviet scene. The department even assigned two young officers to learn Mongolian, but years went by and nothing happened. Not until 1987 did we agree to exchange diplomats. Every major country had long recognized Mongolia. Not us. This stupidity (there is no other word for it) is exceptional in the catalog of American diplomacy. At first it was explained that we could not do it, because it would anger Chiang Kai-shek. Later, it was claimed we could not do it because we would offend Beijing which, of course, had long had its own diplomatic ties to Mongolia. The real answer may be buried in inertia and possibly the veto of some individual with unfathomable personal resentments. It's a real puzzle.

Our trip to Ulan Bator in 1969 proved a ten-strike. The border fighting had begun between China and Russia in the winter and seemed to be escalating. In Hong Kong on our way to Ulan Bator, we had seen Chinese newsreels of the fighting on the Ussuri and the Amur. The Chinese had attacked Soviet positions on the Ussuri islands in heavy snow and white camouflage uniforms. They destroyed Russian tanks, armored troop carriers, and artillery posts. It looked like large-scale warfare. On the Amur, Chinese in rowboats and launches sallied out against Russian gunboats. The Russians, grins visible in the pictures, turned high pressure water hoses on the Chinese, but the Chinese had the last laugh. They clambered aboard and cut the hoses with axes. The Chinese audience in Hong Kong cheered and leaped to their feet.

The casualties in this were not small. I heard that they ran into hundreds and thousands and that one Soviet division had been badly cut up.

The propaganda between the countries escalated. The Chinese called the Russians the "New Czars." Moscow called Mao "an Asian Hitler." Each contended the other had abandoned Communism and embraced Capitalism. Moscow claimed Mao had never read Marx. Beijing said Moscow's god was Wall Street.

As our plane touched down on the familiar Ulan Bator airfield, I was astonished to see a squadron of Soviet advanced MIG fighters parked at the edge. A Soviet military transport came in as we gathered our luggage. Soviet Army trucks loaded with troops and supplies passed us on the aspen-lined asphalt road into Ulan Bator.

In the days that followed, we traveled widely. Never before had I seen the *purga*, the duststorm of the Gobi, great brown clouds that smeared a dirty scum over the sky, reaching to the horizon. There was dust between our teeth. A gauze nose bandage did not keep it out of Charlotte's lungs. At night we hardly dared open windows. Just a crack let in three or four inches of dust. The whole Gobi was blowing off to north China, the grass steppes ravaged by Russian plows.

But it was not the dust that captured my attention. It was the Soviet army. It was everywhere. Here they were rushing to build a *voenny gorodok*, a military encampment, a permanent camp with wooden houses (the lumber must have been brought from Siberia), there an air strip on the flat steppe. Along the roads technicians were installing complex equipment in cement chambers buried in hillsides facing away from China. I had never seen such equipment, but I knew it must relate to an advanced weapons system. (When I got back to the U.S.A., I telephoned the CIA and said that if they would tell me what the equipment was, I would tell them where I saw it. They refused, so I called a friend at the Defense Department who readily explained: It was high-tech transmission relays, for use, he felt certain, with nuclear missile installations.)

Diplomats in Ulan Bator told me the buildup had been begun during the winter in such a hurry and in such numbers there could be no concealment. Travel south to the Gobi was interdicted. Everywhere the diplomats went, they found the Soviet military, airfields being built, barracks complexes, the streets of Ulan Bator roaring with military trucks and tanks. "They are getting ready for war," one diplomat said. So it seemed to me. This was not a Potemkin show, a show to frighten the Chinese. This was for real. No disagreement among the diplomats about that. When I got back to Moscow, I found plenty of support. The Soviet military were, I learned, advocating a "surgical blow" against China, a calculated nuclear strike to "take out a few Chinese cities" including Beijing. Better strike now, they said, before the Chinese get too strong. It reminded me of what some U.S. generals were saying about Russia at the end of World War II.

War was in the wind. Of this I was certain by the time I got back to New York. It well might break out at any time. The fighting on the Amur and the Ussuri was followed by fighting on the Xinjiang-Kazakhstan border. By this time I was at work writing a short book about the background of the Russia-China conflict, the ancient national enmity, going back to the earliest contacts of the two powers along the Amur River in the summer of 1650, at a small settlement called Albasin. Neither side had any notion of the identity of the warriors it was fighting: The Chinese had never heard of Russia; the Russians had no idea this was an outpost of the new Manchu dynasty of China.

I traced the hostility between the empires, recalled the unequal treaties imposed on China through the nineteenth century, under which she was compelled to cede to Russia possibly 1.5 million square miles of territory—the emirates of central Asia, the Maritime Provinces, much of Siberia east of Lake Baikal, and Mongolia. I explained the conflict of the two Communist parties and of Stalin and Mao (I didn't know much about the early rows of the 1920s and 1930s). I offered my hypothesis of the double-dealing by which Stalin maneuvered the Chinese into war with the United States in Korea.

351

And I recited the steady rise of hostility in the decade since the 1959 break between Khrushchev and Mao. It was succint, concise and complete. I proposed to call the book *The Coming War Between Russia and China*. My editor, Evan Thomas, was so alarmed by what I wrote he feared that war might break out before he could get the book into print. He changed the title to *War Between Russia and China*. The more phlegmatic British brought it out under the original title. Breaking every rule known to the publishing industry, Thomas managed to get the book out by mid-October 1969.

By that time, as is now evident, the peak of the crisis was passing. Ho Chi Minh had died September 3, 1969. The chiefs of the Communist world gathered at Hanoi for the funeral. With border fighting escalating, Moscow had sent a circular telegram to the Communist countries of Eastern Europe and the big parties of France and Italy, warning that the situation might lead to war. The Chinese were feverishly building air raid shelters under their big cities. They knew they had no defense against the nuclear weapons Moscow had targeted on the main Chinese cities. The whole population, school-children and all, was thrown into the task. The lovely old city walls of Beijing were tumbled down and the stones used to hold up the shelters. When I finally got to Beijing in 1972, stacks of stones and steel reinforcing rods lined the streets, shelter building was still going on. We were taken to the busy shopping center, and there, from a trapdoor in the rear of a dress-goods shop, entered the labyrinth of the multilayered shelter system, complete with electricity, power plants, water supply, hospitals, workshops, dormitories, and factories. We saw a shelter at Huhehot in Inner Mongolia big enough for trucks and buses to drive miles under the city to deep mountain caverns, blasted from granite, far outside. (I still doubt that many would have survived a Soviet strike.) The Chinese had zeroed their own nuclear missiles on industrial cities in the Urals and Siberia. Their rockets could not yet reach European Russia.

The moment I heard of Ho's death, I cabled Pham Van Dong for permission to come to Hanoi. I got no reply. Several months later I learned from Marc Ribou, the French photographer who had hap-pened to be in Hanoi at the time, that the Vietnamese had cabled me to come but, alas, the cable must have gone astray.

At Ho's funeral the Communist leaders called on Moscow to make one more effort to avert war with China. Zhou Enlai had deliberately left Hanoi before the Russians could arrive. Now Kosygin cabled Beijing asking permission to fly there and meet with Zhou. The Chinese response was delayed (deliberately?) until Kosygin was airborne on his flight back to Moscow. The message, however, was forwarded, and he received it at a refuelling halt at Tashkent. He switched plans and flew 2,500 miles east to Beijing and met Zhou in the lounge of Beijing airport.

By this time the Russians had massed a million or more troops on the China frontier, including crack armored divisions, missile forces, and their most advanced air elements. They were poised to strike. The Chinese probably had close to 2 million on the frontier. Their equipment was far inferior. Their hope was to make up in manpower what they lacked in metal.

Zhou and Kosygin talked for six hours. They did not leave the airport. They agreed to engage in diplomatic talks to attempt to resolve the border disputes. The talks were to open in late October. It was, in essence, a standstill agreement for one last effort to avert war. When the Russians and Chinese met in late October, they agreed on only one thing—to meet again. They could not even agree upon an agenda. The meetings would continue intermittently for the next twenty years—they were still in progress in 1987. No agenda had yet been agreed upon. For two decades nothing happened.

I took a sardonic satisfaction in these endless, frustrating conversations and the frozen faces which the Chinese brought to the conference table. Leonid F. Ilyichev had been named chief Soviet negotiator. For years he was put through a devastatingly rigid diplomatic experience. It was cruel and inhuman, but I thought he deserved it. He had been editor of *Pravda* before Stalin's death and then was shifted to head the Soviet Press group under Khruschev. He and I had become enemies. He, it was, who had barred me from Moscow for many years. He had sworn that I would never set foot on Soviet soil. It seemed to me fitting that he be subjected to the Kafkaesque trauma of meeting again and again with Chinese diplomats who never smiled, never spoke an unnecessary word, and never budged from their position during the sixteen years in which he was compelled to meet with them.

The war between Russia and China did not come to pass, but long before I arrived in Beijing, my book, as I was to discover, had made its way there, had been translated, read by Zhou Enlai and the highest government circles, probably including Mao himself, and had been made compulsory reading for everyone in the Foreign Office. The first hint I had of this came from Scotty Reston, who got to Beijing in July of 1971 simultaneously (although he did not know it) with his friend Henry Kissinger, who had slipped into China secretly via Pakistan in the first move of President Nixon's "opening." Zhou told Scotty that he and others had read my book and found it good.

What Zhou did not tell Scotty—and what I later learned from Qiao Guanhua, China's foreign minister who later fell from grace for casting his lot with Mao's widow, Jiang Qing—was that my book had become the subject of dispute between the Russians and the Chinese.

Objective as *War Between Russia and China* was, in my opinion, the Russians disliked it as much as the Chinese liked it. At a session of the Sino-Soviet border meetings in 1970, Soviet Deputy Foreign Minister Vasily Kuznetsov marched into the conference with a copy of *War Between Russia and China* tucked under his arm. He slammed it on the table and charged that it was a cooked-up work of propaganda, a provocation that the Chinese had put me up to. Delightedly, Qiao Guanhua told me, the Chinese assured the Russians they had nothing to do with the book, had never met me, but thought I had done an excellent and objective job.

After I came back to the United States from China in 1972, I chanced to mention to a Soviet diplomat that I was interested to know that my book had become the subject of a dispute between Moscow and Beijing.

"Who told you that?" the man said angrily.

"Well," I responded, "I heard that in Beijing."

"Oh," said the Russian, "I thought that must be the case. The Chinese have done it again. They have broken their word. We have an agreement that neither side will say a word about what happens in our talks. Now the Chinese have been talking. It's typical of them. You can't trust them."

So it is possible, I suppose, that Zhou Enlai was speaking the plain truth when he said I had lost my chance to be No. 1 into Beijing, because the Chinese thought that my notoriety with the Russians would put another drop of vinegar into an already high acid mixture.

But I think the situation more complex. The final dash to Beijing was touched off by the Ping-Pong Championship in Tokyo in April 1971. When the Chinese won the championship, most of the teams asked if they might visit Beijing. Zhou Enlai put the matter to Mao

Zedong. Zhou—so he told me—didn't think much of the idea. Mao did. He said: Why not? Then he wanted to know about the Americans. The Americans hadn't asked for a trip. Mao said, never mind, get hold of them. Let them come too. Which they did, and when that news became public, half the reporters in the United States (myself included) cabled Beijing seeking permission to come to China.

Once again Zhou bundled up the requests and went to Mao. Once again Zhou, or so he said, was negative on the idea. But Mao overruled him. Let them come, Mao said. Give permission to some of them.

In reality, it is easy to see now, Mao—and I have no doubt Zhou— were opening the way toward relations with the United States. Mao had hinted at this to Edgar Snow in the fall of 1970. He had said that President Nixon was welcome to come to China for a vacation—a phrase that had not escaped the notice of Mr. Nixon and Henry Kissinger. I am sorry to say that the *Times* did not carry Snow's interview, after a squabble supposedly over the sky-high price demanded by Ed's Paris agent. I say "supposedly" because at one point, Ed offered to let the *Times* print the Mao interview for free. It was a document of world importance, but the text was ultimately run only in *The New Republic*.

So—despite Zhou Enlai's disclaimers—I think that the Chinese were carefully orchestrating signals to the White House that it was time for a change.

When Mao gave Zhou the go-ahead (and this comes from Zhou himself), he decided that the first wave would be Old China Hands, men and women who knew China, who had been there in the 1930s and through the war years, and whom Zhou knew personally. Telegrams went out to a handful of them including Jack Belden, once a *Time-Life* man, long since ill and retired in Paris, and Tillman Durdin and his wife, Peggy, of *The New York Times*. The Durdins had become ardent supporters of Chiang Kai-shek and the Nationalists and violent critics of the Communists. Never mind, said Zhou: Find Till Durdin. I want him and Peggy in the first group to come to Beijing. This was not easy. Durdin was finally located in Sri Lanka. He and Peggy did, indeed, join the first wave, although because of Peggy's illness, their stay in China was cut short. Belden made it, but wound up with three months in a Beijing hospital.

Till got into China April 15 and was followed by a small covey of

*Times* people. Audrey Topping, wife of Seymour, foreign editor of the *Times,* arrived in China ten days later with her father, Chester Ronning, born in China of a missionary family, an old friend of Zhou Enlai and former Canadian ambassador. In a couple of weeks Audrey's husband, Seymour, joined the party at Zhou's invitation.

Then it was decided, probably by Zhou, that there should be a second wave—not of old-timers but of new men, men of influence, columnists and/or editors. First, Joseph Alsop was considered. He was an Old China Hand, in a sense, having been in China during World War II on the staff of General Claire Chennault. He was a distinguished columnist, had a wide following, but he had become so violently anti-Communist and pro-Chiang that his name was put aside for that of James Reston, who had equal distinction as a columnist for *The New York Times* and, so far as was known in Beijing, a reasonably objective point of view. That was how Reston came to get the nod, I was told by the Chinese.

So it turned out that I became a tortoise and not a hare on China.

# Chapter 31

# The Long March

In the winter of 1972 Charlotte and I made plans to visit Italy. Charlotte had lived there for a while, and she wanted to introduce me to the Renaissance. Then I got the letter from Moscow on March 20, and everything changed. The North Koreans were inviting me to come to Pyongyang.

My interest in Korea, north or south, I confess, was not intense. We had visited Seoul in 1966, and Charlotte had suffered a stomach upset so severe I feared for her life. It was over in a few days but left an aftershock. Neither of us was in a mood to trade Leonardo for heroic statues of Kim Il-sung, the North Korean dictator.

But there was a catch. To get to North Korea I would have to transit China, and at this late date I had not yet managed to get to Beijing. In fact, the invitation to North Korea was the product of a convoluted strategy I had initiated in 1970 about the time I launched the Op-Ed page of the *Times*. I had become convinced that my sometime hero, sometime nemesis, Abe Rosenthal, had decided to get a correspondent other than me—anyone would do—into China before I got there. Today this may seem a paranoid notion, but at the time I believed it might be true. So, in my usual contrary fashion, I decided to try the back door to Beijing—via Pyongyang.

Of course, North Korea had been on my shopping list for a good many years, but now I began to forward hand-carried messages to Pyongyang, reminding Kim Il-sung of my deep interest in North Korea, especially now that, as it seemed, the glaciated texture of Communist Asia was beginning to thaw a bit. I subjected him to the usual barrage of cables, renewing a campaign I had carried on at intervals since 1961 or even before.

So when one morning I found on my desk an invitation to Korea, postmarked Moscow and signed by the North Korean Journalists Association, Charlotte and I set about rearranging our lives. Whether I could turn the two-bagger (Pyongyang) into a homer (Beijing), I did not know, but I would give it a college try. Charlotte went off to Italy

357

with her daughter, Charlotte, and I stayed behind to negotiate with the Koreans and the Chinese.

May 1, 1972, found me aboard Northwest Airlines Flight 3 to Anchorage and Tokyo, Charlotte in Italy with her Charlotte, and my mind pounding with unanswered questions. Could I get a transit visa through China to North Korea, or would I have to go by way of Moscow? Would the Russians, who had been remarkably hostile to the ideas of visas for me in recent years, give me one if the Chinese wouldn't? Would the Chinese let Charlotte and me make a reporting trip in China after Pyongyang? If they wouldn't, could I go back to Vietnam (Nixon had just escalated the war again)? Could I, if all else failed, go back to Mongolia for a new look? (Tsedenbal quickly said no.)

I had mixed feelings, I noted in my diary, as we flew northwest following the still frozen Mackenzie River. I was meeting John Lee, the *Times* correspondent in Tokyo, who would accompany me. There had already been publicity in the Japanese (and some European) papers, and my trip was being taken as having an important diplomatic significance—which, I supposed it had, although exactly what that significance might be I did not know. There had not been an American reporter in North Korea since World War II (except for the war correspondents who accompanied MacArthur in the swift American drive to the Yalu river followed by the even swifter American retreat when Mao sent 1 million Chinese "volunteers" over the border). As far as I could discover there had been no U.S. or western non-Communist correspondents in North Korea since the 1930s. The Japanese had kept the area tightly sealed. So, if nothing went wrong, the trip would be another "first" for me, another hermit kingdom penetrated, a good and important story, but, as I noted, "not a great consolation prize for the loss of being first in China—but a nice one, an interesting one," and I should at least get a glimpse of China even if I didn't win permission for a real look. The permit for Korea was, I knew, a tail to the opening up of China. If Nixon could go to China, well then, I could go to North Korea.

I thought of the many times I had set out on missions like this, how many times I had sat in the plane, taken out my notebook, and tried to pull my thoughts together and figure out what it really meant to me. I had been doing this since 1942 when I flew to England in the marvelous old flying boat with the built-in bunks and lounge and white-jacketed stewards, fine steaks, very dry martinis, vintage wines, and overnight stops at Bermuda, the Azores, and Lisbon. In those days I was an excited youngster off to the great adventure of my generation—the War. Now another kind of war, Vietnam, was still in progress. "It is the bitterest taste of my life," I wrote, "on, on, on, in spite of all we do."

A North Korean delegation met me at Tokyo airport with a great bouquet of red carnations—there would be red carnations all along the route to Pyongyang. I got to the Okura Hotel about midnight. Hardly had I dropped off when David Schneiderman, my assistant at Op-Ed, called from New York. Mr Kao of the Chinese embassy in Ottawa wanted to talk to me. In ten minutes I had him on the line. I noted: "The jackpot! Chinese transit visas for John Lee and myself and a trip through China for Charlotte and me when I return from Pyongyang. Now the trip begins to have a real purpose."

Next day I telephoned New York and caught Charlotte as she walked into our house at 349 East 84th Street from Italy. She had just put her bags down when the telephone rang—me, calling from Tokyo: "Go up to Ottawa to the Chinese consulate, get your visa, and meet me in Beijing."

I had made the trip to Lo Wu, the Hong Kong boundary town, in 1966, climbing to the security deck of the railroad station and peering gingerly into Shum Chun, seeing the grim-faced PLA men, the barbed wire, and the peaceful peasants tending water buffalo and chickens along the little creek that separated Communist China from Hong Kong's Leased Territories.

Now, heart racing with excitement, I rode the suburban electric train toward China, passengers thinning out until only a handful were left at the border. John and I picked up our bags and typewriters, marched out across the railroad bridge, halted by solemn PLA men, waved on inside the Shum Chun station. Miraculously we walked into China!

Veteran of a hundred crossings into Russia and other Communist countries, I dreaded the grim customs examination. I hauled my bags up on the counter and started to open them. A young Chinese woman smiled at me and said, "The customs examination is completed."

I could not believe my ears. But it was true. So it was all the way to Beijing—and beyond. Good humor, courtesy, charm, informality, problems dissolving with a word and a smile. *This* was Communist China? This was the forbidden land of the red peril? This was the scene of the *luan*, the madness of the Great Proletarian Cultural Revolution?

Something was wrong. Of course I had read all the accounts by my colleagues, but nothing prepared me for this benign atmosphere. John and I had hardly gotten to Beijing when we were received by Ma Yuzhen, the Foreign Office press chief. That evening, with no interpreter, no guide, I called a taxi at the Hsin Chiao Hotel (I hardly knew the name) and drove off under a velvet sky through streets so empty I thought I had come to the end of the world, no policemen at intersections, millions of people sleeping all around but not a sound, hardly a light in the buildings, two solitary bicycles the only sign of life. I knew not a word of Chinese, my driver not a word of English. No one knew where I was, not even myself. A quick turn from dark street into a darker *hutang*, and I could vanish beyond any finding. Just vanish.

The Foreign Office was bright and alert, Mr. Ma on duty, brisk and smiling, newsmen bustling in and out, a Japanese from the Kyoto news agency, an Agence France-Presse man, a North Vietnamese, I was in the traffic stream, no big news, but a good page 1 story, a Chinese protest against Nixon's escalation in Vietnam. I rode back to the hotel, called New York, got the desk in twenty minutes, dictated my story, and lay awake for hours excited as a child on Christmas Eve. I was in China at last. I was in Beijing, the enormous and mysterious city of which I had dreamed all my life. I was covering the news, writing stories, plunging out into the unknown streets to a Foreign Office whose name I could not say in Chinese, whose location I could not have told if my life depended on it, writing and dictating as I had for a lifetime. Of course I could not sleep. I heard a deep rhythmic pounding. I thought it was my heart, but when I went to the window, I heard a switch engine in the distance chuffing away as the switch engines had in the railroad yards just beyond the old house at 107 Royalston Avenue in Minneapolis.

I lay back in my snug bed and relaxed. My worries about Charlotte arriving alone in Beijing dropped away. Mr. Ma had asked about her before I could even raise the topic, had promised to take care of her if I was late in getting back from Pyongyang. He asked me to telegraph him from Pyongyang what I would like to do in China and he would make the arrangements.

I was on a high. I was still, I thought, a romantic, but I was something else as well. I had not engaged in this long, long struggle with all its dramatic twists and turns just for the sake of adventure. I believed then (as I believe now) that the world's future lay in Asia, that Asia and specifically China would determine our fate. This, I thought, was the significance of the century—not, as Henry Luce had thought, the American century but the prelude to the Asian century. We were witnesses to a tidal shift in world power, comparable to the shift to Europe when she mastered the technology of the gunpowder which China had invented, when she armed her galleons and frigates and privateers and adventurers with their letters of marque and set them to plundering the East.

No, I was confident, the Asian renaissance was at hand. World War II had liberated the continent. Every great nation had won its freedom. We Americans had fought the final battles: we defeated Japan only to lay the basis for her extraordinary rise; we had tried but failed to dictate the future of China; we had tried but failed to hold the line in Korea; we had lost in Indochina although the terrible toll was still going on.

This was what underlay my interest in the continent. With all of China, as it seemed, asleep around me, I was so wide awake that I did not drop off until I heard the first sounds of the waking city, coughing and hawking, the shuffle of slippers on the sidewalks, the creak of carts, the muffled greetings, the dim clang of tin pails, and the slowly rising rustle of people riding to work on their bicycles.

I spent two weeks in Korea, angered by gross anti-American propaganda, hating the *kimchi*, the Korean national dish, a kind of pickled cabbage which seemed to me to smell like an open sewer, and revolted by the manner in which children were taught songs such as "Let's Mutilate the Americans" and the "fact" that the U.S. had been the enemy since the visit of the warship *General Sherman* in 1866. On the night before we were to meet Kim Il-sung, I got into such a row with my escorts that I expected to be hurled over the border at dawn. In the fortnight's stay I had not met a single Korean peasant and not a single worker, until I had protested so loudly that they turned up four men carefully rehearsed to denounce the United States and its capitalist, imperialist leaders. When I told them that President Nixon was then in Moscow engaged in cordial discussions with Brezhnev, they were nonplussed. The event had not been reported in Korea.

One afternoon in Kaesong, John Lee and I slipped out of the hotel and got 100 feet down the street before an alarmed escort caught up with us. It was our only unescorted walk. We were warned that we might be attacked by North Koreans, whose hatred for Americans could not be restrained. I hardly endeared myself by suggesting that there was much in common between Koreans and Americans— both of us were violently disliked by the Japanese. A poll had rated Koreans the most disliked foreigners, with Americans a close second.

There were a few light touches. We did meet Kim Il-sung the morning after the big row and had a long dull interview. We were late because our escorts had never been to Kim's palace and took the wrong turn. Kim opened the conversation by saying I had written him ten years before (actually it was eleven) saying I had some questions to ask: What were they? When the official photograph appeared in the paper next day, I was puzzled. It showed me sitting next to Kim—which I hadn't been. I looked more closely and saw that the picture had been spliced to eliminate the interpreter (English very poor) who sat between us. Kim Il-sung's photo dominated every issue of the newspaper. Most of them displayed spaces where participants had been blanked out.

Despite the show of bad feeling, the Koreans hounded me to stay longer. I refused, saying I had a date to meet Charlotte in Beijing. Finally Kim put a personal plane at our disposal. Even so Charlotte had been waiting a day in Beijing alone before I got back.

It was drizzling as the Korean plane touched down on the runway and taxied to a halt. I saw Charlotte standing on the airport steps with red umbrella and raincoat under a great protrait of Mao Zedong. I jumped out and raced to hug her. Rendezvous in Beijing! It took a few moments before I saw two Chinese and two Koreans (with big bouquets of red carnations) waiting to shake hands. One of the Chinese was Yao Wei, the Foreign Office man who was to be by our side for nearly two months and became a close friend. We rode to the Chien Mien Hotel, a marvelous grubby place, filled with PLA men and Overseas Chinese, dirty table linen and cheerful carefree waiters. I can't remember when I have been so happy as when Charlotte and I made our way to the big plain room with its big plain furniture, its big plain bed, its big green thermos jugs of hot water. We couldn't open the windows at night, the fumes from the next-door chemical plant were so gaseous.

I had telegraphed Ma Yuzhen of the Press Department a few days after getting to Korea with suggestions for what I wanted to do in China. "I would like very much," I said, "to visit the route of the Long March and Yenan as well as Chairman Mao's birthplace (Shaoshan)." Of course, I wanted to talk with Zhou Enlai and Madame Soong Chingling and to catch a glimpse, even at a distance, of Chairman Mao, but the Long March of Mao and the Red Army in 1934–35 was No. 1. It had been on my mind for years. Charlotte remembered me "babbling about it" as I came out of the operating room, still under ether, after a minor operation in 1971. And it was still on my mind when we dined with Zhou Enlai. I noticed that he wore leather sandals and walked with an easy gait, which I imagined he developed on the Long March. I felt sure that despite the years he could pick up his pack and start out in the morning and walk all day without a pause. When I said good night to him that evening, I told him I very much wanted to retrace the Long March and talk with the survivors. He looked hard at me under his inky black eyebrows, a quizzical look which I could not fathom, and made no reply.

I mention my request and Zhou's reaction not to demonstrate once again my habitual perseverance (stubbornness, if you will) in working toward reportorial goals, but as a sign of my ignorance of what had been and was going on in China.

I learned a good deal about Mao in China. I think I began to understand his character, his early character, after visiting his birthplace, Shaoshan, and the city of Changsha, where he began his career as a teacher and as a rather eccentric reformer and revolutionary.

I knew about Mao's struggle in the 1950s with the hero of the Long March, his old associate, General Peng Dehuai, and I knew something of the rise of the enigmatic Lin Biao whom Mao had named as his successor. I knew that Lin Biao had vanished from the scene in a mysterious plane crash in Mongolia in September 1971. But I did not understand what connections, if any, existed between Peng Dehuai and Lin Biao. I sensed there must have been a struggle between Lin Biao and Zhou Enlai, but I had no measure of its depth. Even now the circumstances of Lin Biao's death were a matter of rumor, and there would be no official announcement until after I left China in early July, quixotically believing it more important to get back to the U.S.A. and the national political conventions than to stay on and get more insight on China.

I did not know that the Cultural Revolution, in effect, *was still in progress.* It had, I thought, come to an end in 1968 and 1969, sort of petered out. Lin Biao? Well, he seemed to be an aberration. Now he was gone. The term "Gang of Four" had not come into use. Zhou Enlai seemed very much in charge. He had, I believed (and still think), engineered Nixon's visit to China. He was, so far as I understood, riding high in the aftermath of the Nixon rapprochement. It seemed to me that Mao was quietly receding into the traditional role of Elder Statesman and that Zhou in the chairman's name had his hand on the helm. Zhou publicly adopted a reverential attitude towards Mao. "We are all his students," he said solemnly during our dinner at the Great Hall of the People, "but we cannot do as well as he." I accepted this as a sincere expression of Zhou's devotion to his teacher. Now when I know so much more about Mao, the terror and paranoia of his last decade, the very strong signs that he sided with Lin Biao against Zhou (Mao was "jealous of Zhou's reputation in the world," one of the Old Guard told me in 1984), the petty (and not so petty) torment Mao inflicted on Zhou in the months before Zhou's death—well, I wonder. I wonder a great deal, and I wrestled with the enigma of Zhou almost every foot of the way when Charlotte and I finally took the Long March in 1984. I must have asked a thousand questions about Zhou and got no very convincing answer. I tried and tried to interview Zhou's widow, Deng Yingchao. She was one of the handful who did not see me. She had nothing to add to the official record. I wonder about that. No one—well, only one survivor of a martyred Party leader—was willing even to hint that Zhou had failed in any way to meet his high ideals. No one, I came to believe, was going to raise this question. In the debris of the Cultural Revolution and the Gang of Four, Zhou Enlai provided an icon for China to live by.

There is so much to ponder. Take the question of the Long March and the proposals I made the moment I got to Beijing in 1972 to retrace its path and its politics. What naïveté! No wonder Zhou looked at me with that Mona Lisa smile. I did not know that the Cultural Revolution (if we are to use the conventional phrase— "Mao's Vengence" might be a more accurate one) was far from over. Yes, some victims had been released from prison and hard labor and placed under forced residence, usually in remote places in the countryside.

But what I was asking of Zhou was something of colossal gall— that Mao give me permission to exhume the bodies and reputations of his most illustrious victims, the men (and women and children), tortured or left to die in appalling circumstances. All of this Zhou knew, all of this had been done by his "teacher," part of the continuous struggle, sometimes hidden, sometimes not, which had been in progress for fifteen years and would run another four years until 1976, the year in which both Zhou and Mao would die.

What can I make of this? Was it one more case of ignorant journalist and sophisticated diplomat? Or was it, as I believe, something more complex. I had been through this kind of thing in the Soviet Union, the paranoia of Stalin and the outrages perpetrated by him on his people, those closest to him, his long-term associates.

Was I simply unwary in this new situation? Or did I face again a Rashomon in which the truth was so bent by refracting crystals of distance and time and space that there was no real way to relate Zhou's truth and my truth.

I have not found the answer to this question, but not from failure to talk to men and women who were Mao's victims, the walking wounded, the crippled survivors of the Cultural Revolution. I spoke with many on every trip we made to China and particularly on the Long March in 1984, but there are still gaps in the patchwork.

Perhaps naïveté has its uses. It held me on course—the course to the goal of retracing the route of the Red Army in 1934–35. Within a year or so I understood much of what lay behind Zhou's quizzical smile. I knew enough about the Cultural Revolution to realize I was not likely to achieve my ambition while Mao lived, but I plowed ahead. In 1973 I acquired an ally—John S. Service, the famous Old China Hand, the diplomat the State Department expelled in McCarthy days but who fought in the courts and got his job back. Jack was born in Chengdu where his father headed the YMCA, had lived in China much of his life, and walked the mountains of Sichuan as a young man, knew and loved the country. In Yan'an days, he met Mao and the other Communist leaders, and his dispatches to the State Department are classics of information and judgment. No one—Chinese or American—can write about China without drawing on Jack's insight.

Jack and I knew each other only casually, but when my book, *To Peking and Beyond*, was published, he liked it. He wrote that he and his wife, Caroline, were thinking of another trip to China (they had been there in 1971) and perhaps we might join forces. He liked to walk. How about going on a walking trip along the Yangtze? I liked to walk too, but I had a better idea.

"One thing which I thought would make a wonderful framework for a trip," I wrote, "would be a reconstruction of the Long March. We could do that, walking, in part, jeeping in part, and covering other areas by train or plane so as not to take two years! I was thinking about the possibility of doing this this coming fall. What do you think?"

I told Jack that Yao Wei, our friend and companion of 1972, had just been to the United States. I had discussed the March with him. He thought a walking trip would be too hard. We didn't, he said, understand how difficult conditions were in the countryside. Yao Wei, I conceded, might be right, but why didn't we try anyway? As years went by, Jack and I lobbied our project with any Chinese official who would listen.

The more I learned, the more I wanted to document the odyssey of Mao and his Communist movement. I had to begin at the beginning, and the beginning was the Long March. That had given birth to the movement, that had shaped its form, had crystallized its spirit, and placed Mao at its head. It was, I was convinced, an epic of our time—the 6,000-mile retreat over terrible mountains, terrifying deserts, devilish rivers, impenetrable swamps across China's outer reaches, the lands which climb up to the mountain core of Asia, the heartland of which MacKinder wrote, the Himalayas, the Pamirs, the Tien Shan, the cruelest barriers nature has erected against the passage of man.

Again and again Charlotte and I went back to China. We traversed the length of the northern periphery with the Soviet Union—Manchuria, Inner Mongolia (so like yet so different from Outer Mongolia where we had often been), the endless deserts and oases of the Northwest, the old Silk Road, Xinjiang, and up to the Soviet frontier, Tibet and the then almost impassable stone trail from Lhasa under the brow of Everest to Kathmandu (we had to hike around great landslides like those that had barricaded us in Sikkim). There wasn't much of China we hadn't seen—except the beauty spots.

With Mao dead, Zhou dead, Zhu De dead, so many of Mao's heroic Long March commanders dead, I confess I began to wonder if our Long March would ever come about. Charlotte hoped the project was dead. She didn't think we could survive it. We were too old. I had acquired a pacemaker. Jack Service had had a bad heart attack. Neither his wife nor his doctor thought the Long March would be a good idea.

So on August 17, 1983, I got a telephone call from a Chinese correspondent in New York. Was I still interested in going on the Long March? Will a duck swim? If so, I was invited. Could Charlotte come, too? Of course. How about Jack Service. No problem. To say that Charlotte was overjoyed would not be correct. I was coming up to seventy-five, and, as it transpired, she would celebrate her seventieth birthday in Beijing as we prepared, in March 1984, to take off. Jack, a year younger than I, miraculously got the agreement of both wife and doctor and joined us.

The Long March was difficult. I developed a heart irregularity in the back country, but thanks to Charlotte's nursing (the Chinese called her "a model wife"), some fine Chinese doctors, and long distance consultation with my doctor, Peter Schrag in New York, it did not prove serious. We continued the March, and it was, in the end, worth the grinding pressures, the years of nagging, the physical stress of saw-boned mountains, jungle heat and June blizzards on the bend of the Yellow River. "I enjoyed it," Charlotte said. Jack agreed. It was the experience of our lives—and those of our remarkable Chinese companions, General Qin and interpreter and friend, Zhang Yuanyuan. We emerged with the story—not just the exploration of 6,000 miles (we traveled 7,400 miles on land by jeep, land rover, minibus, mule, horseback and by foot) but the historical record, all that was preserved in the memories of the survivors, high and low, the top men of Deng Xiaoping's government, and the ordinary men and women who made the march at sixteen or seventeen and lived to become the steel core of Mao's government. We explored the archives, such as there were, correlating our findings with those of the official historians.

It gave me not only a cavalcade of the history of China for the past half century but an extraordinary insight into China today and its problems, a panorama of life in the remote, almost medieval back country, where we were the first Westerners since the missionary era, a territory long off-limits, visited by few Chinese from outside. Not until we blazed the trail had a Chinese (or anyone else) thought to follow in those footsteps of 1934.

Edgar Snow, after hearing tales of the Long March from Mao and Zhou and Zhu De and the others in the caves of Pao'an in 1936, wrote in *Red Star over China:* "Some day someone will write the full story of this exciting epic." He had hoped to write the story himself but never did, and not until *The Long March: The Untold Story* appeared, had the narrative been put together. Only when the book was translated and published in China, first serialized week by week in a publication called *Reference News* (circulation 5 million) and then in hard cover and paperback editions by the Military Publishing House, did Chinese readers have access to more than brief reminiscences, usually of hortatory character (*Chairman Mao on the Long March*, written by his batman). Publication of *The Long March* in Chinese generated a powerful demand among Chinese historians and scholars that they be given equal access to sources and equal freedom to publish factual history.

China specialists and nonspecialists have asked me how I knew I was getting at the facts. Good question, one I have raised myself. Of course I did not get all the story. But I got a great deal more than anyone ever had before—including the Chinese. Again and again by dint of questioning, of skepticism, of what I can only call police reporter tactics, of comparing and contrasting differing versions, I have been able to get close to what really happened. Again and again Chinese specialists who helped to dig out the facts were astonished to find that, after I had rejected the first version and insisted on deeper digging, they did in fact find evidence that made sense.

The Long March raised more questions than I could possibly answer. There remain passages of Chinese history with which I am not satisfied, including those shadowy patches in the biography of the man whom I so admire—Zhou Enlai. There are the contradictions in the philosophy of Mao Zedong. There is the still puzzling story of Lin Biao, of Chiang Kai-shek's kidnapping December 12, 1936, at Sian, of the rivalry between Mao Zedong and Zhang Guotao (did Zhang really plot to kill Mao?), of Zhu De and Mao, of Jiang Qing and the Gang of Four. There are 100 unanswered questions still waiting, and there is China, the giant of Napoleon's epigram, no longer sleeping, shaking off the sloth of centuries, moving ahead under that contradictory and extraordinary little man, Deng Xiaoping, five feet tall and packaged like a bundle of dynamite. Nothing will keep me from going back again and again to China so long as those questions haunt me.

# Chapter 32

# A Verray Parfit Gentil Knight

He moved, I thought, like a panther, puissant, supple, swift, his dark eyes showing flecks of gold, a man of grace, a man whose wit flashed like a tanager's wing, hands sensitive and lips that could be cold as iron. No man I have met in a lifetime has left so deep a mark on me. He was Zhou Enlai, scion of a decayed noble family, Premier of Communist China. For nearly ten years, 1965–75, only his pliant mind and steel will kept his country from the abyss.

The image of Zhou as I saw him first on the evening of July 28, 1954, at Spiridnovka House in Moscow is fixed in my eye as though with an engraver's tool. He was fifty-six years old, dark hair not touched with gray, face smooth, heavy black eyebrows, sparkling eyes. In the half-hour I observed him at a reception given by Vyacheslav M. Molotov, there was not a pause. He was moving, gliding, talking, teasing the Russians, sometimes Peck's Bad Boy, sometimes grave as Buddha. Like so many Americans—Edgar Snow, Teddy White, Anna Louise Strong, John Hersey, General Stilwell—I fell in love with Zhou on first sight.

July 1954 was a moment of triumph in Zhou's life. He was on his way home from Geneva, where he had negotiated the accords that ended (for a time) hostilities in Indochina. By Zhou's side that evening in the old Spiridonov Palace in the Arbat quarter was Pham Van Dong, the Premier of North Vietnam, whom twelve years later I would meet in Hanoi in the midst of the war. On this evening he was quiet, retiring, almost an invisible tail to Zhou's comet.

It was an evening that stayed in my mind, and as I was to discover, it did not vanish from Zhou's. I remembered it with delight, Zhou with sadness not for the prankishness with which he tweaked the Russians but for what had happened to Vietnam after the agreement which he persuaded Pham Van Dong to sign against Pham's better judgment. But that came later. On the night at Spiridonovka, he was skittish as a colt, taunting the Russians. The party was given by the stone-faced Molotov, who hadn't laughed since Lenin died in 1924. The whole Politburo was there: Nikita Khrushchev; Georgi Malenkov, soon to depart for distant Kazakhstan to run a power station, confessing, in his letter of resignation, that he lacked the experience to be Premier; Anastas Mikoyan, dark, cynical, looking, as his comrades often said, like an Armenian businessman ("In America," they said, "you'd be a millionaire"; they probably were right). There were the others: Lazar Kaganovich, not yet ousted by Krushchev, tall, heavy-shouldered, glum; Nikolai Bulganin, drinking a little too much as always; and improbably, the British, Indian, and Swedish ambassadors, invited because they maintained diplomatic relations with China.

I was not invited to this inner circle, but in my reporter's way I had sidled from room to room, from the big reception hall where I was supposed to stay, through the outer inner reception room, filled with low-ranking Chinese and low-ranking East Europeans, through the middle inner chamber (higher-ranking Chinese, Russians, and East Europeans), and to the holy of holies, the inner inner room, the Politburo room. A plainclothesman barred the door, but I could look over his shoulder and see and hear what was going on. I got an earful.

Zhou Enlai was gliding about the room, clinking glasses with the Russians, but he was saying, "Bottoms up!" not the Chinese *Gum Bei* or the Russian *Do adno.* He was speaking English, which none of his hosts understood. The only ones who knew what he was saying were the Western ambassadors—and myself, leaning in the doorway.

His hosts were not exactly pleased. "Why don't you speak Russian, Zhou?" Mikoyan said testily through an interpreter. "You know our language perfectly well."

Zhou responded saucily, "Look here, Mikoyan, why don't you learn Chinese? I've learned Russian."

"Chinese is a difficult language to learn," Mikoyan grumbled.

"No harder than Russian," Zhou snapped. "Come down to our embassy in the morning. We'll be glad to teach you Chinese."

Kaganovich, never noted for drawing room manners, exploded with a bit of Russian *mat',* a coarse mother oath. Zhou was not ruffled. He went on speaking in English, his remarks translated into Russian by a deft Chinese interpreter. "There's no excuse for you people," he said. Then he drank toasts with the ambassadors, the soul of politeness and protocol.

I was astonished. I didn't know whether Zhou was just indulging in high spirits or whether, as I suspected, he felt tired of Russian chauvinism and that, after China's debut on the international stage of Geneva, it was time that Russia began to treat China as an equal. Zhou believed then that China had scored a success at Geneva. The negotiations had brought the French war in Indochina to an end. There would, he seemed to suggest, be more victories in the future. No longer was China just a junior partner to Great Russian seniors.

There were many undercurrents that evening. One was Zhou's pride that he had met and bested John Foster Dulles. I learned a lot about that after Zhou's death from Wang Bingnan, one of the bright young Foreign Office men who accompanied Zhou to Geneva.

Wang had been entrusted with preparations. It was China's first appearance in the international world. She had been in purdah since October 1, 1949, and Zhou was determined that she would display her maturity and sophistication at Geneva. The Chinese delegation must be properly dressed and properly briefed. Wang was sent to the best Beijing tailor and ordered severe, dignified black tunics and trousers for everyone. When the Chinese went for their first stroll beside the lake in Geneva, the Swiss doffed their hats and bowed. Later the Chinese learned that the good burghers had taken them in their solemn black clothing to be a delegation of Chinese clergymen.

One thing, Wang told me, the world got wrong. John Foster Dulles did not snub Zhou by refusing to shake his hand. Zhou never offered his hand. In fact, Zhou had formally instructed all of the Chinese delegates and, indeed, Chinese diplomats around the world, not to shake hands with Americans unless the Americans extended their hands first. The rule was strictly followed at Geneva. Moreover Wang selected a route from the Chinese delegation office to the council room that avoided the path Dulles would follow. If, by chance, Zhou saw Dulles approaching, he would quickly turn away so no informal encounter would occur.

But, Wang, said, the No. 2 in the U.S. delegation, Walter Bedell Smith, did not follow Dulles' stern example. Smith had told reporters that the closest contact the two sides had was that they used the same roller towel in the men's room. But one day, after Dulles had gone back to Washington, Bedell and Zhou met in the delegates lounge and exchanged small talk. There was no handshake because Smith had a cigar in one hand and a coffee cup in the other.

On the last day Bedell sought out Zhou and told him of his pleasure at meeting with him and his high regard for Chinese art and culture. He did not shake hands with Zhou, but he seized Zhou's arm and shook it several times, emphasizing his personal friendly feelings.

Despite the nonsense about handshakes, Zhou was pleased. The French and the Vietnamese had agreed on an end to the fighting and on elections. Informal diplomatic contacts had been made with the United States—quiet talks about exchanges of prisoners and detainees—and a threshold had been crossed which soon would lead to open and formal diplomatic meetings, the fifteen years of talks in Warsaw, conducted on the Chinese side by Wang and on the American side by a succession of ambassadors.

A lot of history rolled by before I would see Zhou Enlai again, much of it history which I perceived only dimly (or not at all) at the time. In those years China went through the Great Leap Forward, the Blooming of 100 Flowers, the Great Proletarian Cultural Revolution, the fall (and death) of legions of the Old Guard, Ping-Pong, Henry Kissinger's secret 1971 trip to Beijing and the visit by President Nixon to China in February 1972, before I got to China and saw Premier Zhou again. He invited Charlotte and myself to dinner in the Great Hall of the People, and as was the imperial custom of the day, we were recalled from Sian to Beijing, traveling by train because the Chinese did not trust their air service to insure our presence in Beijing. We were not told until a few hours before that we were to dine with Zhou, but we guessed from hints and protocol that this was what awaited us—at the end of a day spent in seclusion at our hotel expecting a telephone call summoning us into his presence.

Zhou Enlai had gone through much since I had seen him. There were times during the Cultural Revolution when he seemed, so far as I could discover, the only sane man in China's leadership. He looked older but relaxed and as self-confident as he had been at Spiridonovka House. Charlotte spotted a button missing from his tunic and later I heard stories of his dropping in at the kitchen of the Beijing hotel, just off Tiananmen, for a quick bowl of noodles before the nightly state dinner or political session at which he would be too busy to catch a bite to eat.

I did not know then, as later was revealed, that during the Cultural Revolution, he had once been surrounded at the Great Hall by 1 million Red Guard demonstrators—the same mob that had forced so

372

many of his comrades to bow in the "airplane posture" (arms fiercely drawn behind the back and the victim's head shoved to his knees, deluged with filth, verbal and literal, tortured and sometimes killed). He engaged in fierce debate with his tormentors for more than twenty-four hours before he finally talked his way to release. Zhou's wit and tongue saved him from a howling mob, just as his wit and tongue had saved China from anarchy in those days, without a hand being raised to support or rescue him by Chairman Mao and his right-hand-man, Lin Biao.

I did not know on that night in the Great Hall, so elegant behind silk-embroidered screens depicting the wonders of ancient provinces, sitting at the great round table with its silent, efficient waiters, tasting delightful unknown delicacies with ivory chopsticks, that my host had for months and years walked a tightrope between life and death, between honor and dishonor, somehow keeping a balance which, I am certain, no one in China could have managed. He had saved—for a time—the life of a Long March hero, He Long and his wife, hustled the famous writer, Ding Ling, to safety in a remote Manchurian military camp, tried vainly to soften the torture of Liu Shaoqi, the fallen Party leader, sent a threatened diplomat to the countryside to protect him from torture by the Red Guard, warned an exposed cabinet minister to take refuge before the storm broke, and, alas, only too often found no ingenious way to save old comrades and their children, try as he would.

I could not have guessed that many close associates, old Party leaders, grizzled commanders in the battles of the Long March and the anti-Japanese War had been tortured and killed (or still languished in prison or camp) nor how many wives and children had been sacrificed, their blood swelling the terrible toll of those years.

There was no sign of this in Zhou's suave behavior, his quick compliments, his politeness to the ladies, in the charm and vitality of a man relaxing in an evening of banter and occasional seriousness, which he said reminded him of what now seemed the golden days of Yan'an, the days in the caves of northern Shaanxi in the 1930s and 1940s when he first learned to enjoy Americans and their freewheeling talk.

When I match the Zhou Enlai I met that night, June 16, 1972, with what he had passed through—and indeed with what lay ahead in the last four years of his and Mao's lives—my wonder mounts.

Neither I nor anyone could have been aware that 1972 was Zhou's last good year, the last before the diagnosis of cancer of the bladder numbered his days and cut short the energy which he had ceaselessly poured out for China. Even with my limited knowledge of the complex, hidden mysteries of Chinese politics, I knew that the death of Lin Biao, once Mao's constitutionally designated heir—in a phantasmagoria which (if the official version is true) included a Wild West plot to dynamite Chairman Mao's train and Lin Biao's fatal aircrash in Mongolia (after Zhou himself had penetrated Lin Biao's plot and raised the alarm)—had given Zhou a clout he never before possessed. That evening Zhou looked and acted like a man in command. It was easy to believe that nothing was beyond him, that if he had not formally displaced the ailing (some said doddering) Mao, it was simply because of his exquisite tact.

Zhou Enlai had never wavered in his support of Mao since late 1934—almost 50 years. Before the Long March of the Red Army began in October 1934 Zhou Enlai had been a competitor of Mao's. He had stood with Mao's enemies who had removed Mao from leadership of the Communist Party and its Red Army. But only a few weeks after the March started Zhou began to incline toward Mao and at the decisive meeting in Zunyi in January 1935 when Mao Zedong was again placed in command Zhou stood at his side, never wavering no matter what the crisis, what the pressures, even in the worst days of the Cultural Revolution. Zhou had been at Mao's side for many years. He would not humiliate the old man in his last lingering years. If this is what Zhou decided it was the first time his quicksilver mind had betrayed him.

What did we talk about on this sultry summer evening of 1972 when the men, at Zhou's command, liberated themselves of ties and jackets? What didn't we talk of! There were eight Chinese and nine Americans, some Old China Hands like John and Wilma Fairbank, some new like Charlotte and myself, and Dick and Helen Dudman. We talked about Chinese students coming to the U.S.A. Zhou worried that they would bump into Taiwan Chinese; he did not foresee the thousands from mainland and Taiwan who would fill our universities, mingling freely. Cigarette smoking (he was almost as much a chimney as Chairman Mao and didn't believe in any connection between cigarettes and cancer). Nixon (whatever Americans might think, Nixon had done the right thing in China and China wouldn't forget). Mao Zedong ("We are all his students"). The

Vietnam war (I said it never should have been started and could be ended any time the United States wanted it to; he agreed). The Korean war (he quoted American generals who said it was the wrong war in the wrong place at the wrong time). American politics (he didn't understand our politics). China and Vietnam (China had invaded Vietnam many times over the centuries but, Zhou said, finally gave up because of the fierce resistance).

No subject so preoccupied Zhou as Vietnam. He took upon himself great blame for signing the Geneva accords of 1954 and persuading Hanoi to withdraw its forces from the South; his only excuse was his inexperience. "We were deceived [by Dulles]," he said. As he spoke of the massacre of North Vietnam families left behind in the South, his voice shook. "We made a mistake," he said. "We were greatly taken in at that time." He paused. "We must stop this discussion, or it will become too emotional."

Zhou's mind ranged over the horizon. He philosophized about the role of accident in man's affairs, paying only lip service to Marx's theory of the inevitability of economic-social change. Chance, he thought, was the main thing. It was chance that Mao had suggested that the American Ping-Pong players be invited to China, chance that telephone communications with Tokyo were good, chance that word caught the Americans as they awaited the bus to take them to the airport and a flight back to the United States. It was chance that had triggered Chiang Kai-shek's kidnapping by the young marshal at Sian in December 1936, chance that Chiang was compelled to join the Communists in fighting Japan. If Chiang hadn't gone to Sian to organize a campaign against the Communists, the opportunity would not have come. It was chance that China got into the United Nations in 1971 instead of 1972 as he had expected (he admitted his younger colleagues had predicted it, but he did not realize events were moving so swiftly).

"All events," he said, "have an inevitable cause, but it may be through an accidental turn that the inevitable happens."

I thought that Zhou in a few words had summed up the Chinese view of the dialectic: pragmatic, sensible, nondidactic. Marxian theory was OK but good luck helped a lot. Yes, the Russians were Communists and, yes, the Chinese were Communists, but a continent divided their way of thought.

Zhou pondered the difficulty of forecasting events, the difficulty of foreseeing the future. Neither Chiang Kai-shek nor he could have forecast the Sian kidnapping nor the speed of the United Nations action, and no one could have predicted that poor Prince Sihanouk of Cambodia would be ousted from his country and spend year after year in exile in China.

No one could have predicted the last years of Zhou's life. A year after our dinner, by which time he had been given the diagnosis of his illness (but showed no outward sign), he dined with his old friend, Chester Ronning, onetime Canadian ambassador, born in China of missionary parents, and Iphigene Ochs Sulzberger, the irrepressible daughter of Adolph S. Ochs, founder of the contemporary *New York Times*, paying her first visit to China at the age of 81.

To make small talk, as Iphigene said, the Premier asked about her family. She said she had all kinds of racial and ethnic strains among her descendants. "But no Chinese. How can I get a Chinese?" The Premier said he didn't know. "Can I advertise in the newspapers?" Iphigene inquired.

"No," the Premier smiled. "Our papers don't print ads."

"What if I should put up a Big Character poster?" Iphigene asked.

"Heavens," said Zhou. "Please don't do that. It would cause a riot."

Zhou was the parfit gentil knight and so would glow in Iphigene's memory. No hint of illness, no hint of problems. Within the year, his prestige still unimpaired, he summoned Deng Xiaoping back from exile to share his burdens. But treacherously soon, the fateful knives of Mao's wife, Jiang Qiang and her comembers of the Gang of Four, were being sharpened. New winds of persecution had begun to blow. The first whispers of an assault on "Confucius"—Zhou Enlai—had begun in the feverish corridors of Chinese power.

On June 9, 1975, Zhou struggled out of his sickbed and attended a memorial service for He Long, his Long March comrade, one of the great heroes. Despite Zhou's best efforts, He Long had been tortured to death by Mao's men. On this day, so weak his trembling hand could hardly sign the memorial book, Zhou spoke to He's widow, Xue Ming. "I failed," he told her, voice quivering. "I failed to keep him out of harm's way."

Zhou lay dying. The "struggle with Confucius" raged on. Zhou asked that they play for him "one more time" a classic song of the Long

March written by a Red Army general, Xiao Hua. No, ordered Jiang Qing, wielding her Dowager Empress' power. Zhou lay dying, but Mao Zedong did not visit his bedside. Zhou died January 9. Mao did not show himself at the mourning ceremonies. Jiang Qing did, wearing a casual body-glove sweater. That evening Jiang Qing arranged to have two of her favorite Western films shown in her residence in the Western Hills.

On Qingming, the April holiday for "sweeping graves" and showing respect for the departed, China erupted. Millions thronged Tiananmen in tribute to Zhou; mountains of flowers were heaped at the heroes' monument; thousands of poems were placed on the walls. After four days, a midnight sweep by police cleared out the flowers, tore down the posters, scrubbed off the slogans, beat and arrested those standing vigil.

The tribute to Zhou was erased. His right-hand man, Deng Xiaoping, once again was hurled from office. The Gang of Four reigned supreme, but only for a moment in time. Mao died September 9 and China reclaimed Zhou for her own. The Gang was arrested, tried, and imprisoned. Deng returned to Beijing and power. Zhou was hailed as China's true patriot, the man who kept the faith, who served the people and the Revolution.

## Chapter 33

# The Little Man Nobody Mentioned

I confess that, when I went to China for the first time, the name "Deng Xiaoping" rang no bells. Yes, I had heard of him. I knew that he had been a target of the Cultural Revolution. President Liu Shaoqi was called the No.1 Capitalist Roader and Deng was called the No.2. The pair were supposed to have conspired to turn China away from Communism and back to Capitalism.

That was about it. In the tens of thousands of words I jotted down you will look in vain for the name of Deng Xiaoping. I never asked a question about him, and if he was mentioned, it was only as a hyphenated add-on to President Liu Shaoqi. Deng is not even listed in the index of my *To Peking—and Beyond*. It had never occurred to me in March 1953 that Nikita Khrushchev would succeed Stalin; it didn't occur to me in May 1972 that Deng would succeed Mao.

I try to keep this in mind when I am tempted to make prophesies. Grand politics is beyond tidy formulations. The odds defy even the science, if that's what it is, of advanced polling technology. No one in 1987 knew who would be elected U.S. President in 1988.

No one in China in 1972 was eager to talk about what would happen after Mao Zedong, but I concluded that he would probably be succeeded by Zhou Enlai, then in vigorous health, no hint of the cancer yet. Mao looked slack and sloppy, overweight and tottery, sprawling in his armchair in baggy clothes, his mouth slightly agape. I thought Zhou had pretty much taken over the day-to-day running of China and that before long Mao would shuffle off the stage. It would be a long shuffle. Mao would hold the spotlight for four more years, and Zhou would precede him to the land of the immortals by eight months.

My idea was that Zhou would have a free hand and time to tidy up the mess left by the Cultural Revolution, then the era of the Long March, of the men who had come to power with Mao, would end.

378

The successor generation, I came to believe, would emerge from the dynamic Shanghai leadership, which had carried out the Cultural Revolution.

This notion was reinforced by a meeting in Shanghai with a man called Zhu Yongjia, dark-haired, handsome, quick grin, sharp wit, a non-nonsense way of talking. He wore a well-tailored gray Mao tunic, and I guessed his age at thirty-two or thirty-three. He held one of those cumbersome titles which seemed to disguise more than it told. He was a member of the Standing Committee of the Shanghai Revolutionary Committee. That meant he was one of the top men running Shanghai, just below those soon to become known as the Gang of Four.

Zhu Yongjia looked me in the eye as he spoke, and I could see that his frankness was rooted in both authority and knowledge. We dined in a cream-and-gold suite in the Park Hotel (now the Peace), a first-class English residential hotel before 1949 and still, if a little déclassé, a four-star establishment. We dined well, the linen white, the silver gleaming, the waiters quiet and efficient, one splendid dish after another, a menu in exquisite calligraphy on rustling sheets of gold-and-red paper. The pièce de résistance was a vegetable plate decorated with twin pheasants carved from winter melons, a trompe-l'œil of the kind Shanghai hotels had been famous for long before the Revolution.

After this glorious meal, seated in an adjacent room with a bowl of fruit, fine cigars, and brandy, Zhu turned to me and said quietly:

"I can tell you something about the Cultural Revolution in Shanghai. I only participated in it here. I wasn't in other parts of China. But it is true that it all began here."

It had been, as he recounted it, the splashiest Revolution since the Paris Commune of 1870.

Again and again I had asked to be given a briefing on the Cultural Revolution. Now, in a swift and flowing narrative Zhu told the story. It was a lucid, logical account of extraordinary complexity, but he danced through the twists and turns without hesitation. He met my skeptical questions in stride, never the slightest hesitation, like a runner taking the high hurdles. It was, I thought, the kind of briefing a young Andrei Vishinsky might have given me on Stalin's purges, every point neatly tucked in place, no loose ends.

The conversation went on until 1 A.M., an outlandish hour in a city that went to bed by 9 P.M. He and I were prepared to go on to dawn, but Yao Wei was exhausted. So was Charlotte. I was enthralled. Zhu seemed as fresh as when he started.

379

The story Zhu Yongjia told was a classic exercise in paranoia. If you accepted his basic premise—that Liu Shaoqi had been a hidden traitor from the earliest days of the Revolution, say, since 1927—the rest mortised like a Chinese puzzle box. But the premise was as bizarre as the premises of Stalin's delusional apparatus. It was cut from the same psychotic cloth. Zhu's tale reeked of Othello, the sickly suspicion with which I had become so familiar in Moscow, as dark and dangerous a drama as any of those confected by Stalin and his murderous executioners, Yagoda, Yezhev and Beria. All this Zhu Yongjia presented to me with businesslike assurance, a total commitment to his tale that took my breath away.

As I traveled back to our hotel past the haunted pillars of Britain's once imperial establishments along the Bund, I felt I had caught a glimpse of China past and China future. Perhaps I was wrong, perhaps Zhu only affected to believe the story he had so deftly spun, but I doubted that. He plainly was a major player in what I thought (and feared) would be China's next act—the coming to power of a band of thermidorian revolutionaries, armed with intelligence, driven by paranoia, superior, I suspected, in every way to Stalin and his cronies but infected with the same lunatic views and possessed of far more vigour than any other group I had found in China. That long talk at the Park Hotel, I thought, had lifted a curtain and given me a glimpse of what to expect.

I recall no mention in Zhu Yongjia's narrative of Deng Xiaoping nor do I find his name in my notes.

The ambitions of Zhu and his Shanghai associates were not to come to pass. There were many reasons for this, but the most important had to do with the little man who was not there, Deng Xiaoping. In the days after the death of Mao Zedong, September 9, 1976, it was a very close thing, very close indeed, as to who would win out. But the chips fell against Shanghai and Jiang Qing, and as I ultimately was to discover, Zhu Yongjia would play out the last scene in the fall of the Gang of Four.

Things moved with great speed after Mao died. Everyone knew that supreme power was up for seizure. It was the moment Jiang Qing, Mao's widow, had been awaiting. Her forces were ready. But so were those of the Old Guard, the handful of survivors of the Long March who still held key positions, military men and an equivocal politician named Hua Gaofeng.

By lightning strokes, cloaked with deceits straight from that classic of China *The Romance of the Three Kingdoms* (so long a favorite of Mao's), the Old Guard arrested Jiang Qing and her three Shanghai collaborators on the evening of October 7, 1976, in Beijing—a secret sweep not revealed to anyone outside the core of the Old Guard. In Shanghai the second tier of leaders—suspicious but unaware—stood by awaiting a call to action. One by one they were summoned to Beijing on plausible pretexts and placed under control of the Old Guard.

Finally, Zhu Yongjia, my cool confident Gang of Four man of the Park Hotel, was left in charge by the conspirators, to handle whatever might come: a rising against the Old Guard in Beijing, an order to mobilize against attack—who could know what might happen in these frightening times? It was his duty to call out the workers' militia (some estimated the Shanghai defense force at 1 million), to prepare for combat, to rally the masses behind Jiang Qing and the Gang (not a whisper of their arrest had seeped out) and to hold the Shanghai bastion of Revolution, come what might.

Single-handedly, no directives from his chiefs (now held incommunicado), unable to reach any reliable ally in Beijing by telephone or coded message, Zhu Yongjia pulled together the remaining cadres of conspirators, suppressed all news coming from Beijing (propaganda had been his special responsibility), invoked a blanket censorship, halted the Shanghai edition of the *People's Daily* (the national Communist Party organ), jammed all incoming radio transmission, distributed arms, placed defense detachments at newspapers, radio stations, communications centers, battened down the hatches.

For five days Zhu Yongjia held the fort in the face of waves of rumors that the cause was lost, hoping against hope, drafting proclamations declaring that Shanghai had taken up the flag of the Revolution against usurpers.

This was his final act. On October 13, one week after the arrest of Jiang Qing and her collaborators in Beijing, Shanghai capitulated.

Much of the detail about Zhu Yongjia's last stand was reconstructed by Roger Garside of the British embassy in Beijing. I am not certain of Zhu Yongjia's fate. Probably he is still in prison.

So ended the ambitions of the bold but fatally paranoid group that hoped to ride into power with Mao's death. And so much for my ability to fathom the complexity of China's politics. I had sensed correctly that Zhu Yongjia and his associates were high rollers.

But not one item of my scenario came true. Nor did theirs. Instead we had what came close to a Chinese version of *Aida*.

Who did become Mao's successor? Not the ambitious men of Shanghai, not Jiang Qing with her hope to become China's new empress, not the slow-moving, uncharismatic provincial politician Hua Gaofeng, whom the doddering Mao had improbably installed as surrogate in his last days ("With you in charge I am at ease").

The one who leaped to the top was Deng Xiaoping, the man whom nobody had mentioned in 1972.

I make no apology for the blank page in my 1972 portrait album. In that time not a word, not a line about Deng had appeared in the Chinese press for years—not since he was thrown out of office and daubed with wagons of verbal nightsoil in 1966. Deng had vanished, just as the No. 1 Capitalist Roader Liu Shaoqi, had vanished. Not a word of the fate of either had circulated outside Zhongnanhai, the government compound within the Forbidden City. The two men had slipped from the face of the earth. Liu Shaoqi was dead, dead since 1969 at the hands of Mao's torturers. No one knew that. Deng Xiaoping was alive. No one knew that.

My ignorance was total in those early days. I didn't even know what questions to ask. In fact it was not until 1984, when I took the Long March and met the colleagues and friends of Liu Shaoqi, Deng Xiaoping, and Mao Zedong, that I was able to put the picture together. When I did that, I found the rise of Deng beat the traditional Chinese classics for pure melodrama.

In the quiet late spring days of 1972, when I first came to Beijing (as Deng's daughter, Deng Rong—"Maomao" was her family nickname—was to reveal in 1985), Deng's spirits had begun to rise. After his arrest and disgrace in 1966, he and his wife, Zhou Lin, had been kept under twenty-four hour guard in Beijing, subjected to interrogation and physical harassment. Then, without warning, they and Deng's elderly stepmother were bundled onto a plane under armed escort and flown to Nanchang, capital of Jiangxi province. Here they were harangued by the governor-general, then taken to an abandoned infantry school in Xinjian county closed down in the Cultural Revolution in 1966.

They were confined in a brick house, which once had been the residence of the school's director. In this remote spot, forbidden to speak to anyone except their guards, cut off from communication with any authority, virtually without money, they had to struggle for existence. In a nearby tractor plant, Deng got a job as a machinist, a trade he had learned as a work-study student in France after World War I. His wife worked as common laborer, washing and cleaning coils of wire. They dug a vegetable plot and raised chickens, selling the eggs in hopes of putting by money to bring their children to them. Deng broke up ten-kilo hunks of coal to feed the stove.

The five Deng children had been scattered to the winds. The oldest son, the brilliant Deng Pufeng, a physics senior at Beijing University, had been hurled from a fourth story window by the Red Guards. His spine was damaged, paralyzing him from the waist down. Denied medical treatment, he was confined to a dirty hostel north of Beijing. He lay flat on his back weaving baskets of thin wire, which he sold to buy food.

In 1971 Pufeng was permitted to join his parents. Medical aid was still refused, but Deng bathed his son and massaged his back and legs. That year, too, the youngest daughter, Maomao, was permitted to join them. The Deng family will always remember November 5, 1971. Guards escorted Deng and his wife to a Party meeting. They had no idea what might be happening—perhaps another struggle session. The children waited in concern. About noon their parents returned, saying not a word, their manner grave. Maomao caught a signal from her mother and followed her to the kitchen. The guards were still in the house, but her mother seized Maomao's hand and traced on her palm four characters that meant: "Lin Biao is dead." Then she put a finger to her lips. When the guards went outside, Deng let his emotions come to the surface. "Justice could not have allowed Lin Biao not to die," he said. "Even heaven won't tolerate him."

Things began to move. The Lin Biao officials who had held Deng and his family in custody were replaced. The new officials paid a formal call and apologized for the harsh regime. They removed the armed guards. In April 1972 permission was given to bring Pufeng to Beijing for treatment. Maomao accompanied her crippled brother.*

In Beijing there were more signs that the clouds were lifting. Wang Zhen, one of Deng's comrades of the Long March, sent word that he

---

* Deng Pufeng was brought by his father to America for diagnosis. U.S. physicians said nothing could be done. He did undergo physical therapy in Toronto. Since 1979 Pufeng has headed an association for aid to the disabled, the first China has ever had.

wanted to see Maomao. Himself a victim of the Cultural Revolution and still "set aside"—that is, forbidden to work—Wang Zhen told Maomao that times were changing. He was writing to Mao asking that Deng be reinstated. (Later, with the death of Mao, Wang Zhen entered the Politburo.) Maomao told her father, when she went back to Jiangxi, that not since the start of the Cultural Revolution had anyone treated her so warmly.

All of this was going on while I was having my long talk in the Park Hotel with Zhu Yongjia.

For the Dengs life went on in the red brick barracks near Nanchang, cultivating their garden, Deng reading at night from books he had been permitted to bring with him, sometimes Marx, sometimes not, listening to the evening news on the radio, following events with great care.

In December 1972 they had a vacation—a sightseeing trip to the mountain top of Jinggang Shan, 200 miles southwest of Xinjian county, the redoubt where Zhu De and Mao Zedong assembled their ragged bands in what would become the first formation of the Communist Red Army. Deng had served in the Red Army through the Long March, the war against Japan, and the final victory over Chiang Kai-shek and was one of those who stood with Mao on October 1, 1949, in Tiananmen.

After the visit to Jinggang Shan, Deng and his family went back to the Xinjian barracks, back to their quiet routine. In late afternoon as the declining sun cast long shadows on the courtyard, Maomao watched from her window as her father emerged for his constitutional, forty turns around the square. Deng, head slightly bent, hands clutched behind his back, walking briskly in the path his feet had worn in the red soil, day after day, deep in thought.

"Watching his sure but fast-moving steps," Maomao recalled, "I thought to myself that his faith, his ideas and determination might have become clearer and firmer, readying him for the battles ahead."

Deng was pondering, there can be no doubt, the future of China—what must be done to set the country back on the track, what steps he would take should he once again rise to leadership.

One evening in April, 1973, a banquet was given at the Great Hall of the People for Prince Sihanouk. Nothing special about the banquet. Sihanouk was periodically so honored, partly to boost his morale, partly as a gambit in the complicated political games around

Vietnam and Cambodia. Nothing unusual about the dinner except for one guest—Deng Xiaoping. The Little Man (Deng is slightly under five feet tall) once again had bounced back. No explanation, no reversal of the verdict which had declared him a vile traitor, a scab, a pernicious weed. Deng simply walked in and sat down at the table as if he had just returned from a long vacation in the country—as, indeed, he had, but of a special kind.

No one, except perhaps Zhou, knew China and its problems as did Deng. There was not much of China he had not seen since his birth in Paifang village a few miles from Guang'an, a district town in Sichuan about sixty miles north of Chongqing.

No one had been up and down the political roller coaster so often. Deng was small physically, but when I finally met him in 1977, he had the bounce of an India rubber ball. I could imagine him on the court in his favorite sport, basketball, and I wasn't sure he could not hold his own against the six and seven footers. Years later a Russian told me of an encounter between Deng and Mikhail Suslov, the tall, gaunt six-foot ideologue of the Soviet Union. The two men, Deng so short and Suslov so long, had engaged in violent debate over Soviet and Chinese versions of Marxism in the late 1950s. Suslov was Moscow's premiere dialectician, but Deng had boned up on Marx. Nikita Khrushchev later grumbled to Mao: "Your little guy floored our big guy." Mao smiled. "Never underestimate our little guy. Our little guy led the Second Field Army in a battle with Chiang Kai-shek in which Chiang lost 1 million troops." Deng was political commissar. One-eyed Liu Bocheng was the general. Together they won the Hwai-Hai battle that sealed the defeat of Chiang Kai-shek.

To underestimate the little guy was a common mistake. Deng was small, but his energy never ran down. When he entered a room, he charged the air with electricity. When I saw him in 1977, he bounced across the floor and I felt vibrations on the back of my neck. We shook hands, and the current flowed up to my shoulder.

When Deng was knocked out politically, he came back on his feet—always. Most people talked about Deng having been knocked down three times. They didn't know what he had survived in his early years. In 1926, having made his way back to China from France via Moscow (he studied for a while at the Sun Yat-sen University, where Jiang Jingguo, Chiang Kai-shek's son, was a classmate—"not a bad fellow," Deng recalled sixty years later), Deng was sent into a very tricky area on the Vietnamese border. Twice he was dragged into inner Party intrigues, but both times he shook off the charges and moved on up the ladder.

On the eve of the Long March, Deng was arrested on trumped-up charges (actually because he supported Mao whom his accusers did not dare attack openly). He was beaten, held in a bare-walled room, and given only a cup of rice and a cup of water a day. He refused to confess any crime (he would do the same when he was accused in the Cultural Revolution thirty years later). So he was beaten again. One day, as he was being led back to his cell, he encountered a Communist woman who was an old friend. "I'm starving to death," he told her. She bought two chickens, cooked them, and made his guards give them to him.

Deng's persecutors stripped him of rank and sent him to duty in a dangerous no-man's-land. They hoped he would be killed. Deng's principal accuser persuaded Deng's wife to get a divorce and marry him.

Of all Deng's downs this was the most dangerous. But he survived. He was brought back as a common soldier when his enemies became fearful he might defect to Chiang Kai-shek. Deng started the Long March like all the other soldiers, carrying his own pack, a twenty-pound food bag, forty rounds of bullets, and his rifle. There were rumors he was made to serve as one of the 5,000 porters who toiled under 200-pound burdens. That doesn't seem to be true. His load was heavy enough, but he had developed strong muscles working in the Renault factory in Paris and as a locomotive fireman in France.

The Long March gave Deng the brisk pace Maomao noticed as her father walked around and around the barracks courtyard. He learned a lot in those years.

The first thing I heard about Deng in 1974 was that he was a man in a hurry. "Sometimes he moves too fast," my Chinese friend said. Deng had just become Zhou Enlai's chief deputy. "That's what I am afraid of now. He may get into trouble."

He did. But Deng could no more take a snail's pace than he could transform his hot Sichuan temperament. Mao cursed at him, said that Deng was deaf and that he deliberately sat in the back of the room so he could not hear Mao's instructions. But Mao also said that Deng was like "a needle wrapped in cotton." He was a sharp man but gentle, "a rare and talented man." Deng had ideas, and he was capable of finding responsible solutions to difficult problems. He was a good fighter. He was a good fighter against the Russians. Not many like him, Mao said.

Deng did move fast. Possibly it had something to do with his stature—very small, very quick. He thought his growth had been stunted by his student years in France when he worked as a laborer and often had nothing but a croissant and a glass of milk a day. He developed a fondness for croissants, and when he finally made it to the United States in 1974 for a United Nations session, he went home via Paris, bought 100 croissants, and took them back as a gift to Zhou Enlai and others who had been his comrades in France.

I learned a lot about Deng as time went on. He had started the Long March under an evil cloud, but he bounced back. When Mao took command in January 1935, Deng was pulled out of the ranks and resumed his own long march to the top. By the end of the epic in October, 1935, he was a trusted young lieutenant of Mao's. He went on to play a leading role in the battle against the Japanese in 1944–45 as Liu Bocheng's political commissar in the famous 129th Division. At the close of World War II the 129th Division was expanded into the Second Field Army for the struggle against Chiang Kai-shek. When Mao proclaimed the People's Republic in 1949, he named Deng proconsul for the vast regions of China's South. Up and up and up Deng rose only to fall to the depths in 1966. Again he went up in 1974, taking charge from Zhou's failing hands, then with Zhou's death in 1976, he fell to the pits where he would have perished but for Mao's timely death a few months later.

Why, Charlotte asked a Chinese official, do you respect Deng so much. He has been up and down so many times. "Ah," he said, "that's why we trust him."

In 1976 it was a question of life or death; he fell like Lucifer. Whether he would survive, no one could be certain. He had one advantage. He had never lost his friends in the Red Army. After Deng returned to power, he demurred at becoming chairman of the State Defense Committee. "It should go to one of you military," he said modestly. But the military men smiled. "You are one of us," they rejoined. With his life in danger from Jiang Qing, Deng was given protection by Xu Shiyu, commandant of Guangdong and South China, one of the toughest Red Army commanders, called Old Ironsides by his troops. In Guangdong Deng had the support of the Party Secretary Wei Guiqing. All this would have availed Deng nothing had Jiang Qing won. It gave him temporary protection, and in Beijing he had the quiet backing of Ye Jianying, second only to the ailing Zhu De in the armed forces. Other stalwarts secretly sided with Deng, including Li Xiannian who was to become President.

The three great men of China died in 1976—Zhou in January, Marshal Zhu De in July, and Mao Zedong in September. Deng resembled none. He set himself four-square against Mao's leadership style. No cult of personality. You could travel from one end of China to another and never see his pictures or statue. The old Deng home in Xiaxiang village housed three families, no museum, no little Red Book of Quotations from Chairman Deng, no calligraphy on the walls, no poems by Deng. He didn't give interviews, and he refused to have his biography written. He was not effacing. He just didn't want to be overblown like Mao. He had a flair for easy relations. He liked to play bridge, had liked to since his days in Yan'an where bridge and poker were introduced by Americans like Edgar Snow and Anna Louise Strong. But Deng was no ordinary bridge player. He was world class. He played to win. And he played two or three times a week with some of his old friends like Wang Li. No money stakes, but the loser had to crawl under the table. Deng seldom lost, and when he did, his friends told him he didn't have to get under the table. No, he would insist. "It is a rule of the game," and would crawl under—not so difficult for a man of his stature.

"I concentrate on the cards," Deng has said. "That way my mind gets a good rest." Deng likes to swim, too, and has told his friends "The fact that I can swim especially in the vast sea [the Yellow Sea, at Beidaihe] proves that I am healthy; the fact that I play bridge means that I still have a clear brain." He fell in love with soccer (European football) when he was in France and once pawned his jacket to buy a ticket for an important match. In later years he watched championship games on TV. He took a daily cold water bath until he was seventy-five. Mao also liked to swim. Cold baths and calisthenics were closely linked with revolutionary activity in China. One of Mao's early works was on physical exercise. Deng comes from sturdy Hakka stock, the Hakkas being a special ethnic group of Hans who migrated from north to south many centuries ago. They are usually small, dark in color with ruddy cheeks. They are numerous in the area around Hong Kong and Canton, the women wearing fringed lampshade hats. Deng came from a middle peasant family. His father led a local defense detachment.

This was the background of the Little Man Whom Nobody Mentioned in 1972, the Little Man who could never be kept down. It took him about two years to reach the top after Mao's death, and he was already racing ahead with the pragmatic, daring program which he had turned over and over in his mind as he paced those forty rounds of the courtyard on his barracks home. It was a fast track program, and it broke through conventions, both Communist and Chinese. It was, in a sense, more Chinese than Communist, and that was not, in the tradition of the Chinese Communists, Marxist but *Chinese* Marxist— Marxism of a special kind, building a Communism tailored to Chinese needs (which is one reason why Stalin and his successors disliked and distrusted China).

Deng said: "It does not matter whether the cat is black or white so long as it catches the mice." What he meant was that, to drive China to technological rationalization by the year 2000, he was ready to take techniques, methods, devices, ideas where he found them. If that meant abandoning Mao's blue-ant communes for private farming and private profits—OK, he did just that. When I followed Mao's Long March into the deepest and most remote places in China, I saw the results: booming market towns, private houses going up like Levittown, television antenna thick as willow branches, red-slippered girls trotting off to the paddies to transplant rice, more money than the countryside had seen in the last 5,000 years. The slogans: "Make the Peasant Rich—Make China Strong," "To Get Rich Is Glorious."

Deng opened the doors to foreign investment, private industry, joint ventures, "special economic zones" (free trade areas where Chinese and foreign entrepreneurs operated in a style more like Hong Kong than anything seen since 1949 in mainland China).

New stock exchanges in Shanghai, Tianjin, and Shenyang, private trade, private business, private restaurants, private beauty shops, private shipping companies, private production contracts for factory workers.

It happened so fast it took China's breath away and possibly even Deng's: stock market reports in the official English language newspaper, a bridge column, beauty hints, classy international style hotels, a golf course beside the Ming tombs. Well, it took my breath away, too. It brought with it a husky dose of graft, corruption, prostitution, black marketeering, smuggling, foreign porn and VCRs.

Deng's new China dazzled my eyes when I first saw it. I discovered

389

I missed blue ants, hundreds, thousands of peasants bending over in the rice fields, no way to tell man from woman, the plaintive strains of Jiang Qing's primitive eight operas, *The White Haired Girl, The Taking of Tiger Mountain by Strategy, The Red Regiment of Women.*

I found it hard to imagine a man better suited than Deng to guide China into the passing lane, to overcome the devastation of the Cultural Revolution and motivate 1.1 billion Chinese to the tasks of what he called The New Long March.

I was not confident that Deng would succeed in all his goals, but I did not think there was anyone in China so competent. When in 1986 and 1987 there arose a moving and shaking in China, when Hu Yaobang, Deng's handpicked chief lieutenant, was compelled to resign as Party secretary, when a miniwave of repression was ordered against the more free and talented writers, when young people were reined in (a bit) and some brakes applied to the economic joy ride, I did not see Deng Xiaoping as threatened. More likely, I thought, Deng and his old Army cronies had decided to pull up before China took off into the clouds.

I was prepared to believe that the new mode had been touched off by pragmatism. Deng headed a coalition government even if his voice was the most powerful. I did not have to believe that a group of Party Old Boys (and women), led down to Shenzhen to see Hong Kong honktyonk flourishing under the aegis of Communist puritanism, had risen up against Deng. Rather, it seemed to me that they had done the job (if they had done it) *for* Deng and not *against* him.

China, so I thought, would stay on Deng's course, the one he worked out during those long walks in the Jiangxi courtyard, the one which had already won him three *Time* magazine cover stories (one excerpted from my *The Long March*) and the title of 1985's Outstanding Achiever, awarded by *Success* magazine, the trade journal of young U.S. executives, which voted him the Success Story of the Year and ran a profile written by me under the title "China's CEO."

Success he surely was. CEO he was. I put my money on his getting China up and away toward a new kind of economy, which might be Socialist in description but one seasoned with enough free enterprise to place China firmly among the rising Pacific rim powers, Japan, Korea, Taiwan, Hong Kong, Singapore, which would make the twenty-first century their own.

## Chapter 34

# Where's the Rest of Me?

The evening of April 25, 1984, Charlotte and I had reached a place called Xishui on our 6,000-mile journey retracing the route of Mao Zedong's Long March of 1934–45.

We were deep in Guizhou, a province where, tradition says, there are no three li* without a hill, no three days without rain, and no man has three silver dollars in his pocket. It was back of beyond. In prerevolutionary days everyone smoked opium, and babies became addicted at the breasts of their half-naked mothers. We halted overnight at Xishui on our way to Mao Tai, a village where the Red Army on its long march first discovered a local booze called mao-tai, made from sorghum mash, said to be 190 proof. It became the national drink, imbibed (usually) in minute quantities at official banquets. I wanted to check a dubious rumor that Mao's teenage soldiers were so naïve they soaked their blistered feet in mao-tai instead of pouring it down their parched throats. They may have, I found, used some mao-tai on their feet but more went down their gullets.

Charlotte's meticulous diary records the events on the evening of April 25. She saw her first rat in China, and she saw Ronald Reagan on Chinese TV. She was not making a political comment. The rat, a greyish creature, flashed across her feet when she visited the improvised toilet that had been set up for her use. (Charlotte knows rats; she has lived on a farm and in New York City and has coped with rats in both places.)

Ronald Reagan was making his first trip to China, and in remote Xishui, roughly 1,000 miles west of Beijing, we had hardly expected to catch a glimpse of him. I was interested in the President's visit. Nixon had left an indelible mark on his 1972 trip, and I wondered how Reagan would play in Beijing. He was more anti-Communist

---

* The li is a Chinese unit of measurement, about half a kilometer long. Three li is the rough equivalent of a mile.

than Nixon and on entering the White House had made no secret of his preference for Taiwan. Some Reagan friends were last-ditch Taiwan supporters. I knew that many Chinese were excited about the President's visit, but I was amazed when our hosts told us that he was going to be on TV and that somehow in this remote corner they had obtained a set so we could see him.

Sure enough, after dinner they led us into a kind of barren lounge, and there on a table in front of a lumpy davenport and several chairs was a small TV. Quite soon, Mr. Reagan appeared on a grainy screen, a bit ill at ease, but Mrs. Reagan seemed to be having a fine time. I thought that was very important.

Charlotte and I and our Chinese friends listened to the end. Our companion, Jack Service, former Foreign Service officer, Old China Hand, McCarthyite victim and Californian, fell asleep. The Chinese seemed amiably impressed with the President, but not until we got to Xi'an seven weeks later did I talk to a Chinese who had actually seen him in person. The President, like most tourists, had made a side trip to Xi'an to see the famous terra-cotta warriors.

Reagan had left a strong impact on Xi'an and, as I later found, in Beijing as well. The Chinese had been amazed at the remarkable security arrangements and split-second timing. They had never seen anything like it. They could hardly believe that the President's bullet-proof limousine had been flown across the Pacific to Beijing and then to northwest China for the short ride from a military airport to the archaeological museum.

And the President himself. "Oh, that wonderful cowboy smile," one young man explained. That was it, the cowboy smile, even in post-Mao China, it was the symbol of America, etched deep by thousands of Western movies. Here was Mister Cowboy himself, Mister America, if you will. How could they not like him? They went for him for the same reason so many Americans did—for that smile, for his big American image, his friendliness, the wave of his hand, and all the imperial trappings.

I was not as surprised as some might have been. I felt that, except perhaps in England and Western Europe, Reagan's cowboy image was a national heritage. It reminded people of the cowboys and Indians they had grown up with, the Lone Ranger, all the wonderful child's mythology. When Reagan or his handlers or Nancy Reagan nixed a proposal that he go to Moscow for the Brezhnev funeral, I could hear the Kremlin sigh with relief. His cowboy smile on Moscow TV would have been worth a thousand Star War pitches. No Russian man or woman could have been convinced after seeing his "wave from the saddle" that he had ill intentions toward what he had foolishly dubbed "the evil empire." If Nixon had wowed the Russians, Reagan would have knocked them dead.

Reagan scored a hit in China, but not with everyone. In Beijing in June we dined with Hu Yaobang, general secretary of the Communist Party, in his residence in Zhongnanhai, in the Forbidden City. Hu told me he had met three American Presidents—Nixon, Carter and Reagan. He rates Nixon No. 1, Carter No. 2, Reagan No. 3. Nixon had made the "opening" to China, Carter had established diplomatic relations, Reagan still had not lost all the aura of his Taiwan sympathies. The upper Chinese were still a bit suspicious.

I had never been close to Reagan. My opinions were all second-hand. I saw him as one of those special products of California, which in politics as in plants are distinguished by showy colors, uncertain flavor, and dubious nutritional values. The politicians had not come out of the plant-breeding experiments of Luther Burbank, but they somehow seemed related to boysen berries, pomatoes, and avocados.

The first California politician I heard of as a child was Hiram Johnson, a Bull Moose Republican, always out of step with everyone; he eventually helped Henry Lodge to scupper Woodrow Wilson's League of Nations. There were Californian politicians and business-men involved in the Teapot Dome scandal of Handsome Harding. Herbert Hoover, disguised in starched collars, was half do-gooder, half entrepreneurial pirate, a lot more California OJ in his veins than Iowa corn.

The depression brought the California quirkies to the top. It gave us Upton Sinclair, socialist muckraker, author of *The Jungle, The Brass Check*, and the Lanny Budd series, as governor. Dr. Townsend scared the daylights out of solid citizens by proposing $200 monthly pensions for the elderly. All this, I thought, was natural in the land of Aimee Semple McPherson, a new frontier of low-budget imagin-ation, populated by a mixture of the elderly and the young in search of nirvana and a free ride.

When a new generation of California politicians began to sprout after World War II, they seemed to me to wear the colors of their predecessors. Richard Nixon fitted in nicely, although on the other side. He defeated Helen Gahagan Douglas, too sensible a lady to make it in day-glow politics. Nixon had no easy time, but thanks to his dog Checkers stayed on Ike's ticket and entered the realm of destiny. He was followed by the song-and-dance man, George Murphy, who managed to serve in the Senate without leaving any detectable trace of having been there. Then came Jerry Brown, a true product of Luther Burbank, a cross of 1960s rebel, Hollywood, the Jesuits, and Zen. And no one wore the California colors with more flash than Tom Hayden and Jane Fonda.

It was within this framework that I placed Ronald Reagan, first as governor, then coming on like Gangbusters—real Gangbusters—against the unfortunate Jimmy Carter, who may have had the last laugh, having bequeathed Iran to his vanquisher.

To find the real man within the cocoon of political legend is never easy. The politician himself loses his ability to tell what is flesh and what is plastic. The task is even more difficult if the man is both politician and actor. There is, of course, a close connection between acting and politics. One element of the art of politics is to create an image that is attractive to the general public and wins their backing for the politician and his policies. Harold Macmilliam put it neatly in answer to an American reporter's question as to what he thought of electing an actor President. Macmillan smiled behind his bushy moustache and said: "Why, my dear boy, we are all actors on the world's stage, aren't we?"

He was right, and television has brought more and more stars of the electronic world into public office. The blending of stage and politics is not without hazard, of course. Introspection and self-examination are not highly developed on the stage. There are apt to be more Jesse Helmses than James Madisons in the future.

Before Mr. Reagan launched his Hollywood career, he spent some years as a sports announcer on WHO radio station in Des Moines, Iowa. He broadcast football and baseball games play by play with the aid of telegraphic bulletins. The report was offered with all the excitement of the real eyewitness play by play, although the listeners were told it came off the wire. There was no deceit in this, but the announcer's trick was to make it sound so exciting the listeners forgot it was all secondhand.

Early in his career Walter Cronkite performed the same chore in Kansas City. One evening after a White House interview, Walter told the President about the awful moment when his telegraph line broke down. He expected it to come back in a minute or two and went ahead, making up trivial detail, five-yard penalties, incomplete passes, failed line plays, time-outs. It was the Notre Dame–University of Southern California game, and to Walter's horror the wire stayed down—five minutes, ten minutes, fifteen—finally coming back after a twenty-minute interruption. He discovered that Notre Dame had scored a touchdown in the interim. In Walter's imaginary game, USC had the ball deep in Notre Dame territory. It took him another three nervous minutes to get Notre Dame's touchdown racked up. It was, Walter said, the worst time he had ever had on the air.

A few weeks later, Walter was going over some outtakes of a minor speech by Reagan and heard him telling about "my worst moment as a sports broadcaster." It was, Mr. Reagan said, during a Notre-Dame—USC game . . ." Reagan told it very well, Walter conceded.

Actors and politicians take their materials where they find them. Cronkite suffers from loss of hearing in one ear. He told Mr. Reagan he dated the trouble to a moment in World War II when a GI on the battlefield discharged a shot only a foot from his ear. Not too long after that, Walter heard the President talking of his hearing difficulty, which was caused, he thought, by a rifle shot close to his ear. The President, to be sure, saw no combat during World War II. He was first assigned to a cavalry unit and then to an Air Corps detachment, where he made morale films for the troops.

A storyteller's tales are not necessarily true, although he may earnestly assure his listeners that they are. He consciously heightens suspense, colors the drama, and often casts his story in the first person. It was *his* adventure, *his* escape, he it was who slew the dragon. We do not mind the deception. We suspend belief in order to increase our own enjoyment. This is tradition, and this is how the bard held his place at court, amusing the king and his courtiers.

No one minds if Reagan puts on the mantle of Cronkite to tell a good joke. But where to draw the line? A friend of mine had a magazine assignment to interview Mr. Reagan. He was well received. Mr. Reagan enjoys telling tales. The conversation strayed onto race relations. Well, said Mr. Reagan, this America of ours is a wonderful place. Do you remember how on the day after Pearl Harbor, FDR integrated the U.S. Armed Forces—just like that?

But, demurred my friend, I think there is something a bit off here. I believe that President Truman integrated the military, and there was quite a row over it.

Mr. Reagan was patient with the writer. Oh, no, he said. You must remember that Negro cook on the battleship at Pearl Harbor? The Japs were attacking, the crews had been killed or wounded. He picked up a machine gun and shot down a Japanese Zero. The very next day FDR integrated the armed forces.

My friend did not press his point. He knew exactly what Mr. Reagan was talking about. The President had it dead right. But he was talking about a movie, not real life.

Or there is the story about the Israeli Prime Minister who was seeing Mr. Reagan for the first time. He came out of the White House aglow. He told the reporters that the President had described how he took part in the liberation of the Buchenwald concentration camp. "I'd never known that," said the Prime Minister. Back at the embassy his colleagues explained to the Prime Minister that the incident had not happened that way. Mr. Reagan had not been in Europe during the war. The liberation occurred in a movie, not at Buchenwald.

I was in Moscow just after the Summit at Geneva in 1985. One of Mr. Gorbachev's close aides invited me to his office. He was walking on air over the Gorbachev-Reagan meeting. They had been very worried. It was Gorbachev's debut. How would he stand up to Reagan? They briefed him to the ears with everything they could think of about Reagan. Then the two men met, one on one, an interpreter, no aides. Gorbachev was on his own. So was Reagan. They began with small talk, then Gorbachev switched to the subject of movies. He told the President he had seen some of his films (as he had in the briefing sessions). Mr. Reagan beamed. Hollywood was home ground. Yes, Gorbachev mused, I have seen some of your movies. "There was one," he said, "which I liked best. I think it was called something like 'The Best of Me'."

That was the ballgame. Gorbachev was talking about *King's Row,* the best picture of Reagan's career, an adult, dramatic totally professional performance. Reagan had not been nominated for an Oscar, but he might well have been. On late night TV reruns the picture is sometimes called *The Rest of Me*. In it Reagan undergoes a double amputation, both legs off above the knees, wakes up from the anesthetic and exclaims: "Where's the rest of me?" It was the best line Reagan ever uttered, and he knew it. In 1964 when politics began to preoccupy his mind, he called the biography which a free-lance writer named Richard Hubler had turned out for him: *Where's the Rest of Me?*

*The Rest of Me,* I think, was a watershed in the life of Ronald Reagan, as much of a watershed as the poliomyelitis attack which FDR suffered. True, it was not a real amputation. It was make-believe, but it was an experience that changed everything, philo-sophy, role, expectations.

Gorbachev and his advisers were shrewd, well-informed, but I do not think they were *that* shrewd or *that* well-informed. I do not believe they understood that *King's Row* opened a direct route to the Reagan psyche. It put Gorbachev and Reagan on a plane of intimacy and understanding. Fears melted. Each man now felt he knew who he was talking to. It was not just Reagan who had seen the image of the Evil Emperor dissolve. It was Gorbachev who saw the Capitalist Enemy vanish. They went on to talk of critical matters like Star Wars. Reagan spelled out his views and his vision of a world from which nuclear peril forever vanished.

As he listened, or so my Moscow friend told me, Gorbachev made a profound discovery. Reagan really believed in his dream. He was not dissembling. He saw Star Wars as a peace project, not a device to bring the Soviet Union to its knees. "Listening to Reagan talk, Gorbachev understood that this was no trick," my friend told me. Reagan might be mistaken. He might be ignorant. He might be badly served by his advisers, but he was not trying to wipe out Moscow. He wanted to saddle up and ride into the golden west of Peace, stirrup to stirrup with his Russian *friend.*

I do not know whether this is the whole story. I don't know whether Mr. Reagan was as naïve and sincere as Gorbachev was represented as thinking. But I do know that the two men hit it off. For a while until the wrecking crews on both sides—the professional arms experts, diplomats, ideologues, and military—got to work, it looked like a real breakthrough.

I think that the intimacy of the talk about *The Rest of Me* was genuine and that it underlay the curious events of Reykjavik when Gorbachev and Reagan, again one to one, negotiated a virtual nuclear-free world to the amazement, alarm, and horror of their advisers, who rushed into the breach and torpedoed the friendly, human, and mind-boggling achievement.

Yet, it was not entirely smashed, and as time went on, quiet words, hints, and a little hardball applied to the antagonistic negotiators freed one element after another for a new and grandiose deal. Edged by memory of an event that never happened—an almost catastrophic but theatrical amputation—the world moved inch by inch toward sanity.

I did not meet Mr. Reagan until 1985 when (to my surprise) I was twice invited to the White House. It had been years since I had been a guest there, and I found a lot of changes. In New Deal days and until the Kennedys, there was a kind of Jacksonian scruffiness abut the place, especially backstage, in the offices and press quarters: cramped cubicles, reporters dashing for phones, impromptu news conferences, people sauntering in and out of the offices of the President's staff, little or no security, a pleasant, sleepy White House policeman at the door. People left tennis rackets and packages from Woodward & Lothrop's department store on the big Philippines mahogany table in the entrance hall. Copypaper was balled up and tossed toward the cuspidors beside the old leather chairs, where visitors waited and waited for their appointments, which were always late.

All that was gone now—most of it before the Reagans, but the President and his wife put a seal on it. The press quarters reminded me of CBS at 524 West 57th or the *Today* studios at 30 Rock, combed down, hot lights, security guards, no wandering.

I found the social quarters of the White House spiffed up and very well run. Efficient, pleasant, well-groomed young men and women of the armed forces escorted guests through the metal detectors and up to the reception rooms. Quiet, careful waiters and an air of relaxed elegance I'd not seen even in the Kennedy era, smooth as a Cunard liner in the great days. The White House had become, if you will, an excellent stage: superb dinners, fine after-dinner entertainment, lots of show biz guests, Liz Taylor, Beverly Sills, Robert Mitchum, you name your favorite.

My first visit was a luncheon honoring the Eagle Scouts. I had been one a great many years ago. The President had a handsome black Eagle Scout at his right, an elderly Jewish scoutmaster from the lower East Side on his left, and at the table a button-eyed black Cub Scout and a brace of towheaded Nordics. A balanced selection.

I couldn't place one guest at my table, a French lady, author of a book about nuclear war. I couldn't figure out how she related to the Scouts. Why was she there? Pat Buchanan filled me in. She was going to have a quick photo opportunity when the President left the room, a little promo for her book. I thought of that later on when stories appeared about people wangling Reagan handshakes through low-ranking White House officials.

Still, I liked the way the Reagan White House ran, except for the press part. The grubby old days were better.

I got a closer look at Mr. Reagan and his White House July 23, 1985, when Charlotte and I were invited for the state visit of President Li Xiannian of China. The President had been operated on for cancer of the colon ten days earlier, and this would be his first public appearance.

His gesture would long be remembered by the Chinese, who venerate age. Mr. Reagan turned it into a tour de force. He had never seemed more fit. (Although I spotted a fold-up wheelchair just inside the entrance to the East Portico, where the elderly Chief Executives met, whether for Reagan or Li who could say?)

We spectators had been handed tiny red flags with golden stars to wave when President Li appeared. Red flags in the Reagan White House? What next? I wondered. Then I remembered that Mr. Reagan had shown his friend Warren Beattie's picture *Reds* (about John Reed and the Bolshevik Revolution) in the White House. When someone asked him how he could show such a Communist paean, he responded: "But I thought it was *anti*-Communist!"

Wave our red flags we did when the Presidents emerged, Mr. Reagan bouncing up the four steps to the rostrum, Mr. Li assisted by an attendant. There was a twenty-one-gun salute and the respective national anthems. When "The Star Spangled Banner" rang out, the Americans briskly placed their arms over their hearts, all but Charlotte and me. We hadn't been brought up to do that. We stood at stiff attention. A hundred times I had seen President Reagan thrust his arm proudly across his breast. Not today. For the first and only time, he betrayed a reality beneath the hearty exterior. He must have had his mind on his operation. Like Charlotte and me he stood with hands firmly at his sides. Only Donald Regan's quick eye caught the President's lapse. He too stood at stiff attention. Going down the steps, Mr. Reagan gave President Li a hand. Another fine mythologic photo opportunity. No White House correspondent bothered to report Mr. Reagan's single lapse. Perhaps they did not even notice it.

It was, all in all, a good performance, and in the evening he gave another. He and President Li made a private pact to skip the entertainment. His decision should have been shared by Charles Z. Wick, USIA director, who snoozed through Grace Bumbry's songs from *Porgy and Bess* despite Mrs. Wick's repeated jabs of the elbow.

The evening had the identifiable Reagan signature. At my table I sat beside Mrs. Michael Deaver, worrying about the fallout from the Bitburg scandal. Her husband had vetted the President's ill-fated visit to the Nazi cemetery, and there had been some talk about Deaver's purchasing several BMWs at export prices for Washington friends. I told her not to worry. Little did I know what lay ahead, the indictment for perjury.

Earle Jorgensen, an elderly, frail but frisky California businessman, was standing alone at Table 8 when I approached. He introduced himself as one of the five men "who got Ronnie to run for governor."

"At that dinner," he told me, "I told Ronnie, 'You will be in the White House one day.' I didn't believe it, and he didn't believe it. None of us did but here he is, and here I am."

He explained that he had grown up poor, hadn't money to pay the rent when he went into business. He had two suits. He pawned one to pay the first month's rent on his office. "And now," he said proudly, "I have forty-two suits in my closet. That's America for you."

I agreed that, indeed, it was America. As other guests joined us, I heard him repeating the story. Finally, he came back to me, introduced himself, and told me the story again. I thought it was a pretty good story. I knew that Mr. Reagan's kitchen cabinet was made up of self-made men, some more self-made than others. Mr. Jorgensen was a good example of the Horatio Alger legend, and he had every right to be in this house, which was—as John Hersey pointed out to me that evening when we were wondering a bit sheepishly how we happened to be there—the People's House, not just the President's House.

It seemed to me that the Reagan saga was a blend of legends, not just the cowboy legend but the rags-to-riches legend, the clean-scrubbed Boy Scout legend, the Ah, shucks, high school football hero legend. All of it. I grew up reading *The American Boy*. Mr. Reagan could have been the hero of every one of the Clarence Buddington Kelland serials, his legend every bit as rich an American invention as those banana splits the corner drugstore used to serve, marshmallow and cherry topping, a sprinkle of nuts, and maybe a dash of chocolate sauce. There was a lot of boy in Reagan. In Sacramento after dinner with legislators in the Governor's mansion he used to invite them down to the basement to enjoy his electric train. It was a super-duper.

How could anyone—the President, his wife, or his California friends—know what was real and what was dream, where reality and unreality met? There was no way of sending it to the laboratory for scientific analysis.

As I tried to grasp the secret of it all, I found myself again and again sucking air like a pump in a dry well. I turned at last to Mr. Reagan's one effort, with the help of his ghost writer, to discover himself and put it down on paper. Early in the pages of *Where's the Rest of Me?* Mr. Reagan or Mr. Hubler had written:

> So much of our profession is taken up with pretending, with interpretation of never-never roles that an actor must spend *at least* [my italics] half his waking hours in fantasy, in rehearsal or in shooting.

This, he added, gave to the imaginary world an exaggerated importance. It became harder and harder to distinguish between real life and imaginary life on the stage. In fact, he said, it was the very trauma of his experience in *King's Row* that caused him to decide to leave the film world for politics.

Now, as the political leader of the greatest nation in the world, as the leader of what he liked to call "the free world," could he distinguish the boundary between fact and fiction?

Sadly, I concluded, he probably could not. He could rise from a cancer operation, his life in danger, and play a glittering role of a President overcoming the harsh reality of the physical world. He could, when the political world was collapsing about him, telephone Colonel Oliver North and congratulate him as a "real hero," adding the greatest of accolades: "It would make a great movie." But was there, indeed, a line between what should have been in his mind, the real world of the White House, and the "never-never" world in which he had spent most of his adult years?

Did Mr. Reagan know that the answer to his cry "Where's the Rest of Me?" was a terrible truth: It did not exist.

# Chapter 35

# "Death for Noble Deeds Makes Dying Sweet"

By spring of 1971 the view from 43rd Street was tinted with alarming colors. President Nixon's Cambodian "incursion" hit America and the university campuses with an explosive power not unlike that unleashed by the B-52s in the jungles. Kent and Orangeburg rocked the country. Sitting in Taconic, I wondered how we were going to get out of this— and if we would. I could not admit that thought to myself, but in spite of everything it crowded into the edges of my mind.

I had not felt such agony since February 1933 when, every bank in the country closed, I rode the train from Chicago to Detroit bringing a satchel of nickels, dimes, and quarters so the UP bureau could go on covering the news. As I rode into Detroit, I saw a city abandoned, not a factory wheel turning, not an assembly line moving, tens of thousands of men huddled around pots of slumgullion in the Hoovervilles along the banks of the dirty Detroit River. I thought the factories were closed for keeps. I didn't think the chimneys would smoke again. I didn't believe the men would work again. America was busted, its spring broken like a mechanical toy. The system could not be fixed. That is what I thought.

Cambodian spring was, in a way, more terrifying. Detroit had been passive. Now smoke and fire and rifle volleys echoed over the land, soldiers shooting young people. I thought of St. Petersburg in 1905. Could our nation be made whole?

Events rushed forward. In a sense the publication of the Pentagon Papers in June 1971 prepared the stage in a Sophoclean way for Watergate a year later. The Pentagon Papers were LBJ, Watergate was Nixon, but both were rooted in the desiccation of American political morality, the growing gap between our belief in American virtue and the spirituality of the democratic process and the reality of a society turned sordid. Long since we had moved away from that soaring vision of John Winthrop, drawn from Matthew:

402

Wee shall be as a Citty upon a Hill, the eies of all people are upon us; soe that if wee shall deal falsely with our god in this worke wee have undertaken and soe cause him to withdrawe his present help from us, wee shall be made a story and a by-word through the world.

We had dealt "falsely" in Winthrop's words, and we had become a "by-word." If Pentagon and Watergate were personal shocks, there was little in me to indict only two men, Johnson and Nixon, and their associates.

I might find blame in Rusk and Rostow and Westmoreland; I might shudder at the thought of men like Mitchell and Haldeman and Ehrlichman in the White House circle. But what of us—of myself and my fellow citizens? We had elected Johnson and Nixon. It was our choice. Yes, they were flawed men. So was Reagan, waiting in the wings, but were they more flawed than the society for which they spoke? We Americans had collectively chosen them out of the 200 million men and women of our nation. Each was elected by a landslide. It was, I thought, too cheap, too slick to put the blame upon these men alone. We had made them Presidents. We had voted them our proxy and our power. We knew their flaws. They had not sprung unknown on the scene. They had been around for years. We could not pretend that we had been deceived. I didn't think we had much to cry about—except our own sorry selves. Mr. Nixon had not suddenly become a sly political trickster when he walked into the White House. Nor had LBJ. We knew their character. On balance, matching Nixon's wisdom in foreign policy (except for Vietnam) against his abuse of the secret agencies (CIA and FBI) and the creation (like Reagan) of his own private security apparatus, I think he performed better than we had a right to expect.

We cannot cast off our responsibility by saying, Well, I didn't vote for him. We live in a democratic world, and if democracy provides us with ignorant, incompetent, and venal leaders, we have no one to blame but ourselves.

Not long after Watergate, I rode one evening through the bluegrass country of Kentucky with a college student. He came from Pelham, New York, son of parents in the publishing world, product of what he called a wonderfully comfortable and even exciting home.

"My God," he told me, "you don't know how lucky I've been with parents like mine and a younger sister and younger brother."

403

We drove through the October dusk, and he talked and talked.

"I like it a lot here in Kentucky," he said. "I might even relocate here. I've learned a lot. Not so much in classes [he was a sophomore at Centre College] as out. Do you know there are people here in school who watch daytime television? Honestly. Daytime TV. TV—that's what saps our imagination. It turns our minds into jelly."

He turned to me, lumbering the big college station wagon into the fast lane.

"You were lucky," he went on. "You grew up on radio. That extended your imagination."

"True," I told him. "Radio was like the old-fashioned story-teller. It gave you the words. You provided the pictures."

He had been, he told me, a Nixon supporter, a believer. He worked in the campaign of 1972. He hadn't thought a word of Watergate was true. Then something happened. He and some others were called in by the Nixon staff. There was going to be a breakfast meeting. They wanted the young people to help, to come in as waiters. Of course, everyone volunteered. Then they were told to wear suits and jackets and ties. He thought that was peculiar. But when they turned up, he saw that the neatly dressed young Nixon people were being used to demonstrate that young people were still supporting the President—nice young people, the right kind of white button-down shirts and rep ties and J. Press suits. It gave him a strange feeling, he said. Then came the tapes and all the rest.

"You don't know how that made me feel," he told me. "I felt as if I had been betrayed. It was terrible. I can't get over it. Sometimes I read Lincoln, the Gettysburg address, and I get all choked up. And I have a tape of President Kennedy—the inaugural address. I can't play it without crying."

Sometimes, he said, he felt so bad he even thought of joining the Socialist Party or the Communists.

"Don't do that," I said.

"No," he said, "I won't. But you don't know how terrible it is. I'm only nineteen, and what is there to believe in? I don't think much of Ford or Reagan or any of the Democrats. I haven't any faith. Not in anything."

He told me that the people of the 1930s like myself were the lucky ones. Things were bad then, but we had faith. We weren't disillusioned. We believed that things would come out all right in the end.

"That's right," I told him quietly. "That's right."

But was it right? Today I am not really sure. I had never expected to see the Ford assembly lines working again or smoke from the River Rouge plants. Did I have faith that everything would come out right in 1931 when I scampered down the staircase to lower Michigan as the mounted police were riding into the demonstrators outside the *Chicago Tribune* tower? Did I have faith when I walked past the silent rows of jobless men sitting on the curb of Halsted Street in Chicago? When I found my father had pawned his gold watch and cufflinks and was borrowing money from the loan sharks to make the mortgage payments?

No one looking back on these last years can give us high marks. That cliché of Pentagon, Watergate, and the Reagan days—"the system worked"—is true only by the kindest extension of belief. The system has been abused by people, ordinary, middle, and high, who put their personal interests ahead of those of the country. There was and has been an abandonment and/or distortion of patriotism—twisted away from concern for all to the interests of the few or the individual.

I see this not as an indictment of the system but of society—of bigness and greed, selfishness from vulgar top to wasted underclass.

I see myself as constant critic of American life and of American institutions. And as their strongest supporter. I have examined the other systems at first hand and conclude with Winston Churchill that there is no poorer system of government than democracy—excepting all the rest.

On the Fourteenth of July, Bastille Day, 1975, I tossed a notebook and a briefcase into a rental Chevy and headed up the New England Thruway. I had embarked on a journey of discovery—Good-bye, Moscow, Good-bye, Beijing, Good-bye, Hanoi and the uglies of the world, I was taking the high road back in time and space to explore my own country.

My first stop would be Chepachet, Rhode Island. No one had heard of Chepachet, but that was where the Salisburys spent the first 150 years of their life in America. I was going to follow the Westward Ho! of their trek across the continent and then retrace my own peregrinations from the Hoovervilles of depression days to the battlegrounds of civil rights and Vietnam, Birmingham, Berkeley, and the rest. I would use this as a chart to the two centuries of the

American experience. Not exactly the way De Tocqueville and Trollope had done it, but the best scenario I could invent to expose the hardscrabble of American history.

The great hero in the America which I portrayed was my "Uncle Hiram." It was on his account that I had headed for Chepachet. Actually he was my father's great-uncle, born in 1779, three years into the Revolution. He died in 1860, one year short of the Civil War, a span of extraordinary years in American history. The more I discovered about Hiram—and eventually I discovered a great deal—the more he came to symbolize for me that early breed which had laid the foundations of the country.

I arrived in Chepachet with a copy of Hiram's journal in my briefcase. The parts which I possessed began October 19, 1815, describing a journey from Chepachet to Buffalo, New York and back—a peddler's trip. He wrote his account (I later found), in a neat hand, with black, slightly rusty ink in a small calf volume which he had purchased in Providence October 6 "15 days after the tornado of Sept. 23rd" as he noted. He kept that journal until May 9, 1819. A second segment began January 1, 1825, and ended December 20, 1844. Two or three segments were missing. So were the original rag-paper journals.

Hiram kept a day-by-day record of his life. He was thirty-six years old in 1815, and he would write regularly, journal and letters, until he died at eighty-one. His last letter was posted only three months before his death. His style was sparse, exact, thrifty, details of his work, sums earned, sums owed, salty comments, horizon narrow, not a mention of Europe, seldom of Washington or national affairs, the record of a yeoman's life and times, debts, weather, deaths, births, crop failures, bank failures, suicides, and occasionally crimes.

Hiram was all the things my generation was not. He went into the woods, hewed timber, fashioned chestnut and oak into lumber, trimmed beams with his ax, raised houses, forged his nails, gathered old iron and smelted it into bolts and hinges, surveyed the land, built gristmills and schoolhouses, constructed coffins (a steady source of cash), fashioned chests of drawers and bedsteads, plowed the land, cut the hay, sowed wheat, barley, and oats, planted beans (his winter fare was beans and molasses), chipped a plow, carved a gunstock, fixed clocks, built wagons for himself and his neighbors, collected taxes, wrote deeds—not much he could not do. I listed seventy-eight skills in a casual run-through of his journals. He sheared his sheep, made cheese from the milk of his cows. Hiram was that "upstart American" of whom Daniel Boorstin wrote—Mr. America of his day. He fought in the War of 1812 as his father had fought at White Plains with George Washington, as his grandfather had fought in the French and Indian war, and his great-grandfather and uncle (I believe) had fought and died in King Phillip's War in 1675.

Like his family, Hiram was plainspoken, never rich, never poor, working every day, Sundays included, no holidays, no vacations (once he took a three-day trip to Boston), celebrating only Independence Day, the Revolutionary War still close, drinking a little too much rum on New Year's Eve. No Christmas. No Easter, an ecumenical man who heard every preacher who came to Chepachet, once or twice a Catholic and once a Jew preaching a Sunday service.

He possessed a small, serviceable library, a speller bought for half a shilling (he was a good speller except for writing "choir" for "chore"), an almanac, a couple of arithmetics, a trigonometry, a psalter, a book on elocution, and a couple of readers. He was a literate, well-spoken man.

The life of his wife, Diane, was hard, and like so many she went mad and died early. Death was close to women in those times, especially in childbirth. In Hiram's day the babies died, one after another. In the cemeteries you find graves of three or four wives, and a tatter of infant children with their tiny stones. When I learned of the peril which the Chinese women faced on the Long March, the danger of pregnancy, of death and the death of the babies, I thought of Hiram, his wife, Diane, and the other wives of those grubbing days.

There was no way in which I could have written or understood the 6,000-mile Long March of Mao Zedong's Red Army without crossing the 100 rivers and 1,000 mountains of the Chang Zheng. There was no way in which I could understand the origins of the American legend without walking in the footsteps of the men and women who created it. I followed every step of the ice-clad roads from Chepachet west across Connecticut and Massachusetts, over the Hudson and along the Mohawk trail west to Canandaigua and north to Buffalo, traversed by Hiram in his peddler's ventures. I journeyed along the Erie Canal and the Great Lakes to Milwaukee, where my great-grandfather Amasa removed in 1843. I inspected the house in

Oregon, Wisconsin, where he lived and the little red brick house in Mazomanie, Wisconsin, where my father was born. I went to Minneapolis where I was born, the old Victorian home bulldozed with the whole Victorian neighborhood, curved streets, elms, and all.

There was continuity in this progression. I am not so certain of the continuity of my own life: my childhood in the Jewish ghetto Royalston Avenue became; the straight-arrow Scandinavians of high school days; my North High School classmate, Farrell Dobbs, catapulted out of the teamsters' strike of 1934 to Trotskyite leader (he had never heard of Trotsky before, had barely heard of a strike or a union), who went on improbably to run four times for the Presidency as candidate of the FBI-ridden Socialist Workers Party; my university political mentor, Harold Stassen, as bright a man as ever came out of Minnesota, who ran even more times for the Presidency than Dobbs but failed, sadly and finally farcically.

I tried hard to define what I called the Minnesota spirit. I conceived this as an amalgam of Hiram's work ethic—honesty and pragmatism—blended with the Scandinavian socialism of the 1880s and the flinty doctrines of the Mainites, Vermonters and Massachusetts men who came to Minnesota a bit earlier and grabbed the iron ore, savaged the timber, and milled the wheat.

I believe in it as an entity, the agrarian ecleticism which has given us honest, rather lumbering politicians: Humphrey, Mondale, Eugene McCarthy, Stassen, McGovern, and earlier Floyd Olson. None quite made it.

The heroes who made up my iconostasis were not, in any case, mainstreamers, those who made it to the top. There had not been in my family a professional man, a man with a college degree, until my grandfather got his M.D. at Michigan after the Civil War. Until then it had been a yeoman's family, farming the land since we arrived from England in the mid-seventeenth century and probably for generations before. The first deviation came with my Buffalo great-uncles, Smith and Hezekiah, and their newspaper.

Lawrence and Sue Brooks, when Charlotte and I met them, were in their upper eighties. Each died at over 100. If Hiram was Mr. America of the 1800s so the Brookses were the flame which lived on into the late twentieth century, pure Quaker honesty, pure New England ideals, clear blue eyes that spanned the years from the Civil War to the dying embers of Vietnam.

But they were hearty, laughing people, mountaineers who took us into the Adirondacks to Putnam camp, where they had first met in 1905. Lawrence and Sue led us up the twisting trails, surefooted as goats, each with a cane, never faltering, never breathing hard as we puffed and slipped behind. And on the Cape, hurrying down the steep path to the beach before seven in the morning for a quick dip before the water got warm, and sailing summer-long back and forth across Pleasant Bay in their skipping *Quawk,* a catboat cousin of the one Charlotte had sailed on Buzzards Bay in her teens.

We worshipped the Brookses and their covey of children, grand-children, great-grandchildren, their oatmeal porridge, race ribbons bedecking the living room, the judge sitting at the Yamaka piano which he got for his eightieth birthday, hammering out the songs of the 1880s as the family joined in chorus.

I cannot say that Lawrence or Sue had much use for our more recent national leaders. Both had been brought up as staunch Republicans (as had I). Judge Brooks had known Teddy Roosevelt. The judge felt confident that a sense of equity and justice would return to public life, that fortunes like those of Getty and Hunt would wither away (as has Hunt's), that in another fifty years the rich would not be so rich, the poor would not be so poor, that education would begin to bring us up from the doldrums.

One cool autumn day I followed Judge Brooks' path on his favorite walk on Boston Commons. I stood before Saint-Gaudens' bas-relief of Robert Gould Shaw and his mounted black infantry. Some sidewalk artist had carefully embossed a heart in blue crayon on Shaw's horse and each trooper's canteen carried a white crayon star, circled in blue. Not defacement, homely enhancement.

Three young people were sitting on a bench beside the statue, eating their lunch. They moved aside so that I could copy the inscription: "Death for Noble Deeds Makes Dying Sweet."

I thought then, as I think now, that the heritage of our first 200 years is not going to be eroded by the sleeze of speculators, corruption of men in high office, the hypocrisy of television, or the aimlessly evil deeds of random actors on the national stage.

I agree with de Tocqueville:

Future events whatever they may be, will not deprive the Americans of their climate or their inland seas, their great rivers or their

exhuberent soil. Nor will bad laws, revolutions and anarchy be able
to obliterate the love of prosperity and spirit of enterprise which
seems to be the distinctive characteristic of these men or extinguish
altogether the knowledge that guides them on their way.

# Chapter 36

# The Winged Eye

On a sunny morning before Christmas, 1985, I was entering the hall of Botticelli in the Uffizi in Florence, my eyes adazzle and my head spinning. I had never seen Florence, the Uffizi, or Botticelli, and I thought I could stand in that doorway forever, transfusing into my consciousness the glory of Venus and the poetry of Primavera.

I knew as I looked into that room, inspired by Michelangelo and designed by Vasari for Cosimo, that I would never be the same; I had crashed like a jerrybuilt condo. I felt, it seemed to me, as Moses must have felt in the presence of the Revelation. Nothing I had experienced possessed any weight on these scales of gold.

As I stood intoxicated, my eyes brimming with joy, my mind in turmoil, I bumped—literally—into Christopher Lydon, he too in a trauma. I had last seen him when we were making a television record, June 8, 1978, of the commencement in Harvard Square, listening to Aleksandr Solzhenitsyn intone his indictment of the West, pronouncing anathema on that mixture of Good and Evil which he proclaimed "made space for the absolute triumph of absolute evil in the world."

It was the voice of doom arising from the bowels of Russia, resounding like the iron bells of Moscow's 700 churches, proclaiming the Apocalypse.

The decline of the West, Solzhenitsyn thundered, began in the Renaissance with the birth of a humanist view of the world, the abandonment of the absolutes of the Middle Ages. We had taken the wrong turn. We had raised the false banner of a philosophy which, he believed, had caused the West to abandon in totality "the moral heritage of the Christian centuries."

I had not entirely understood what Solzhenitsyn was driving at, standing in the gusty spit of rain in Harvard Square, aware (because I had tried to reassure his wife) that he feared he might be pelted with stones and hurled down by the ranks of radical youth, professor-atheists, and debauched citizenry which he imagined to constitute the

411

audience for the hallowed Harvard ceremonial. It was a moment. I felt as though I was witnessing Savonarola preaching perdition as he was led to the flames in Signoria Square (not five minutes from the Uffizi where I now stood).

I sensed the relief (and puzzlement) with which Solzhenitsyn concluded his address. He was received with the polite applause due a celebrity, the courtesy (a few boos very faint from the extreme rear) awarded a great man, and congratulations (many had not really understood his words, the loudspeakers, as usual, defective). The temple had not fallen and its elders, if later to express some irritation, had not been shaken.

Oh, to have Aleksandr Isayevich beside us now in the Uffizi! I exclaimed to Christopher. Oh, that he might breathe into his lungs the joy of man's most soaring creations, savor the Renaissance at its ultimate eloquence. How would he respond? I did not believe mortal soul could come into this presence without being born anew. But that most stubborn of men? The iron will of Aleksandr Isayevich had not been bent by Stalin, and his spirit, snug and secure in the granite hills, snow, and birches of Vermont, had not been lured by the sirens of American materialism. To Aleksandr Isayevich, the spot where Christopher and I stood truly marked the Great Divide of Western civilization, that place at which the Church of Rome turned west. The Church turned to humanity (away from revealed truth, as Solzhenitsyn believed), embraced the explosion of human talent, the broadening of human minds, which under Cosimo and the others created in Florence and Italy and Europe that civilization (so deeply fertilized by Athens and Rome) that gave our modern world its exhalted spirit. For the Renaissance was as profound an event (I believed) as the birth of Christianity itself.

Solzhenitsyn was not mistaken in his remarks at Harvard. Here at the Uffizi, we did stand beside the crevasse that sundered the world, Rome looking to the future, the Church of Constantine looking inward to the past, to that literal doctrine which the missionaries Cyril and Methodius preached to the Slavs, founding the Orthodox faith of Russia. A faith untouched by the Great Rebirth of human vigor and thought, by what, as I now realized, had been a Revolution as profound as if the earth had been struck by a comet. In that moment I realized, how absurdly pedantic and teutonic had been Karl Marx. What a coven of pretentious bigots he had summoned forth, the believers and the antibelievers. How Cosimo would have laughed at the spectacle, Botticelli turning his head in embarrassment at such mawkish naïveté.

It is a measure of the poverty of my education and, I'm afraid, the narrowness of my preoccupation with the contemporary that Renaissance had been for me a word without content, the Medicis only a synonym of wealth, Lorenzo a metaphor of cloth-of-gold magnificence, Cosimo only the faintest of echoes.

I did not know that the wisdom, the classics, the literature, the philosophy, the culture of Greece and Rome had been strangled by the Dark Ages as if it had never been. I did not know that Cosimo and his friends, Niccolo Niccoli and Poggio Bracciolini, had ransacked Europe to discover, preserve, and revive the art and knowledge of the classical world—as if Dante, Villon, Chaucer, Boccaccio, Shakespeare, Michelangelo, and Botticelli had vanished without a trace for hundreds of years and suddenly been found by an expedition financed by J. P. Morgan.

Only now at the Uffizi, under the impact of Solzhenitsyn's words at Harvard, did I comprehend that the Renaissance *was* a Revolution, *the* Revolution. It recaptured the human body and human spirit for art and man and God. It broke the one-dimensional parameters of a Church sunk in blackness. It blasted open minds like pockets of ore. It created a tide on which, 500 years later, our society still rode at flood. The humanism against which Solzhenitsyn inveighed had become the way of mankind from the day Cosimo began to reclaim those worm-eaten parchments from the stone cellars of the mordant monasteries of Switzerland and Greece.

Only in Florence did I realize that the Revolutions of my day—1917 in Russia, 1949 in China, and all the sputterings before and after— were only summer squalls on sand-saucer lakes. Only, perhaps, the American Revolution, its founders familiar with Greek, Hebrew, and Latin, conscious of history and philosophy, caught a whiff of what had been born in Florence in the fourteenth and fifteenth centuries.

Florence illuminated like lightning the essence of the modern debate. Solzhenitsyn's argument echoed that of the Albizzi family, the enemies of Cosimo, who hated and feared the wildfire spread of the new philosophy, contending that the Greek and Latin classics threatened the pillars of Christian faith. But the Church followed Cosimo, not the Albizzi.

Russia knew neither Renaissance nor Reformation. It plodded on in the tracks of the Middle Ages, arguing whether the sign of the cross should be made with two fingers or three, spawning schismatics who believed in self-flagellation, self-castration, immolation by fire (the congregations assembled in their wooden churches and burned themselves up), and in redemption through sin, as Rasputin preached to the Romanovs.

I cannot but wonder whether Lenin's Marxism, its intense insistence on purity of dictum, discipline, the "divine word" of Party, did not have its real roots in that Eastern Orthodox world which had never known challenge, change, or Florentine charisma. Florence taught me how shoddy are our discussions of the political issues of our day, how poorly we reason, how shabby our education, how weak our standards, how little I—who have spent a lifetime on the pseudo-ideological frontiers of the world—know of genuine thought, of history, and of the rich, exquisitely convoluted society which we humans have created.

Charlotte and I spent not quite two months in Florence. How could I have taken so long to let her lead me there? How could I have visited Tirana, 100 miles across the Adriatic, in 1957 and not see Florence till thirty years later? What sense did it make?

How could I have spent my life arguing about Democracy, Fascism, and Communism and never studied the originals of these doctrines in Athens, Rome, or Florence? What manner of world have we Americans created with our opulent universities, brimming museums, extraordinary electronic skills yet nurture a people as ignorant as myself.

I have watched our parades for popes and pennant winners, our Presidential polls and electronic politics. But what about our minds? My mind in particular. How can we expect to create a new or better world if we possess only cartoons of what is going on—an image of the American flag, buoyant in the breeze, patriotic bombast, talk of morning in America, commercials of cowboys riding into the Golden West, peddling light beer, low-tar cigarettes, and ever-lower taxes?

This is what Florence has come down to? This is why Hiram spent his life plowing the land, building houses, and selling notions on icy trails until he died at eighty-one in 1860?

I sit at this Remington portable which I have used for forty-five years. I have spent hundreds of dollars to keep it going. I hate to think how many words I have pounded out, how many ribbons I have worn to rags, how many quires of paper I've used. It has been been faithful to me, has responded when I battered at it in deep Siberian forests, on a plane I thought for sure was going down over New Guinea, in an air raid shelter in Hanoi, in a pigsty on Roswell Garst's farm in Coon Rapids, Iowa.

It has been faithful to my use. Have I been faithful to it? I am not so sure. It seems to me that a lot of mile-wide, inch-deep conclusions have sailed off these keys. How often have I got down to bedrock? Not as often as I would like to remember, except when I reported what I saw or heard, the Hanoi bombing, the *Andrea Doria* disaster, the bloated German bodies gently rising and falling in the Black Sea off Sevastopol, the Shook-up gangs in Red Hook. I can tell you what Stalin said and looked like, the way he held his shoulders, but it took me five years to realize that no one in the Politburo was taller than he (he was very short) and that this was no accident. I knew Nikita Khrushchev better than I have known most American Presidents. I never did a portrait of him in words that caught his schoolboy's gaucherie, his sly peasant curiosity, and the haunting look in his eyes. I thought Ike was a naturally nice guy who turned into a kind of a fake because of his ambitions. (Never put that down on paper until now.) I think Richard Nixon is the most complicated, smartest, and stupidest President of our times. (Never wrote it before.) I thought Carter (before he was nominated) was the most attractive candidate since Wendell Willkie. I didn't write it and am glad I didn't. I was wrong.

I've been writing and talking and arguing about Russia for nearly fifty years. I know what I am talking about. I've never found the right words to convince people that it is Russia's burden of history, not Communism, which makes her so difficult. No one likes to hear that there is more Mongol than Marx in Communism. We clutch our clichés to our bosoms, and I have never found a grenade to blow them free.

I look out over the orchard and wonder if we'll have any apples in the fall. Often we don't, I haven't a clue as to why. Neither, it would seem, do the cheerful young men who come to prune the trees. I would not think of writing an article on apple culture. But I will analyze the Afghan situation at the drop of a hat. I once spent ten days in Afghanistan; I love the Afghans; I shouldn't open my mouth about their plight. Of course that doesn't keep Presidents, Prime

Ministers, and Pundits from uttering long, weighty, didactic absurdities. They don't have to know a thing to pontificate. Sometimes they get us into wars.

I do know a lot about Russia, China, and the United States. I am sitting right at the apex of that triangle. I have spent three decades studying the United States, China, and Russia. I have been over the ground. It is my territory. I have seen it from every side and over a long time. I know the history. I have known a great many of the players, the men who have made policy, who have committed troops, who have disposed their forces. I have known many of the diplomats who have negotiated on the problem or segments of it. I have even, at times, been part of the problem in polemics between the Russians and the Chinese.

The US-USSR-China triangle weighs more heavily on the world's future than Grenada, the Falklands, the Persian Gulf, the India-China frontier, the trumperies of North and South Korea, the edgy debate over Libya or the question of bugs at the American embassy in Moscow. I speak about it frequently, but no one in government *thinks* about it. The press doesn't devote five minutes a year to it; the public never asks about it.

The rottenness in our government, the growing deceit, blundering, and hypocrisy since World War II has made me a First Amendment absolutist—that is, I oppose any government retrictions on the press except for what is called the "troopship exception." No one, I hold, has a right to publish the date of a troopship sailing in wartime or war crisis. I agree with wartime censorship but only on military operations. I would forbid publication of the fact that we have broken a hostile state's code but insist on publication of bumbles of our own expensive intelligence apparatus, even if sometimes this seems harmful to immediate interests, in the long run it would serve us well. I would prohibit the government from concealing its blunders and embarrassing mistakes. I believe with Jerome Wiesner, former head of MIT, that democracy and secrecy are incompatible, that people will not in the long run permit the kind of government cover-ups which have become so common. Without William Howard Russell of the London *Times,* the command-made horrors of the Crimean war (including the Charge of the Light Brigade) would never have come to light. Newspapers revealed the rotten beef and dud bullets of the Union Army. Without Upton Sinclair the meat industry would have buried its victims unheeded. The presses exposed Teapot Dome. It alerted the nation to the incompetence behind Pearl Harbor, and tardily it began to tell the truth about Vietnam and is still getting hell for it. The press brought us the Pentagon Papers and Watergate and trembled at its audacity. It exposed the Bay of Pigs but tread softly about Grenada and Nicaragua. To its shame it has never told the full story of the United States in Iran (where the money went). It hasn't bothered to winnow the thousands of documents exhumed by Tehran from the secret files of the U.S. embassy.

*The New York Times* electrified the nation in 1871 when it exposed the financial crimes of Tammany and the Tweed ring. It dozed through the Koch years, even sending its outraged and brutally honest columnist, Sydney Schanberg, to the showers. The press drowsed along with the government and its opulent contractors until *Challenger* blew up. Nearly twenty years ago Emma Rothschild in *The New Yorker* forecast the demise of Detroit. It took David Halberstam's book to detail the sordid story not of Japanese skill but of American sloth. The press slept.

I could go on and on. The world of electronic journalism, once sparkling with men like Edward R. Murrow and Walter Cronkite, slipped into the gray wasteland, with bottom-line barons taking it over, men whose testicles seemed to have been replaced by puffballs. No one in the Fourth Estate ventured to don the mantle of the certifiably eccentric Colonel Robert R. McCormick of *The Chicago Tribune.* McCormick wittingly or unwittingly gave away, in anger at Roosevelt, the secret of our breaking Japan's Purple code. FDR decided not to send the Colonel to jail, for fear of tipping the Japanese to what they had missed. J. Edgar Hoover has been in his grave for a decade. Mysterious events—fires and strange deaths— have, it is said, burned the archives and eliminated witnesses. The press yawns. Candidate after candidate rolls out of the electronic image processors. Nobody hires Sy Hersh to see what skeletons lurk behind their gussified hairdos. I mean real scandals, not Gary Hart trifles.

And no one complains of all this. Not the public, not Congress, not the White House—heavens, no, not the White House. Not opposition parties. Not the princes of the press—with a few honorable exceptions: *The New York Times, The Washington Post, The Boston Globe, The Los Angeles Times.* The others are too busy with their accountants and tax lawyers. We sleep. Oh, a few eccentrics raise a paranoid cry of Conspiracy. But nothing breaks the somnolence. We are, it seems, as Lincoln Steffens found Philadelphia, corrupt and content.

If anyone had a clue to national interest and national security, he would be spending, let's say, billions analyzing and studying this country itself, the United States. The menace of our own malfunctioning, it would seem to me, is the only serious menace to our own well-being and survival. We spend tens of billions on ultratechnology, pennies on those who are supposed to manage it. Schools close, universities turn into drug-ridden, commercial sports farms, and only a dwindle of men and women capable of manning new-age miracles escape the rush to Wall Street's megabucks.

We can do anything. We possess the know-how, the manpower, the thought power, the laboratories, the concepts. We do nothing. We rarely even bring to trial the men in government and out whose concentration on self-promotion and extravagant profit margins trash our prestige abroad and our integrity at home.

There is no story—literally none—which the great electronic news media and the billion-dollar press aggregates cannot extract, be it from the Kremlin or the Pentagon, and bring to the public of America. Instead, they tinker with sitcoms and four-color ad pages. Priorities? Forget it.

On Christmas Eve, 1985, Charlotte and I walked through the streets of Florence, awash with people, young, old, rich, poor, gay, and serious, through the throngs and into the great Duomo, that wonder of the world, where Florence has gathered on this holy eve since the fourteenth century. Tonight the vastness is filled, and the music lifts up to heaven. We stand breathless as the priests and princes of the church utter the incantations, the prayers, the music swelling, the tapers alight, the incense filling the air.

Finally, we make our way back through the people, very close, walking slowly, the sense of the moment filling our hearts, out into the square, deep with young people, happy, abandoned, holding hands and arms around waists, teasing and joking, no ribaldry, a festive night. We walk down Via Santa Maria, in the center of the street, no traffic, only sauntering people. We walk up onto the Ponte Vecchio, as lovers have for a thousand years, pausing in center bridge to look up the Arno to Ponte Santa Trinita and beyond, one bridge after the other, each a work of art, each as it has been for centuries (but rebuilt and rebuilt, especially after the German destruction) and then around the corner to our *penzione* just down the street from Pitti Palace, looking out over the slanted gray roofs, just as did Cellini and Leonardo and Brunelleschi and Donatello and, I suppose, Cosimo. It is a long, long way from Minnesota. Or even Boston. I know that Florence possesses us and will to the end of our days. We are very close.

I read a good deal that winter about Florence. I could not get enough. I was transfixed by the city and its men, none more than the architect Leon Alberti and his concept of man, unlike any I had ever heard. He saw man as a ship, designed for long, arduous voyages, sailing to the edge of the earth, and back, driving himself each year of his life, because there was so much to do and so little time in which to do it. He was painting a self-image I am certain. For his own device he took a winged eye because only an eye with the wings of a bird could see as much, see as far, and see as fast as man could travel. He borrowed, he said, a concept from ancient Greece, the idea that "man is born not to mourn in idleness but to work at magnificent and grandiose tasks."

That, I resolved, was a theorem for me. So much in the world to see, so much to report, so much to write, so pressing time and strength. I must hurry if I am to return quickly to Firenze and walk again the ancient stones of the pavement and let my imagination float freely over the beauty and wisdom of man's finest hour.

# Index

**421**

# Index

Parker, Ralph (*The Times*), 131–2, 318
Pasternak, Boris: 186–7, 190; *Doctor Zhivago*, 178, 190
Patch, Ike, 89, 91
Pearl Harbor, 34–5
Peng Dehuai, 363
Pentagon Papers, 267, 294–6, 402
Persia, 76
Pham Van Dong, 369
Pieck, Wilhelm, 130, 131
Pinkley, Virgil (UP), 71
Pol Pot, 263
Poland, 231–8
Popham, John (*NY Times*), 199
Popkov, Pyotr, 95–6, 101, 104
Poskrebyshev, Aleksandr, 146
Post, Robert (*NY Times*), 61–2, 65
*Pravda*, 144–5, 146, 154, 328
Pulitzer Prize, 234, 237, 298–9
Pursley, Robert F., 267

Qiao Guanhua, 354
Qin, Gen., 367

Reagan, Ronald: 306; and Gorbachev, 396–7; in China, 391–3
Reston, Scotty (*NY Times*), 146–7, 246, 250, 251, 354, 356
Ronning, Chester, 264, 266, 267, 356, 376
Roosevelt, Eleanor, 28
Roosevelt, F. D., 32
Rosenthal, A. M. (*NY Times*): 198, 235–7, 247–8, 251, 255; Pulitzer Prize, 237
Rostow, Walt, 294, 296
Rusk, Dean, 296, 297, 330–1
Russia: 77–87, 92; agriculture, 182; air power, 64; Astrakhan, 77–8; Doctor's Plot, 105, 147–8, 156, 164; foreign policy: China, 112–13, 243–4, 323, 328–47, 348–56, 371; Germany, 29–30, 32–4; Nazi-Soviet Pact, 29–30; Sino-Soviet Treaty, 112, 244, 335; US, 107, 113–15; Katyn massacre, 79–84; Leningrad, 93–7; Nineteenth Congress, 142, 143; poets, 185–6; pogroms, 3, 106; Presidium, 142, 143; purges, 94, 104–6, 141, 145–6, 338, 340–1; quality of diplomatic corps, 138; war preparedness, 117–20, 350–1

Sakharov, Andrei, 192
Salisbury, Andrew, 9, 25
Salisbury, Charlotte, 241–2
Salisbury, Harrison: childhood, 9–14, 313–14, 408; family history, 406–7; patriotism, 9–18, 38; reading matter, 6–7, 36, 99; FBI record, 40–4; house searched, 31, 40–2; war correspondent: 38–97; in London, 45–74; in Russia, 77–97, 116; Birmingham libel

case, 209–10, 213–14; in Southern states, 197–217; Kennedy story, 221–6; foreign correspondent: Asia, 249–58; Hanoi dispatches, 275–8, 289–300; Poland, 231–8; Vietnam, 275–300; Yugoslavia, 227–8; *900 Days: the Siege of Leningrad*, 97, 106; *The Long March*, 368; *To Peking and Beyond*, 365; *War Between Russia and China*, 352, 354
Salisbury, Hiram, 406–7
Salisbury, Janet, 2, 9, 20, 39
Salisbury, Mary (aunt), 9, 25, 116
Salisbury, Mary, 70, 116, 147
Salisbury, Mary Pritchard (grandmother), 6, 24
Salisbury, Michael, 6, 28, 115, 147, 269
Salisbury, Percy Pritchard, 6, 9, 19–20, 23–4, 39
Salisbury, Stephan, 147, 269
Salisbury, Sue, 9, 13
Schlesinger, Arthur, 219, 309
Security Index, 42
Service, John S., 365–6, 367, 392
Shapiro, Henry (UP), 33, 77, 84, 88, 102, 134
Shapiro, Ludmilla, 88, 91
Shehu, Mehmet, 228, 229–30
Sholokhov, Mikhail, 178
Shostakovich, Dmitri, 189
Sihanouk, Prince, 273, 376, 384
Sikkim, 249–53
Simonov, Konstantin, 188, 191
Sino-Soviet Treaty, 112, 244, 335
sit-ins, 200–3
Sitton, Claude, 199–200, 204, 214
Smith, Walter Bedell, 371–2
Snow, Edgar: 311, 316, 355, 367, 369; *Red Star Over China*, 311, 368
Snyder, Fred B., 12, 14
Sohlman, Rolf, 138
Sokolvsky, Gen., 152, 165
Solzhenitsyn, Aleksandr: 139, 191–2, 411–12; writings, 192
Soviet Union *see* Russia
Spaatz, Gen. Tooey, 37, 62
Spry, Constance, 67–8
Stalin, Joseph, 90, 114, 151–66, 415; and China policy, 319, 333–4, 336–7; and seige of Leningrad, 95, 97; anti-Semitism, 106, 139; illness and death, 155–66; Leningrad affair, 105; Nazi-Soviet Pact, 29–30; on German invasion of Russia, 32, 33, 79; purges, 104–6, 145–6, 338, 340–1; talks with Mao, 112–13, 334; power in Congress, 143; views of Germany, 130–1, 135
Stalin, Svetlana, 105–6, 148
Stalin, Vasily, 152
Stallworth, Clark (*Post-Herald*), 210
Steiger, Andy (Reuters), 102, 144

423